M A Y
SARTON

Selected Letters

1 9 1 6 – 1 9 5 4

Miss Pickthorn and Mr. Hare
The Poet and the Donkey
Kinds of Love
As We Are Now
Crucial Conversations
A Reckoning
Anger
The Magnificent Spinster
The Education of Harriet Hatfield

Nonfiction

I Knew a Phoenix
Plant Dreaming Deep
Journal of a Solitude
A World of Light
The House by the Sea
Recovering: A Journal
At Seventy: A Journal
After the Stroke: A Journal
Writings on Writing
May Sarton—a Self-Portrait
Letters to May by Eleanor Mabel Sarton
Selected, Edited and with an Introduction by May Sarton
Honey in the Hive
Endgame: A Journal of the Seventy-ninth Year
Among the Usual Days: A Portrait
(edited by Susan Sherman)
Encore: A Journal of the Eightieth Year
At Eighty-Two: A Journal

For Children

Punch's Secret
A Walk through the Woods

M A Y
SARTON

Selected Letters

1916–1954

edited and introduced by

SUSAN SHERMAN

W. W. NORTON & COMPANY

NEW YORK • LONDON

For information about permission to reproduce selections from this book,
write to Permissions, W. W. Norton & Company, Inc., 500 Fifth Avenue,
New York, NY 10110.

The text of this book is composed in Bembo
with the display set in Castellar
Composition and manufacturing by the Haddon Craftsmen, Inc.
Book design by Chris Welch

Library of Congress Cataloging-in-Publication Data
Sarton, May, 1912–
[Correspondence.   Selections]
Selected letters / May Sarton edited and introduced by Susan Sherman.
      p.   cm.
Includes index.
Contents: v. 1.   1916–1954
ISBN 0-393-03954-4 (v. 1)
1. Sarton, May, 1912- —Correspondence.   2. Women authors, American—
20th century—Correspondence.   I. Sherman, Susan.   Title.
PS3537.A832Z48   1997
811'.52
[B]—DC20   96-43614
CIP

W. W. Norton & Company, Inc., 500 Fifth Avenue, New York, N.Y. 10110
http://www.wwnorton.com

W. W. Norton & Company Ltd., 10 Coptic Street, London WC1A 1PU

1 2 3 4 5 6 7 8 9 0

CONTENTS

EDITOR'S PREFACE
AND NOTES

May Sarton's dedication to letter writing began in earliest childhood when she was frequently separated from her parents for long and lonely periods. Her father, George Sarton, eminent professor of the History of Science at Harvard, traveled widely lecturing, as well as researching his monumental four-volume *Introduction to the History of Science* and his projected nine-volume history of all sciences. When her mother, Eleanor Mabel Sarton, was not away recovering from illness, she was caring for her aging mother in England, traveling abroad with her husband, and commuting monthly to the firm of Belgart in Washington, D.C. which she and Margaret Gillespie had founded. There she taught employees how to execute the exquisite embroideries she designed for the elegant coats and dresses sold to Neiman Marcus, Lord & Taylor, and Marshall Field.

Thus alone, packed off to camp, theatre school, and the homes of friends, young Sarton found letters her only true connections, her bridges to family and friends, her way of "touching wings." The historian in George Sarton passed on to his daughter a respect for chronicling and dating. As artist and eloquent letter writer herself, Eleanor Mabel Sarton sensitized May to the art of celebrating the ordinary.

Gradually letters became a cornerstone of Sarton's routine, a means of transcending and distilling experience, of coming to terms with the events of her world, of venting every mood, of "having a good think," and later the means of setting wheels in motion for work; ultimately they became the richest of communions and the heaviest of burdens. But always letters remained absolutely central to her life.

Having read letters from every stage of that life, I continue to be moved by the immensity and intimacy of their content, their richness and radiance, and the vivid sense of her presence they evoke. The pages of handwriting and primitive typing bring back a voice and an era now gone, an art form lost. Beyond her honesty, her political conscience, her incandescent spirit, her art of friendship, her legendary generosity; beyond her passion, her struggles and victories, her lifetime of reading, her evolution as a writer, beyond *all* that, there is an ineffable aspect of Sarton which letter writing alone freed. "It was always a bloodrush," says Bill Brown, "to find a letter from May in the box. I would open everything else first, and then take her letter to a private place and savour it alone, like a wonderful meal."

This volume of *Selected Letters* came about as part of a larger ongoing project of editing a far more comprehensive *Collected Letters*. Already fifty-seven libraries have yielded letters to scores of correspondents while hundreds of additional correspondences have come to hand directly from their recipients. Readability, a wish to cover as many aspects of her life as space would permit, and consideration for those living were the guiding factors. It was Sarton's own quintessential art of autobiography, her epitomizing a "life examined" that finally dictated the design of this volume. And of that art Carolyn Heilbrun writes, "I would name 1973 as the turning point for women's autobiography. The transformation in question can be seen most clearly in the American poet, novelist, and memoirist May Sarton . . . the publication of *Journal of a Solitude* may be acknowledged as the watershed in women's autobiography."[1]

Her memoirs and journals distinguish Sarton as one of the great autobiographers of our time; this first volume of *Selected Letters* reveals her as a preeminent letter writer as well, for whom letters were a devotion, a discipline, and an art. It is their scope and richness which constitute her ultimate autobiography.

Throughout her life Sarton was intensely objective and self critical; her expressions of doubt are an intrinsic matter of temperament, a measure of her purpose; far beneath them existed an abiding belief in the lasting value of her work.

For the sake of consistency I have corrected certain idiosyncracies such as her not capitalizing English or Jewish, or characteristic misspellings such as negros for negroes, snyde for snide. I have, however, retained her anglicizations such as Elisabeth for Elizabeth Bowen, humour for humor, and so on. I have left her French as she wrote it except where the meaning was obscured and in translating, have tried to approximate as closely as possible her own voice and locutions, even when that somewhat departs from the literal meaning of her French. These French versions of her letters can be found at the back of this volume. It was Sarton's custom in early years to sign letters

---

[1] *Writing a Woman's Life,* Carolyn G. Heilbrun. W. W. Norton, 1988, pp. 12–13.

with a hieroglyph, usually a lily-of-the-valley, sometimes a mouse or bird. Such instances are indicated with brackets [   ].

Her lifetime of letter writing, begun in childhood and nurtured as a central and sacred part of her routine, continued to the final days when even though tenuously, as seen in brief and barely legible notes written days before her last trip to the hospital, they still connected her to her friends and to what Virginia Woolf called her Common Reader, to whom not responding constituted for Sarton a flagrant betrayal of the trust her life of work had inspired.

From her father she early inherited her life-long habit of spending Sunday mornings at her desk for what she called "my Sunday religious service, devoted to friendship." That Sunday in July of 1995, when she made her final brave journey to the hospital, was the only Sunday I ever knew May not to attend that service.

Susan Sherman
Riverdale, New York
June 1996

CHRONOLOGY

It was Sarton's custom to set out on lecture tours in the fall and spring of each year; I have recorded only the first such tour, in 1940.

Annually, with few exceptions other than the years of World War II, Sarton returned to England and Europe to visit the Limboschs, her second family; Jean Dominique, her beloved friend; and a host of others. Despite her relationships in America, and her home with Judith Matlack, it was in Europe that Sarton's passionate attachments flowered, and where each year she watered the sources of her poetry.

1912 Born 3 May, Wondelgem, Belgium, daughter of George and Eleanor Mabel (Elwes) Sarton

1915–1919 Immigrates, via England 1914, to Washington, D.C., and later moves to Cambridge, Massachusetts.

1924 Becomes naturalized American citizen. Attends Jean Dominque's Institute Belge de Culture Français, Winter 1924–1925.

1926–1929 Graduates from Shady Hill School; enters Cambridge High and Latin School, graduating in 1929. First poems published in *Poetry.* Joins Eva Le Gallienne's Civic Repertory Theatre in New York City first as apprentice, then as member of The First Studio, and finally as director of the Apprentices.

1929–1933 Member of Civic Repertory Theatre as actor; Director of Apprentice Theatre.

1933–1935 Forms Associated Actors Theatre which fails in 1935.

1936 Decides to pursue writing career. Spends April–August in England and Europe, meeting the Huxleys for the first time.

1937 *Encounter in April* (poems). Spends April–September in England and Europe, meeting Virginia Woolf, Elizabeth Bowen, Vita Sackville-West, James Stephens, S. S. Koteliansky.

1938 *The Single Hound* (her first novel). Spends April–July in England and

Europe meeting Grace Dudley, Lugné-Pöe, Camille Mayran. Begins teaching at the Stuart School (until 1942).

1939 *Inner Landscape* (poems), *Fire in the Mirror* (novel, unpublished). Spends June–August in England and Europe, meets Bill Brown.

1940–1941 Begins first lecture tour through South and Southwest wintering in Santa Fe, New Mexico and continuing through Midwest the following spring. Virginia Woolf's suicide. Death of Lugné-Pöe.

1942 Death of Edith Forbes Kennedy.

1943 Various residences in New York City, including Muriel Rukeyser's apartment. Works for Pearl Buck's East & West and Office of War Information (OWI). Launches New York Public Library's "The Poet Speaks" readings.

1944 Returns to Channing Place, Cambridge which parents buy after years of renting.

1945 Spends April–July in Santa Fe, meets Judith Matlack. Resides with her at 139 Oxford Street, Cambridge from November through 1950.

1946 *The Bridge of Years* (novel). Poet-in-Residence, State Teachers College of Southern Illinois at Carbondale. Sells first story to *Colliers*.

1947 *The Underground River* (play). Spends April–July in Europe meeting Brancusi, Malraux, and Spender while staying with the Huxleys, and meeting Ruth Pitter in England. Golden Rose Award (poetry).

1948 *The Lion and the Rose* (poems). Spends April–September in England and Europe meeting Sitwells, Auden, Freya Stark.

1949 Spends April–August in England and Europe meeting Eugénie DuBois.

1950 Deaths of Eleanor Mabel Sarton and Grace Dudley. Moves to Maynard Place with Judith Matlack where Elizabeth Bowen stays with them. *The Leaves of the Tree* (poems) and *Shadow of a Man* (novel). Bread Loaf Writers' Conference. Teaches at Radcliffe (until 1953) as Briggs-Copeland Instructor.

1951 Spends June–August in England and Europe, staying with Meta (Budry) and Mark Turian in Switzerland in July.

1952 *A Shower of Summer Days* (novel). Moves to 14 Wright Street with Judith Matlack (Sept.) Death of Jean Dominique.

1953 *The Land of Silence* (poems). Meets Louise Bogan. CBS Interview. Bread Loaf Writers' Conference. Boulder Writers' Conference. Named Lucy Martin Donnelly Fellow, Bryn Mawr College; receives Reynolds Poetry Award.

1954 Spends August–November in England and Europe, meets Janet Flanner, Leonard Woolf. Travels in Italy with Eugénie DuBois. Meets Cora DuBois. Guggenheim Fellowship in poetry.

KEY TO ADDRESSES

22 East 10th St.
> On September 3, 1943 Sarton found this apartment into which she moved on September 19.

23 Taviton St.
> The boarding house in London where Sarton lived in 1936 and first met John Summerson.

239 East 17th St.
> 239 East 17th Street, New York City.

43 York Street
> 43 York Street, near Baker Street, London W.I. A rooming house where she stayed briefly.

54 West 10th
> 54 West 10th Street, New York City. An apartment Sarton shared with Theodora Pleadwell.

59 Acacia Road
> 59 Acacia Road, London. Home of S. S. Koteliansky where Katherine Mansfield had lived in 1915.

94 Macdougal
> The McLean Club, 94 Macdougal Street, New York City. A residence for women where Sarton lived while working at the Civic Repertory Theatre.

Austria
> Sommerheim Seeblick Am Grundlsee, Steiermark, Austria. The summer home of Hermann Schwarzwald, Austrian director of finance in the 1930s, and his wife, Dr. Eugenia [Nussbaum] Schwarzwald, teacher and social worker; during the first four decades of this century it served as an inn for writers, intellectuals, and musicians, including Thomas Mann, Rilke, Brecht, Sinclair Lewis, Dorothy Thompson, Rudolf Serkin, the Huxleys, and May Sarton.

Belgium

> Among Sarton's juvenilia, George Sarton marked the letters simply "Belgium," although the reference is undoubtedly to the Limbosch's at Le Pignon Rouge or at their summer home in Knocke.

Belgium (C)

> c/o Mme. Céline Dangotte [Céline Limbosch's maiden name], 65, Ave. de la Toison d'Or, Bruselles, Belgium. Home of Arts Décoratif.

Black Mountain

> Black Mountain College, Black Mountain, North Carolina.

Bread Loaf

> Bread Loaf Writers' Conference, Middlebury, Vermont.

Carbondale

> State Teachers College of Southern Illinois, Carbondale, Illinois. Sarton was Poet-in-Residence, June 8–25, 1946 and returned for frequent appearances.

Channing Place

> 5 Channing Place, Cambridge, Massachusetts. Home of the Sartons.

Cobbs Mill

> Cobbs Mills, Nyack, New York. Possibly an inn. Margaret English lived nearby on Old Mill Road in West Nyack.

Chicago

> Allerton Hotel, Chicago, Illinois.

Detroit

> Women's City Club, 2110 Park Avenue, Detroit, Michigan.

Dublin, N.H.

> Lerned House, Dublin, New Hampshire. Home of the Henry Copley Greenes.

Florence

> Pensione Picciolo, 1, Via Tornabuoni, Florence, Italy.

Fredericksburg

> Mary Washington College, Fredericksburg, Virginia.

Gloucester

> Gloucester School of the Little Theatre, Rocky Neck, East Gloucester, Massachusetts where Sarton studied and performed during summers. She took board at the Theatre Teakettle, and room at the Inner Harbor Inn.

Hampstead

> 35, Rosslyn Hill, London N.W.3.

Hartford

> Specific location unidentified; stayed here while her Associated Actors Theatre played at the Wadsworth Athenaeum.

Jamaica Plain
> Jamaica Plain, Massachusetts. Home of Elizabeth McClelland.

Le Pignon Rouge
> Le Pignon Rouge, 16, Avenue Léquime, Rhôdes St. Genèse, Brussels, Belgium. Home of the Limbosches.

Linkebeek
> 12 Longue Haie, Linkebeek, Brabant, Belgium. Home of Jean and Eugénie DuBois.

London (GH)
> Garland's Hotel, Suffolk Street, Pall Mall, S.W.I.

London (JS)
> In London Sarton often stayed with her friend Jane Stockwood who lived at various addresses over the years.

Lourdes
> Specific address unidentified. Visited there with her father.

Maynard Place
> 9 Maynard Place, Cambridge, Massachusetts. Home of May Sarton and Judith Matlack.

Newcastle
> Newcastle, New Hampshire where Sarton and Muriel Rukeyser lived over Mr. Amazeen's lobster house.

New Orleans
> Warren House, Sophie Newcomb Memorial College, New Orleans, Louisiana.

New York (HA)
> Hotel Albert, 65 University Place, New York City.

New York (HT)
> The Hotel Tudor, Tudor City, 304 East 42nd Street, New York City.

New York (MHH)
> Murray Hill Hotel, Park Avenue at 41st Street, New York City.

Ogunquit
> For several summers the Sartons rented Lucy Stanton's studio in Ogunquit, Maine.

Oxford St.
> 139 Oxford Street, Cambridge, Massachusetts. Home of May Sarton and Judith Matlack.

Oxon
> Far End, Kingham, Oxfordshire, England. Home of Jay and Basil de Sélincourt.

Painesville
> Lake Erie College, Painesville, Ohio

Paris (H-SS)
    Hotel Saint-Simon, 14, rue St. Simon, 7e.
Paris (Huxley)
    In 1947 the Huxleys occupied an apartment at 2 Avenue Alphand. After
    1947 they lived at 38 Quai Louis-Blériot.
Paris (P)
    In 1931, before moving into Willem van Loon's flat, Sarton lived in a
    pensione (unidentified).
Paris (vanL)
    42 Places Jules Ferry, Montrouge (Seine), Paris, France. The apartment
    of Willem van Loon, son of Hendrik Willem van Loon, Dutch-born
    American journalist and author.
Poughquag
    Muffet Farm, Poughquag, New York. Theodora Pleadwell's farm.
Rathfarnham
    Rockbrook House, Rathfarnham, County Dublin, Ireland. Home of
    Lady Beatrice Glenavy.
Raymond St.
    103 Raymond Street, Cambridge, Massachusetts. Home of the Sartons.
Rockport
    Straitsmouth Inn, Rockport, Massachusetts.
Rowley
    River Houslin, The Turnpike, Newburyport, P.O. Rowley, Massachu-
    setts. Summer home of the Henry Copley Greenes, which Rosalind
    Greene lent to May Sarton during the summer of 1934 for rehearsals
    of the Associated Actors Theatre.
Rye
    Samuel Jeakes House, Rye, Sussex, England. Home of Conrad Aiken,
    which Sarton and three friends rented in the spring of 1937.
St. Petersburg
    Boca Ciega Inn, St. Petersburg, Florida.
Santa Fe (AS)
    724 Canyon Road, and later 600 Canyon Road, Santa Fe, New Mex-
    ico. Homes of Agnes Sims, painter and sculptor, where Sarton stayed
    as a paying guest.
Santa Fe (ER)
    940 Acequia Madre, Santa Fe, New Mexico. Home of Edith Ricket-
    son.
Sudbury
    Box 128, RFD 1, Maynard (Sudbury), Massachusetts. Home of Anne
    Thorp.

Vermont
    The Hockings had a summer home.
Vineyard Haven
    Sarton visited there from September 1–7, 1946. Specific location
    unidentified.
Vouvray
    Le Petit Bois, Vouvray, I & L, France; home of Grace Eliot Dudley; see
    "Grace Eliot Dudley: Le Petit Bois" in *A World of Light*.
Washington
    The Sartons lived briefly in Washington, D.C. where May attended
    nursery school. Later, Eleanor Mabel Sarton returned frequently to
    work at Belgart for whom she designed dresses.
Whipsnade
    An open zoo on the Bedfordshire Downs where the Huxley's kept an
    apartment 800 feet up, overlooking its 500 acres.
Wright Street
    14 Wright Street, Cambridge, Massachusetts. Home of May Sarton and
    Judith Matlack.
Yonkers
    Home of Dr. Leo and Céline (BoBo) Baekeland.

The arbiter reviews a face
Flawless in its partial knowing:
"Child, think well of me or try.
I must be going."
                    —James Merrill from "On the Block"

M A Y
SARTON

Selected Letters

1916–1954

TO GEORGE SARTON   [29 July 1916]
[Ogunquit to Cambridge]
     MY · DEAR · DADDY I · AM · SORRY · I · DID · NOT WRITE · VERY
OFTEN · I WANT · YOU · TO · COME · QUICKLY · MAY

TO GEORGE SARTON   [Received in Florence 24 October 1919]
[Belgium to Florence]
     Dear Daddy thank you very much for the book and the little books and
cards. My little sister and brother play alot outofdoors. because it is so fine.
Iv found that at home its really lazey I'm allways play Iv worked so well today
day. Im going to make you a picture and here it is. Im writing very little we
are going to have a little fate for mother. We are going to make the cake alone.
are you working well. it really is very fine here. with lots of work to do. with
best love from may

———————

The Limbosch children: Jacques, Claire, Nicole, Jacqueline.
Work ethic: as a child Sarton understood from her father that to work was to be good.
Fate: fête.

TO GEORGE SARTON   [26 June 1922]
[Ogunquit to Cambridge]
Dear Daddy,
     It is lovely ~~whether~~ weather here, Mother is feeling much better and looks
very well. I keep wishing you were here so that I could go for long walks
with you. I have built a sort of a house in one of the trees nearby our house,

I am writing in it now I get wild strawberries and other eatables and have feasts up here, or read, or draw, or write; it is lots of fun. I saw a large sailboat out at sea this morning. When will you be back? I hope before the fourth of July. Yesterday we went to miss Wheelers she has a lovely old long white house with fruit trees at one side. ~~That~~ Mother said she pointed it out to you on the way to Wells station. Mother went in bathing yesterday, she enjoyed it very much. I hope thou art feeling well this merry day.

> much love from thy little daughter
> May

TO ELEANOR MABEL SARTON   July 17, 1923
[Woods Hole to England]
Dear mother,

I galloped on the pony! At first I was scared but then I sat up and held the reins tight. On Friday ~~(I)~~ we went for a sail it was peachy it was quite rough coming back we had a picnic. On Bastille day we went to Waxmans, friends of the Merciers, who have just been in Spain Daddy came to. There was a Punch and Judy Show and I sang then we all sang together we each had a surprise. Have you seen Grannie Yet? Please write.

> lots of love from
> May

TO GEORGE SARTON   July 25, 1923
[Gloucester to Cambridge]
Dear Daddy,

Miss Coit has written and says she wants me on the 30th of July to the 17th of August. Please write to me your plans as to how I am going to get there and whether i am going on the 30th. I would like to ~~see you~~ be with you before I go. We are going to Plymouth this morning. ~~yes~~ on the 23rd there was a party here for me it was lovely I met some of the Merciers friends, and I got a lovely prize.

> lots of love and kisses from your loving little daughter May

---

Miss King and Miss Coit: They made careers of training children to perform beautiful and highly stylized plays for one performance each year. This summer when Eleanor Mabel Sarton was called to her mother in England, May was shipped off to Miss King and Miss Coit at the Gloucester School of the Little Theatre who cast her as the manager and interpreter in *Nala and Damayanti,* a Hindu play, adapted from the Mahabharata. As manager, it was Sarton's role to hand each child her flowers. She was the only child not given flowers; her parents sent her a beautiful book instead.

TO GEORGE SARTON   [12 October 1924]
[Belgium to Cambridge]
Dear Daddy,

how are you? I am not very well as I have a little stomach upset. We are now at Aunty Lino's as we arrived (last) yesterday morning. The crossing was awful mother was very sick and I was quite sick and we have not quite recovered yet. Aunty Lino and the children were much surprised to find that I could speak french so well! They are much as I imagined them. Jacquot is still beautiful and Clairette more so than last year mother says. The little ones are darlings, Nicol dark and much like an elf, and Jacqueline chubby and fair with blue eyes and two little light pigtails. Uncle Rámon has a wonderful wireless and every morning we hear Westminster Abbey <u>ring</u>! You can hear it all over the house and it seems very strange.

I am keeping a diary now and I put the clipping you sent in it! I pasted a few postcards too and I wrote quite a lot. I wish you were here.

Uncle Rémon, Auntie Lino, Jacque, Claire and Nicol all came to meet us at Antwerp in the car. And we had a lovely drive back. Thank you for sending the letters and my Youth's Companion. This is not a very excellent letter for composition but I am just putting down what comes into my head.

Mummy has gone to Brussels to look at schools, Uncle Rémon drove Aunty Lino and her there. The children have lots of animals: 8 ducks, 8 pigeons, 2 hens and 2 roosters and their dog "Rouly." He is a dear and I walked to school with the children this morning and ran with him. Soon I hope I shall write in French to you.

                                   avec beaucoup d'amour ta petite fille
                                   May

TO ELEANOR MABEL SARTON   Février [February] le 28, 1925
[Belgium to England]
Dear Mother,

I am a little upset because they don't want me to open Daddy's letters it costs to much to send them! And I have no more money because I gave my ten francs for the big present for Claire. Bobo said I could but Aunt Lino didn't say anything, so I thought it was better to say they could send them straight on.

Your card came just now with Daddy's letters, thank you very much. Do you think it will be 10 days or two weeks before you come back? I am really quite happy so don't worry if you can't come back for two weeks. Don't forget the stamps. How is Grannie? And that buziness?

Quite early this morning we went for a walk all together, it was great fun except that "Rouly" chased lots of chickens! By the way, all the little dogs are gone! and Rouly is a little lonely.

Yesterday Aunty Lino took us to see the exhibition of portraits of the father of "Roudouce," you know; wasn't that nice.

Please send daddy's letter to me, on.

> With best love to Grannie and you
> from
> little May

"Bobo": Leine van Loy, the Limbosch's governess.

TO GEORGE SARTON   May 1, 1925
[Belgium]
Dear Daddy,

We have been back from Knocke for quite a few days. At Knocke Clairette and I made a real pavement with bricks and cement, it was great fun. The garden is glorious, the fruit trees are in flower and it is full of daffodils, jonquils and forgetmenots and all sorts of bright flowers. The ducks and hens are laying many eggs and the pigeons have little ones.

Claire and I have been working in the garden of lately, we transplanted the "poirots" the white cabbages and red cabbages. We hold in the ~~flowers~~ strawberries too. I am delighted that the spring is there and that in six weeks we will be together.

                                                                     May 4
I am continuing today. I had a ~~lovely~~ happy birthday and thank you ever so much for the lovely white roses that you sent me. "The Sprite" is a delightful book and I am afraid you will scold me, because I have already finished it. E. Harold Baynes had begun a book on "Animal heroes of the great war." Unfortunately he died before it was finished, but my Youths' Companion is printing as much of it as is finished; it is extremely interesting.

Mother has given me a dear little ~~wat~~hch! and Granny an interesting Persian box full of little surprises! There is a little box made with silver filagree, with inside ~~a~~ two of the smallest dolls in the world; [   ] as high as that, and all dressed.

Aunty Lino gave me a curious and beautiful present; being three tsoubas or this part of a sword. [   ] They come from China. And are made of a kind of wrought iron.

Our plans are these: the 15th of this month Mother will go to England (without me) and come back for the 1st of June. Then we will go to Mons to Tante Vera. And on the 14th come and get you.

A <u>big</u> kiss on each cheek and a <u>big</u> thank you from your <u>big</u> daughter

May

(Just think Daddy I am thirteen years old)

———

Tsuba: A metal plate that serves as a guard on a Japanese sword. Eleanor Mabel Sarton writes this marginal note to her husband: "tsuba—from *Japan* tho' I imagine in China similar ones exist."

Vera Bouny-Tordeur: Friend of Eleanor Mabel Sarton whom May called "aunt."

TO CÉLINE LIMBOSCH,   15 August 1925
[Lourdes]
My dear Auntie Lino,

If you don't receive this letter today, it is because daddy has been distracted and kept a letter in his pocket until 6 P.M.! Yesterday afternoon we rested until 4 and then Mother and I had tea, and then at 5 we met Daddy here at the hotel. The weather is so hot that in the middle of the day one must rest from 11 til 5. We went to visit an old castle that overlooks Lourdes and has been changed into a Pyrenéen museum. It was very interesting, showing the furniture, tools, clothes and customs of the Pyrenéen peasants from the past. In the most important room there was actually the history of science! They showed notebooks, tools and pictures of the greatest explorers of the Pyrénées, and there is a library. When I said "explorers" I meant not only those who were first to climb these mountains but also those who drew the first maps, who reached the heights, and who studied the plants and minerals. It was really very exciting. Then we came back and had supper. Then we went out to see the cave where Bernadette saw the Virgin. When I told this story I did not know that she had seen the Virgin many times. The first time the Virgin did not say anything, the second time Bernadette said, "If you are from God come forward, if you are from the devil leave" and the apparition smiling, came toward her. The third time Bernadette asked the Virgin what she wanted to write. The Virgin answered "what I have to tell you does not need to be written. Come here for 15 days and I will make you happy, but not in this world." After that Bernadette saw her several times, and on Sunday a large crowd accompanied her and the Virgin said "pray for the evildoers." And on Wednesday she told Bernadette to tell the priest that a church will be erected here and that processions will take place there. On Friday she told her to wash herself and drink from the fountain and to eat the grass by its side. The child dug the ground and a little stream appeared; it is the famous holy water of Lourdes. Later on, Bernadette asked her what her name was, and the apparition, with her hands in a humble position answered "I am the Immaculate Conception." This is a true story. I find it extraordinary that a child can have such faith and imagination. There was such a crowd getting ready for the evening procession that it was difficult to reach the grotto. There must have been at least a hundred people on their knees. The walls on the left are covered with crutches, casts, braces etc of people who were healed there. It is extraordinary how many there were. But when the procession started it was like a river of gold. Everyone sang "Ave, ave Maria," and it was a moment of such beauty that I don't know how to explain it. This morning we went to the Cathedral and the Church of the Rosary which are below. All the stones of the walls of the Rosary are full of votives. The cathedral is filled with votives of all kinds. The architect who built the cathedral is a real genius I must say. I'll send you a postcard of the way he drew it. I'm so hot that Mother told me to stop so I kiss you.

Your little girl,
May

TO ELEANOR MABEL SARTON   Thursday afternoon
[Cambridge to Washington, D.C.]   [July 1, 1926]
Dear Miutsie,

Just think tomorrow at this time I'll be almost at camp! My trunk's off and my suitcase packed. I bet you can't guess where I was at 8:15 A.M. today! Well I was in Miss Taylor's apartment. Yesterday when I went to say good-by to her she asked whether I wouldn't like to borrow some of her poetry books from her. Of course I said yes and as she had no other time I went then. She is so gay! I took 9 books! I have started on my third poetry book.

Miss Taylor also said that if I wrote anything to show it to her and she would correct it. There is a contest in the Youth's Companion which I believe you could win a prize in but alas! I have just seen that the age limit is 21, and I'm afraid you couldn't quite pass for that.

Much love to the Gillespies and a hug to you.

May

_____

Miutsie: One of Sarton's names for her mother.

Miss Taylor: Katharine Taylor, succeeded the Hockings as director of the Shady Hill School. May sometimes refers to her as K.T. in later letters. See "I Knew A Phoenix in My Youth" in *I Knew a Phoenix*.

Gillespies: Margaret Gillespie, Eleanor Mabel Sarton's partner at Belgart in Washington, D.C. where they designed clothing for women and children. Eleanor designed the embroidery and trained women to execute it; Gillespie and Sarton sold their work to such stores as Lord & Taylor, Neiman Marcus, and Marshall Field's.

TO MARY GARDEN   [7 February 1928]
[Raymond St.]
Dear Mary Garden,

I am pretending that you are not tired yet of being thought exquisite. Friday night I went to the "Jongleur" and came home determined not to write to you although I was bursting with joy and amazement. In vain, however, and I remind myself that I am almost sixteen and should have some sense; in vain did I attempt to convince myself that you wouldn't care anyway. It was impossible. At present I am proud of not having spent a fortune on flowers for you or forcibly burst in and demanded to see you. As for the letter, I assure you it was impossible not to write. The more I think of the "Jongleur" the more I want to see or hear it (what does one say of opera?) Again, I am furious because I can't go to Carmen again this year! How perfectly delicious it must be to be able to both sing and act so that one can't help writing and telling you how entrancing you are.

I must ask you one question. Did you feed the donkey? I have been arguing about it with my friends since Friday. So you see, you must answer so we won't come to blows! There is no use in my hoping for a chance to see you even for a minute I suppose. Dreams, especially such heavenly ones, are horrid about coming true. Oh, yes, one more thing, I think your French is charming.

Sincerely, hopefully yours,
May Sarton

"Jongleur": The Juggler of Notre Dame, by French composer Jules Émile Frédéric Massenet (1842–1912); a miracle play with music composed originally for male voices. American operatic soprano Mary Garden (1877–1967) persuaded Massenet to adapt the title role for soprano and sang it for many years with great success. With her retirement, *The Juggler* vanished from the repertoire.

TO KATHARINE WARREN   [12 February 1928]
[Raymond St.]
Dear Katharine Warren,

Jean Tatlock having gotten (how could I make such a mistake, I only thought of it when the letter was mailed) your letter is in heaven and I am on the edge out of sheer joy that such a great dream could come true! I have kept this letter, at least the last part of it, for a week because I am trying to be more controlled. I am much too emotional, but this is off the point which

I shall blunder out in a minute. Why can't I send you a snow-flake, clear and frosty and fine-wrought instead of words and words.

Ibsen at present makes me burn to act—Hedda Gabler, Hilda Wangel, Nora, Rebecca West—but especially Hedda Gabler. There is no reason for my telling you that you were exquisite almost hurtingly beautiful as Hedda Gabler but I will tell you it. The only thing I can send you that will not be self-conscious is a poem I wrote. It is poor, but I feel as if it were the nearest thing to a snow flake I have to give you. (Then I copied my "Hedda Gabler" poem). It lacks restraint and precision. (I can't remember what came next.)

Mayn't I come to see you and ask one or two questions about acting. I am going away this Thursday for a week dash it all! But please, write or just send a post-card with yes on it if I may before then. At least there I go again That is what the impetuous part of me is singing but my sensible part says, very shocked "People don't do such things!" I am going to pretend they do— by special delivery!

Hopefully,

Katharine Warren: Chief actress of the Boston Repertory Theatre.

Jean Tatlock: Friend of May's from Cambridge who committed suicide in 1944.

Parentheses: This letter is copied out in a 1928 holograph journal. The parentheses in each case are notes to herself.

Hedda Gabler poem: There are two 1928 "Hedda Gabler" poems. See Appendix for text.

TO EVA LE GALLIENNE   [17 February 1928]
[Raymond St.]
Dear Miss Le Gallienne,

I am not long in writing, as you see, but I was afraid you would forget who I was.

I am seriously thinking of acting as a profession. I want something that I may throw my will, my whole soul into—I could certainly do that with acting. The frightening part of it is that I have no reason for thinking I have any talent. I have will enough and intelligence enough. I honestly believe, but that only means that I would make a good stenographer.

When I spoke with you with Mary Hotson after "Cradle Song" I didn't ask was still so full of Teresa and Joanna of the Cross that I didn't ask half of what I wanted to. You did disadvise college. I have been thinking about that since. I want to get to work, to really start putting effort in something besides algebra and latin. On the other hand I am thirsty for more English, more depth and that I would get at college. Do you really think I would have little chance starting at twenty two? (If you haven't got time for more just send a card with yes or no for the questions—but <u>please</u> have time for more!) Is there anything I can do right now that will help me along? I am learning as much as I have time for by heart. You don't by any heavenly chance have a school in the summer do you? I suppose anyhow you are swamped with youthful and illusioned females.

This is a barren letter. Here is a try at Hedda Gabler that I wrote after seeing it in Boston. It's Ibsen that I want most to act. I wish I had something more beautiful to send you to thank you for those few minutes after "Cradle Song."

Are you coming to Boston this year? If so do bring an Ibsen. How does one find out if you are going to lecture? Last year I missed you.

[no signature]

––––––––

Eva Le Gallienne: London-born American actress (1899–1991), producer, director, writer, and teacher. Daughter of the English novelist and poet Richard Le Gallienne. Trained at the Royal Academy of Dramatic Arts. Founder of the Civic Repertory Theatre in New York where Sarton worked first as an apprentice, then as a member of the First Studio, and finally as director of the Apprentice Group for four years before starting her own company.

Mary Hotson: Taught fourth grade at the Shady Hill School in its earlier days. She and her husband, Leslie, an Elizabethan scholar, were friends of the Sartons. In 1936 they sent Sarton's poems to Vita Sackville-West, whom Sarton later came to know through the Huxleys.

A transcription of this letter to Le Gallienne appears in the 1928 holograph journal. The only single extant letter to Le Gallienne appears later in this volume.

TO ABBY AND MARY DEWING   [after March 1928]
[Raymond St?]
Dear Abby and Mary,

I am writing this in spare moments at rehearsal. We are working on "Madame" every single minute today and the first performance is tonight. The dress rehearsal, as usual, was hilariously bad. I'm quite worried about it, even the business was perfectly insane and most of the time they used their books. Wish me luck!

Well, here goes for Mrs. Evans. It'll take pages I assure you. First I read her the Miss Cunningham one; she said that she had always thought of her in much the same way, as a sort of sprite dancing on waves. She read it aloud in a very bad way as it was the first time she had seen it. She thought "almost-too-careless-smiles" was good and also "the flash of crystal appreciation." She said she thought I had much the same idea only I had developed it and perfected it. She said that analogies were <u>essential</u> to convey thought. Then that I am all-apparalled for a poet or function as a poet. She gave me this as the functions of a poet:

1. tints commonplace
2. finds life pulsating beneath style
3. is the most broadminded of people
4. is essentially an economist

She said my voice showed that I had economized and used every experience and therefore was much more mature than Peggy Leland. (I'm tired of saying "she said" so when she says anything I won't put anything and when I say anything I'll put "I think" and "I said"). Deterioration would be infinite without poets. Joyce Kilmer called poets "glorified reporters." Writing is such an excellent detective of your development.

I showed her "A Sense of Proportion." She was delighted. She loved "tread on the very hem of truth." She asked me if I had always written and I explained that Shady Hill really started me. I remarked that its purpose was not to teach information but to teach how to get information for yourself. She was very interested. When I said that I thought it sometimes lacked discipline she said that the subject was the only discipline necessary. The objective of education should be, she said:

1. vitality
2. courage
3. sensitivity
4. intelligence

She asked if I were going to college. She said immediately that she thought I ought. But I explained all my reasons that I have told you often and that I would follow a more or less regular course of study alone. She thought a minute then "I can't say right off for you as I did for Beatrice 'G', because of your background and character. But don't decide until you have to. Keep your mind open. It will cut you out of precious things not to have a degree." She was much surprised that I am to act instead of write. I guess she thinks I can't do it. She said I might find that I only wanted to act as a way of getting experience for writing. I was rather amused.

I read "Hedda Gabler" but told her that it is rather an idealized version. She said that the pistol was the symbol of the play, and that if Eva Le Gallienne had given the picture of a cruel, cold explosive person then her interpretation was right despite the criticism of critics.

Once she asked if I knew E. St. V. Millay. There we absolutely agree. I offered to lend her Millay's article "Fear" which she had not seen. She was pleased that I read the newspapers enough to have seen that. She said that few kids my age read them, but it seems to me all my friends do. She wants me to read Tennyson's "Rispah" as an example of the difference between modern and classical poetry. She said that poets today do not write with the purpose of educating or reforming but for the purpose of interpreting life. This she thought the true way of making beauty.

I then read "The Tower." She said it had a mysticism that reminded her of Maeterlinck. We discussed its meaning a little. I said I meant by the tower falling that once beauty was unessential it had to crumble. As a partial explanation of what she thought I was trying to say she gave me this:

"Love of life, personal at first, desire for a subject, personal growth and positive achievement in that subject, out of which beauty must come."

"People kill time, spend it, only a few use it and you are one who uses it."

She likes "Monday" very much. She seemed rather surprised. She was greatly touched by "A Friend" and loved the symbol of geranium leaves. I can't remember what else she said about it.

Best of all I think she liked "When something beautiful makes a hush." She sort of caught her breath.

At the end we shook hands twice. She said we'd have great times together next year. And that school opened on Oct. 1st. Cheers!

I miss you both terribly—the room seems so huge and empty and still.

Best love to your mother and piles to you—

May

Abby and Mary Dewing: High school friends of Sarton.

Mrs. Evans: Florence Evans; co-director of Gloucester School of the Little Theatre and director of the Boston School of Public Speaking.

Miss Cunningham: Florence Cunningham, whom Sarton called Ariel, co-director of Gloucester School of the Little Theatre; had studied with Copeau in Paris.

Peggy Leland: Fellow actor at Gloucester.

See Appendix for "A Sense of Proportion."

E. St. V. Millay: Edna St. Vincent Millay, 1892–1950, American poet, famous during the 1920s for her poems celebrating love, unfaithfulness, and the right of women to as much freedom in matters of morals as men; her work of this period influenced Sarton's early poetry.

Rispah: Rizpah

See Appendix for "The Tower."

Maeterlink: Maurice Maeterlink: 1862–1949, Belgian poet and dramatist known for the delicate fantasy, mystery and dreamy melancholy of his famous symbolist plays such as *Pelléas and Mélisande* and *The Blue Bird*.

See Appendix for "Monday," "A Friend," and "When something beautiful makes a hush."

TO KATHARINE TAYLOR   [June 1928]
[Raymond St.]
Dear Miss Taylor,

This is a book (Une Syllabe d'Oiseau) that I reread on very special occasions when I am in need of a beauty like white poppies. Marie Closset, "Jean Dominique," gave it to me herself. I love to think of your reading it lying in a steamer chair with only sea around you—no telephone, no inquiring parents, no tired prospective teachers, no loquacious alumnae!

I also enclose poems. Some of them are very poor but I couldn't leave them out, so here they are wagging their tails behind them. I realize more and more that nothing I have written is poetry because it never sings, it never goes beyond words chosen to convey a meaning. The 9th ("Flowers After the Ball") is to Eva Le Gallienne. All the group about her were written in my wild week. It's funny how fast a thing like that goes even out of one's mind. You just have to kiss its wings and let it go, I suppose. I almost sent the second one alone (prayer). I would like it to represent me more than any other. It doesn't.

I guess there's no need of my saying "Have a glorious time!" I hope you have some adventures besides illimitable sleep. Give my love to the Greenes.

Great love,
May

Marie Closset: The Belgian poet Jean Dominique. Founder and director of the Institut Belge de Culture Français in Brussels and one of the most important influences in and throughout Sarton's life. Doro in her first novel, *The Single Hound*.

See Appendix for "Flowers After the Ball."

The Greenes: Rosalind, her husband Henry Copley Greene, and their daughters Katrine, Francesca, Ernesta, and Joy, were friends of the Sarton family. Sarton wrote "For Rosalind"; see *A Grain of Mustard Seed*.

TO ABBY DEWING   Tuesday [end of summer 1928]
[Gloucester]
Dear Abby,

I have been waiting for time to copy the Kahlil Gibran parables so that I could return them to you but I think I'd better answer your letter now and send them along afterward. I'm delighted to have them.

You said in your letter that Gibran looks like any <u>Swede</u>. He's Syrian! I adore the poem and am sending it to Jean T. [Tatlock] with some of the parables. I think all that group: the human philanthropist, the Puritan etc. are awfully good. I think it means by the optimist that he is trying to sweeten the entire ocean by putting in perseveringly pinches of sugar but the pessimist sees only the existing evil and even adds to it by his pessimism. I must say I don't understand the crucifixion one, especially the end interests me. I think "War" is tremendous and "The Fox" delicious.

I have a copy of the lecture letters, thanks. I used to spend about half the summer at the foot of Black Cap with the Boutons, so your description of climbing around there made me quite homesick. Isn't it terrible about Francesca? I wrote a long letter to K. [K. Taylor] who had not yet received my first letter about our night escapade. I think the one comforting thing of Bunny is that such an illness should happen to someone who is plucky enough to get something out of it and whose sense of humour is without bounds.

After closing up—I've never worked so hard in my life as those two days—I had the lovely surprise of being carried off to Bobby's farm in Franklin N.H. Her family came for her in their car and drove all the way back through the most gorgeous country. I stayed two days and then came home. Cambridge is positively desolate—there isn't a soul here so I am rather lonely. (a gentle hint for a quick answer)

I almost telegraphed that you must come to the last night of "The Taming of the Shrew." The Fiera was perfectly scrum and after the play we had a party and stayed up till nearly two o'clock dancing and talking. Mrs. Evans and Stuart danced. They were absolutely sweet—sort of trotting round in a business-like little way. Edgy came back especially for the last night.

Ted was so exhausted after the play that he fainted dead away, causing great excitement. However he was revived sufficiently to dance wildly the rest of the evening.

The sweet one avoided saying goodbye to everyone she could—It was quite funny. I hate goodbyes anyway and escaped to the kitchen when most of them left. I wrote a steamer letter to Miss Cunningham instead.

I enclose some poems by George Dillon that Mouse showed me. I had a long walk with her that last Sunday night until half past twelve. I got to know her better and like her awfully well.

Heaps of love to you all—May

---

the Boutons: "Aunt" Mary (Mrs. Charles) Bouton and her daughters, Charlotte and Margaret, were family friends from Cambridge.

Francesca: Francesca Greene was suffering from tuberculosis of the spine.

Bunny: Pet name for Francesca Greene.

Bobby: Probably Bobby Yerkes. Sarton met her at Gloucester in July 1928. She was four years older than May, and about to enter her senior year at Bryn Mawr.

The Fiera: Spanish for the mad, wild one. Sarton was probably referring to the role of Kate.

Stuart: Probably Stuart Avery who later became Abby Dewing's husband.

Ted: Ted Adams, to become business manager of the Apprentice Theatre and later, a writer and director.

T O   K A T R I N E   G R E E N E   [n.d. summer 1928]

[Gloucester]

Dear K,

I couldn't imagine whom your letter was from when I reached into my cubby hole and saw its fat self lying there. Mail time here is the most exciting time of day: our little boxes are in a tiny hall sort of place called "The Porthole" which cannot comfortably hold more than three people, so when 26 determined and eager boys and girls suddenly all rush into it you can imagine the result. Everyone insists on seeing for himself whether he has mail or not even if he is told by well meaning friends that he hasn't. Not only that but he seems to be determined to open his letter, if he has one where he is and peruse it to the final word despite damns and kicks from the rear. You can imagine the triumph with which I bore your letter from the battle to a shady tree and read it.

You sound as if you were having a glorious time as I am if that is possible. Quite apart from the theatre Gloucester is a scrumptious place. We live on a point where you can't get away from the sound of water plopping and squidging round piers, the chugging of motorboats, bells and buoys, and always over the tops of houses the straight geometrical lines of masts. There is no smell of fish, only salt and the hempen smell of ropes, and the hot smell of tar. The old sailors are great fun to talk with about the weather—this eternal subject. The theatre itself is almost completely surrounded by water as it is out on a pier.

The thing I have to tell you which can most nearly approach the wonderful tales you have heard about the camp is our one and only big adventure. Mary and Abby and I are the youngest here and had been terribly good for the first month so we were getting the reputation of being goody-goodies. (Don't smile. We really had been extraordinarily quiet though it may seem unbelievable). One night in solemn conclave we determined to put an end to this. Unfortunately it was a Saturday night so that to break any rules we had to stay out till after twelve instead of after half past ten. After the play at about eleven we went to the "ship," famous on Rocky Neck for late suppers and dancing. We tiptoed to the door dressed in our regular boys trousers and peeked. Then with great fear and trembling we walked in and sat down on the porch outside. Quite a few of the actors were there. For awhile we sat and looked about us at the tables lighted by a candle which showed us only circles of faces. Some terrible jazz was being screamed in jerks from a victrola. This was all very well but no one approached us to take our order. We felt exceedingly out of place and got farther back out of the light. We waited uncomfortably; nothing happened. We talked a little about nothing. Then with as much nonchalance as ~~possible~~ I could muster I sauntered up to the waiter and ordered ice cream and brownies. Ah! we breathed again. At least, we comforted ourselves, this was taking up time. It was now nearly half past eleven. By quarter to twelve we had finished and, very much relieved, got back into the cool dark night. We thought we'd walk around the neck until about twenty minutes past.

The stars were multitudinous and big as summer stars are. We explored a cavernously dark road shaded by trees, then climbed about on the rocks at the shore. For awhile we sat and watched the water creeping up and splashing into a fretwork of white spray. It's awfully hard to judge distances at night—I caught myself imagining rocks to be several feet away which were right beside me. We clambered up a precipitous wall into an uncannily quiet garden and house and ran to another road. We were all tingling and prickly with excitement, all our senses on the alert. At a street lamp we looked at our watches and decided we might return.

Luckily the door wasn't locked. We crept upstairs to be met reproachfully by Mrs. Goodwillie, the housemother. Then we tumbled into bed and stayed awake talking for hours.

The best part was to be when we told Miss Cunningham but she was away over Sunday so we waited peacefully until six o'clock. O! I wish you could have been there! We sat on her bed and laughed until we cried and until we could hardly breathe. It was only then that we fully appreciated the humour of the situation. Between gasps she suggested various worse things we might have done. Ever since we have regretted that we didn't go in swimming and come back by the fire escape. However our reputation is now established as un-goody-goody so our chief end is accomplished.

[unsigned]

———

The Rocky Neck story: This incident was inspiration for "Picnic," Holograph Journal 1928, see *Among the Usual Days,* p. 20.

TO ANNE THORP   [4 April 1929]
[Raymond St.]

Here we are plump in the middle of spring almost without knowing it! Things happen so suddenly, so unaccountably these days. The amazing grass is now bright emerald in every garden; crocuses overnight have shot their purple and orange flame through the earth, and even snowdrops. I have seen primroses and countless anemones in shop windows that made me think of woods and a brook in Belgium. But this is horribly old news for you, who must already be in summer, half the world away from early English spring.

This, as a matter of fact, is a very English day, not the nicest. It is warm and gray; no one seems to get anywhere but to be having a very hard time getting there. Dreaming becomes the preeminent fact of life. One sits and wonders about silly things like will two times two equal four instead of five. It is also the sort of day when one half expects Pelléas and Mélisande to wander down the street or to hear Roland's horn across the hills.

Nothing terribly exciting has happened since Christmas, but the time has slipped away with lambish and gamboling little adventures. One is that Jane Cowl and Philip Merwall gave "Paolo and Francesca" here—Stephen Phillips' version. It was beautifully done, so beautifully that one was completely swept away from life into its stream for days afterward. Jean T and I went three times; she is living with us you see. The wonder of it was that, with the exception of a few perfect lines the play is not overwhelming; but somehow the actors caught every spark and intensified it so that they seemed fused into the words, and one could no longer separate beauty from beauty.

Then another scrumptious part of life is that we are all furiously writing and dash over to each others houses laden like bees with our honey—we being Jean T., Letty F., and myself. It's such fun to see what other people are thinking about the important things—spring for instance. And really you never know quite until you've seen the people's poems. I'm getting to know Triggy Clark much better; she reminds me of Emily Dickinson.

I'm reading Amy Lowell's "Keats" whenever pressing engagements into gardens or the river don't demand my immediate attention. It's marvelous, although rather long. She spends pages in reporting some authority or whether Keats ever read a certain book. This is important, but in spring it annoys me. She does have wonderful passages, though and sees with devastating clarity as well as with great love.

Anne Thorp: Anne Longfellow Thorp, grandaughter of the poet Longfellow, and May Sarton's teacher at Shady Hill. She was a friend of the family and a heroine of Sarton's novel *The Magnificent Spinster.* This letter appears in a holograph journal.

Letty F.: Letty Field, her brothers Herman and Noel, and sister Elsie were friends from Shady Hill.

Triggy: Margot Clark's nickname. She and her sister Jean, who later married Herman Field, author of *Angry Harvest,* an autobiography about his imprisonment, were friends from Shady Hill.

TO ELEANOR MABEL SARTON   Sunday, June 2d. [1929]
[Raymond St.]
Dear Miutsie—

I was glad to get your note from the ship. I hope the people haven't turned out too badly and that the captain is as nice as he sounds. Here it has been frightfully hot. One felt suspended in a kind of Hell. But today it is so cool that I am wearing a jersey dress. Cambridge is luxuriantly green as if the heat had fattened every leaf and blade of grass.

On Friday night Jean and I went to a concert at Symphony Hall, given by the Radcliffe and Harvard choirs and the symphony orchestra. It was perfectly marvelous. I have rarely seen orchestra and players so perfectly blended. They gave three things never before played in Boston. The first was a piece of exultation composed for the fiftieth anniversary of Radcliffe's founding which the concert commemorated. It was very beautiful, not too decorative, not childishly simple.

Then a Vaughan Williams little oratorio adapted from "Pilgrim's Progress." The soloists as usual weren't anything extra. But the great moments of the evening were the singing of the "Hymn of Jesus" by Gustav Holst. It is frightfully thrilling, as Hilda would say. The words themselves are wonderful. Here is a little part.

> "Divine Grace is dancing:
> Fain would I pipe for you: Dance ye all!
> Fain would I lament: Mourn ye all!
> The Heavenly Spheres make music for us;
> The Holy Twelve dance with us;
> All things join in the dance!
> Ye who dance not, know not what we are
>   knowing.
> Fain would I flee: and fain would I remain."

Miss Taylor was there in a heavenly blue dress <u>and</u> Mary Hotson. We were in the second balcony, but when I saw her on the floor I dashed down stairs to speak to her. I am going to see her this morning, which is jolly.

Yesterday in the morning I went to town to get some things for Gloucester. I bought a white felt hat for $1.69 also a shirt for the same price, and a delectable powder blue ~~jacket~~ tailored jackety coat ($2.25) to wear with sailor pants and in general at Gloucester. ~~Then I we~~ (these all in Filene's basement.) Then I went to Raymond's where I got two pairs of real boy sailor pants for only $.95 each. Isn't that marvelous? I won't need anything more for Gloucester except perhaps stockings which I'll get at the last minute.

Mrs. Dodd called up, much surprised to hear you were gone, to say she had sold both dresses. She is mailing you a check, I believe. I gave her Grannie's address.

Yesterday afternoon—rehearsal. We did the first act with the whole cast. It was supposed to be without books, but when we stop so much for corrections you really have to have them. It didn't go very well, though I got on very well. Mrs. Evans was beaming. I'm beginning to get awfully excited, as I really think it's going to be great. Heaps of love to all the children and Uncle Raymond, Lino, and Bobo, and Grannie.

A great hug,
May

TO ELEANOR MABEL SARTON   Sunday, June 15th [1929]
[Raymond St.]
Dearest Miutsie—

Graduation is over—I am now a dignified alumna of C.H.L.S. and never, never shall I have to go to school again. You can't imagine how happy I am! It all went very well. Sanders Theatre was absolutely jammed. There must have been about 1500 people. I have never spoken before such a large audience before so it was awfully thrilling! I think the poem went well. For the Caroline Close prize I got Stanislavsky's "My Life in Art"—perfectly marvelous. You must read it when you get back. This last week has been the busiest of my life, for I have had to be cramming furiously for Chem. besides rehearsals Friday, Saturday and today! It is awfully hot, which makes matters worse. However I begin to breathe more comfortably now I have completely reread the Chem. book and studied it pretty thoroughly. Did I tell you that I got 80% on a practise college-board we took? I was awfully surprised.

If only we could both get the lines, the play would be going very well. Mrs. Evans is delighted with the acting, but of course it is impeded at every move by our forgetting our lines. After this ordeal of exams is over I shall have time to concentrate and then I hope with a day or two's work I'll get them firmly stuck. I am going to wear a lovely deep blue suit of Ibby's in the second act in which I have to have a skirt. It suits me and fits me to perfection.

Aunt Lucy gave me a darling little fairy garden for graduation. I think it was dear of her to think of it. It is a delectable little elf sitting on a snail's back. And Mrs. Ekern sent me $5.00—a huge sum. I have spent it on a wonderful book of oriental poetry. Here are a few—

This is by a Japanese—Buson

HOKKU
Granted this dew-drop world is but
A dew-drop world—this granted, yet . . .

and this little Chinese one by Li Shang-yin

THE FIGURED HARP
I wondered why my figured harp had
fifty strings,
Each with its flower-like fret an interval of
youth - - -

The sage Chuang was day-dreaming, bewitched by
                    butterflies,
The spring-heart of Emperor Wong was
                    crying in a cuckoo,
Mermen wept their pearly tears down a
                    moon-green sea,
Blue fields were breathing their jade to
                    the sun - - -
A moment that ought to have lasted
                    forever
Had come and gone before I knew.

Jean left yesterday. It's awful without her—except that I'm so busy. I'm going to K. T.'s on Wed.—And I guess that's all the news. Love to Grannie from whom I got a dear note last week. I shall write to her as soon as I have time. Best love to the Limbosch's—

And needless to say oceans for yourself—

May

C.H.L.S.: Cambridge High and Latin School.

poem: Sarton delivered the class poem.

Ibby: Ibby Tracy, a friend of May's from Shady Hill.

Aunt Lucy: Lucy Stanton, a miniaturist, aunt of Stanton Forbes. Her works are in the collections of the Metropolitan Museum of Art, the Philadelphia Museum of Art, the National Portrait Gallery, and Emory University. She and her husband owned the cottage in Ogunquit which the Sartons were invited to use for many Augusts.

Mrs. Ekern: Alice Ekern, friend of the Sartons.

TO ELEANOR MABEL SARTON   Friday Eve. [23 August 1929]
[Raymond St.]
Dearest Miutsie—

Thanks for your note. A rather thrilling thing has happened. Daddy and I went Wed. night to "The Playgoer's Theatre" and afterwards I went backstage to see K. By a strange coincidence they were frantic for an ingénue in their play "Pygmalion and Galatea" next week. Almost in spite of myself I was dragged into it and am rehearsing now. I couldn't think of any excuse, though I really didn't want to do it. I did <u>so</u> long for a peaceful week. Well, anyway it will be good experience. They are making me do the part very melodramatically which rubs me the wrong way and I am rather tired. But don't worry I am really very happy and glad to be home—and I have some free time.

I am reading "Jean Christophe." I absolutely adore it.
I am longing to see you—

Love,
May

K: Katharine Warren, chief actress of the Boston Repertory Theatre.

Pygmalion and Galatea: (1871), adaptation of the greek legend by Sir William Schwenck Gilbert (1836–1911).

Jean Christophe: Novel series by Romain Rolland, (1866–1944). A favorite of George Sarton's who gave it to his daughter.

TO PARENTS   Sunday 5:20 p.m.
[94 Macdougal]   [1 September 1929]
Dears—

Here I am, safely ensconced in my room. It is really quite sweet and I already feel very much at home in it. I don't think I'll have to get a bookcase because there are two shelves under the window which give ample space for my books. Here is a plan of the room:

[   ]

This is somewhat out of proportion as the cupboard is quite small and the room only a little wider than the window, which is quite big. I may finally get rid of the armchair—it is rather in the way.

I had to leave my trunk downstairs and carry every single thing upstairs in my hands! I finished all that this morning when it was quite cool. Now it is fearfully hot. I have been sleeping all afternoon until now, as I slept badly on the train.

Lunch was very good—they have a cafeteria system, rather fun. I ate with Mrs. Baldwin and her daughter. After supper I think I'll go for a little walk.

The people outside fascinate me. They look out from their windows—little old ladies, babies, fat women, canaries and cats, while the men talk vociferously below, very conscious of their Sunday clothes. It is quite foreign. Right opposite is a little café (also a "speakeasy") called "Dante Alighieri"!

Well, heaps of love to you both.

Write soon,
May

Mrs. Baldwin: Mrs. Julia D. Baldwin, director of the McLean Club at 94 Macdougal Street, New York City which advertised itself as "A Place to Live in New York For Young Business Girls and Students."

TO PARENTS   Saturday
[94 Macdougal]   [7 September 1929]
Dears—

I met Miss Cunningham at Grand Central last night and we had supper together which was great fun. Then I took her to the boat. She looks tired but is gay as usual though a bit sad to be going alone. It was awfully nice to see her—she's such a darling.

Of <u>course</u> I can manage with the money I have—I'll draw on my account at the bank if necessary. Also next month I wish Daddy could put in another $50.00 and have the $100.00 simply as a reserve fund to be used only in an emergency. Because they charge me if my balance gets below $100.00. This month of course it will get way below because I shall have to pay three weeks board—but I don't think they'll charge me very much. At the end of the month I'll send you an exact account—I am keeping a very careful one.

Did I tell you that later on we are to give "The Lower Depths"? I am awfully excited—I'm getting a copy today. The library, by the way, is simply marvelous. I have such fun browsing in it!

Next week we start dancing and fencing with Blake Scott—there has been no mention of charge so I think it's free. You see they use us in plays as return.

There, I must go to dress-rehearsal of "Cradle Song"—

Great love
<u>May</u>

J. Blake Scott: Actor and dancer, member of the permanent company of the Civic.

TO PARENTS   [probably September 21, 1929]
[94 Macdougal]   Tuesday
Dears—

Yesterday was an exciting day—In the first place my poem "Friendship" has been accepted by the "Harp"—a poetry magazine. There is no remuneration, worse luck, except extra copies. People never pay for poetry. Isn't it disgusting? Anyway I'm awfully thrilled.

Then I went to buy my victrola—I have finally bought a Victor portable, $35.00. The $25.00 one had metal fixtures inside so that it reverberated as if against tin and the other is *so* much better I thought you'd agree that it was worth it. If not I can still change it. The Cortina course has come and looks very good—yesterday I didn't have a moment as a friend came and stayed the whole afternoon and for supper—she is very nice, a Southern girl, Helen by name. But I can hardly wait to begin. I am buying the Oxford Book of German Verse—a second hand copy in excellent condition for $3.00. You see it starts with very simple old lyrics which are easy and delightful to read and gets harder as it goes on. So I shall use it as a reading book. Then I wish if you have a German Bible and a dictionary you would send them because there doesn't seem to be a dic. with the course. Also while I think of it—the records I most want if you can spare them are the Brahms first symphony and "To the Memory of a Great Artist." It will be marvelous being able to hear music.

Last night was the first night of "Sea Gull"—it went marvelously and the papers are unanimous in praise. When Eva came on at the beginning there was tremendous and unceasing applause—it was really very moving, and at the end people simply wouldn't go away. Mrs. Fiske, who is a relation of Merle Maddern's, came to the dress rehearsal. She seems very charming.

Today I shall be awfully busy—at 9:30 the first dancing lesson, at 12 dress rehearsal of "Cradle Song," and tonight my first appearance behind New York footlights! Thank heavens it isn't hot because the nuns' costumes are frightfully hot.

I enclose an account of the first two weeks—I have tried not to be extravagant. "The Admirable Crichton" and the "Moscow plays" I had to buy for the student group and Descartes I wanted to study. Verlaine and "Crime and Punishment" are the only things I've had that I haven't needed. It's appalling how fast money goes!

Heaps of love,
May

———

Helen: Helen Brewer.

Eva: Eva Le Gallienne.

Mrs. Fiske: Minnie Maddern Fiske (1865–1932), actress whose career spanned half a century.

The Admirable Crichton: (1902), a Dramatic fantasy by J. M. Barrie (1860–1937).

TO PARENTS   [23 September 1929]
[94 Macdougal]   Monday
Dears—

Today I found four fat letters in my box—it was such joy! Thank you for sending the checks early because since I have to pay my lodging one week in advance I would have had to pay the first week of October out of September's which would have brought me rather low. I think I shall be able to cut down this month—I'm getting into the swing of things. Also I think I'll pay the whole of October for my board and lodging at once so's to have it off my mind.

I can hardly wait for the records—it was sweet of you to send them so soon, and the books. I am getting on finely in German and eagerly await the dictionary. The Cortina system is excellent I believe. Are you sure the first volume of "Jean Christophe" isn't somewhere there? It may be in my room, in fact I think it is. I'm sure it's in the house somewhere. I have so fallen in love with French that I hate reading English—it is such a vague inadequate language compared to French.

I am dying to see the kitten—it sounds sweet. Do name it "Carmen" if it's a girl and anything like its mother in character. Don't bother to send the certificate. I'll see it when I come home. Yes, my bed is very comfy and the food on the whole good. I haven't found out about Messendinck [?] because Miss Cunningham said that it was bad to take fencing at the same time and we are having fencing. <u>Do</u> forward the letter from Aunty Lino and Oncle Raymond!

I got a dear little note from Miss Cunningham from the boat on Friday— perhaps I told you.

Yesterday I had a very quiet day doing German and reading Descartes— and finishing volume VI of Jean Chr. I'll mail the two I have in my next batch of laundry and would you ~~give~~ send me the remaining volumes in the same way? Last night was the dress rehearsal of "Cherry Orchard"—It was agony because Merle Maddern wore all Nazimova's clothes and did it atrociously!—

Heaps of love
May

First week

<u>on hand</u>	
<u>10.95</u>	
lunches	3.05
carfare	1.50
food (at night)	1.37
~~taxis~~	~~.45~~
eau de cologne	.75
~~shorts (for dancing)~~	~~.85~~
~~telephone~~	~~.25~~
~~Verlaine~~	~~.60~~
Admirable Crichton	1.00
~~socks~~	~~1.00~~
- - - - - - - - - - - - -	
total	10.97

<u>Second Week</u>

drew from bank	23.00
	also $5.00

" " "	18.50
paid in checks for Cortina	
and Vic.	60.00
board	13.35
"	13.35
lunches	2.90
carfare	1.85
food (at night)	.30
Lower Depths	3.00
Sea Gull ticket	1.00
odds	1.00
taxi	.35
head of Beethoven	.50
by Bourdelle	
map of N.Y.	.35
Descartes and	3.00
"Crime and Punishment"	
Guest's food etc.	1.50
dancing slippers	1.65
---------------	
total	41.60

TO PARENTS   [before 27 October 1929]
[94 Macdougal]
Dearest Miutsie and Daddy—

I've seen a coat that was made for me—it's chezkoslavakian [sic], dark green leather goatskin with the fur inside—all curly and white. It has marvelous embroidery in two panels down the side and a high collar and ruff at the bottom of black curly fur—and the sweetest little hat to match. I've never seen anything before that I felt was meant for me—really. I tried it on and it suits me to perfection and will last for ever—much longer than a fur coat— But and I realize how terribly much it is—it costs $175—I'll be willing to go without any luxuries all winter if I may have it and no Christmas presents and could perhaps earn some of it in the summer. O please, please I've never been in such ecstasies over a piece of clothing before and you know I wouldn't ask unless I felt that it was really worth it. I suppose it's frightfully extravagant. But if you could see it I know you'd say yes, it isn't gaudy—it's really very sober and distinguished. If you could advance me the money I think I could pay it back on the installment plan.

This is just a wild hope, because I know we can't afford it. It's a pity I can't just offer her (the lady in the shop) a sheaf of poems and say here is my greatest beauty—now give me yours—

Mrs. de Neeregaard and Beatrice are still abroad. Yes, Jo Hutchinson is charming—You know, Leona Roberts is her mother.

I did tell you that I am to be Dunyasha the maid in Act I of "Living Corpse."

> heaps of love
> May

P.S. I wrote most of this at the theatre where I didn't have any other paper.

––––––

Beatrice: Beatrice de Neeregaard, member of the permanent company of the Civic. Frequently visited her native Copenhagen with her mother.

Jo Hutchinson: Josephine "Josie" Hutchinson, intimate friend of Le Gallienne, and her mother, Leona Roberts, were actors in the permanent company of the Civic.

TO ABBY DEWING   November 31st [1929]
[94 Macdougal]
Dear Abby—

I adore your description of Ariel's smile—it's such fun to get news from you all! Especially as every now and then I get a tooth-achy twinge for Cambridge. I think I'll be able to come home for a day and half at Christmas time, leaving on the midnight Monday and coming back Wednesday afternoon. You see they're giving "The Living Corpse" Christmas night and I have to be back for that.

I have just finished Proust's "Swann's Way"—I adore the style. He has the best sense images of any writer I know, especially of smells. For instance this description of rain "A little tap at the window, as though some missile had struck it, followed by a plentiful, falling sound, as light though, as if a shower of sand were being sprinkled from a window overhead; then the fall spread, took on an order, a rhythm, became liquid, loud, drumming, musical, innumerable, universal. It was the rain." and this of the smell of a quilt—"the nondescript, resinous, dull, indigestible, and fruity smell of the flowered quilt." But I think I wrote you about it before. Now I'm reading Galsworthy's "Modern Comedy"—I don't like it as well as "Forsyte Saga" but it gives the same keen pleasure, the same sane wisdom, and subdued shiny wit. Somehow Fleur's generation seems terribly self-centered and artificial—and I suppose we are.

Since I last wrote to you thousands of exciting things have happened—which is a slight exaggeration, but you know that characteristic of Snabs. One of the girls was suddenly called home and I have inherited both her parts—so I have graduated from the insignificant rôle of wolf to that of Indian in "Peter," and am Natasha in Gorky's "Lower Depths" which the students are giving. It's a marvelous part—the sort of one where you feel that you really become the person—like Hilda. But the most exciting has just happened today. I am to play Francesca in "Paolo and Francesca" by Stephen Phillips! I've never even dreamed of playing such a part—but today between two performances of "Peter" we had try-outs and just by luck I got it. You can't imagine how happy I am!

I must read "A Preface to Morals" [Walter Lippmann]—everyone says it's so marvelous. I guess I told you that I've been reading Uncle Ernest's new book "Types of Philosophy." I like it more and more. He says such things—things that you've always known but never formulated. But with rehearsals all day of "Living Corpse" and performances of "Peter" I have to squeeze time in for reading, and it's a very tight squeeze!

I'm playing a heavenly Schubert quartet on the vic—it's so wonderful having one in my little room where I can [listen to] music whenever I choose. When Kousse was here with the Boston symphony I went because of the Beethoven 5th. It was heavenly—like a first fall of snow or a sudden spring day transplanted into winter. It must be simply thrilling—singing with Doc. You're going to sing the Requiem aren't you? When? I've simply got to come.

I'm sure Eva will come to Boston, but I don't know when or what she'll bring. I want her terribly to bring "Inheritors" by Susan Glaspell—but I haven't dared to ask yet. I suppose she'll bring one new play—perhaps "Romeo and Juliet" which opens in the spring, or "The Living Corpse." I don't think they'll decide until after Christmas. O, I just thought perhaps "The Would-Be Gentleman." I hope they do. Brecher is so good in it.

I got a note from Judy the other day asking for information—I haven't answered yet—I simply haven't had time. Anyway she couldn't get in this year. Isn't it strange that she's thinking seriously of going on the stage? I don't think she'd like the student group, but she might.

I have made some awfully good friends, though when I came I was so spoiled by you all that everyone seemed terribly stupid and uninteresting. I really am having a glorious time—

Heaps of love and write soon
May

The Forsyte Saga: A series of novels by John Galsworthy (1867–1933). Fleur is one of the characters who appears throughout. *A Modern Comedy* was a second series of novels about the Forsytes.

Snabs: The name Sarton used for Jean Tatlock, Letty Field, and herself.

Uncle Ernest: Ernest Hocking, who with his wife Agnes founded the Shady Hill School. Sarton called him "Uncle." For more see "I Knew a Phoenix in My Youth" in *I Knew a Phoenix.*

Kousse: Serge (Alexandrovitch) Koussevitzky (1874–1951), American conductor and composer of Russian birth, conductor of the Boston Symphony Orchestra, and founder of the

Berkshire Music Festival at Tanglewood. See "Koussevitsky" written at age 15 in *May Sarton: Among the Usual Days.*

Brecher: Egon Brecher, member of the permanent company of the Civic.

Judy: Unidentified.

TO GEORGE SARTON   [4 January 1930]
[94 Macdougal]   Saturday
Dear Daddy—

I forgot to tell you that the bank's address is: The Amalgamated Bank of New York, 11–15 Union Square: I have at last been able to cash on your check so I am returning the $5.00 you sent—thank you piles—it really pulled me through.

With the money that Aunt Louise gave me I have just ordered Katherine Mansfield! A week from tomorrow I am going on a walk on the Palisades with some of the students, you could ask Catherine to send my Hilda clothes special delivery—my boots, blue flannel shirt, knickers, and brown cap, and my old knapsack? They are either in my room or upstairs in the flat trunk.

O yes, before I forget, I have been thinking of what records I want next— I think the pastoral symphony, and Tchaikovsky overture to "Romeo and Juliet," and if there is any more room a few Chopin preludes. I play the ones I have everyday—I love particularly the Brahms.

I've just heard that Eva isn't coming to Boston this year—they're only going to Philadelphia for two weeks. Isn't that horrid? In that case, I may have to stay here until the end of May with a two weeks vacation when they go to Philly. I had so looked forward to their coming to Boston. Isn't it beastly?

I'm so glad you like the Sigrid Undset book. I have just read Radclyffe Hall's "The Unlit Lamp." I think it's the most devastating book I've ever read—but exquisitely written.

It's a glorious day with a deep blue cloudless sky and lots of wind—now I'm going to Peter Pan—

Heaps of love
<u>May</u>

Aunt Louise: Louise Inches, a Cambridge friend of the Sartons whom May called "Aunt Louise."

Catherine: The Sartons' maid.

Sigrid Undset book: Probably one of the Kristin Lavransdatter series (1925–1927) by the Norwegian novelist.

[94 Macdougal]
Dearest Miutsie—

Tomorrow Eva is going to give us criticisms—it's really terribly thrilling. Yesterday we had a meeting of the students and I pleaded to have a work-shop or laboratory where we should try problems instead of trying to finish easy little plays to show our ability. Eva was there without our knowledge and said I was absolutely right! Isn't that nice? I guess she was just passing by and got interested in the discussion.

Today has been warm like spring and pale gold—I didn't have to go to the theatre at all so had a lovely fine time just reading and writing letters and doing nothing.

I have bought K. Mansfield's letters with the money given me by Aunt Louise and Aunt Mary—they are utterly heavenly. She says things like "My roses—my roses are too lovely. They melt in the air (I <u>thought</u> that in French where it sounds sense but in English it's nonsense.)"

You must read it when I come home. I paid the rest of the month's board in advance so that's off my chest!

Do write soon
Heaps of love
<u>May</u>

TO PARENTS   [1 February 1930]
[94 Macdougal]   Sat. Eve—
Dears—

Today has been a large orange marigold—mummy's telegram arrived this morning with the money and started me off grasshoppering to the theatre. I bought a bunch of marigolds on the way home. They look glorious in my pewter jug.

Last night I saw "L'Invitation au Voyage"—by far the most profoundly poignant thing I have ever seen. I think I must have dreamt it—there couldn't <u>be</u> such a play. Eva was more than herself.

The coat is perfect—I am going to get a wide belt to wear with it, like a trench coat—I tried it with a belt of mine and it looked just as I had dreamed about.

O yes, could you send me two copies of the <u>nicest</u> of the three photos you took on Christmas day—you know, the smiling one.

Tomorrow's Sunday—I am saying over that little poem of Davies (in the book Daddums sent) isn't it exquisite—

"Sweet Chance, that led my steps abroad,
  Beyond the town, where wild flowers grow,

A rainbow and a cuckoo, Lord
How rich and great the times are now!
Know, all ye sheep
And cows that keep
On staring that I stand so long
In grass that's wet from heavy rain—
A rainbow and a cuckoo's song
May never come together again:
May never come
      This side the tomb.

          Love and love—
          <u>May</u>

———

Davies poem: William Henry Davies (1871–1940), "A Great Time" in *Great Poems of the English Language,* Harrap & Company, 1928.

TO PARENTS   Monday, [17 February 1930]
[94 Macdougal]
Dears—

   "Poetry" has accepted some of my poems! Here is what Harriet Monroe said in her letter—"Although we are accepting almost nothing because of congestion, your two poems seem to me too beautiful to decline. But I warn you that it may be a year before we can use them. Perhaps by that time there may be more. We pay on publication"—Isn't that thrilling? I can still hardly believe it—even though I have to wait some time before publication, the main thing is that I've really broken through. "The Harp" is nothing—but *Poetry* has a very high standard—and is the only poetry magazine that pays. The awful thing is that I can't remember which two I sent—when I send in the little biography they require, I'll ask—though I feel an awful fool. I think they may be these two—

              AFTERMATH
Let me rest now, let me lay my hand
In yours, as cool as smooth as stone—
Keep it, hold it as holds ribbed sand
A wave's shape after the wave has gone.
Let no wind come to blow the lashes down
Between our eyes, who look each into each
As a fawn looks at that sea-changed fawn
In a rock-pool. Let the bronze beach
Color our mind alone with sand and space.
All we gave, lost or took in pain

Forgot as the wind in this windless place,
Forgot as noise of wind during the rain.
Let us rest now. Let me lay my hand
In yours like a smooth stone on the
smooth sand.

I haven't time for more as it's "Living Corpse" tonight—Daddy's gay letter arrived with the "Poetry" letter—making a lovely day. The broken record is in the 6th symphony which I'll mail probably tomorrow morn. or the next day. Love

May

I adore the Chopin things!

Harriet Monroe: (1860–1936), American editor and poet. Known chiefly as the editor of *Poetry* which she founded in Chicago in 1912, an immensely influential magazine often introducing the work of leading American and British poets.

"Aftermath": Published in revised form in *Encounter in April* as sonnet "Now let me rest. Now let me lay my hand." Also enclosed, "First Love" published in *Poetry* December, 1930; a.k.a. "First Snow."

TO HARRIET MONROE   March 1st, 1930
[94 Macdougal]
Dear Miss Monroe—
    Would "Let No Wind Come" do for a title instead of that stupid "Aftermath"? I am very brazenly enclosing the other three sonnets that belong with it, on a chance. If you like them, the whole group could be called "This is Not Less than Love" so that each one wouldn't need a title. I hate titles— they always seem to be either advertisements or explanations, both of which should be unnecessary.
    Thanking you again, most fairy lady—

Sincerely yours,
May Sarton

TO ELEANOR MABEL SARTON   [13 March 1930]
[94 Macdougal]   Thursday
Darling Miutsie—
    I just got Daddy's letter saying you were ill—O, I wish I could fly to you on the March wind and shower you with daffodils and anemones—
    I began this last night before you telephoned—I'm so relieved—and this morning came your letter. How annoying about Jean's dress—she really is unthoughtful in some ways. I would simply say that you haven't time to arrange for another—regretfully.

I had Strawbridge again yesterday—it really is marvelous. I feel absolutely relaxed and yet straight and fine when we're through. He uses lovely images. For instance to get the feeling of holding one's head high, he said, "Pretend you have wings behind your ears like Hermes." And we did a thing of swinging our arms which he described as "lassoing a chair, a table, an elephant—lassoing the earth, the universe" till we get terribly excited.

Ross is I think, going to cast "Outward Bound" today—he's kept us in suspense so long I'm afraid I won't get Ann, as there's another girl a good deal older who read with more ease and finish than I—though less feeling. I'm sure. <u>Do</u> get hold of the play—it's very good—it's by Sutton Vane.

I'm awfully sorry I've forgotten each time to speak of "Poet Lore," Daddums. I would love to have it—they don't have it at the theatre. They print excellent plays in it, I think. I hope the Providence lectures take a sudden leap forward, now that Mummy's better.

Abby D. sent me a program of the Brahms festival. How frightfully tantalizing! I hope you are going—my victrola is broken again. I can't understand it—I always wind it very carefully.

I'm awfully excited about Philadelphia. I think I'll get about $20.00 a week, and the Cushman Club, where I'm staying, charges $17.00 for room and board! Isn't that excellent. Most of the people from the theatre are staying there. I'm going to room with Renée—not one of my best friends—but I like her very much. Helen, the little Southern girl, isn't going. Isn't that tough. Of course they take as few people as possible because of the expense.

When you're better, Miutsie, could you send me some piece of silk or crepe that I could make a tunic out of—it can be quite little as the tunic is just a short straight up and down one with a hole in the middle for my head and a belt.

Heaps of love
<u>May</u>

Queen Elizabeth has come—thank you. O, <u>do</u> get Daddy to get K. Mansfield's "Bliss and other stories" from the library. It's perfectly charming.

Strawbridge: Edwin Strawbridge, dancer, choreographer, actor, and director of children's theatre.

Ross: Robert F. Ross, member of the Permanent Company of the Civic Repertory Theatre and director of the First Studio Group.

Sutton Vane: (1888–1963), English playwright, wrote *Outward Bound* at twenty-six.

Renée: Renée Orsell, member of the Civic Repertory Theatre; later stage manager of the Associated Actors Theatre.

TO HARRIET MONROE   April 6th [n.y.]
[94 Macdougal]
Dear Miss Monroe,

Here are four for spring—perhaps you will like one of them. I have suddenly come to an unrythmic [sic] and jagged place I'm afraid.

I am not for Mr. Zukovsky. It seems to me too intellectual and too deliberate an attitude to make for great poetry. Poetry is not an orchid, but a crocus. Simplicity is the very essence of poetry, and cleverness and simplicity have very little in common. And I blame his intolerance. O well—I mustn't go on. This sounds like a middle-aged adorer of Tennyson, I'm afraid.

Yours sitting under an azalea-tree
May Sarton

A perfectly heavenly white one

––––––––––

Louis Zukofsky: (1904–1978), American poet, translator and editor. His major work *"A"* begun in 1928 was a free verse journal of meditations.

This letter was found in holograph journal.

TO RENÉE ORSELL   [23 July 1930]
[Gloucester]
I've been in too much of a fog to deal with words even to people like you, whom I love. Letty Field died early in June. There seems to be nothing else to say. It's queer how one goes on living.

There are more stars in this sky than anywhere in the world, I think, and such sunsets. I'm soaking in sunlight, it intoxicates the earth. There are people here whom I love. I think as little as possible, so deep down, I'm probably as happy as I'll ever be.

––––––––––

Letty Field: On June 9, 1930 at the age of 18, Letty died of endometriosis.

TO HARRIET MONROE   October 13th, 1930
[94 Macdougal]
Dear Miss Monroe—

These really belong with the two of mine you so graciously accepted last year. I feel as if they went a little deeper. From this peak of 18 years last year already looks very far away. You grow so startlingly—by leaps.

And—dare I ask—when are the other two appearing? You said "next year" an eternity ago.

I send you a wind full of leaves—

May Sarton

TO HARRIET MONROE   October 26th, 1930
[94 Macdougal]
My dear Miss Monroe—

You have put wings on my shoulders, so that I'm really flying in your window to say this. Does it sometimes terrify you to have such power of joy or despair?

Yes, I am George Sarton's daughter—but really a black sheep as far as science goes, except in love for it. Then perhaps pure science and pure art are rather close, so that, in going into theatre, I'm really not right-about-facing but simply running parallel with my father.

This has been a thrilling week—the first reading of "Alison's House," Susan Glaspell's new play about Emily Dickinson. I think Emily herself is not far away. When you're in New York, come, <u>do</u> come to the Civic Rep. to see it.

Thank you again for simply existing, for being so bounteous and exquisite a person—

                                                    <u>May Sarton</u>

TO PARENTS   <u>Sunday</u> [9 November 1930]
[94 Macdougal]
Dears—

K.T. came unexpectedly to N.Y.—I had breakfast and a long talk with her on Friday. Isn't that fun? It was like manna from heaven.

Today I'm going to break in the first act of "Marceline," and at four a reading of "Alison's House." Monday night "Three Sisters" with Jo back—I have a funny little maid's part, and a delicious costume—no lines, but much lighting of lamps and trotting around.

I feel very drowsy—I think I'll go to sleep. It is a very pale Sunday day.

O, Daddy, I got an album for $1.25. I sent some records back last week. Have they come safely?

In three weeks I'll be seeing you!

                                                    Heaps of love
                                                    M—

Jo: Josephine Hutchinson.

TO PARENTS   Sunday [30 November 1930]
[94 Macdougal]
Dears—

My heart <u>did</u> leap when "Poetry" came. Have the ten copies come? I want to send one to K.T. Did you see the note at the back—which said "She is a daughter of the distinguished scientist, George Sarton"? I'm writing this in the Grand Central waiting for a train to Yonkers.

Friday night after "Three Sisters" I had a rehearsal of "Marceline"—in the middle of a scene there was suddenly a screeching crash—and a chair broke, (the boy who is playing Phillippe sat on the arm). It was a very valuable old chair, and more than that is used in "Alison's House" which opens tomorrow night! We were so "ahuri" that all we could do was laugh—finally Pete, the Korean, went to Tupper Jones (he is stage manager) and routed him out of bed. He is a perfect darling, came right over, and started to mend it then and there. At last at 4 A.M., you couldn't see where the break was! No one is to know, said Tupper. So we are mum except for occasional shivers whenever anyone leans heavily on the break. It was really terrible, but great fun, I must admit.

I have been busily making cards—they're going to be quite sweet. Mum, could you send me some of that bright blue Japanese paper for mounting? I'll pay for it—and (if it's not too expensive) about 12 sheets of that beautiful Italian paper for my poetry books. I'm using the bird as an end-paper and the peacock as a frontispiece. The cover will be very plain with no design, I think.

I have to go—

Heaps of love
M—

Yonkers: Home of Dr. Leo Hendrik Baekeland (1863–1944), the Belgian-born chemist and inventor of bakelite, the material which gave the great impetus to the modern plastics industry and Céline (Swarts) "Bon Bon" Baekeland, his wife; together they opened their home in Yonkers to the Sartons when they first immigrated from Belgium. Sarton stayed there as a child when her parents were away. See "O My America!" in *I Knew a Phoenix.*

ahuri: Bewildered.

Pete: Peter Hyun (1907–1993), stage manager for the Civic Rep, director of The Children's Theatre of N.Y. Federal Theatre, and later organizer and director of the Studio Players in Cambridge, Massachusetts.

TO PARENTS   8:30 P.M. [13 June 1931]
[on board S. S. Lapland]
                                    LOG

Saturday—June 13th—
Weather—clear, transparent sea, and sky—the horizon melts away—pale, still—un peu triste but in a deep peaceful way.

I just went to see if by any chance there were more mail, though I was spoiled already. And lo! three letters from 103 Raymond—Saturday Review refuses "Leopard"—and handkerchiefs from Mummy—and a Marconigram from Renée. She and Helen came and saw me off—we nearly waved our arms away, and altogether managed things gaily and gallantly.

I only have one cabin-mate who seems jolly in a nondescript and harmless sort of way. My cabin was <u>full</u> of bundles and flowers—The Dewings sent red roses and Robby (the darling) a bunch of ragged orange African daisies, Bon Bon a great basket of fruit (I sit and read and spit cherry stones out of the porthole.) I'm using the top bunk because of the porthole and anyway it adds to the zest of nautical life to have to clamber up and down and hoist my belongings by imaginary hawsers.

My table companions are about the worst possible and service interminable—I left before dessert after ogling them silently for an hour. A Belgian family—two girls—one of whom is tiny and frightfully spoiled and the other about my age sits at the far end so I can't speak to her. They sit opposite. On my left is a middle-aged middle-western society woman who spends the time either in complaining about the food or minutely studying the menu with lorgnettes, and her blue-eyed fat husband. Finally just as my salad came a fair young man came and sat at the end in my right but he looks frightfully dull and besides shyer than I—so I went out on deck to feed my spirit.

It's incredibly calm—no movement at all, and a good steady salt breeze.

I have just begun "Far From the Madding Crowd"—and like it enormously. Frank Blake sent me the short stories of Saki. O, two very sweet people have chairs beside mine. A young woman and her mother-in-law. They are the only people I have met really.

The Noyes family are here. But I'm not sure they remember me (from Intervale) and anyway I'm not very interested.

I'm still in a daze about Eva—in fact, I don't think about U.S. at all or I feel rather "mizzy" as Eva says. 15 months is a long time.

But on the whole it looks like a "bon voyage."

Bonsoir—

Sunday, June 14th

Weather—grey with squalls and a bank of mist—the waves are lovely—and I don't feel a bit sick. I got up at seven-thirty, had a delicious salty bath, and walked for an hour before breakfast—noone was down at my table. Then I wrote letters a little while and settled for the morning in my chair about ten-thirty. My companions are charming—(a mother and daughter) they come from Portland and know Maggie Clifford who was at Gloucester two years ago. They will introduce me to a lady in Paris who has a very cheap delightful pension and knows theatre people.

I am beginning to have a sense of the future—after rather a long wrench away from U.S.—what fun it's going to be looking for a job. I determine more and more on Paris—if not the English theatre then as a student under the Pitoëffs or Copeau—

I didn't tell you that Mary Henderson called Actor's Equity for me—and it's absolutely impossible even to <u>enter</u> England as an actress looking for a job. The man didn't know about France—but I think they will be more lenient as the problem can't be as bad due to language difficulties.

I like "Far From the Madding Crowd" more and more, though I haven't been reading much. This afternoon I slept for three hours.

The Belgian family is warming up—tonight we had quite an interesting conversation about India and Russia. The blue-eyed man has travelled a great deal.

We arrive Monday the 22d I think, so I'll cable Aunty Lino on Saturday I think. Don't forget Renée's birthday the 20th—I shall cable to her too.

Voilà—I'm not in a very talkative mood, you see.

Bonsoir, mes chéris—

Monday, June 15th

A heavenly sunset—pale yellow and an angelic blue with great purple clouds over the sun so that the rays spread underneath in a great fan.

I wrote to Anne and read a little, but am being very lazy. What a difference a blue sea makes! It is really not the sea itself that is moving I think, but the <u>light</u> over the sea—the wonder of light. It's like living in constant view of the anatomy of lights—you see it nakedly. But I am not like Daddy, a sea-child. I always feel a little strange and adventurous, like a foreigner who understands but cannot speak the language.

I'm looking forward immensely to seeing Aunty Lino and the children. There is really nothing much to say tonight. I am happy in a suspended sort of way.

Tuesday, June 16th

I got up early because it was such a heavenly day—and played three sets of deck-tennis and some golf (à la Sarton) with the result that I felt far too energetic for this cup of coffee, this cigarette, this desk, this abominable orchestra and these boring people.

Great event—the first ship we have seen. An Italian boat twice the size of ours and looking like a shell that the first wave would bear away.

I shall finish "Far From the Madding Crowd" tonight—it's a great book.

Goodnight—

Wednesday, June 17th

I'm writing in the most awful bedlam—an auction which might be a funeral or at best a Ladies' Aid society—I listen with half an ear and watch with half an eye—the most horrible American politician middle-west woman with a bull's neck and—

Friday, June 19th

I didn't have energy yesterday to gather words into sentences. In the morning I played five sets of deck-tennis—and in the afternoon had tea with a Madame Carola B. Ernst—a Belgian woman who knows Daddy. It was good practice for my French which is worse than I thought. She is a very intelligent person, and knows many French writers including Claudel and Verhaeran.

Saturday—

We arrive in Plymouth early tomorrow morning so this is the last day I can write a log. It's really terribly exciting now that we're almost there—I am sending a telegram from Plymouth as wireless from the ship is ruinous. It cost $5.00 to send Renée two words for her birthday!

This morning we passed a submarine "Nautilus" but I was fast asleep—losing an hour every night is no joke—yesterday I stayed in bed till lunchtime.

Today is quite grey with an unpleasant ground-swell.

Do write often—and I will—

and come soon—

All my love
<u>May</u>

Robby: Leona Roberts.

Bon Bon: Baekeland.

Frank Blake: Unidentified.

Pitoëffs: Georges Pitoëff (1887–1939), Russian actor and director whose work had an immense influence on the French theatre. His company did much of their best work in the Théâtre des Arts and the Mathurins in Paris.

Copeau: Jacques Copeau (1878–1949), French actor, director, and critic whose ideas influenced the theater throughout Europe and America.

Mary Henderson: Friend of May's, later a member of the apprentice theatre.

Anne: Anne Thorp.

Claudel: Paul Claudel (1868–1955), French poet, dramatist, and diplomat. Ambassador to Japan 1921–1926; to U.S. 1927–1933.

Verhaeran: Emile Verhaeren (1855–1916), Belgian poet and author.

August 2d, 1931
[Belgium (C)]
My dear Miss Monroe,

I sent a bunch of poems in June to go with "Antelope"—but no sign of a refusal card, nor more hopeful words have I had. Perhaps I didn't enclose a return-envelope. I have a sort of suspended feeling until I receive the ultimate syllable and can throw it into the wastebasket and begin again. So here they are—again.

We have migrated to Europe for the year. Daddy goes to Beirut to study Arabic—the second volume is at last finished and indexed. I am hunting a job in Paris. They are as rare as the fabulous Snark and usually turn out to be Boojums at that. But there is one slim hope—a theatre is being built for experimental American plays, to be given in English. They cast in September. If not there are endless things to be done and to venture. I would like to get into the Pitoëff's rehearsals.

The human landscape is discouraging. People wait for the debacle—there is a sound of breaking, and no real contact possible between the nations. They are all so afraid, and fear cramps life. Here in Belgium they say "Now Germany is starved into peace, but what will happen when she is strong again—young, powerful? What has always happened." And they wait for it. There is no trust in each other—only a sense of the uselessness of it all and the inevitability. But I'm too much in the middle here to be able to see far. You have a bird's eye-view, and perhaps it is more hopeful.

Most sincerely yours,

May Sarton

I find I have no American stamps to put on the envelope!

––––––––

Snark and Boojums: In a holograph journal letter to "Miss K" Sarton writes in April 1932: "*The Hunting of the Snark* [Lewis Carroll] is a profound tale. I find it applies to every occasion (much better than the Bible) & Snark being so much more elusive and charming than the God of David who would never have the imagination to turn into a Boojun when in a tight place, but content himself with obvious roaring and pulling of his beard. The power of the Snark is great, for he has never been seen nor heard."

TO MARIE CLOSSET, MARIE GASPAR AND
BLANCHE ROUSSEAU   August 26, 1931
[Le Pignon Rouge]
Dear Mademoiselles,

All my apologies for not having written to you earlier, but it seems that I have spent an entire month eating (those endless dinners!) with relatives—those stuffy rooms filled with knick-knacks, where even the windows are hidden behind lace and heavy silk, and which one leaves feeling a little like a stuffed parrot! Finally it's over—and one has time for one's friends.

Here are some poems—I'm sad that they're not better. Actually as I was typing them up I was struck by how little one can actually achieve when one wants to achieve so much.

I return again and again to Puits d'Azur and Une Syllabe d'Oiseau—such treasures—one never tires of them, rather they enrich one newly with each reading. Thank you for having written them is all one can say. Speaking of matters of the heart is impossible, but at least one can write a poem or send a flower.

The kitten has fallen asleep on my lap—his nose buried in my arm, one ear standing up, the other hidden. I can't budge.

I send you a butterfly—perhaps he will come in through the window, and land lightly on your cup for me.

May

Closset, Gaspar, and Rousseau: The three women Sarton came to call the Peacocks, and who appear as the Owls in *The Single Hund.* See "A Belgian School" in *I Knew a Phoenix.*

Puits d'Azur *and* Une Syllabe d'Oiseau: Titles of books of poetry by Jean Dominique, published by Mercure de France, the former in 1912.

TO HARRIET MONROE   October 6th 1931
[Paris (vanL)]
Dear Miss Monroe—

Great joy! Of course I am more than willing for you to publish anything and everything—in fact dancing up and down with delight that you should want any of them—I've been in empty bogs and marshlands of mind for ages. But now with autumn and leaves and your word floating in the window, we can really <u>dance</u> on fine ground again! Such an autumn too! Worth the whole summer of rain.

Are there three that you want "We came together softly"—"If I have poured myself" and "Leopard"? I'm not quite sure what order I sent them in, for the record. Also could perhaps "Antelope" be published with these? one that you accepted long ago in the spring—

I am having a heavenly time, hoping to have a book when I come back next summer, and meanwhile studying theatre with the Pitoëff's, and scuffling leaves in the Luxembourg, and sipping crème-de-menthe.

Again—a whole row of flower-pots of joys on my window-sill thanks to you!

Yours
May Sarton

O, has my subscription run out? I haven't seen the shadow of a poem for months. I guess I'd better enclose a note for the bus. man—forgive my bothering you—

TO PARENTS   Oct 6 [1931]
[Paris (P)]
Dears—

Please take my <u>not</u> writing as a good sign—I'm feeling quite settled down except for the job, which still looks far away. Still Mr. Gladstone will be back before the middle of the month and might do a play before the theatre itself is finished. For the present I go to the Pitoëff's rehearsals! I just went to the theatre and asked if I might and he said, "Of course"—they are rehearsing "La Locandiera" of Goldoni which I imagine is not their genre at all. Madame Pitoëff is tiny and very simple like a child, having fits of laughter—she looks about 18—a little thin face with a large mouth, and eyes and forehead reminding one of Duse—Mr. Pitoëff has an enormous head with curly black hair which looks strangely square and bull-necked from the back—tiny feet and beautiful hands—he directs very much as Eva did only with more impetuosity—often he runs onto the stage and does what he wants of the actor—this marvelously with a sort of abandon and un-self consciousness that's charming. Ludmilla plays almost <u>too</u> naturally, especially for this part—which really consists of artful flirtation and she doesn't flirt <u>at all</u>, so that one would imagine her to be really in love with the Chevalier—it spoils the whole point of the play. She has a strange rather flat voice which she lowers at the end of every sentence monotonously. Which sounds as if I didn't like her—I do really. I think she might be great in Tchekov and perhaps Ibsen. But she has very little technique from what I can see—is simply <u>feeling</u> projected—she holds herself badly, walks and moves badly except for her hands—and seems to have no sense of costume.

Anyway it is thrilling to be in a working theatre again—they are going on tour Nov. 25th and only coming back in February. But before that I shall have a chance to see them rehearse "Doll's House" and two other plays which I don't know.

The day before yesterday I was walking along by the stalls scuffing the leaves when I saw two strangely familiar ladies looking at some bright pictures of costumes that looked like Aucassin and Nicolette—I followed them and discovered F. C. and Roswell Hawley! a heavenly middle-aged person at Gloucester (she played the old woman in "Enchanted April"—Mrs. Fisher). We went and sat in the Tuileries by a fountain for a little while—and then I had to fly off to lunch. But I shall surely be seeing them again.

Then on top of that Laurette and her husband are here! I had lunch with them yesterday outside of a café in heavenly blazing sunlight—we were really roasted! Autumn is making up for the summer—day after day, clear blue and Luxembourg afire with all the oranges and golds of turning leaves, <u>besides</u> very green grass and all the flowers which mysteriously stay on.

Here at the Pension I have made two friends—a Mrs. O'Sheel (ex-wife of the poet Shaemus O'Sheel) who paints rather well in an amateurish way and is very responsive and tactile—we get on very well. Then there is a young American girl studying in very advanced classes at the Sorbonne, who is quite shy, but awfully nice too.

We three have little smokes and discussions together after dinner.

I've practically decided to get a victrola which I shall give away or sell at the end of the year—I can get one that isn't too bad for 175 fr. and Willem has piles of records which he will leave in the apartment. I'm so used now to having one—it fills up any solitude one may feel—I really think I'm not being extravagant. And I can save it in a few months by not having tea.

I've done almost no writing either—working and writing go together somehow—the less time I have the more I seem to write—It's funny. And here I have days and do nothing.

But here is one to go with others—:

> We who had been so wounded and so cloven
> Were grafted like two trees into one bark
> And our two colors sharply interwoven
> The delicate and bright, the tawny dark—
> Out of our mingled blood petal and flower
> With a strange fertile perfume of its own
> Love came upon us softly in that hour:
> We did not see that love lay there alone.
> And when we woke out of the dream she made
> Nothing had changed—the earth was just the same
> And we, so wounded, strangers and afraid,
> Standing apart saying each other's name,
> Looked down and saw love luminous and wild
> Lying between us like a sleeping child.

I haven't heard from you at all since Daddy's on the way—it's frightfully tantalizing, since I haven't the remotest idea how your landscape looks—

I'll try and be better about writing—at least once a week—and please do too—and heaps of love and anxious thoughts from

Your increasingly Parisian daughter
M—

I wrote to M. Delaisi <u>last week</u>—and no answer—I think he must be away, because he was so nice about asking me to come and see them, that he would surely answer. I've sent off also several introductions and have received no answer, which is a little discouraging. Perhaps you might send a word to De-laisi- 11, Place St. Michel VIe—

———

Mr. Gladstone: Unidentified.

Goldoni: Carlo Goldoni (1707–93), Italian dramatist, creator of comedies in the style of Molière.

F.C.: Florence Cunningham.

Laurette and her husband: Unidentified.

Shaemas O'Sheel (Shields): (1886–1954), New York poet whose work is in the tradition of Yeats and the Irish renaissance.

American girl: Mary Chilton, a friend Sarton met in Paris and greatly admired; she died in July, 1932. See "That Winter in Paris," in *I Knew A Phoenix.*

Willem: Willem Van Loon, dancer, son of Eliza and Henrik Willem van Loon, Dutch-born American journalist and author; the Van Loons lived in Washington when the Sartons arrived there in 1915 as refugees. Willem and May went to the same kindergarten where May proposed marriage sitting beside him on a laundry basket.

The apartment: Willem van Loon offered Sarton, now at a pensione, his flat in Montrouge while he was on tour starting October 22.

poem: Appears in *Encounter in April.*

M. Delaisi: Francis Delaisi (1873–1947), political reformer, labor leader, spoke at international conferences, wrote many important works. Friend of George Sarton.

TO ELEANOR MABEL SARTON   Sat. morn Nov. 21st—[1931]
[Paris (vanL)]

Darling little Miutsie—

Daddy left yesterday for Egypt I guess—I hope you won't be too lonely—do a lot of "settin'." Is there a library there [Beirut] where you can get books? I must say the descriptions of your Sunday excursions are <u>marvelous</u>—I suddenly feel tempted to fly down for a month—

There isn't any particular news except that I seem to be frenziedly pursuing time and it always escapes. I really almost never have two consecutive hours entirely alone and without interruption which is the only way I can work at all. This is partly because of the Polish boy who comes every morning to play the piano.

This morning is Marché—I usually spend Saturday entirely in the house and get up rather late. Marché is great fun—this time I came back with a basketfull of mimosas, narcissus and marigolds for 3 frs. 50 isn't that amazing? I've put them together in a blue-green jug—it's a little hard but nice.

Today I hope to make the drawing for a Christmas card—no more angels this year. But I don't know quite what. O, before I forget—Couldn't I get you material for Anne's coat here in Paris and mail it? Or any other things like cut-paper that you might need. It's horrible that the package got lost.

There is a very thrilling plan about the Tyrol—a Dutch boy here, friend of Willem's, knows a place in the Austrian Alps where you can get full pension for 1.60 a day counting tea and the ten percent. And there is a plan that a group of us would go up there for Christmas for a week—I must say I have a longing to be out of doors in sun and snow without houses or people. There is wonderful ski-ing. Mary Chilton—the nice quiet girl at the club—I like her more and more—well, she and I and T. (the Dutch boy) and his mother and some German boys, friends of his who live in Germany could have great fun together. T. is awfully nice—very correct European manners, and quite intelligent—a "good sport" but nothing special. I am working on a play with him for his audition for the student group of "Les Quinze"—a typical description of him is that he always brings cookies and things for tea when he comes to work with me—so sweetly.

This place sounds quite "Ark"-ish—no dressing for dinner as in the fashionable places, and no amusements and very few people and breath-taking country, T. says. It sounds perfect. In the evening you all sit around a great stove playing chess, or reading, or dancing in ski-boots to the victrola! Of course, the great expense is getting there (It's probably about $25.00 round-trip third-class, which we would do) then $15.00 for board for eight days with a little extra for drinks and cigarettes, and for hiring skis. The other great expense is ski-trousers, boots, socks and mittens. I have sweaters. I think I could do this for $15.00—T. knows a place there where you can get boots for $7.00 (they're usually ten) and this after all is a thing that lasts all one's life. The trousers I could get for five I think, maybe a little more. So all together with all expenses it would make about $60.00—it seems a huge sum. But I am hoping Anne and perhaps Bon Bon will give me money for Christmas. I could give $20.00 out of my savings and perhaps Daddy would give me twenty for Christmas instead of the pictures. (I have turned against the pictures because in the first place—they are huge and I would be a little shy of giving such a large portrait of myself. Also <u>very</u> expensive I think. Later I am going to look up Taboo.) But really I long to have this ski-trip—here I do no sports—and for two or three summers I haven't done any very much. What do you think about it? If it seems awfully extravagant I'll give it up immediately—we thought perhaps of going to Chartres for the week-end of Christmas if not. But it's being out of doors in sun that sounds so marvelous. I don't want to go to Belgium at all—though perhaps they will be disappointed. But they would understand a chance like this. I might perhaps go for two weeks in the spring. I feel very far away from them—and so close to Méta—it's very strange. I wrote again to Méta about a week ago to ask if there were any chance of her coming in Nov. as she had half-said she would.

But there is no answer. It seems strange. Have you heard at all? I sent a whole bunch of poems as a "Bon Voyage" which were never acknowledged.

I went to a dinner the other night—given by Rousseau (director of Guaranteed Trust) for the playwright Savoir (who wrote "Lui")—His daughter (Rousseau) is a Duncan dancer—I met her through Willem. It was quite exciting there were only the daughter, I, and an elderly banker's wife as women—and Irene had lent me a perfectly stunning black dress with a top of a Chinese embroidery applied onto it—I can't describe it but it's really stunning—lots of style and yet interesting. It has long sleeves. The men were Savoir, Rousseau and a charming French boy composer, Prix de Rome. The horrible thing is that they tried to get Eva to come—she's in town—but couldn't get hold of her in time! It would have been like a fairy-tale to meet her there, I must say. Savoir is a typical successful playwright, content to be merely witty, and very "mere" wit at that. I learned afterwards from Lugné-Poë that he is only interested in money. The boy played some Bach on the piano. It all went off very gaily—I felt well-dressed and looked quite lovely, if I do say so—and I managed to feel very much at ease (or they managed it for me). It's always rather an ordeal, but awfully good experience for your unsophisticated daughter!

I haven't seen Mlle. Sumpt for ages—I think she must be very busy because I sent her a little note asking her to come to tea ages ago, and she hasn't answered.

Affairs with Lugné-Poë are very amusing—he's really an extraordinarily kind person. But I doubt if he can get me a job. I left him laden down with plays and promises of tickets for tonight, but he hasn't telephoned as yet about that.

Yesterday I had tea with a very charming person—Germaine Swarts (daughter of a professor of Daddy's)—the first intellectual French person I've met, and I hope it will mean some contacts. She lent me a lot of books, and gave me the address of a library where I can get almost anything. She teaches and seems very jolly and extremely intelligent—it's a whole world of thought to explore which I haven't been able to find as yet.

Today came a letter from young Louise Inches—relating the great delight of a letter from you which they all savored extremely—and also the Van Cleve poem. I guess she wrote you too though. She told me to look up two people who both sound as if they might be amusing—an old man who is one of the curators of the Beaux Arts, and an Elizabeth Clèvenot described as follows "She dresses like a scarecrow, weighs 250 lbs. and has the energy of a cyclone and tornado combined." I am sending a note to both of these today. (Telephone!)

Bob Kennedy just called up and I'll have dinner with him on Friday which is a very nice prospect. Thursday is Thanksgiving—and Mary, Irene, Betty

Blake and I are all going to an American place that serves Thanksgiving dinner and then to the circus (Irene says it's the best theatre in Paris)—

As to the Van Loon's—Mrs. is in Munich and will probably go to Berlin for the winter. Willem is in the South with a German writer-friend—and is probably coming back to Paris for the winter with the friend, but he doesn't want the apartment thank heavens. I think Mrs. feels a little lost—she has no work—and Willem runs off of course (it can't be helped) and she really hasn't got a great many friends. You ought to write her a word someday—but I don't know her address—probably "Dresdene Bank, Filiale München, Promenade Platz, Munich would always reach her.

I got a dear little letter from Grannie which I shall also answer today—I owe fifteen letters (and all such long ones to write!) Grannie is worried about Hugh—

I must stop because I have <u>got</u> to practice—it is terribly hard to squeeze in the time!

> Your mouse
> with a thimble

(It was great to find the Mercury book of poems the other day—I haven't seen any poetry for ages—thanks piles, Daddums—and I like the idea of a book sent from Syria to Paris via London so to speak!)

"Les Quinze": Copeau's nephew, Michel Saint-Denis formed the Companie des Quinze in 1930 with members of Copeau's defunct Vieux-Colombier. By the time it disbanded in 1934 the Companie des Quinze had become internationally famous for its lively productions.

Méta: Méta Budry Turian for whom Eleanor Mabel Sarton was a dear friend and confidant. After Eleanor Sarton's death Méta became close to May Sarton. Her marriage to Marc Turian, a vigneron, is the subject of Sarton's "Marc, the Vigneron" in *A World of Light*.

Lugné-Poe: Aurélien-François Lugné-Poë (1869–1940), French actor, director, and theater manager.

Mlle. Sumpt: Mlle. Lucille Sumpt, a social worker whom Sarton had known in Cambridge as a child and saw several times in Paris after World War II. A friend of George Sarton.

Germaine Swarts: Daughter of the brother of Mrs. Leo "Bon Bon" [Céline Swarts] Baekeland.

Louise Inches: A Cambridge friend of the Sartons whom May called "Aunt Louise"; her daughter, Louise, was a friend of May's.

Van Cleve: Joos Van Cleve (1485–1540), Flemish painter known for his portraits of royalty and his religious paintings. Called "Master of the Death of the Virgin" because of two famous triptychs of the death of the Virgin.

Bob Kennedy: Robert Kennedy, architect. Son of Edith Forbes Kennedy.

Mary: Mary Chilton.

Betty Blake: Costume designer, Gloucester School of the Little Theatre.

Hugh: Hugh Geoffrey Elwes (1878–1953), brother of Eleanor Mabel Sarton; a mining engineer in Mexico.

[Paris (van L)]
Bel-Gazou—

What joy to find a yellow envelope slid under my door in the wee small house where all good children are in bed—and only elvish things abroad! Munich sounds good. I always think of people lying on the grass in the Englischer Garten and troups of blond athletic men running in the streets, all of them looking like Siegfried himself in a blue shirt—of bicycles—and Tyrolean hats—and postcards of Marlene Dietrich—<u>marvelous</u> city!

The great event of the last days was that Eva telephoned me suddenly and said, "Come over to dinner tonight"—so I jumped into a taxi, picking up an azalea tree on the way—and found her in a delicious apartment high up overlooking the Seine. She and Josephine had just come back from fencing and looked wonderful—except Eva's hands. They were quite a shock to me, entirely out of shape and horribly red, some of her fingers she can hardly move. But people who saw her six weeks ago say the improvement is incredible, so I guess there's hope. Fencing seems to help. They were both very gay and decided in the middle of supper that we must go to the circus, so off we flew, fed the horses, talked a long time with an old cockney clown, and altogether behaved like four-year-olds. It was good to see her again. And, what is hopeful—I am to go back whenever I like for a really serious conversation. I have a feeling that in spite of all reasonableness if she offers me a contract for next year, I won't hesitate a moment, nor even look at it, but simply turn a somersault and give a grand yell of joy—I find myself really enormously bound up in that theatre, especially looking back at it and comparing with theatre here. It is something to stick by for a few years at least. And a great sense of security. After all, it is <u>assurance</u> of a season's work—and even if one were lucky enough to get a part in a Broadway show, chances are it would close after three weeks, and you'd be lucky if it ran as long as that even—

Having said all of which she no doubt has no intention of asking me—so—

I got a nice letter from Willem—he seems very happy in a quiet way—Ernst evidently adores him.

Lydia said she was writing (only I forgot to give her your address—but shall tomorrow—She and Irene and two other friends and I are going to Elsa's for Thanksgiving dinner—turkey and everything apparently! And then on a grand bat, beginning with the circus and ending God knows where, perhaps caviar and Scotch somewhere where there's dancing. One meets entirely too many nice people to do any work, you know. And I'm fast becoming a dissolute character—circles under the eyes and all the rest—nothing lacking but a Camille-cough and a rose in my mouth! Which reminds me that we saw the most horrible performance of "Camille" the other night at the Odéon with Ida Rubenstein—finally one of the sets fell down upon which we decided to adjourn and tell funny stories over a cup of coffee, as being far more amusing (even though they weren't very funny, or half as funny as if you had been there).

There is a plan, still very much under the hat, that T and I and Mary Chilton (a rather sweet girl who was at the Pension with me) will go to Brand—a place in the Austrian Tyrol—to ski for two weeks at Christmas. It sounds wonderful—no dressing for dinner, few tourists—just sun and snow and mountains with a warm fire to come home to. But $60 is rather a lot for the family Christmas present, I'm afraid. And, as a matter of fact, we could have great fun here, a party in the studio etc. Where will you be? Can't you be in two places at the same time?

I re-read this letter, and it's mildly feeble-minded—I'm horribly sleepy.

Do you remember the portrait by Van Cleve of himself that's in the Flemish room of the Alto Pinakotek [Munich]—I wrote it a poem this summer. Perhaps you would like it—as a matter of fact I read it one night on the Rue Velambre with a glass of Malaga in one hand—

Voilà! I think that is all the news—Daddy has gone off to Egypt with a bachelor-friend for ten days—letters from mummy continue to be full of gaiety and lovely descriptions of excursions into the country—and a sense of rest.

Your loving
Elf—

———

Eliza Van Loon: Eliza Bowditch Van Loon, mother of Willem. Sarton called her "Bel Gazou."

Josephine: Josephine Hutchinson.

Eva's hands: In Weston, Connecticut on June 12, 1931 Le Gallienne went to check the hot water heater in her caretaker's house which she had learned from her maid would not light. Descending the basement stairs, she struck a match; there was an instantaneous, deafening explosion. Le Gallienne suffered massive burns to her entire body. It was not certain if she would live; her hands were particularly maimed.

Lydia: Probably Lydia Rotch.

Elsa: Elsa Ide.

Ida Rubenstein: A member of the Ballet Russe, is described by Jean Cocteau in *Misia: The Life of Misia Sert* by Gold and Fisdale: ". . . as she confronted the stunned audience, she was too beautiful, like a too potent Oriental fragrance."

T: The Dutch boy.

poem: See "Portrait of the Artist (Joos van Cleve, fifteenth century)" in *Encounter in April.*

bachelor-friend: Dr. Max Meyerhof, a medical historian, old friend, and collaborator of George Sarton.

TO PARENTS   Mon—Dec. 14th [1931]
[Paris (vanL)]
Dears—

This ought to get to you about Christmas day—what will you be doing? I—guess! You never could—I shall be with Eva and Jo and Irene! Isn't that fun?

I'm just starting out to send you a telegram about next year—and here is the tale. One morning Jo telephoned to ask me to bring some poems over as Richard Le G. was coming to lunch and would like to see them. So I quickly typed out a bunch and took them over—he has bronchitis and was feeling very mizzy but he took them home to read in bed.

When he had gone they asked me if I wouldn't like to come to their fencing-lesson and then stay to dinner and go to a play, which I accepted with delight. We had a lovely time—very quietly—Jo playing the Moonlight Sonata—Eva chuckling over the Shaw-Terry letters, and I looking at a book by Copeau, each with a glass of brandy. Then we supped—I felt like one of the family. You know—it was lovely. After supper we decided to do something gayer than a play—so we went to hear Dora Stroeva sing at a place called "La Fourmi" extraordinary half-vaudeville place, it was very funny. Then we went to a cabaret—and there—a great event—Eva said she wanted me to come back if I could at a small salary though she couldn't afford more than thirty-five a week (this is a fortune to me of course!)—she said I wouldn't have many parts although she had a few in mind, and that I should be her representative with the students! This is what is thrilling because it is virtually an experimental theatre in my hands. I am full of plans.

The days are horribly full just now because of Xmas—I'm afraid I haven't been writing as often. But neither have you! I am frantically making Christmas cards and must write three or four letters before Wed. when the *Bremen* goes.

Then there seems to be someone to tea every day—and a stack of books three feet high to read! Add to this that I have the "worst cold" on record with a horrible sore throat—and forgive me if I've been bad about letters—

I must fly to mail this and send the telegrams which will probably arrive incomprehensible—they are so stupid at this post-office—

Enfin! I'm so happy about next year. You can't imagine!

I wish you joy, and I wish I were there

                                                      Your elf

(My present which, I will confess is a small photograph by Manuel—will be late, and probably awful. They are <u>ruinous</u> and then take only two proofs in about five minutes with your head held in an iron thing! I'm in despair—

I haven't seen the proofs—I shall tomorrow and I think they should be done by Thursday.)

———

Richard Le G.: Richard Le Gallienne (1866–1947), English writer, father of Eva, enthusiastic about Sarton's poetry.

Shaw-Terry letters: The correspondence between George Bernard Shaw and the brilliant and distinguished actress Ellen Terry published in 1931 is rich and luminous on both sides in grace, humor, and critical acuity.

Dora Stroeva: Russian cabaret singer whom Sarton went "quite mad over," and who sang only at 1 a.m. She gave Sarton special rates to enable her to go more often.

Bremen: A mail-carrying German ship.

"worst cold": A family joke that whenever George Sarton had a cold it would be "the worst cold I've ever had."

TO PARENTS   Thursday—New Year's Eve [1931]
[Paris (vanL)]

And such plans for the new year! I've just been talking with Miss Le G— about next year. I am to have <u>entire charge</u> of the fifty students!—and I can tell you it is a terrifying responsibility, especially that noone has yet made a success of it. I shall choose the plays, cast them, direct them—have, in fact, the whole business to manage as if it were a theatre of my own.

The thing I have to do now is gather material, especially one-act plays which are difficult to find, and begin planning the first production. All this in previous years has been started much too late, and I want to have the first play on in November before "Alice" opens (Dec. 10th).

Le G's plans are to start rehearsing the second week in August, then go on the road for four or five weeks to get in form again and only open in N.Y. in October.

She thinks it would be a good idea to get stock for the summer if it was only Gloucester again just to get my "hand in" so to speak. Which means that <u>I must</u> be back before the 15th of March to go to managers. Meanwhile I wait for definite news from Grace—I don't know what I'll do if she does finally come in Jan. but I rather think not.

You see, I really have to be back also to look for plays—there are so many I can't get hold of here, and about the most essential thing is to be well-loaded so to speak and be able to start off with a blaze and good momentum, as there are so many practical difficulties that begin with the season (company rehearsals, dissatisfaction etc.) If I can get a head-start so much the better.

If you agree to this—(I have qualms at leaving all this so soon, but it seems practically necessary. The stupid thing is of course that if I get a job I'll be free at least until June with nothing in particular to do—and yet—impossible to negotiate from here. It would be better not to go straight back to Gloucester unless they promised me one or two leads—but I know the ropes too well now. And that is the only one where I could arrange by letter.) For plans until March 1st—I think I would spend the first two weeks of Feb. in Belgium (really have to)—then go to Elsie's for a month sending my baggage straight to the boat and going to Cherbourg or Havre straight from Pontivy. I still long for that month of peaceful concentrated writing. What do you think?

In N.Y. I would of course go back to the Club, at least temporarily as it's certain and inexpensive and I like it.

And now I've said nothing of Christmas, which was perfectly lovely from beginning to end. Mary Chilton hired a car and chauffeur and drove us to Chartres Xmas Eve—stopping on the way at a heavenly inn at Jouy called "De La Providence." The whole personnel ran out to greet us as if it were stage-coach times and brought us hot bricks to warm our feet on and the most fairy-meal. Going off we passed a tiny church with all the village streaming to it from every path and hedge, muffled up children singing. Then out into the country again—we left the car and walked up the hill to the cathedral—all you could see was something looming tremendous into towers over one's head. Inside it was horrible—lit by electricity till it looked like the bald skeleton of itself. But an extraordinary service—we stayed and stayed until all the faithful had gone and we could sit in the front row like children at a pageant—and finally to our great terror the Bishop walked solemnly down the aisle followed by yards of purple train and a multitude of singing boys in vermilion and lace—to bless us—we were very much embarrassed like peasants in a palace, not knowing what to do. But isn't it extraordinary that there was no one else? Although there were crowds at the beginning of the service.

We went to bed about two and got up early on the coldest wettest Christmas morn I've ever seen. (How was it in Beyrouth? [Beirut]) Climbed the hill shivering and unenthusiastic to find the cathedral there burning with life—of course the windows of which we had seen nothing by night. Really he who thought of putting glass in stone, letting it flower into glass—is blessed. It was more than you could believe. We stayed until we felt quite drunk with sights. But I must go back still once to study the portals more carefully. (Here is Aristotle for Daddy.) O, very naughtily, I got as part of your Xmas present—instead of pajamas—a wonderful book for 100 frs. "L'Art Religieux du XIIIe. siècle en France" by E. Mâle—full of illustrations and apparently both scholarly (he is the main authority) and beautifully written. It commemorates Chartres you see and besides is invaluable to me who know nothing really. Also I am hoping to find a "Mystère" to do very simply with the students as a Christmas present to Miss Le Gallienne and the company next year. Apparently it's difficult to get hold of texts which of course were fabulously long. If not I thought we might do the old English one of the Chester players that they do at Shady Hill. But anyway this book will be a help. Irene would design the costumes for me—and it would all be a surprise.

We drove back another way stopping at Rambouillet for lunch. Then a snatch of sleep and Eva's for dinner. She gave me this pen—a lovely thick one (not fountain) some sort of transparent browny shell with a gold band and my initials—to write poems with. Wasn't it sweet?

It's very sturdy and simple, and I'm quite fond of it already. Some pens one <u>never</u> is.

We came home rather early as we were all sleepy—they had been out late the night before. But it was great fun—lighting the tree—a really family Christmas.

You haven't written for ages. Tomorrow I think is a boat from America, but I'm bereft of mail.

Various exciting packages have been arriving—first the two dresses of Mummy both of which I wear with great joy (But Miutsie aren't you missing them awfully?) Then the book of English poems from D—which I am delighted to have, thanks piles.

Otherwise there's no particular news. I drop in on the Kennedys every now and then, for warmth and exciting conversation. Am going to lunch there on Sat.

M. Brown and her husband are here and she might possibly stay over with me a few days after he leaves on Friday. I hope so.

Tonight Irene and I are having a grand celebration—dancing etc. to see the new year in.

Willem comes back Jan. 16th—

<u>Write!</u>

Your elf—

M—

———

Miss Le G: Eva le Gallienne.

Grace: Grace Marie Daly, who was to become muse for the sonnets in *Encounter in April.*

Elsie's: Emil and Elsie Masson, at Pontivy, Brittany, were longtime friends of the Sartons.

the Club: McLean, 94 Macdougal, New York.

Chartres: The Cathedral of Notre Dame at Chartres, 100 kilometers southwest of Paris. One of the most beautiful and best preserved architectural monuments of France.

the Kennedys: Edith Forbes Kennedy, who was in Paris that winter, had three sons: Fitzroy, Edmund, and Robert. Sarton grew up with them in Cambridge. Edith Forbes Kennedy, for whom she wrote "Evening Music," was a great friend and influence in her life.

M. Brown: Margaret Brown was prompter at Gloucester School of the Little Theatre.

TO MARIE CLOSSET   19 February [1932]
[Paris (vanL)]
Dear Jean Dominique—

I hoped I would find a poem like a flower to send you but words do not come to me these days. Perhaps one's soul must first cross the desert to taste the fresh spring water at the end. It is true that at the moment I am in such a desert.

Perhaps that is why I cried rereading your letter. It is such a miracle that you exist, that you are here, that you write to me and that I can answer you— that you actually *are* and that I haven't imagined you—because sometimes I think I had to invent you out of a great need to have you. Don't go away— I would be afraid of my soul's loneliness.

I reread this and it is not what I meant to say. One wants simply to open one's heart, but stops confused, lost among words and thought—because the heart is simple but everything around us makes it complicated, and we don't show what we really feel.

Here is an anemone—it is my heart—I would like to give it to you.

[ ]

I ate the crumb.

TO PARENTS   Thursday [14? April 1932]
[Florence]
Dears—

Here I am in Florence—after an incredible journey—the Alps at 6 A.M. after a fresh fall of snow looking like January—the Mediterranean emerald-green at noon—orange-trees, palms, groves of olives and paper-looking houses painted pink and blue that looked as if they might fold up at any mo-ment—an August atmosphere—and finally in a blaze of sunset Florence, the very April-est Florence—Irene met me at the station and brought me here to a room adjoining hers (it is 32 lire a day with all meals)—a table to work at looking out on a tiled roof and a lion and sky—she had put a great jar of iris by my bed and through the door I see the shadow of cherry-blossoms in her room. The flowers are incredible. In the morning we got each other a gardenia to wear. They are 1 lire each—isn't it amazing? The whole day is scented with gardenia—I'm sure I shall never be able to separate it from Flo-rence—

Here I have come to try and find some peace and draw up an account with myself. The last months have been strange—I don't think I have ever been in such a continual suspended state of pain and anxiety in my life. The elasticity of the mind is amazing—it can stretch and stretch and not break. But I shall be all right. I only look a little thin and pointed at the moment and not too beautiful—so don't expect much.

I had hoped to get through it all on my own but I think now it is better that you know all about your only daughter—Being so far away is horrible. Grace's coming, as you know, more or less disrupted this year—firstly because I waited and waited for it as the great event and anything else was really filling in time. Secondly, because when it happened it all went wrong. It's extraordinary how little two people can understand each other and how cruel two people who are fond of each other can be to each other—There is practically no cruelty so awful because their <u>power to hurt</u> is so great. And I suppose there are times when one's <u>whole basis of living</u> disintegrates under the disintegration that this sort of misunderstanding brings about in one part of one's spirit. I can only explain what follows in that way and beg you to understand—it seems to be part of a great mistake!

I found myself getting rather badly into debt at the end of February. There was no understanding between G. and me about money. I paid laundry and bills I had not foreseen at all and lived at a higher standard than I could afford because to argue about money on top of everything else was more than I could bear—this was very weak and wrong, ~~but I felt like a caged animal.~~ Then I borrowed a hundred dollars from Willem with the understanding that I would pay him before January of next year on my salary.

That paid my debts and took me pretty well through March—(I forgot to say that before G. came I was unusually low because for two weeks I had been rather often to Stroeva—flowers etc) Then suddenly G. announced that she had no more money and must stay until April 19th because of return passage ~~blaming me, God knows why, for the fact that she~~ there was nothing to do in honor but offer to support her until then. This I did. And here another misunderstanding. She had considered it a loan, I a gift. Neither of us knew what the other's basis was. Of course I didn't have that seem necessary—she would need about a hundred dollars counting tips on the boat, train-fare to Havre, etc. We had to leave Montrouge—the lease was up. M. Brown had invited us to Northampton—we thought it the best thing we could do and I cashed two-thirds of my April allowance and wrote to you explaining the situation. Meanwhile Grace, considering the money a loan, bought quite a lot in London. I was rather shocked and finally said something. She explained but by that time there was very little left. When we got to Paris I had a check for eight hundred francs and ~~way~~ over that in bills due at Montrouge.

Mrs. Kennedy	300	
piano	276	
laundry	250	
telephone	150	(this I can't
gas, elec. etc.	200	understand.
concierge	50	I think the
milk, bread	50	concierge cheated
		me)

We stayed in Paris at the cheapest hotel we could find. Then came your cable. I saw no way out. There was literally nothing and I more or less responsible for another person. We sat in the hotel. It rained. We had no cigarettes—had our food sent up, hardly spoke to each other, and I thought I'd go mad. Finally I cabled Anne that you were too far and could she cable me 150 dollars. At one on Tuesday it arrived—I threw clothes into a bag, ran about paying bills, gave Grace ~~everything~~ what she needed and took the 8:30 P.M. for Florence—I don't know how I got onto it. But the result is that I am $250 in debt and I had told G. that I would try and pay 200 of the 400 she originally borrowed to come over here with. She owes me ~~fif~~ some of that, but I doubt if she can pay more than fifty, so it makes four hundred dollars.

~~Meanwhile I have 400 francs to live on until the end of the month and owe Willem 700 francs and Irene 800. Irene's 800 I can pay out of next month, and she will lend me~~

So much for the past. I still owe Willem 700 francs and Irene 800 francs—Irene is lending me enough to pay Willem and enough for the last week in April to live on. But she really shouldn't as it leaves her just enough to finish this month and almost nothing for May. If it is in any way possible could you send me fifty dollars before you come. If not I don't know what I can do as I must get clear and even then will have just seventy left for May.

Now I must think of the future—none of the 400 is expected until the fall. By then could you afford to loan me that sum (it would be so much better to owe one person)—on the understanding that I save five dollars a week until it is paid off. The first year I could pay 200 and perhaps more if I can get a stock-job. Meanwhile the only thing I can think of is to go back third-class which would save almost a hundred dollars—and please let me do that.

This is so awful that I can only put it baldly—anything you may say I have no answer for. It's a sort of nightmare like a quicksand—the more I struggle to get out the deeper I sink. The only thing I can promise is to be absolutely independent next year and live simply and work hard. But I can't believe just now that next year will ever come. There is nothing to say. I don't know where to send this or when it will reach you.

Yours,
M—

Montrouge: Willem Van Loon had lent Sarton his apartment at 42, Place Jules Ferry in the Montrouge section of Paris while he was on tour.

Anne: Anne Thorp.

Sarton's father: In a letter to his wife in June of that year, George Sarton wrote from Palermo: "Should I give her an allowance in order to make the payment of her debts more easy, it would simply mean that I would be paying the debts. Will she ever learn anything if *I* am punished for *her* mistakes? Of course whatever happens, everything that hurts her will hurt us, but I would like her to feel the pinch of her own debts as distinctly as possible."

TO ELEANOR MABEL SARTON   Thursday, July 28th [1932]
[Jamaica Plain]
Darling little Miutsie—

I fear this will reach you long after it should to tell you that I love you more than ever on your birthday—and hope it is full of birds and cherries (are they ripe?)—and letters, and poems.

Guess where I am! You never could—in Elizabeth's little house in Jamaica Plain—spending a most heavenly week of reading plays in a luxury of time. I begin to feel quite settled about things. In the first place I've decided definitely to begin with "The Brothers Karamazov"—and that is a great relief. Now it's a matter of planning that, and then finding something for those not in the cast to work on—Pogo got me all the books I needed from the library. I have <u>treasures</u> here—and some of them ones I couldn't have got hold of in N.Y.

Anne is around doing research in the library—she and Harry and Eliz— all came to "Silas Lapham" which was a great success. People liked the costumes (I'll have pictures of them to show you)—and the atmosphere—I suffered at having to say idiotic sentimental lines, but people said I was convincing—Anne cried (which pleased me!)—F. C. says I have improved in bodily grace a great deal—Mrs. K. said my diction was the best of the lot— but I know I was jerky in parts—not enough ease etc.

But O, that feeling of power, that I'm beginning to have more and more on stage—an unrestrained feeling, as if here one could pour oneself out fully into a form without resistance. I always forget the difference of having an audience—it's as if an electric current were set on things then.

Tomorrow night Anne, Elizabeth and I are going to a German film "Der Kongries Tanzt" together—and picnic on the back porch. I wish you were coming! Elizabeth says she is suddenly so impatient for you! When exactly do you arrive?

This is a delicious time of suspense for me—the days are so quiet and full at the same time, although I occasionally get panic-stricken. But work is antidote for that.

K.T. went yesterday somewhere North—to Canada—laden with every kind of book—I didn't see her, but hardly expected to.

I have your Greek boy on my desk. It reminds me strangely of Mary Chilton.

This is a brief note, but really time stands still for the moment except the inexplicable things that are happening inside.

Love to the Limbosch tribe—Your large and healthy daughter

With a hug—
M—

I've been dipping into Milton. This sounds good. "The mind is its own place"—

Elizabeth: Elizabeth Keats McClelland (1890–1936), taught at Shady Hill; in 1927 lived with the Thorps in Cambridge; in the winter of 1929 lived in London with Anne Thorp. Author of *Medieval Merchants and Markets,* unpublished.

Pogo: Alexander Pogo, George Sarton's assistant.

Harry: Harry Dana, grandson of Henry Wadsworth Longfellow.

"Der Kongries Tanzt": Grune's world famous *Der Kongress Tanzt* (Congress Dancers), 1931.

Milton quote: Paradise Lost, Book I, 1.253 ["And in itself can make a heaven of hell, a hell of heaven."]

TO MARIE CLOSSET   27 December [1932]
[94 Macdougal]   Tuesday evening
Dear Jean—

You can't imagine the delight with which I sit down peacefully to write to you—"Sand without flowers" at my side—and in front of me the young Persian man casually reading under the budding tree. It is evening and raining. For the first time in weeks I have three hours of absolute peace. O Jean, Jean—if only you were here (you would love this room—it is small but the walls are blue—there are books—and Botticelli's melancholy "Spring")—if you were here in the big chair, I would turn off the light: I would play Mozart on the gramophone—I would sit very close to you and there would be no need to speak. You must forgive me but tonight it is very difficult to open my heart as I would like—especially in French my thoughts dance—I've lost the ability to put them into words. (Forgive this scribble).

It is strange how the atmosphere surrounding this young man reading suggests Proust's search for the past—perhaps it is the same precision of images and details—for example the acute sensibility he had for flowers—flowers which he loved but had to get away from—perhaps there is something similar in the soul of the Persian painter—I like to believe it.

Last week we had a magnificent snow—really dazzling—I went to the country with a friend—there for the first time this winter I wrote something, it's not very good and I must try again—dig deeper with a lantern before I lose the source. But it is there and it's not going to dry up. And perhaps it's good to live in this feverish way for awhile—because the theatre is like a fever. And everything is going marvelously well. For the first time I begin to live as I've always dreamed of living—working a great deal, loving a great deal, without a break. Now I must build a place of peace and certitude within myself. It's intoxication—and dangerous too, but I think I understand the danger. It's just hard to find time to be alone. I am in the theatre from 10 in the morning til two or three the next morning, almost without a break except for two hours at dinner. But then we are too tired to create anything more than an inner peace, and even that is difficult.

At the beginning of the year I'd hoped to study Greek history for a complete change of intellectual nourishment but I just can't get to do it—lack of time? lack of focus? I don't know. At any rate the theatre absorbs me body and soul for the moment. I like the fifty apprentices very much and they like me and believe in me oddly enough (because really I know nothing) but nevertheless I feel a strong bond with them and given the power, one finds the strength one needs. I've already directed them in three plays—La Mauvaise Conduite by Variot which I translated, Brothers Karmazov and for Christmas an English miracle play—now I have two projects for myself—as actress (I'm afraid of becoming too critical)—we're beginning rehearsals of Shaw's Saint Joan (I play Joan) and later Pelléas and Mélisande (I've always wanted to play Mélisande) all very natural and simple, just in front of a black background with no costumes—Someone just telephoned me that Miss Le Gallienne is sick and I must take her role in Alice in Wonderland as the White Queen—they're waiting for me at rehearsal—I must fly.

Oh, write me a word. I love you so—
May

A kiss for Titi—warm regards to Mme. Rousseau—and a joyous new year with a spring full of flowers for the three of you!

Titi: Marie Gaspar.

TO GEORGE SARTON   Sunday—Jan. 29th [1933]
[[94 Macdougal]
Dearest Daddums—

Your duck has been rather desperately paddling through work that had to be done before this week—Mother probably told you that I had been sent to Yonkers for three days—it was really great fun—sitting in a tower looking on the Hudson—and working pretty steadily on a translation of "Les Ratés" of Lenormand. Once in a while Mummy and I would set out down the hall for a look at the river in the evening, but otherwise I lived like a monk in a sort of artificial security. I almost thought for a moment that I would be willing to give up everything for this sight of a river and time to go very deep down in one still place—one has great hunger for this peace— But now I think the problem for one living in this age is much more complex. That one must be able to create a still point in oneself, contain somewhere within, this river and this timelessness, and learn to withdraw into it out of chaos, that to deny the chaos, and refuse to live in it is simply not to face the issue. For two years I have been restlessly trying to arrive at this place in myself—but perhaps it takes five or ten—Le Gallienne I believe only reached it about five years ago—and yet an artist never comes to his full power until he has managed to create it—Monet is an excellent example of this.

The theatre is for the first time in great peril. I have never seen Le Gallienne really discouraged before—to raise the subsidy necessary to continue is practically an impossibility this year. People's answer is "but I have just given 10,000 to unemployment"—not realizing that the failure of this theatre would put over a hundred people out of work, besides a certain spiritual starvation to thousands who come to it for more than amusement. So I face the possibility of having nothing to do next year. It's a grave prospect.

Otherwise what news? I am longing to hear more of the California adventure—and Hollywood? You know I have never heard you lecture—

I feel very tired inside—

Your duck
M—

Mother has gone to Washington.

———

Yonkers: Home of the Baekelands.
Lenormand: H.-R. Lenormand (1882–1951), French playwright.

TO PARENTS   [April 1933]
[94 Macdougal or Cobbs Mill]   Wednesday
Dearest Daddums—and Miutsie—

Thank you very much for the check—it tides him over almost two weeks more—and I think the theatre may fork out another $20.00 as he has a real part in Alice now. Anyway you have saved the day.

The future for all of us is bewildering at the moment. I had a long talk with Le Gallienne in which she told me in confidence that she will probably take three plays on an extensive tour of the country next year—that she would take me if I wanted to, but I advised against it as it would mean security but no advance from the artist's point of view. She said she would help me in every way to get a job on Broadway. But, God knows, they are scarce enough and even with her influence I could hardly hope to have enough parts to support me for the whole season.

Going on the road would mean giving up my cherished plan of continued work with a group of students towards building a theatre—also I feel very strongly that the time has come for me to go somewhere else—I have seen too many people comfortably settle into the company in comparative security and more or less—rot away.

But from the group point of view this seemed at first a knock-out blow. Some of them will be taken on the road and for those who have had only one year's training it would be foolish to refuse it. For those that stay in N.Y. it is more than ever important to give a chance of going on somehow. My plan is for everyone to try to get a job on Broadway, walking on or something and go on working at the studio at the same time, giving a series of matinées as I had planned and the summer stands as before—we will try to have two plays to present to Le Gallienne before she goes.

There is still the question of raising about $7000 to support these people for a season—and that, as you know, is quite a question. However Dr. Flexner is doing his best.

I had the first meeting of the group on Monday. It was rather thrilling. It is always thrilling to be at the beginning of something.

I will send the records as soon as I have time—although some of them I plan to bring in my case.

Do you think you would be able to help me at all next year during the months I am without work? I was quite terrified by your letter, coming as it did, just when solid earth seemed to be slipping out from under my feet—but I do understand that life now is difficult for everybody, and if you can't, I shall just have to manage—the fund should mean about $15.00 a week per person.

All this, however, we can better discuss when I come home—

Your self—
M—

Miutsie—How marvelous to have cushions—I am longing to be home in an overall with a little can of yellow paint!

————

it tides him over: A boy in the apprentice group had told Sarton he would have to go home, as he had no money. Sarton was trying to raise enough for him to finish the year.

Dr. Flexner: Dr. Abraham Flexner, director of mathematics research lab at Princeton; father of Eleanor Flexner, member of the apprentice group, and then the Apprentice Theatre.

TO DR. LEO BAEKELAND   Saturday, August 6 [1933]
[Dublin N.H.]
Dear Dr. Baekeland:

You remember me perhaps as a little girl who was frightened of you and hid behind "Teddy"—now Teddy is dead and I am grown-up—although perhaps still a little frightened of ~~writing to~~ you—and particularly when writing of my work, as I am now going to do. Try and imagine a very serious young lady (O, at least as serious as my scientific parent) who would sit down opposite you and say "Dr. Baekeland, I am creating a theatre for America and I need $5000 with which to begin work." You would look over your glasses and either laugh indulgently or be furious (as you can be!) and roar "Young lady, you are quite mad!" But please do neither of these things and let me explain a little further before you judge me impudent or scatter-brained.

As you perhaps know I have worked for the past three years at the Civic Repertory Theatre in N.Y. first as a student, then as a member of the company, and finally as director of the student-group. This theater comes the nearest to the European idea of any theatre in America. It was excellent training.

But I feel there is a future for a young theatre—a theatre of children like myself (I am 21) who would work together for five years in an almost medieval spirit of apprenticeship to one of the most difficult and delicate of arts. I have started by taking twelve of my students away with me to this little town of Dublin for two months of rehearsal. Since that time we have been offered the wonderful opportunity of playing 10 performances of 10 different European plays at the New School for Social Research <u>as one of their courses</u>, this winter. We hope to launch ourselves as an apprentice company in 1934–35, but until then, during this year of preparation and training we cannot hope to support ourselves. We ask to be given one year of grace— and for this we need $5000—I think it is a small price to pay for giving 12 young people a chance to establish themselves as <u>workers</u> in this day of unemployment—and eventually perhaps make for America a creative theatre comparable to the Irish Abbey Theatre.

I enclose a brief statement of our plans—and a copy of the announcement being sent out by the New School in their fall circular. Would you be able to help us at all? I realize how difficult it is in these days to do anything—

but I believe we deserve it—and I ask you, not from friendship, but from faith in the idea, to consider it at least. At this moment any sum from $100 to $1000 would be a godsend!

Sincerely yours,
May Sarton

Teddy: The Baekeland's dog, a St. Bernard.

students: Among them were Margaret English, Eleanor Flexner, Theodora Pleadwell, Henry Green, Norman Lloyd, and Alexander Scourby.

Irish Abbey Theatre: An outgrowth of the Irish Dramatic Movement begun by William Butler Yeats and Lady Gregory, a repertory theatre mainly Irish in its repertoire.

TO HALLIE FLANAGAN   August 16, 1933
[Dublin, N.H.]
Dear Mrs. Flanagan:

Katharine Taylor told me she was writing to you, and I hasten to add a word for myself—I might further introduce myself by saying that Margaret Clifford once played and suffered with me in the Philpott's long-winded Yellow Sands at Gloucester.

A group of Miss Le Gallienne's former apprentices are trying—after the fashion of Copeau's children, the Compagnie des Quinze—to make themselves a place in the theatre. Three years ago I was an apprentice, and this year became director of the group of fifty. It has been brought home to me that there is no place for the young actor to grow up in—one year of observation in a working-theatre, like the Civic Repertory; the playing of, shall we say, five walk-ons; and several parts in student productions—is an excellent introduction, little more.

In looking back to Europe I became aware that the creative theatres such as Copeau's had nearly always started from a small group of amateurs who were willing to take a long time about growing, and finally arrived, through trial and error, to a foundation-technique and the personal timbre of their playing.

The group at the Civic last year was full of good material: I became more and more anxious to keep some of them together for at least another year and the idea has now grown to a definite plan. Twelve of us have come here to Dublin to rehearse three plays, do a series of experiments in impromptu, read and discuss the immediate winter plan. We have just had the great luck to be asked to give a series of ten rehearsal-performances next winter at the New School of Social Research as one of their courses. This assures us of an adventurous audience, at the same time providing a solution to the problem of keeping it a laboratory year.

It is about this that I am writing to you. The enclosed information will tell you more exactly what we are doing as well as our general line of action. I wondered whether you would be interested in our doing one or two of the rehearsal-performances at Vassar in connection with your course. As they require no costumes or scenery, the expense and trouble would be very small: we need a stage, a black curtain to play against (or any permanent set which happens to be in the theatre)—and an audience!

Look over the list of plays.—Schönherr, Lenormand and Pirandello are in rehearsal now. We will be doing a performance of them in New York for Miss Le Gallienne about September 15th, and would love to have you come. Any of these three plays we could do any time after September 15th; Knock will be ready in the middle of November.

What do you say?

Sincerely yours,
May Sarton

Hallie [née Ferguson] Flanagan: (1890–1969), author, teacher of the theatre, director of experimental theatre at Vassar.

Yellow Sands: (1926), by Eden Phillpotts (1862–1960), British dramatist.

Knock: Knock, or *The Triumph of Medicine*, by Jules Romain.

TO PARENTS   Sunday [Dec. 9, 1933]
[54 West 10th St.]
Dears—

We came up yesterday to see "L'Aiglon" and are staying at Andy and K. Butler's (friends of Theo's—he is an etcher). I have just had a huge breakfast and feel very purring and catlike.

"L'Aiglon" was quite thrilling, and I had a good short talk with Le Gallienne afterwards—she looked marvelous in it, and plays with sweep and magnificence and a very touching soft quality too. At the same time it creaks a good deal in the English version, and seems a bit theatrical all the way through. She should be breaking new ground. The actual production—scenery, etc. is very poor I think, no distinction.

I saw Robbie for a moment—she sent her love to you.

Hartford seems miles away this morning: the circulars go out on Tues. and it is only then that we shall get some idea of how tickets will sell. Adams is turning out to be a treasure—he is extremely efficient, and I like him better everyday.

The play is going well, though these first two weeks are the hardest and it takes a great deal of actual coaching. A graduate of Avon, a Charles Trowbridge has joined us at no salary—his family is very well-off—he seems very serious and nice, and will play a small part in "Conduite."

I am quite terrified of the actual <u>execution</u> of the costumes—20 to be made in 12 days: we shall have a seamstress sew all day long for that time and are making one of the dressing rooms into a work-room. I can hardly wait to see what the production will look like.

Everyone seems very happy—Kap and Margaret have found a complete tiny house in the country for $20.00 a month! But still I like our ample space.

I had dinner at the Austen's last week. They are really dears—I liked her very much.

I am reading a thrilling book which I shall send you—it is Theo's— Haskell's "Balletomania"—it is a good complement to the Nijinsky book. We are going to the Monte Carlo Ballet in Hartford tomorrow night (this is a gay week-end!) We are dressing in our most gala clothes—it is our first "occasion" in Hartford and will be very exciting.

The voice teacher is splendid. Now I am trying to find someone to give us dancing or fencing—there is a Wigonian pupil who might be able to work with us as a group.

Heaps of love
M—

Theo: Theodora (Theo) Pleadwell, sculptor, apprentice at the Civic Repertory Theatre, and later member of the Associated Actors Theatre.

"L'Aiglon": L'Aiglon (1900), by Edmund Rostand (1868–1918), French dramatist known for his wit and satire.

Robbie: Leona Roberts Jo Hutchinson's mother.

Adams: Ted Adams (died 1995), business manager at the Civic; later writer and director.

Kap: Kappo Phelan, member of the Apprentice Theatre.

the Austen's: A. Everett "Chick" Austin, Jr., of the Wadsworth Athenaeum in Hartford, Connecticut.

"Balletomania": Balletomania (1934), by Arnold Lionel Haskell (1903–?), English writer and critic, and biographer of Diaghalev and others.

Wigonian: Probably reference to Mary Wigman (1886–?). German dancer whose theory was that movement must evolve from emotion. Great influence on modern dance.

TO PARENTS   July 5th [1934]
[Channing Place]
Dears—

First, I discovered a new volume of "Histoire du théâtre" yesterday! And am thrilled—I think it is a splendid history. Thank you, Daddums.

Aunt Mary is here and was very much upset to hear that I had arrived, as she had planned to put flowers in the rooms etc.—which was very sweet.

This morning I picked a small bunch of flowers in the garden and went to call on Miss Hayden—shall try to get her and Mrs. Chapman over for tea some afternoon next week if I can escape from Rowley for a day.

I marvel more and more at all that Mummy accomplished! The things are now all piled neatly in the cellar waiting for Mr. Haley—(it is now Friday 12:00 P.M. and I am waiting for Kappo and Margaret to arrive).

July 12th

I haven't had a moment to finish this in—just as I was writing they drove up in an enormous 1927 open Buick which seems to have an infinite capacity, and which is brilliant robin's egg blue.

Since then we have settled into the house with a fat Irish woman as cook and a girl to clean and wash dishes—they seem excellent and are very cheerful and sweet.

The sofa <u>makes</u> the living room, and I am hanging the bunch of flowers which is in our living room [drawing] over the mantelpiece—the chief difficulty was silver and cooking utensils—I've had to buy quite a lot.

The house was frightfully dirty and a little discouraging at first—there was so much to do. But now 3 of the boys are there putting up screens and all that, while Renée and I are making visits to the Morgan Memorial to find tubs, vegetable dishes, etc.

Le Gallienne may come up for a weekend at the end of the summer to see what we are doing! She is on her way to England now to work on the "L'Aiglon" translation with Clemence Dane. This is a tremendous incentive to work.

We are starting work on Clemence Dane's "Will Shakespeare" (Kap directing) and the "Master-Builder" (me directing, Margaret playing Hilda) right away. Cabot comes on August 1st and then we shall have to concentrate on "You Never Can Tell" in which I have a sweet part. We are trying to get the Oceanside for the week of Sept. 1, 2 and 3rd—Maude Adams is playing there the week before in "Twelfth Night."

I went to Widener the other day—Miss Welborn was there and seemed very cheerful. Tonight I am supping at the Dewings—I met Mr. Dewing in the Coop and he bellowed across the aisle "Are you in the red?" I didn't know what it meant and he was much amused.

Everyone is delighted with Rowley and Kap wants to get someone to buy it for us as a permanent summer place—it certainly would save a lot of buying and moving each summer.

I am very happy at the thought of starting work again—shall write bet-

ter letters when things get a little settled: this has been written in snatches—
  Perhaps there will be a letter from you tomorrow—

love and love
M—

Miss Hayden and Mrs. Chapman: Friends of Eleanor Mabel Sarton.

Clemence Dane: Pseudonym of Winifred Ashton, English novelist, poet and playwright.

Cabot: Eliot Cabot (1899–1938), theatre director and leading man.

You Never Can Tell: (1899), by George B. Shaw.

Maude [Kiskadden] Adams: (1872–1953), American actress known for her roles in Barrie plays.

TO PARENTS   Saturday, July 21st [1934]
[Rowley]
Dears—

At the end of this first week of the new Apprentice Theatre, I am beatifically happy. We have never been such a gay family—the new boys are grand. One very tall blond has bummed all over the earth and done everything from dish-washing to exhibition-tango (he is teaching me to tango!) he is a most extraordinary character and keeps us all amused—he is perfectly naive but an encyclopedia of facts—You have no sooner to say "cider" than he will tell you in detail how it is made and everything about it. He draws quite well, makes figures out of soap, can howl like a wolf (he frightened us to death one night) and is ready to give a decided and refreshing opinion on any subject at all. His name is David Gressen. Another is Saul Nash—who looks very much like me—slight and dark (he is playing my twin in "You Never Can Tell") with a great deal of charm—he is a very serious young man! Then there is Dick Freye, rather Jewish but good-looking and versatile—and full of ideas. We have long discussions in the evenings.

There have been several crises however—one was when in the middle of rehearsal our family of swallows fell down out of the chimney into the fireplace—four fat bewildered babies. We put them in a basket and climbed up on the roof and left it near the chimney so the mother would find them—the nest had fallen down!

Then, what is more serious, the well which supplies all our water has run dry. It is really rather difficult as I am so anxious that there be some grace in our living, and especially for the boys a <u>chance</u> to be clean. First we used another spring that we found on the place—and organized a water-brigade after breakfast and after supper to swing pails—we bought bottled drinking water. Now we are going to get two loads a day in George's trailer with a large vat in it which will mean about 300 gallons a day—enough for drinking, flushing toilets, washing hands but <u>no</u> baths. I am appalled at how much water one uses. This will cost $.75 a day which we can ill afford. There is a real drought here.

There is great activity in the barn where we are at work building the stage in relays—George is making 20 platforms 3 by 6 ft. which can collapse and be used later in all sorts of ways—but it is a big job—we all have blisters from putting in screws.

Meanwhile in the house we are reading "You Never" and "Masterbuilder" and Kappo starts on Clemence Dane's "Will Shakespeare" next week. Cabot arrives on Aug. 1st.

The evenings are very sweet—usually we dance for a half an hour or so after supper (the boys are very good dancers) and then some go out on the porch and read while others fence or play badminton out of doors—the reading usually ends in a discussion.

There is one piece of bad news—Florence Cunningham's twin sister was run over by a truck on Charles St. and died two hours later. It must have been a frightful blow for Florence as they were so very close.

Aunt Mary has been a dear and it is good to feel there is someone <u>there</u> for any emergency.

I don't know whether I ever sent you a copy of this but I thought Aunty Lino might like to see it—

Le Gallienne sails today—

Your postcards are treasures—it really sounds the most lovely holiday!

Love and love and love

M—

We go swimming at Salisbury beach a sort of New England Coney Island but much smaller and cleaner—it reminds me of "Liliom"—the water is very cold but wonderful waves—

Theo sends her love.

George: George Wells, company electrician and scene maker.

Florence Cunningham's twin sister: Mary P. (Mrs. Guy) Cunningham, member of the original corporation of the Gloucester School for the Little Theatre; did all the theatre landscaping.

TO PARENTS   July 29th, 1934
[Rowley]
Dears—

Your letters come in batches—three all together—then yesterday a lovely long one, including check from Daddums. How extraordinary to have starless light night-skies! I had such a small insignificant picture of the northern countries in my mind that it has been most exciting to look through your eyes. I'm afraid Belgium will be a depressing place these days with the Austrian situation turning all hearts over in the fear of another war. Even here so far away the air seems to be charged—I am almost afraid to see the paper every morning.

The last week has been full of perils and adventures which have proved to bind us up into even greater friendship—but which were exhausting. First the well which supplies all our water ran dry (I think I wrote you about this) and for three days we had to haul enough in pails from the spring to do the essential cooking and washing—now we buy 300 gallons a day from Mr. Drummer—by hauling it ourselves in George's trailer this only costs us $.75 a day, but it is not enough for baths. You have no idea of the luxury of a bath when you have hauled three pails for it yourself!

On Sunday George was taking everyone over to the beach, and very carefully got two loads so as not to overcrowd the car. About 200 yds. from the beach with the second load two of the first load who had been waiting there jumped on the running board. George drove the 200 yds. in <u>low</u>, which means less than 5 miles an hour.

But the policemen there are notoriously crooked and one of them came up and said, "Pull over. You are endangering the lives of men, women and children." Things were complicated by the fact that although Kap had her license and was in the car, George had left his at home. They were taken to the police station and George thrust into a pitch-black cell with nothing but a board to sleep on.

At this juncture Theo and I came home and I immediately called Mrs. Langdon Warner to get somebody of influence to get George out—she got me in touch with her brother-in-law who is a lawyer. Meanwhile George's brother had arrived and asked me <u>not</u> to get a lawyer—we waited at the station from 8:30 P.M. to 1:30 A.M. to see the chief of police. The bail had mysteriously risen from $25 to $300 cash and we had managed to raise $100. However we finally got him out at 2:00 A.M. for $50.00 bail. The chief of police assured us they would drop the charge of "endangering lives" which carries a penitentiary sentence and a large fine and prosecute only for driving without a license—so we went happily to bed. Next morning in court <u>both</u> charges were read out—and George would now be in a penitentiary if by luck the lawyer I had gotten in touch with hadn't been there—stepped in on his own (knowing how serious it was) and said he was defending the case and asked to have it postponed until Thursday. I have never been so relieved to see anyone in my life. It all bears out my theory that when you are dealing with crooks pleading is <u>no</u> good—you must use their own methods and get someone to out-smart them. Well, to make a long story short—our lawyer got us out "not guilty" on both charges by a mere technicality. The judge was very sweet and amused. But the whole thing leaves a bad taste in my mouth. Man makes laws to defend himself and then has to defend himself against the law! If murder trials are as ridiculous as this was, God help us all—

The lawyer's fee was $20.00 and the bail-woman gets $5.00 out of the $50 (that's why she raised it to $300)—she would have gotten $30.00) so that makes us $25.00 in the hole.

Apart from all this everything is going splendidly, so well that even these events have proved small clouds that soon blew away. Renée is doing splendidly on the budget so that we are saving enough on food to pay for water.

Which brings me to some business. I have charged some things to the Coop (books particularly) and if you will send me the bills I'll give you an itemized account which you can deduct from my Sept. allowance.

Also I have promised $100 toward the summer expenses, so could you send me the saved $25 for July to make it up? If you are short I think I could take it out of my September allowance and don't bother about it anyway until then.

Yesterday I paid a call on the Warners to thank them for helping us out— Mr. Warner was there in a bright blue linen jacket looking very nice. They were both quite cordial and we have asked them to sup with us.

This is such a stupid letter—but there were so many long involved stories to tell!

Heaps and heaps of love (Theo adds hers)
M—

The garden is <u>lovely</u>! We went in to have baths the other day and I picked two great bouquets—one all yellows and bronzes. The other pink and lavender—and the living-room looks like a party.

———

light night-skies: The Sartons are in Stockholm.

Austrian situation: On July 25th, 1934 a band of Nazis seized the radio station in Vienna, entered the chancellery, and shot and killed Englebert Dollfuss, the Chancellor.

Mrs. Langdon Warner: Langdon Warner (d. 1955) was Director of the Fogg Museum. He and his wife, Lorraine, were friends of the Sartons.

TO MARIE CLOSSET   Friday 24 August 1934
[Rowley]
Dear dear Jean—

It has rained all day and now there is a white and blue fog in the orchard, stretching like a long scarf to the river—high tide. Through the poplars we can see a pink moon rising in the pale blue sky. Downstairs the apprentices are reading the 4th act of a play. It is 8:30. After dinner we played Mozart's

"Jupiter" on the gramophone while we sewed costumes for a play of Shaw's which we give four performances of next week. In a corner two boys are playing chess. Noe, the dog, is warming his little black nose by the fire. Bonnet and Feathers, the cats, are playing on the sofa. They are Manx cats, a breed with no tail and very unusual. They are named after a poem of Edith Sitwell.

Oh if only you could open the garden gate and come and sit among us this evening—it's a night full of hope and tenderness. It's terrible sometimes to love in this way and <u>never</u> able to realize the essence of this love, to <u>touch</u>— our connection is all in the imagination but we need the good bread and wine of seeing the eyes, of hearing the voice. It is painful.

Saturday, 15 September

Almost a month has passed and I have been unable to refind that mood, that special <u>voice</u> with which I started this letter. Now Mother writes that she has seen you—and Daddy too—oh how happy I am—my God what joy.

I don't want to go into the details of these past months—it's enough to say that after a crisis when I had to suddenly come back to New York—cross the continent for a weekend (I had been vacationing in California)—when I believed we would not be able to continue as a company, that I was some kind of Don Quixote trying to create the necessary faith and loyalty—Two of the best men in the company wrote me that they would not be coming back. After this blow I finally came to a simpler clearer idea about the future and more than ever I <u>believe</u>, I have *faith* in what I am trying to do. Instead of a <u>rigid</u> company, I am going to create a <u>fluid group</u>, one whose members can come and go freely working around several permanent fixtures— myself, the other two directors, and two or three actors—and that for about four years. In that way we would little by little become a company with a certain permanence, rather than the original idea of a permanent group from the outset. It is more of a temporal rather than an essential change, but still it is a different point of view which took time and energy to arrive at.

It's strange, you are perhaps the only person in the world to whom I wish to tell my life's story in all its most intimate aspects. I have lived a lot for my young age—perhaps too much—lived in the sense of loving, for to live is to love. My poems—poor as they are—are merely reflections of thought, of things lived and felt and suffered and because I share such affinities with your poetic soul. I want you to understand all this. Will I ever one day be able to tell you? I can write of it little by little in poems, in half spoken japanese phrases. I have the horrible feeling that we might die without ever having the time to know one another—profoundly as only love makes possible— it frightens me. Do you understand? Am I wrong in believing, in <u>wanting</u> to believe, that you love me and understand me better than others? and that it does not shock you to be addressed with complete openness by a young girl?—but the question of <u>age</u> has no place here. The soul has no age. And my soul is not young, nor is yours old—they are both fresh and immortal.

For months I hardly wrote anything—nothing of the great event I was going through. But now I want to write, I need to write and I have so little time. Here are a few poems—they are not very good. They don't say much. You see for almost two years I lived with a woman who does not love me anymore. And now I must write about this love—there is nothing else to do. Write to me soon—I am a little frightened by this letter. I love you so!

May

This is a little flower that grows in the fall—and comes in all shades of purple and lavender. It grows tall and is very hardy—frost does not get it.

[drawing of English aster]

There is a whole volume of your poems that I have never seen—Can someone lend them to me if I can't find them?

Edith Sitwell: Dame Edith Sitwell (1887–1964). English poet, critic, biographer, and novelist. Her brothers Osbert (1892–1969) and Sacheverell (1897–1988) were also poets known for their aristocratic eccentricities.

"a woman who does not love me anymore": Theodora Pleadwell.

TO PARENTS   Sept. 1st [1934]
[Rowley]
Dears—

Well, it's over and was a grand success! The hall was sold out last night to the gayest darlingest audience who made it peal with laughter and applause from beginning to end—it really was very exciting! Also it is a big step to have put on a complete production (at dress rehearsals we all <u>wished</u> we were doing a rehearsal-performance!) It is a milestone in our history. ~~Also~~ It is very nice to have three more performances ahead of us and a chance to go on playing for awhile instead of being abruptly shut up just as we have finished! The costumes were charming—Betty Blake did a grand job (we have some pictures): the scenery not so good although it looked much better than I expected. The stage is very small and difficult to use, and the lighting equipment we have is of the very simplest, but out of all this emerged by hook or crook a total effect of great lightness and charm. People were really <u>delighted</u> apparently—and Eliot is determined to raise $1000 here for us before he goes. We would try to get ten people to pledge a hundred dollars each. Beginning tomorrow with two teas, the next week will be spent in interviews— of course I doubt if the $1000 comes true but even $500 would be wonderful. Expenses of production plus the water situation (this house is quite expensive to run) have mounted up to more than we expected. Of course the production-expenses are permanent investments—the scenery we make and buy we can use again and again. We bought a whole set of a carved wood horsehair furniture (a sofa, an armchair and two straight chairs) for $2.50! These are perfect for Tchekov and Ibsen—meanwhile it is Sept. 1st and I am eagerly waiting to hear from Joseph Verner Reed who had promised $1000 today—it is tantalizing not to know even where he is, we are quite desperate. I seem to have digressed into finances again. It is the problem of the moment as everybody has been "put off" until after the performance and now I am faced with the bills! It looks as if when everything is paid we shall net only about $100 and I had hoped for $400. As a matter of fact I think everything will come out all right within the next two weeks, so there is no need to worry. Only I like to know <u>where</u> we stand.

Your letter telling of the Portuguese adventure arrived just after the dress rehearsal and I must say that I suddenly felt it a <u>terribly</u> long time to wait. However I think now that we probably won't open until December 1st, settling in Hartford about November 1st so that I would have at least 10 days with you—also Hartford is so near that I am hoping to come home often for week-ends—it sounds very strange and exciting to be going to <u>Portugal</u>, somehow—

Sunday morn-
[Sept. 2]

I am having breakfast in bed. Last night the audience was completely different—a great many natives—very difficult to play Shaw to—it was really quite terrifying during the first act as there was the silence of a <u>tomb</u>, but gradually they began to chuckle, and by the 4th act were quite hilarious. Nellie and Rose came and Nellie said to me "Sure and ye were wonderful! Like a little turtle-dove!" She is really a darling, which reminds one that she has asked if I know of a place for her and it occurred to me that you might like to have her—she is rather <u>large</u> for our small house, but I think she could fit in, and she is an <u>excellent</u> cook and the most amenable person in the world. She said she would charge $10.00 a week. I said that was more than mother had been paying, but anyway I thought I might as well tell you.

It is frightfully <u>cold</u> here—the nights are like winter nights, and it is never really warm except at high noon—it has been the coldest August in thirty years apparently. We build a fire every night and have coffee and bread and cheese after the play—and the amount of zest we get out of these simple things is amazing! On Monday night we are all going dancing at Del Monte's, the nightclub here—and I shall christen my white dress.

Next weekend I am going to Hartford (provided I can get in touch with Austen) and then onto N.Y. to see Le Gallienne. She hasn't time to come up here but will see the three plays in N.Y. in October on our way South. If I haven't heard from Reed I can also get in touch with him. I think there is no danger of his not keeping his word, but he may have forgotten the date or something. Then three solid weeks of rehearsing here, and then we are off on our second season.

I have been reading a charming book; John Collier's "His Monkey Wife." I don't altogether like the style but still it is very touching—it comes in Tauchnitz, I know, and I thought Daddy might read it on the way to Portugal. Giraudoux's "Bataille avec L'Ange" sounds good too—it is about Briand I think.

I had a short letter from K. T.—she has had a very restless summer, as she is short one teacher (to take Mrs. Hinton's place) and can't seem to find the right person for the job. She finally went to Chicago for a month without having found one—

Aunt Mary looks a different person—I think she has really had a rest, they, Mary and Charlotte, came to the dress rehearsal, and Margaret and Miss Cunningham are coming Monday night to Magnolia. Their season is just over at Gloucester.

I must get up—enclosed is the third of three articles that appeared in the "North Shore Breeze" about us. I must say we have never had so much publicity.

> Dear dear love to you both
> The mouse
> [ ]

Your letters from Belgium are precious—I was very glad to find out about my ancestors—I <u>do</u> hope you saw Marie Closset, but I'm afraid you didn't with so many people to see—Ah well—

———

Joseph Verner Reed: (1902–1973), Producer, philanthropist. Executive Producer & Chairman of the Board—American Shakespeare Theatre, 1962–1973. Backed Le Gallienne, Margaret Webster and Cheryl Crawford's American Repertory Theatre as well as Sarton's theatre company.

John Collier: (1901–1980), English-born, American short story writer and novelist.

Tauchnitz: An edition of British authors named for Baron Christian Bernhard von Tauchnitz (1816–1895) who founded his own publishing firm and brought out his *Collection of British Authors, Collection of German Authors* in English translation and subsequently, the *Students' Tauchnitz Edition.*

Magnolia: Town near Gloucester.

Dec. 7th [1934]
[Hartford]
Dears—

Just a little note to say that the crisis is temporarily over as Paul Koolie, a friend of Chick's, is lending us $200 (to be paid back in installments) and Le Gallienne $100. She sent a darling telegram which greatly cheered us all. It is swell of Mrs. Pickman to be really going at it and there is next week to worry about still, so that if she can raise anything it will be a blessing. I am hoping by next week to hear from Reed. We took in altogether at the three performances $700 which is not bad at all. The production itself including the work on production, serving, building, original designs cost $500 and we spent $200 on publicity, which means that we covered production expenses but not salaries.

The party last night was very exciting—it lasted until 5:00 A.M.—and I have never seen such a chic audience as was at the Ballet with bravos and a real stampede at the end. The Ballet was interesting but in a year they can't be technically good enough.

All sorts of people were at the party—Gershwin, Archibald Macleish, Dali and his wife (Dali speaks nothing but Catalan and a little poor French—he looked very innocent and not at all sur-réalistic). Minna Curtis, George Antheil, Johnson (the head of the Museum of Modern Art in N.Y. who got up and made a speech about fascism) Pierre Matisse and his wife—not to mention the apprentice theatre in full force and of course the Austens.

Jim Soby, who gave the party, has one of the finest collections of modern French painters in the world, and the house is built for the paintings—very plain walls, beautiful rugs and little furniture—it has all sorts of tricks like an immense bar downstairs. It was impossible to look at the paintings but you couldn't turn around without seeing a Picasso, Matisse, and he has a beautiful Lehmbruck that I really had a chance to look at—the torso of a woman.

The party was nice because it was all very easy-moving and nobody got very drunk. We danced and ate and talked and moved from place to place. It is lucky we opened before and not after the ballet as we would all be too tired to move! We had to be at dancing at 9:30 this morning—and there is another enormous party for the ballet people tomorrow night in the museum with dancing in the lobby—they had to go to bed last night to get some rest.

I must write to Le Gallienne—we are going to tea at Paul's.

Your gay daughter
M—

Mrs. Pickman: Probably Mrs. Edward (Hester) Pickman, friend of Polly Thayer Starr.

Gershwin: George Gershwin (1898–1937), American composer.

Macleish: Archibald MacLeish (1892–1982), American poet, critic, screenwriter, Librarian of Congress, advisor to FDR.

Dali: Salvador Dali (1904–1989). Surrealistic artist, sculptor, filmmaker.

Minna Curtis: Mina Kirstein (Mrs. Henry Tomlinson) Curtiss (1896–1985), author, editor, teacher at Smith College. At this time in the 1930s, she was writing scripts with Orson Welles and John Houseman at the Mercury Theatre of the Air. Sister of Lincoln Kirstein, co-founder of the School of American Ballet and the New York City Ballet.

George Antheil: (1900–1959), modern American concert pianist and composer famous for his *Ballét-Mécanique* and his autobiography *Bad Boy of Music.*

Johnson: Philip Johnson (1906–), American architect. Actually he was Director of the Architecture Department, Museum of Modern Art, New York, not head of the entire museum.

Pierre Matisse: Son of French painter and sculptor, Henri Matisse.

TO PARENTS   Tuesday—
[Hartford]   [Jan. 8, 1935]
Dears—

Just a word to say that we are still alive—this is the darkest hour—and there is some comfort in knowing that it couldn't be much darker.

The dress is going to be quite all right—I am having a dressmaker come late tomorrow to fit it a little better and make a broad sash of the velvet. The tunic I shall leave until I can get home and talk it over with you—all this is more fun than bother so don't worry.

On Thursday or Friday I shall have to make some decision about going on—on Friday, my speech—and beyond that I don't think.

Could you send me five dollars of Mrs. B's in case I have to get shoes (I think my gold ones will do) and to pay the dressmaker? I had no salary this week.

I am becoming quite philosophical—we are working on "Siegfried" hard as if nothing were happening. If worst comes to worst, the company will disband temporarily and we would revive "Master Builder" as the third play here, which could be done in a week.

To work—to work!

Your
M—

Mrs. B.: Unidentified.

TO GEORGE SARTON   March 31, 1936
[on board the S. S. Manhattan]
To the Editor of Osiris
Dearest Daddy—Thanks for your long letter which I take to heart. I suppose it is prerogative of youth to be <u>indignant</u>—"the cry against corruption" that Katherine Mansfield speaks of as one of the primary things that made

her write: the other was joy. There is no doubt that many things are unresolved in my mind—the people of my generation are turning almost without exception (among my personal friends) to communism as the next necessary step in the advance of civilization. Much in my education and temperament is revolted by the idea, but there is no doubt—witness innumerable philosophers and thinkers—that we are going through a difficult period with <u>economic</u> maladjustment paramount. This book of [John] Gunther's "Inside Europe" which I have been reading is illuminating.

I have thought often in the last days of Yeats' epitaph on Swift:

> Swift has sailed into his rest—
> Savage indignation there
> Cannot lacerate his breast.
> Imitate him if you dare,
> World-besotted traveler; he
> Served human liberty.

The one thing I can do is write a letter and work in that theatre which is the <u>mirror</u> of the age.

This has been a very peaceful journey—the people are incredibly dull most of them. I played deck-tennis and ping-pong with a very simple Irishman from the north of Ireland. I like him a lot. He lives in a village of 200 somewhere near Cork, in comparative isolation from his fellow men as his family are the only protestants in the village. He owns two stores in Cork and so is able to take a vacation once a year.

At my table is an old man—Harvard grad—who is very sweet but extremely talkative. He tells interminable stories that have no great point, but is very interested in everything. I get on much better with the old than with the young.

At my table also is an incredibly tough English girl who went to N.Y. knowing no one and paid a taxi driver to take her out—she met nothing but gangsters. I have not seen hair or hide of Solomon Gandz.

Have just heard from the Singers and they invite me to stay with them which is very pleasant, so I won't go up to London until Monday I imagine. I am delighted with the thought of some <u>country</u>. One longs for the smell of earth.

Dear love—
<u>May</u>

Thanks for the check and the Root lecture.

Osiris: As editor of *Isis,* in 1933 George Sarton evolved a plan by which the History of Science Society would take over the more lengthy articles and publish them in a separate review at their expense to be called *Osiris*. Sarton loved the implications of the mythic marriage of Isis and Osiris.

Solomon Gandz: Dr. Solomon Gandz, historian of science, member of the International Academy of the History of Science.

the Singers: Dorothea (Waley) and Charles Singer, historians of science who lived in Cornwall.

TO GEORGE SARTON   Easter Monday
[43 York Street]   [13 April 1936]
                              (write to Cooke as I may move)

Dearest Daddums,

I have had an excellent week, a chari-vari of experiences, notably an afternoon with that extraordinary man Fox-Strangways who laughed constantly at my American accent and talked about the Americans as if they were either savages or merely materialists. I've never met anyone quite so insular, so <u>British</u>, but we ended by being fast friends. He read out loud to me from a charming Hindu tale which he has lent me called "A Digit of the Moon" which was a joke, supposed to be a translation from the Sanskrit, but actually written by a man called F. W. Barn. It really has great charm. I poured out innumerable cups of sour black tea, which he sucked down through his moustache—he lives in very sad rooms and seems rather bitter in a porcelain sort of way with a smile. I enjoyed it very much and hope to take the Hotsons to meet him. (I think he would enjoy them as they are both so interested in Elizabethan music and know a lot about it).

He seems lonely and rather pathetic, but with a sharp wit. Mrs. Hotson reads his Sunday articles with great interest and has always wanted to meet him so I hope we can go.

I went to the opening of Clemence Dane's new play which was great fun although it meant having no dinner. The play itself is feeble though it is apparently a hit, but I enjoyed the excitement of the first night and watching the audience as well as the play. It was in a beautiful old theatre "His Majesty's."

Easter I spent with the Hotsons. We had a long bicycle ride and then Mr. Hotson sang with his lute for hours after dinner. This morning Mrs. H. and I went to the small village where Milton lived during the plague in London. We saw his house where there is this excellent portrait (I have never seen it reproduced). I have got a card to the public library here and am going to try to make a study of Milton whom I know almost nothing of—also of Donne and Marvell. It is a good place to do it in.

I went to the National Gallery again—it is a perfect feast, and am glad to see that there is a Chinese exhibition on at the Victoria and Albert, a famous collection now on view for the first time. This makes up a little for missing Burlington House.

O, I had dinner with Stabler who was perfectly charming (and incidentally the only good meal I have had in England since the Singers. The food on the whole is pretty bad, nothing but sausages as far as I can see). He is going to take me to the zoo on a Sunday, and has invited me to go out to Hammersmith for a few days which I might do if I go to Belgium and give up my room for a week. There is a two pounds eleven round-trip which is very possible if I save my room-rent for a week. And Jean Dominique has invited me to spend Sunday the 26th with her. I have also had a charming note from Lugné-Poë who may just possibly come here—he is off on a rest in Madagascar but will be back in May. He said he would give me some introductions.

On the whole I am finding it quite possible to manage financially but it is very close, so if you could be sure to have my May allowance here on the first I would be grateful. I hope to come out ahead and have really been very careful and had no indulgences, or at least what indulgences I have had (one theatre and one very good French movie) I have paid for by forfeiting a meal. I don't really mind doing this in the least and I hope you will be pleased. Mrs. Hotson took me on Saturday to see <u>King Lear</u> at the old Vic—it is a good but not brilliant performance but I was very much interested to discuss it afterwards with Leslie who has a great many ideas of course about Shakespeare. It was really thrilling.

The time is flying so fast I am horrified and there is so much to do. This week-end I am spending with the Bennetts in Northampton (they are old friends) and next week go to Belgium. Then it will be May already, I can hardly believe it. The Hotsons have asked me to go with them to Oxford to hear them greet the May morn from Magdalen [College], but I don't know yet whether it will be feasible with the Belgian trip (which I really feel I must do) as Jean Dominique is so close to me and so old that it may be my last chance.)

I haven't seen anyone about poems yet but am seeing one of the people Greenslet gave me letters to tomorrow. It has been cold here but not one day yet of steady rain so I don't mind. The skies in London are very smoky and turgid with sudden radiances and quite beautiful. I would not change them.

> There is my news. What is yours?
> Dear love from
> May

So far this has been an entirely successful journey—not only am I delighted with all I see but <u>inside</u> I am at peace.

Root lecture: George Sarton had just delivered the Elihu Root Lecture at Harvard.

Fox-Strangways: Arthur Henry Fox-Strangways (1859–1948), musicologist and journalist.

Stabler: Harold Stabler (d. 1943) and his wife Phoebe (d. 1955), a sculptor, were friends of the Sartons.

Leslie: Leslie Hotson.

the Bennets: Margaret Bennett and her husband, Benjy.

Greenslet: Ferris Greenslet, May Sarton's editor at Houghton Mifflin.

TO PARENTS   May 8th, 1936
[23 Taviton St.]
Dears, Mother's cable arrived today and the decision which I have been looking at out of the corner of one eye, must be faced. I think it really is wise to stay in Europe for the summer. If I go back it means sailing the 30th of May with only a slight chance of getting a job, and even then not a job with a great future. The chief thing about a summer acting job was to get my hand in again, and that I can do in the very small parts I shall have next year in New York, if any! Here on the other hand I am "en train" and really working well and very happy. I shall then start in fresh in N.Y. in the fall instead of probably depressed after a summer of nothing to do. I hardly slept all night making this decision and now it sounds so simple.

My plan would be to stay here until June 7th, then to Belgium for two weeks (I shall suggest to Lino that I pay my board there) to see Jean Dominique—and also work. Here I am almost too gay, and there are so many people to see. In Belgium I shouldn't see relations until the last few days. Then I would like to go to Austria for three weeks, to this lovely place in the mountains where Theo went. That would be June 21st–July 15th, coming back to Belgium when you are there in July and sailing from there. It is just possible that I could go somewhere with Marie Closset but anyway have some peaceful times with her as their "vacances" start July 15th. Does that sound sensible? I think the three weeks in Austria will be good as it is real country and by then it will be hot—my plan would be to take a definite piece of writing to do there, where I shall know no one and be absolutely free. The place is very cheap ($8.00 a week I think) and run by a charming woman. I am writing May to find out definitely about it—it would be lovely if she could come too, but I'm afraid she can't afford it. All this sounds like fairyland! I'm not quite sure of your dates, when you will be where? but write at once any ideas you have. I wish you could come to this place in Austria for a week—it is heavenly, Theo says. But I'm afraid your schedule is jammed already. Anyway be sure to tell me <u>when</u> you will be in Belgium. I shall be here now until June 7th anyway.

There are stacks of letters that must catch the <u>Europa</u>. I'm spending the weekend at Stabler's. He is taking me to the zoo on Sunday and to Kew [Gardens] tomorrow which, they say is full of bluebells.

"Come down to Kew in lilac-time
(It isn't far from London)"

So this can't be a real letter. I dined at Huxley's last night—the most exquisite atmosphere—his wife is one of the most charming people I have ever
seen, like one of K. M.'s women (the apartment all pale green and she is like
that). She has a slight accent—I don't know what nationality she is, but I hope
you will see them when you are in London. They have a very beautiful modern apartment with great windows looking out on the long green lawns of
Regents Park. There were two young men there for dinner, an English boy
who is studying medicine (I didn't like him much) and a Viennese whose father was one of the socialist leaders—a fiery creature who talked politics all
the time. But what a frightful life those poor people have led, and with no
hope for the future. He says something will happen in Austria in a year, probably a Hitler coup, and he said that even if the socialists had won there would
be no hope as the country is entirely surrounded by Fascist countries with
the exception of Switzerland and Jugo-Slavia and war would have been inevitable. He is bitter against the German socialists who apparently put up no
fight at all against Hitler although they had tremendous power, but apparently their leaders were weaklings. Huxley unfortunately had to leave after
dinner for a meeting. Their boy was there, very gawky and sweet (he was in
a terrible accident recently, concussion etc.). Mrs. Huxley is a sculptress.

The [Walter] Adams came here to tea the other day. I like them a lot. Next
door to me is a man called Somerson, awfully nice, he is an architect and is
writing a book on five great English architects beginning with Wren. We
nearly always have tea together as I borrow his tea-pot and cups and we both
feel quite convivial after an afternoon's work. He has a long English face, a
little like an intelligent sensitive sheep.

Something rather funny happened yesterday. I have just written a rather
long poem called "Apologia" which is really a letter to the young communists and I sent it off to New Verse. Apparently the next morning the editor
called Somerson up (who is a friend of his) and asked if I lived here. We are
both going to lunch with him next week. I don't know if he hates or likes
it, but anyway it is something that he is interested enough to call up and want
to meet me. All the poems I sent to the magazine have come back, except
the ones Singer sent to the New Statesman. I am suddenly starting out on
some sketches and short stories. I was set off by a series of incredible stories
about Biarritz; which these people told them where I supped on my birthday (friends of May Potter's). I wrote one called "Sic Transit" which I sent
to the New Yorker. I told them to return it to you, so open anything that comes
from the New Yorker. I also sent "Conception" to a poetry contest in the South,
which you may hear from (I don't think there's any hope).

That is the chief news. I can't get <u>enough</u> time to myself and I love working here.

Dear love to you both
May

I have a radio now, and heard Tchaikovsky's <u>Pathétique</u> from Leipsig last
night. The best time for concerts from abroad is after 11:00 P.M.

May: May Potter, a friend.

poem: From "Barrel-Organ", stanza 3, Alfred Noyes (1880–1958).

Huxley's: Sarton had met Julian Huxley (1887–1975), leading biologist, zoologist, and prolific author, former secretary of the London Zoo, first secretary general of UNESCO) a few
weeks earlier on April 1, 1936 at the Singer's in Cornwall. This is her first meeting with his
wife Juliette (1896–1994), Swiss-born sculptor and writer who became and remained one of
the most important people in Sarton's life until her death.

K. M.: Katherine Mansfield.

Somerson: Sir John Summerson (1904–1992), considered the most distinguished British architectural historian of his generation, author and curator of the John Sloane Museum in London. Shortly before his death at eighty-eight, he wrote a sonnet for *Forward into the Past,* the
Festschrift honoring Sarton's eightieth birthday.

TO MARIE CLOSSET   28 June [1936]
[Le Pignon Rouge]   Monday afternoon
                                                     the country

Darling Bluebird—

I am drinking a beer before heading back. The whole day has been radiant starting with this morning with you and Francis—so that the foam on
my beer looks like a miraculous snow, and I am without doubt a Russian
princess—or Eve herself (nobody knows how she died and it's not even mentioned in the Bible so why wouldn't I be Eve?

I thought that if I wrote this letter now perhaps you would receive it tomorrow morning—Vera showed me a picture of you where you look exactly like St. Claire with a herd of children.

I got a letter from my elephant. He writes "<u>mon cher</u> May." He is in Avignon cultivating his vineyard. He seems happy and is <u>sure</u> "we will meet and
that time won't be an obstacle. Neither will the distance." I am happy. I'll
send him your photos of me in the garden. Sometimes I wonder <u>why</u> I get
<u>overcome</u> with joy—and then I remember that you are here like a flame
burning deep inside me, a flame sometimes white sometimes blue and sometimes red but always warm—and that noone can see that I have the only treasure in the world—and that I am illuminated by love, and that *you* are love
and miracle. I can't get over it.

I've missed two trains!

Goodbye my bird, dear heart, you can't really rest these days but let me at least take the weight from your heart—and let this love surround you as you sleep.

(She should have been dancing)

Francis: Francis Jammes (1868–1938), French poet and novelist whose conversion to Catholicism took on the aspect of a literary event, and whose poetry Sarton was reading.

Vera: Vera Bouny-Tordeur, "Tante Vera," friend of the Sartons.

My elephant: May often addressed Lugné-Poë thus.

TO MARIE CLOSSET   12 July 1936
[Austria]   Sunday 2 o'clock
My blue bird,

What a strange day, timeless—with an infinite, long rain like Sunday's—without end. And suddenly <u>torrents</u> of poems flow from me and I can't stop them—it exhausts me but what an exquisite exhaustion.

It's funny that I must always put a human figure into each landscape to see it in its full grandeur—a small detail full of pathos which gives dimension to the mountain. Here there was no one in that way to light things up—and now suddenly Stiasni becomes that figure, the statue at the bottom of the garden which gives everything perspective. It is not love—it is a kind of luminous force without which I am only half alive—and often the person who suddenly becomes this force is not at all interesting and isn't even aware of it. Maria Stiasni is a charming woman like all Viennese, with an odd face, eyes far apart, an asymmetrical but very beautiful face—she has great reserve (her charm is like a mask behind which she hides). I work often now in her small drawing-room where it is warm (my room is cold when it rains). She works all the time, greets the peasants, speaks to the servants, is nervous and pushes herself too much I think. Dr. Schwarzwald, the husband of the woman who founded Seeblicke, is almost always here, too. He is the great "finance minister" of Austria—a sweet and sad little Jew who limps—he reads in a corner while I work on the sofa surrounded by three sleeping Scotch kittens. It is lovely.

Just now a Viennese lady is playing Beethoven sonatas—how I adore the faraway sound of a piano through a house—particularly on Sunday.

The Czech boy left this morning—we had dinner together at Bad Aussee the night before—It was very gay and pleasant—I had spoken to him very frankly the day before and the situation which was becoming a little too serious and "sentimental," as the Germans would say, was cleared up. He is very <u>kind</u> really. But I am relieved he left.

I must change for dinner. Good night, my darling—I am happy—I kiss you—my heart <u>soars</u> when I think that in a week I will see you.

Monday morning [13 July 1936]

Today if it doesn't rain we will make an excursion to the other side of the mountain in Alt-Ausse but the sky is still uncertain—there are flocks of sheep in the blue field of sky. Before leaving I'll work on "Rivalry." I hope there will be a letter from mother telling me all about Wednesday.

How are you? I'm afraid that this week with the parents to see (those wild beasts) will be worse than the last one—when at least you were alone with the students. When you say that you are going shopping, I feel sad not to be there, <u>in</u> the house, to do all those little things for you.

[   ]

I will go for my mail at Taviton Street—every day. I don't leave here until Monday morning. Hotel Russell, Russell Sq., London.

Stiasni: Marie Stiasni ran the pensione at Seeblick am Grundlsee in Austria, the summer home of Dr. Hermann Schwarzwald which served as an inn for writers and intellectuals; she was director of the Schwarzwald school in Vienna. Sarton's "Mountain Interval" in *Encounter in April* was written for her.

The Czech boy: Franz Wiener, whom she met at Seeblick.

Wednesday: On Wednesday, July 8, 1936 at 4:30, George and Eleanor Mabel Sarton visited Jean Dominique.

TO MARIE CLOSSET
[Austria]

Sunday
13 July 1936
9 P.M.

Bobbie—

Perhaps there will be a letter tomorrow—my head is humming—I have worked all day but have achieved nothing so my thoughts are darting like arrows and there is nothing I can do to stop them. I have come down to the village and right now I am drinking a delicious coffee near the lake—everyone coming back from their weekend greeted me with "Grüsse Gott"—I passed a young man sitting on a bench awkwardly holding his girlfriend's hand—it was charming. I can't say enough about the charm and the kindness of the people here. They are the kind of people we think of when we hear those great, simple words from the Bible "love one another" and "Blessed are the meek." They are happy—I think I have rarely seen people who are simply happy.

My short story is at an impasse. I think I've oversimplified it—it's no longer a story—Oh, I'd so love to have some criticism of these stories now. I feel as if I were blind and that what I'm doing is raw, without form or subtlety—sometimes by chance I love composing a line that seems to say what I really mean, but mostly I flounder blindly.

I'm thinking of a long poem which would really be the story of this journey, the inner story—through a series of experiences and questions of modern morality—it would be made up of one or two long sections—for example my experience in Cornwall ends with a section on the Jews (Singer, my father's friend, is completely absorbed in helping the Jews). There would be the children of Belgium, and so on. But it's impossible to do anything like this without being empassioned—I couldn't write it from detachment, and I don't know whether the passion will seize me. I would love while I'm here in the mountains to write something on a large scale. One wants to put a great mournful horn to one's mouth and sound an immense wail, sad and feral and slow. O, I went swimming this morning—the water is absolutely clear and cold—first you're wonderfully chilled and then you bask in the sun.

Sometimes I'm bored and rather sad, but other times I write and feel happy—if only you were here—O darling, Marie, my big sister, my soul—Goodnight—Letters seem so fragile—do they reach you? It must take days and days—and I can't go on sending them airmail everyday. But my thoughts taste your strawberries and cherries, dwell in your garden and hide in each rose you cut—so don't forget to wish them goodnight.

I am going up to bed. I am translating "L'Eventail" rather quickly without thinking too much—then I'll go back and correct it carefully—it's difficult—like a rose that quivers when you touch it—but it's going to be possible. I love doing it—it relaxes and delights me to try, but I'm afraid it may not be good enough. We'll see.

Monday

A <u>dazzling</u> day! I couldn't get anything done this morning—very distracted—finally I read <u>Art and Poetry in Japan</u> and a great peace descended like an owl sitting beside me and staring at me solemnly. I wrote one not very good poem. I copied out a few little Japanese poems for you—do you know them? I have them in English—a translation of a translation (?). I hope there is something left for you, whose eyes can imagine <u>everything</u>.

Your kiss from last Friday arrived at lunchtime—What a joy! But how long everything takes. <u>What does Marianne say?</u>

What do "ombelle" and "décharné" mean? I have only a tiny dictionary with me.

This afternoon I am taking a boatride with a Czech boy—He is sweet and sad and lonely (but not <u>entirely</u> likeable).

I kiss you,

A leaf from my terrace—no news from P—Oh! What does "Le Gaillé" mean in "L'Eventail"? Is it translatable?

————

Marianne: Marianne Delacre, great friend of Jean Dominique and of Sarton as well.

P.: Unidentified.

TO PIERRE DUPRENEUX   11 October 1936
[239 East 17th St.]
Dear Sir,

Lugné-Pöe told me that you might be interested in getting letters from New York for your newspaper the <u>Paris Soir</u>. I immediately thought of those articles that Genêt writes for <u>The New Yorker</u>—it would be something like that, it seems to me. Naturally there are enormous possibilities—for instance a series of very American subjects: an article on "Burlesque," the world of striptease which is as frequented by the literary and worldly as the Fratellinis; an article on Father Divine, a man who is <u>God</u> for millions of black people, enormously rich and has a mission in Harlem called "Heaven" where his "Angels" live (an incredible story); an article on the two American designers, Muriel King and Hattie Carnegie; one of the theatres of the unemployed and the unemployed artists (all government subsidized), etc etc

As you see I stammer in French, but if I were to write articles for you I would have each one gone over by someone here. Please excuse the mistakes in the article I'm sending you—I am terribly pressured right now and it seems wiser to wait to hear from you before plunging myself into this any more deeply.

I look forward to hearing from you with great interest,
Please accept my sincere wishes,
May Sarton

————

Pierre Dupreneux: Editor at *Le Soir.*

Genêt: Janet Flanner (1892–1978), American journalist and novelist; in 1925 she began writing the Paris Letter in the *New Yorker* under the pseudonym "Genêt" given to her by Harold Ross.

Fratellinis: Famous circus performers in Paris since before the turn of the century.

Father Divine: (1882–1965), né George Baker, leader of the Peace Mission, a nonsectarian and interracial movement begun in Harlem in New York City. Many accepted him as the personification of God.

TO WILLIAM ROSE BENÉT   March 30th, 1937
[on board *American Trader*]
Dear Mr. Benét,

Here I am in the middle of the Atlantic wanting to send you a word quickly to thank you for your review of <u>Encounter</u>. It's the first review I have had—the week before you listed a group of books together as of "slight importance" and for hours I didn't dare look at it I was so sure mine was one! I thought what you said about "influences" was very true—most of the book was actually written five years ago when I was nineteen and knew most of Elinor Wylie and Millay by heart. Now it is Donne, Hopkins and (though you don't approve) Auden and Spender. The long poem I am glad you liked—I think it is the big thing in the book, perhaps the only quite original thing, and I agree that it doesn't succeed. I could do it better now and I suppose that is always the way.

<u>Encounter</u> the book as a whole was turned down by every publisher when I first tried to do something with it and only came out because a friend took it to HM [Houghton Miffin] without my knowledge. Of course I can't wait for the second book with everything I am feeling and thinking <u>now</u> in it, though I think it is still a transitional piece of work—I fought against over-decorativeness and wanted bare emotion, so it is a little un-singing. Perhaps eventually every element will fall into place (D.V.). I'm afraid you won't like the second book but don't give me up for lost!

Thanks again for the review—it is a spur! And more than I deserve. I'll be at Conrad Aiken's house in Rye, Sussex for the next two months. Come down if you are in England: address Samuel Jeakes House, Rye Sussex— Conrad is in Boston and I have taken his house as well as Jeakes' ghost for the spring.

Very sincerely yours,
May Sarton

William Rose Benét: (1886–1950), American poet, critic and editor, married for a time to the poet Elinor Wylie. In his column "The Phoenix Nest" in the *Saturday Review* of March 27, 1937 he cites Sarton's "distinctly original power."

Auden: W[ystan] H[ugh] Auden (1907–1973), English poet and dramatist, part of left-wing group including C. Day Lewis, Christopher Isherwood, and Stephen Spender.

The long poem: "She Shall be Called Woman."

D.V.: Deo Volente (God willing).

Conrad [Potter] Aiken: (1889–1973), American poet, writer and critic. In the spring of 1937 he rented his home, the Samuel Jeakes House in Rye, Sussex to Sarton and three friends.

TO POLLY THAYER STARR   April 6th—[1937]
[London (GH)]   11:00 P.M.
Darling—

I've been here just 24 hours and already there is so much to tell and I am so exh-o-sted (as Juliette would say) that I don't know how I can write you a proper letter! First of all we got stuck in a fog at 8:00 A.M. yesterday morning so didn't get in till 8:00 that night instead of in the morning—poor Julian was at the boat at that ungodly hour and then came back again in the evening—I saw this thin figure in a large black hat pacing up and down the dock—but couldn't see his face—the most tantalizing 15 minutes I've <u>ever</u> spent! I was the first off the boat and then we both felt so stiff and funny it was awful. But it <u>was</u> exciting to be whisked off ahead of everyone else in his roadster—he took me straight to the zoo—and we had supper with Juliette smoking cigarettes like a chimney and looking <u>ravishing</u>—one of the boys playing Russian bank with Dora Clark (the sculptress)—the apartment even cooler and greener than I had remembered—but I felt dirty and tired— then finally Juliette as I was putting on my things in her room suddenly hugged me and said she hoped I would be happy. And I feel *nothing* must happen—she is such an exquisite person. I keep thinking of that thing in "Master Builder"—

"Someone I have never seen—yes—But someone I have come into close contact with—Ugh! No—I am going away"—a paraphrase but there is the idea. Julian wrote me a dear letter that night while I was writing one to Juliette—I must say it is an extraordinary situation. The fundamental thing is *I* <u>think</u> that we are three special people (in the sense of specially sensitive to each other) and <u>perhaps</u> a balance can be maintained. If it can, it will be to me a resounding glory—and a sense of what a great satisfying difficult thing living is—how much more real in the end than any easy being-run-away with emotion and the messiness of it—<u>could</u> be.

I had lunch there today—a lovely soft gray day—this hotel is *heavenly*— was designed by Nash—shall we be staying here together next spring I wonder? You will go mad over the <u>light</u> in London—the red sky at night and the thousands of shades of cloud and rain and sun, changing all the time—and the soft seductive air that says "Wait. Wait. Don't hurry."

Then we all went (Julian, Juliette, Dora, Liz, I and the two Huxley boys—) to see a preview of "Tumai of the Elephants" a <u>wonderful</u> Indian picture from Kipling's book. Flaherty was there (he directed it and "Man of Aran")—a big baggy man. I just saw him for a moment.

Julian has just had built a very beautiful modern building at the zoo called "The Studio"—it contains an amphitheatre with a <u>cage</u> instead of a speaker— so that people can come and draw a panther or a bear—isn't that a swell idea?

You had better come over! I am going to draw when it opens—It's so rare that one gets a comfortable quiet chance to draw wild animals. (That is an unintentionally humorous sentence)

At 5:30 John Summerson came for me here—took me <u>miles</u> in the tube to a place called "Olympia" where there was a big cocktail party in connection with an architectural exhibit. I was too tired to enjoy standing up in a *mob* and drinking—but apparently I met the four most distinguished architects in England (John kept assuring me) and one—<u>Wells Coates</u> I made quite a hit with—he looks a little like Pick—he kept saying "You are one of these distinguished Americans." I felt quite proud. I got quite cross with John for being so long so he took me miles in a taxi to a Hungarian restaurant for dinner—and, like Rebecca West, I shall have to sue him for biting my lip. Now it is only 11:00 and I am nursing it in bed.

Polly Thayer Starr: (Mrs. Donald), Boston artist. Did the etching of Sarton used as the frontispiece in *Encounter in April*. Her portrait of Sarton, done in 1937, which hung at York until 1994 and was reproduced on the jacket of *Encore: A Journal* (1993) now hangs in the Fogg Museum, Cambridge, Massachusetts.

Dora: Dora Clarke. Sculptor, friend of the Huxleys. Her bronze of a Kikuyu girl was reproduced as the frontispiece for Julian Huxley's *Africa View,* 1931.

Liz: Elizabeth Johnson, a recent Bennington graduate whom Sarton met crossing on the *American Trader.*

Flaherty: Robert Joseph Flaherty (1884–1951), American explorer, motion picture director, and writer. Considered father of the documentary film.

Pick: Probably Edward Pickman, friend of the Starr's.

TO JULIETTE HUXLEY   [April ? 1937, probably 8th or 15th]
[London (GH)]   10:30 Thursday morning
I am here wrapped up in a quilt thinking how incommensurate I am to the glories that crowd me.

Dear Juliette, I wish I were coming to Cornwall to find a camellia tree with you and make petals drop on your head and walk in the wet grass— and perhaps finally talk, say something that somehow is not possible—words are terrifying. One realizes suddenly how <u>flamboyant</u> they are, how apt for exaggeration when one is dealing with the closer stern particles of the heart.

> Could mortal lip divine
> The undeveloped Freight
> Of a delivered syllable
> 'T'would crumble with the weight.

There has been too much all at once. And I haven't had time to reach any certainty except that I would do anything in the world for you—and for you I could sing hosannahs and praise God. Can you guess—have you ever—how entirely you seem complete and beautiful, how humble you make one feel? How I would like to cover you with roses. And what a terrifying two days this has been. I think I love Julian enough and not too much to build and not to destroy. God, Juliette, I wish you weren't going away. Or that I could write you a poem—and say something completely instead of these sentences finishing in tears because of one's feeling that blur the cool mind senselessly.

The last thing my father said to me which was extraordinary as he never says anything) was "Be as wise as a serpent and as gentle as a dove"—I'll try to be gentle and wise.

I'm sending you some poems with the novel—it is good to think that you will be reading them. They are the best of me, though it is not much—and they are what I would like to give you.

Couvre-toi de roses—

[   ]

---

poem: # 1409 in Emily Dickinson *The Complete Poems of Emily Dickinson.*

TO PARENTS   May 12, Coronation Day [1937]
[Rye]
My dears,

I have so much to tell I don't know where to begin. Last week I went to London on Thursday night as Julian was taking me to Covent Garden to hear Gluck's "Alceste" as a birthday present—It was very thrilling, a really gala audience, French singers (They are having an international season). The music is astonishingly grave and pure and yet really theatrical. It makes most operas look melodramatic and cheap. But none of the singers was really thrilling. We sat right beside Robert Nichols on one side and Herbert Read (the art critic on the other). Nichols is a very nervous strange genius of a man, an old friend of J's—he had seen my poems at their house and immediately starting [sic] talking about them very fast and intimately in the middle of the lobby, suddenly stopping to give a groan as he caught sight of the Sitwells to explain how he hates them; in the five minutes I had with him he had explained that Kit Cornell had just turned down a play of his, criticized my poems, exploded at the Sitwells and darted off suddenly to greet his divorced wife who was there. Afterwards it was pouring but we walked through the Covent Garden full of vegetables and flowers already and had a little supper at Rules, a very old theatrical restaurant full of statues of actors, prints and so on. I stayed at Elisabeth Bowen's—it is really very nice to have a place to go to in London.

The next day I had tea at the Crowthers who have a charming modern apartment on Russell Square. Dorothy Wrinch was there in one of her strange simpering, showing off moods, talking about herself constantly. For some reason it made me feel extremely shy and uncomfortable.

I had dinner with John Crofton, a young doctor Moll introduced me to very nice and went on to see "Balaika" [Balalaika?] the musical comedy that this girl I met in Austria is starring in. I thought the show very bad, in the good old operetta style, royal dukes, ballet dancers, great deal about "Old Russia"—we went back to see Muriel afterwards. She has a whole suite in the theatre. Then J. Crofton took me to the Café Royal, full of green looking intellectuals—then home to bed.

The Huxleys picked me up Saturday morning. Unfortunately a cold gray day but we had a picnic lunch with us and decided to eat it anyway on the way. So we stopped at a lovely old bridge over a river full of flowers (like the pre-Raphaelite painting of Ophelia) and chased each other about to keep warm. I am so happy in this friendship with the Huxleys. Julian's assistant, Alan something or other was there, awfully nice young man who does sculpture. Then on to Whipsnade—Julian immediately took me all round and though I was tired it was lucky he did because from then on it poured all weekend. I was dying to get pictures and of course couldn't. It is a magnificent place—a great green hill looking over the whole countryside, covered with magnificent trees and lakes. There are wallabys with their babies in their pockets running wild and peacocks displaying round every corner, all sorts of deer, flamingos, mackaws all together. Then there are enclosed areas where you can see the lions and tigers walking about. It is so impressive to see them walking past as if they were in the jungle. There is a bluebell wood, and a strange bare pine forest where the wolves wander looking just like the red riding hood wood. In the late afternoon after tea we played a terrific game of patience and Julian read aloud. The restaurant where they have their meals is glassed in and modern and from it you can watch all sorts of animals playing about.

Next morning it poured—we stayed in and worked. I did a whole chapter and felt very pleased with myself. Then Julian had to go to a formal dinner given by Lord Lugard for the Alarke of Abiocoota and we hid behind doors to see him come in. He is a huge nigger (like a doorman in New York) absolutely black, and king of three quarters of a million people in Nigeria. He is escorted everywhere by a black slave holding over his head a huge gold umbrella. He himself wears a fantastic beaded hat with a ridiculous Jay bird sitting on it, a gold cape, beaded boots, and carries a sceptre with a dome on the end which he waves at the populace with an ineffable smile of joy. He has a private motion picture man who follows him everywhere to take pictures with which to impress his people on his return! Really the British Empire is a wonderful thing. I must say he has great dignity and spoke English well but is obviously the most simple and childlike type of negro. He was covered with gold rings on his beautiful thin black hands. When he shook hands with Juliette she complimented him on his English and then he let out a typical darkie high shriek of laughter, which all his entourage echoed although they can't understand English for that is Nigerian etiquette! I took some pictures of him in the rain but I'm afraid they won't come out. After lunch Julian rushed upstairs and grabbed me in my gray slacks to go out in the private bus with them among the shouting populace to see the zoo and I felt quite like royalty! It was great fun and of course the animals were fed wherever we went and I saw the zoo wonderfully. The Alarke kept calling regally for the motion picture to be sure he was taken properly feeding the giraffe, being knelt before by the elephant and so forth. After he had left we went into the cheta [sic] cage. They have two, Castor and Pollux, hunting leopards just like the ones in Persian miniatures, the most beautiful animals I have ever seen about as big as dogs with the teddy bear ears of tigers a soft gold color with black spots. They were very tame and we went into the cage and stroked them under the chin. They purred loudly. Julian said, "Well you have met the Alarke of Abiocoota and made a cheta purr all in one day" which sums it all up quite well!

With all this excitement it is lovely to come back to our peaceful Rye life. I have just heard from Bowen that she is coming down for a few days at the end of the month and Kap is writing a play for us to present for her in the studio. I do find it difficult each time to get back into the stream of the novel. But on the whole it is going very well. I think I can have the first draft pretty well finished by the end of June and then two quiet months to rewrite and revise. I have booked my return passage on "The Importer" sailing from Liverpool September 11th which lands very conveniently in Boston. My plan is to come back to England for a week or so before sailing and perhaps go to the Singers.

I have heard from Greenslet that they have sold 314 copies of the book which is not too bad but I can't help being a little disappointed about reviews. I am waiting anxiously to hear from the Cresset Press which Patience Ross is trying to persuade to take both the poems and the novel.

The weather is awful for May. I hope it is doing better for you. Oh, I was just going to close and quite forgot about the Coronation [George VI] which we have been listening to all day. I guess it will have to wait until my next— it is good to think that Daddy is through his lectures. Have you made summer plans yet? I find I didn't bring my birthday book and have confused your birthday. Do let me know <u>soon</u> which is which.

Love as always
M—

Gluck's "Alceste": Christoph Willibald Ritter von Gluck (1714–87). Austrian composer of operas who innovated a new "reform" style.

Robert Nichols: Robert Malise Bowyer Nichols (1893–1944), English poet and dramatist.

Herbert Read: Sir Herbert Edward Read (1893–1968), English literary and art critic, poet, and author.

Kit Cornell: Katharine Cornell (1893–1974), with Lynn Fontanne and Helen Hayes, one of the great American actresses of her era; although she hated performing, she was more willing than either of her rivals to extend her range and attempt classics from the entire history of the theatre.

Elizabeth Bowen: [Dorothea Cole] (1899–1973), Anglo-Irish novelist and short-story writer with whom Sarton was briefly in love.

Crowthers: Probably Jimmy Crowther who collaborated with Julian Huxley on a survey of British science published under the title *Science and Social Needs.*

Dorothy (Dorothea) Wrinch: Scientist and colleague of George Sarton's.

Moll: Family friend, Mary "Moll" Manning Howe, Mrs. Mark DeWolfe Howe, later married Faneuil Adams.

girl from Austria: Muriel Angelus.

Alan: Alan Best, Canadian, natural historian, sculptor; friend of the Huxleys, later became a zoo director. Taught Juliette the rudiments of sculpting.

Whipsnade: An open zoo on the Bedfordshire Downs where the Julian Huxleys kept an apartment 800 feet up overlooking its 500 acres and where they spent most weekends.

Lord Lugard: Frederick John Dealtry, Baron Lugard of Abinger (1858–1945), played major role in British colonial history (1888–1945) notably in the conquest and administration of Nigeria.

Alarke of Abiocoota: The Alake of Abeokuta, tribal prince, visited the Huxleys at Whipsnade when he came from Nigeria for the coronation of George VI.

the novel: Sarton is working on *The Single Hound.*

the book: Encounter in April.

Patience Ross: Sarton's agent at A. M. Heath in London.

TO POLLY THAYER STARR   May 25th, 1937
[Rye]
Darling,

I have so much as usual to tell you that I don't know where to begin. Last week-end I went to Oxford with J who had a formal dinner there he had to attend—I must say all Virginia Woolf describes about the luxury of a young man's life at Oxford is perfectly true. We had lunch in Christ Church in J's half-brother's rooms there with Solly Zuckerman the zoologist and another Balliol boy, Lord Early (Lord Reading's son). He looks like an enlarged Greek Apollo—Reading is a jew and his son has that slightly heavy fair look some jews have, frightfully handsome and self-assured. Well anyway we were served an impeccable meal with several wines by an impeccable butler and I yearned for the life of Oxford—the cool green gardens, the sense of being part of a distinguished tradition. It is surprising to think of boys having studied in some of the buildings for nine centuries—a sense of privilege, an overwhelming sense of <u>class</u>, of being one of the chosen.

But I am no tourist. I want always to settle down and live in any place I like—I hate being taken around and shown things, of feeling outside and strange and being shown things (though I admit the pleasure of showing things to people is intoxicating as I learned the other day when I took Margaret around London.)

On Sunday we drove all over the place, going out on the Thames high up where it is narrow and slips through green meadows full of buttercups and cows and tasselly elms (so different from ours but nice). The great thing of the day as far as I was concerned was coming on a swan family and seeing the little ones [swan drawing] climb up and sit on the female's back—sticking their silly little heads up through her majestic feathers (about the worst drawing I have ever made but Elisabeth is here typing letters over on the other side of the studio and I am slightly rattled). Anyway they are the most charming things I have <u>ever</u> seen, dove gray and humorous with bright black eyes. Sometimes they follow her in a little string squeaking. Finally at great peril to ourselves and the swans Julian caught one—I have never felt anything so soft in my life—I wanted one terribly. What is it that is so touching about a kangaroo with its baby in its pocket, a swan with its creatures scrambling up its back? I prefer it any day to Magdalen tower or even St. Martin's in the Fields. Great and magical are the inventions of God.

Went also to "Ascent of F6" with Moll's nice Irish doctor friend, John Crofton. I was disappointed a little. I suppose adolescence of outlook can be almost completely camouflaged in poetry but you give yourself away in a play or a novel (God help us)—I thought it was childish though full of his very personal startling phrasing and occasionally good satire of the most obvious kind. Still it set me boiling and belligerent which is more than most plays do and is I suppose sufficient virtue to put him in a class by himself. I am just faintly weary of the mixture of communism, homo-sexuality and a sort of old-school-tie idealism. Also the audience was irritating: they laughed too loudly at everything as if they were thinking "This was written for us and only we understand it"—the smugness of the intellectual radical.

Afterwards we went down and looked at the Thames with the moon streaming down. London is full of unexpected glories—not like Paris laid out before you—it doesn't take your breath away. But it is a secret that you are let into little by little.

Did I write you after the week-end in Paris—I can't remember. It was very peaceful and strange and we had no money because Julian had forgotten the tickets and had to spend all his money getting new ones. It was very sweet. We had tea on the island in the Bois [de Boulonge] which is just like the German romantic paintings—do you remember the willows and mulberrys weeping into the water? We went to Giraudoux's new play "Électre" which is mentally exciting but in the end says nothing and is really a kind of titivation of the nerves I think—it had one brilliant idea, the furies were represented as three little girls in white, horrid precocious little girls who callously predicted everything that was going to happen a little like Princess Elisabeth. We went to see Josephine Baker in her element at the Folies Bergère, witty charming with that strange nostalgia she has—and her inhuman bird-voice.

Then we came back and stayed at Seaford, an incredibly dreary half-baked English seaside resort because we would have had to get up too early in Paris to get back in time on Tues. (it was Whit [Sun] week-end). There was an awful moment when we saw the bleak shingly beach and went into a being-repainted boarding house hotel called undoubtedly "Sea View." It had the atmosphere of the most painful Katherine Mansfield short stories of sea places—I could imagine all sorts of sordid heart-tearing stories. But we escaped and walked five miles through a golden evening across green downs and a little forest to a village which was just like the one in "The Dog Beneath the Skin"—They were having coronation celebrations and were just beginning the wheelbarrow race on the green when we arrive, the curate being judge. The town is a church on a green hill and one beautiful old street ending in a square round a big chestnut like the little French towns. We had a wonderful dinner and then went back to Seaford by bus just in time to see the moon rise.

Time has left me my sweet and I don't know when I last wrote or what I said—did I tell you that we had decided to give up the house? I am going to London for a week and then to Whipsnade for three weeks to really settle down and work. I am suddenly so relieved at the idea of being quite alone (it is just your feeling about Rhode Island I think)

Next day

I have just had a letter from the Cresset Press (Koteliansky is chief editor) and they are liking the poems and the novel—I don't dare say more but will cable to the family if a contract is signed. I am so on edge not being within telephone distance of the Howe baby at this point. I am saying little prayers for it.

Darling, I must send this off—Love and love—you don't spoil me with letters but they are good when they come. Oh, I had a long letter finally from Erika, very sweet—she is staying in New York I think and is very hot and miserable and making speeches all over the country. Gert writes that Cornell is going to make a round the world tour next year taking two years to do it—it sounds too Sarah-ish for words. I am a bit skeptical.

Do write, you beast—

Love, as always
M—

---

birthday confusion: Both birthdays occur in August: Eleanor's on August 3 and George's on August 31.

half-brother: Andrew Fielding Huxley (1917–), a physiologist who won the Nobel Prize in 1963.

"Ascent of F6": The Ascent of F6, by W. H. Auden and Christopher Isherwood.

Josephine Baker: (1906–1975), Née Freda Josephine McDonald. African-American expatriate who made her fame as a singer at Théâtre des Champs-Élysées in Paris; renowned for jazz singing and dancing, exotic costumes, and extravagant gestures; worked with French resistance in World War II.

"The Dog Beneath the Skin": The Dog Beneath the Skin or *Where Is Francis?* (1935), a satire drama in verse by W. H. Auden and Christopher Isherwood.

Koteliansky: S(amuel) S(olomonovitch) Koteliansky. A Russian émigré living in London, reader and translator for the Cresset Press, to which he introduced May Sarton. Friend of D. H. Lawrence and Katherine Mansfield, as well as the Woolfs and the Julian Huxleys. A great supporter of Sarton and her work.

Howe baby: Susan (Sukey) Howe was born in 1937.

Erika: Erika Julia Hedwig Mann-Auden (1905–1969), actress, journalist, and commentator, active in liberal causes and writings attacking Nazism. Thomas Mann's daughter.

Gert: Gert Macy, Katharine Cornell's friend and manager who strongly believed in and supported Sarton during her theatre years.

TO EDITH FORBES KENNEDY   June 17th, 1937
[Whipsnade]
Oh, Edith,

Never, never have I wished more often that you were within train, telephone, or reasonable writing distance—and never have I been more incapable of sitting down and sending off the <u>mass</u> there is to tell. The enclosed, begun two months ago, simply says nothing. And that is the way this will be.

I have fled to this green hill because the life in Jeakes House was a bit dis-tracting, especially with constant weekends away with Julian and another life to pick up when one got back. Here I have an apartment to myself and a whole green hill full of wild animals and a very good restaurant below. I sim-ply work all day and then emerge at the end of the week like a fish for air. It is a good combination. And in two weeks I have done fifty pages on the novel and begin to feel as if I owned my soul again. It haunts me that you once said I led a charmed life because in the last two months the charm has worked almost too well and something awful is bound to happen soon. The Cresset Press (which is Koteliansky's Press, K. M.'s friend) feel pretty sure they want the novel and want it by Aug. 20th if possible. I like having spurs dri-ven into me with a definite end in view—and then when the big work is done I am going to regard it soberly and insist on three months to revise if it needs it. Kot is a darling, a big Russian bear, a gentle Jewish bigness. He says, "Don't worry. You are a writer. Just bear that in mind. Just write." He is sweet. He has got James Stephens (the most gnomish man I have ever seen) to write a swell letter about the poems. I must admit I was a little discour-aged by the reviews—there have been two intelligent ones John Holmes in the Transcript and Benét in the Sat. Review. Eda Lou should have a pin stuck into her—it was such a tired piece of work, prissy and tired. But anyway that is all over. It doesn't matter now and I am thinking of my revenge in the form of a small and much better second volume. (Here, my dear darling, you must sternly advise me when the time comes).

I am realizing once and for all the difference as far as I am concerned of women and men and the necessity for both. With a man, however tender he is, one is feeding him—one is always and eternally understanding, mother-ing, supplying him with faith in himself (not in you). It is very sweet and good but for instance all the inside of me that writes poems simply doesn't exist. It is given out in another way. One is creating with life itself. (This is all my personal problem because other people seem to manage a simpler sex life, but there you are!) and until a week or so ago I thought I was com-pletely happy with Julian until I fell in love with a woman and realized that I had been deathly tired inside and now here was life pouring back in. Now I am writing poetry again and living I suppose in a falsely electric atmos-phere but I feel alive and it is so good, I simply can't tell you.

The whole business with J has been rather walking a tightrope but it has come out in the most civilized possible way—making me sing praises of man and life that such things can be—Juliette knows all about it and occasion-ally we spend week-ends all together, and in many ways I feel far closer to her than to J—she gets the novel read to her and is wonderfully perceptive and sure as a critic. Even as I write it it sounds impossible but it is true that we are really free with each other and have a basis of our own. She is of course extraordinary and I hope to God if I am ever in the same situation that I will be able to master it with that delicacy. At the same time I am tired to death of the continual heights that an affair demands—how one longs for steady rhythmical unforced companionship. I do want to marry.

Elisabeth Bowen wants me to marry Bowra (I can't imagine it except as a marriage de convenance and that is something I shrink from) I met him there the other night but he was completely eclipsed by the presence of Virginia Woolf. Elisabeth has a very high cool drawing-room with great windows looking out on to the green trees of Regents Park and the lake full of boats—the long pink curtains blow in and out. There are usually white peonies very open in a rococo shell on the mantel-piece. It is a formal room with a curious atmosphere of its own—into this stepped Woolf like a sea-horse, delicate and fabulous and <u>exactly</u> as she should be. She went right over to the window and stood looking out until dinner was announced—the room affects her as being underwater and the rest of the evening was Wavesian. She sat eating lettuce with her fingers and drinking white wine and talked about poplars to Elisabeth's fat cheerful husband, Alan. I talked to Bowra as well as I could being constantly distracted by the presence opposite. In her own house Elisabeth brings people together and observes them happily, making no effort once they are gathered—she sits like a cat in a corner and watches. Finally dinner was over and (thank God for the British custom) E., Woolf and I had the submarine drawing room to ourselves. It was really most extraordinary because one couldn't help falling into this stream-of-consciousness conversation. I remember eating two little white pinks in the course of it and thinking it sounded so like a parody of <u>The Waves</u> that she would notice it and be horror-stricken. Well, the evening went on until I finally went and sat down on the floor very rudely and then Woolf turned to me and said, "Are you professional?" When I first came to London I left my book with some primroses at 52 Tavistock Sq. and had had a short note from her about them. I stammered something about it and then she said, "Oh, it was you. It was you."—apparently they had come when she had no flowers and she likes the poems. I'm glad she only found out in the middle of the evening—it meant that one was exploring without introduction, so to speak. I am going there to tea on Monday.

Elisabeth is in Ireland now. I am hoping to be able to go there for two weeks before sailing—I want to meet your friend Sean O'Faolain. Oh my dear, I am dead. I can't go on though this is only the beginning of a long story. I stay here until early July, then to Belgium to see J. D. on my way to Austria. Julian is coming there for two weeks followed by Juliette and the boys for two more.

Here are some poems—I wish you would write to me. Where are you for the summer? I have had to give long ardent descriptions of you to Elisabeth.

Love and love—I am going to stay in Cambridge all winter next year—I am terrified that you won't be there.

M—

[ ]

———————

K.M.: Katherine Mansfield.

James Stephens: (1882–1950), Irish poet and novelist, best known for *A Crock of Gold;* close friend of S. S. Koteliansky. See "A Letter to James Stephens" in *Inner Landscape.*

reviews: Of *Encounter in April.*

Eda Lou: Eda Lou Walton, American poet and critic, in the *New York Times,* May 16, 1937.

"fell in love with a woman": Probably Elizabeth Bowen who had invited Sarton for dinner on June 14th, 1937 with Sir Cecil Maurice Bowra (1898–1971), British classical scholar and literary historian, and Virginia Woolf. This was Sarton's first meeting with Woolf. Sarton had first met Juliette Huxley on May 7, 1936.

Alan: Alan Cameron.

Sean O'Faolain: (1900–91), Irish novelist, short story writer, and biographer of Irish politicians: Eamon de Valera and Daniel O'Connell.

TO THE SATURDAY REVIEW OF LITERATURE
UNIDENTIFIED RECIPIENT   June 24th [1937]
[Whipsnade]
Dear Sir,

Many thanks for the check for my poem "From Men Who Died Deluded" in your May 29th issue. My joy is somewhat diminished however by a <u>horrible</u> misprint in the second line which ruins both the metre and the sense.

It reads "The <u>continental</u> clouds have crept down upon us" which gives it a topical allusion I particularly wanted to avoid and as you see spoils the line. It should read "The <u>continual</u> clouds." I suppose there is nothing to be done but it is distressing.

Very sincerely yours,
May Sarton
c/o Dr Julian Huxley
London Zoo
Regent's Park,
London, N.W.8

[Austria]
O darling—

Your letter came in one of those dreadful mornings when nothing seems
<u>real</u> and one thinks one has been living in a world of illusion—and it was
like one of your old letters (the one from Mt. Desert) and made me feel so
<u>warm</u>—my poor darling you have been having a hard time except that
being alone at Mt. Desert sounds rather good—I have been incapable of writing—and even now I can't—having Julian here, energetic—wanting to climb
the mountains, read aloud, play games—having to finish the novel when what
I really wanted was simply to be alone. Well, c'est la vie—very rarely do things
happen at the <u>right</u> time and yet it was heavenly in a way.

My sweet I can't write—but I can't <u>tell</u> you how I am looking forward
to seeing you—you say "what will you want of me another year"—but my
darling you must realize that nothing has changed—and that I shall always
want <u>everything</u> of you—everything that you can give—it was absolutely
true what I said long ago and have repeated at intervals that you are <u>irre-
placeable</u>—so often in the last months I have enjoyed a thing twice over in
the fun of telling it to you in thinking of telling it to you. I do have what
Juliette calls "Un coeur multiple" but in some strange way there are things
that nothing <u>changes</u> and my feeling for you is one. You must believe it. I
know it so well that I can't believe you would ever doubt it.

I have finished the novel and can only think—I finished it today—how
<u>little</u> it says that I wanted to say—how difficult it is to live but to write about
living, to try to arrive at something, some solution some positive clear and
peaceful statement. God!

My darling, it is true that I can't write these days. But as to Hingham my
plans are horribly vague because mummy has suddenly had to come over to
move my grandmother completely (her housekeeper is dying of cancer) altogether a rather sad and miserable affair. I have bookings on the 10th of September (American Importer) but am trying to get it changed to the 18th—so
anyway I shan't be home before Sept. 20th—I hope there will be a corner
for me to sleep in then.

Here I have lived my usual curious life writing a great many poems to
Maria Stiasni and finishing the novel, thank goodness.

Reading? A quite good first novel called <u>The Hill</u> by a girl called Eleanor
Green. Andre Malraux's <u>La Condition Humaine</u> which is damn good I think
(the best of its kind)—but I can't read. Julian read me <u>Antony and Cleopa-
tra</u> aloud which was really very exciting. I had forgotten that marvelous line
"Music, moody food of those who trade in love" I wish I could describe this
place to you, the people in it. There is of course first Marie herself who is

indescribable being everything and nothing, charm and depth and childishness and withal somehow or other a very efficient hotel manager. There is a very well known German actress Maria Schanda who looks like Saint Joan, brown and simple with high cheekbones and a rugged sort of charm (for some reason actresses in German-speaking countries are so much more attractive, with no chi-chi about them, than ours). Fabrizius (Son of Marietta has just arrived) a nice blond Dutchman who goes off to paint every morning. Erika Mann's sister is here, not at all attractive funnily enough as far as I can see, the black sheep of the family—with a most awful jew who is apparently her lover. Mariette arrives the day I leave—and then there are all the other people—

I must go and pack—am off to Belgium for 10 days—Forgive this letter—there is just <u>too</u> much- and no <u>inner</u> silences for so long. I feel as if there were a whole concert of instruments tuning up in my mind—

Love, as always—
M—

Hingham: Donald and Polly Thayer Starr's country house.

André Malraux: (1895–1976), French novelist known for his Marxist beliefs. *La Condition Humane* was translated in the U.S. as *Man's Fate.*

Mariette: Mariette Lydis, Maria Stiasni's friend with whom she later emigrated to Paris and eventually Buenos Aires, Argentina.

TO ELEANOR MABEL SARTON   Saturday afternoon
[59 Acacia Road]   [28 August 1937]
Darling little Miutsie—

Today came a letter from J. D. with precise details. I can transfer it to <u>Bruges</u> (so keep it in Belgium!). Only certain specific details of the 3rd part to be changed. I feel like a man let out of prison, and I think she has made this sacrifice for me. I simply can't talk about it. I must take out all intimate details of Claire's marriage (there is very little) and everything implicating C-- [?] in the school.

So, I think I can re-do the first part on the boat. And the third part easily in a quiet month at home. Isn't it wonderful? We are hoping to hear from Cohen (the editor) early next week. Kot is delighted with the third part. So I am not going to Belgium (they wired not to come) and will go to Rye instead.

I went to the U.S. Lines to pick up my ticket and discovered that there was 4£ to pay! Horror! But I think I can <u>just</u> squeeze through all right and don't worry.

I arrive at 10:00 Wed. morning and will come straight to 34 Viyls and go over to Grannie's if you are not there.

Love and love—

M

I am so grateful to J. D. I can think of nothing else, but I think in the end she will be glad.

————

J.D.: Jean Dominique demanded certain changes in *The Single Hound* which was based upon her, Marie Gaspar, Blanche Rousseau and her school, the Institute Belge de Culture Français. There was a great to-do, and Sarton rewrote much of the book.

Cohen: Dennis Cohen, editor at the Cresset Press.

34 Viyls: Unidentified address.

Grannie's: Eleanor Mabel Sarton was in Ipswich, finding a place to move her mother; she had asked May to come primarily to comfort her concerning Jean Do's requests. She writes of this time, "Mummy and I tired the sun with talking."

TO ELIZABETH BOWEN   September 25th, '37

[Channing Place]

Oh Elisabeth, sorting out papers and letters (six months accumulation) it came over me with a rush that you were thousands of miles away and I shouldn't see you for ages and ages. How strange these complete amputations are—the difference being that one grows a new limb like a centipede. Already I am deep in a set of habits—work all morning looking out on three very tall poplar trees that are never still making the air seem always alive— then almost always music before lunch when I feel dizzy and silly emerging from the curious madness of writing—I have played the Bruch concerto I wanted to give you and the Mozart clarinet quintet and the Vivaldi con- certo—all the things I have missed at odd times.

Then sleep (which you manage to live without, extraordinary woman!) Then usually a desire for air, a hatred of dirty ashtrays and the mess of a desk and out onto these stately provincial streets, big wooden houses, set back from the road, surrounded with green carpets, and all the trees. Cambridge is peo- pled with trees, arching and heavy now with leaves that have hardly begun to fall. Every day is clear and blue and warm. It is a good life.

Today I went over to see Edith Kennedy. She lives in a very shabby house and when you open the little wooden gate (it has an American "fence" around it) there is a terrific barking which is Chris the biggest dog I have ever seen. His full name is Jean Christophe. I saw him when he was a puppy and thought he was a bear, the nicest I had ever seen. Now he is a dog who seems big- ger than the house and has a long gray beard like an El Greco (he is quite like an El Greco) He makes Edith look even smaller than she is and more touching. (She would dislike that word). The room is shabby. It has grown definitely shabby in the last years—two old sofas and a very big armchair with a hole where it has been sat in off and on by everyone of interest who has come to Cambridge in the last ten years. Perhaps Sean used to sit in it but I was too young to know. Books, records, a victrola always open on the table—usually a pile of manuscripts in front of the wingchair where she always sits curled up like you in a corner and watches. There are two watercolors she did in Paris—one of a green armchair at a window, very cool and sophisticated, the other a street which seems to be everything one loves about Paris—Both have a kind of perfection about them, like everything she does though she does very little. On the mantel-piece there is a copy of an Egyptian head in green stone, a very bright blue-green Mexican glass and a carved wood deer that I gave her (It is so small that it is almost invisible except to the proud donor and the—I hope—pleased recipient). The room is shabby when one goes in and not after one has lived in it for an hour or two.

I have a great desire to tell you about Edith—once you asked me what she was like and I made enthusiastic noises and that was all. Now I would like to tell you really about her. It seems important because of the strangeness of life and because I have never really known Edith until I put together the pieces of Sean, Elisabeth, Edith and saw the pattern they made. This happened the other night.

After supper

It is fatal to begin a letter like this and be interrupted. Then I was just happily talking to you and now I feel self-conscious and I wonder what time of day it will arrive and what you will be doing and how bored you will perhaps be at such a long letter to read when there is an article for "Night and Day" and a book review and a novel all to be done this morning, the hydrangeas, Bea (is she back?) God knows what. I am very jealous and miserable at the idea, (not of Bea but of everything) but I think I will tell you about Edith anyway for my own delight if not for yours. The first person I ring up when I get back is Edith because by the way she listens she always makes things that have happened seem real and when one is just back they seem horribly unreal. So I went over there—it is the first time in years that there has not been one boy in the house. They are all away. Bobby, my age, married a girl I hate but who they say is very nice, last year. He is an architect, Gropius' draughtsman at the moment which is pretty good. He is selfish, entirely absorbed in his work and brilliant. I have great respect for Bobby. Fitzy a year or two younger is the kindest and most charming boy I know and I never thought for that reason that he would come to anything. But he is now engineer with a good radio station in N.Y. and the youngest man there—also, which shows how strange life is—the girl I lived with for years is in love with him. I heard that from Edith also on this curious night. Eddy, the youngest, has red hair and is tennis champion of his school—he is, I'm afraid and so is Edith, a success boy. At twelve in Paris when I first knew him he seemed to be as sophisticated in a nice way as one could be. Well, you can imagine what it is like to have had these three around for years and now none. There is no one living there except Aunty who is 78, deaf, half-mad, very virtuous so that you are always in the wrong. It is a crime that Edith has to take care of her and she is the only thing I have ever heard her be bitter about. Aunty is so miserable away from Edith that if she is sent away for a vacation at great expense she always comes back within two days and there is nothing to be done. (Does this sound like Stevie Smith? I don't know how to write it.) Well, I sat in the hollow of the armchair and had a drink and in the course of the evening rather suddenly because I had been wanting to ask it for a long time and now the conversation was way past the suitable moment I asked "Why didn't you marry Sean O'Faolain?"

Edith was silent for almost a minute and then she said "Noone has ever asked me that before. I think my pride and his inexperience." That is most of Edith. I have never seen her silent like that before. And I felt I had done a very ruthless thing. The silence was emotional. The answer was absolutely clear and I guess true. It is something I shan't forget, like a door opened suddenly and then shut. That is not the whole story. The whole story is none of my business, but even from what you said his marriage was nonsense at the time. Why do people do such things? I can't help wondering a little and hoping you will not be hurt. No, that is stupid. Of course you will be hurt, so I suppose, will he, but it doesn't matter.

I would like you to meet Edith some day not too bright and not too stormy. I suppose it will happen sooner or later. In the last two years she has begun to look much older. I guess it is no joke to have had to feed and clothe five people. But Oh, Elisabeth, what depth she has and what wit and clarity she has. It is curiously moving to find her vulnerable and to set my finger suddenly on her greatness, on a moment set apart like a figure in stone when she might have been womanly and wily and was simply straight.

Is this all nonsense? Why have I written you this letter? Daddy says that he sent letters to you in Ireland for me and if you still have them could you send them on. I thought there might be one from silent Austria. Please write to me soon—don't feel it has to be a real letter. A word or two—a carrot in front of the donkey's nose—please, darling.

And be happy—I think you have an extraordinary life. I am waiting for the novel! Mine is finally sold to Cresset and should come out in the spring in England and here (Greenslet is delighted) but there are still complications in Belgium. I had a letter this morning which resulted in floods of tears. I think it will come out all right. But I feel as if a cup were constantly being snatched away just as it is at my lips! Also I want to be finished with it now—

Love love love

M—

Bea: Probably Beatrice "B" Curtis Brown, a friend of Bowen's of whom Sarton was jealous.

Bobby married a girl: Robert Kennedy, son of Edith Forbes Kennedy; architect, married Gerta.

Gropius: Walter Adolf Gropius (1883–1969), German architect and educator. Founder of the Bauhaus, revolutionary art school which combined teaching of pure art with the study of functional craftsmanship; closed in 1933 by the German government.

Stevie (Florence Margaret) Smith: (1902–71), English poet and novelist known for her quirky, sardonic tone and idiosyncratic readings.

hoping you will not be hurt: Bowen and O'Faolain were lovers at one time.

Belgium: Jean Dominique's concerns were still unresolved.

TO JULIAN HUXLEY   December 26th [1937]
[Channing Place]
Dearest one,

My bear, golden and sweet, the melancholia of festivals is on me. But O how lovely, how perfect the pajamas are there and how I adored looking at the box every day before Christmas and <u>expecting</u> them. I've never seen anything so chic and they fit perfectly, just a little long in the trousers which can be easily fixed. I can't tell you how touched and warmed the cockles of my heart are to think of your searching in shops for me, though you shouldn't have done it. I am sad that you still feel mizzy—I hope you are planning a vacation in the middle of the winter for surely part of it must be long-accumulated tiredness and you might give the treatments a chance by taking a rest! I am anxious to hear about the Christmas lectures, about dinner with royalty, about everything! And I see to my horror that the Bremen goes today and not another fast boat for ages so god knows when you will get this. The thing I enjoyed best about Christmas was cabling you and Juliette— the excitement of thinking it would reach you so far away, so quickly—I should have had Babar deliver it.

I am in the end-of-the-year lower depths. On thinking back I think there is usually a down-curve at this time. But I have just decided to throw out the fifty pages of the new novel and try to do something entirely different even if I have to wait awhile for an idea. There is no point in doing something which I know isn't distinguished, which somehow in the writing hasn't any <u>spark</u>. Partly I think because I forced myself to do it as discipline while Edith was ill and in spite of all one's moral ideas these things of the spirit can't be grown under the whip. I feel so lost when I can't work—suddenly so dreadfully lonely and bored—and everything that I love about this life with my family feels like a prison when I can't work—especially as I can't bear to let them see my depression and hence bottle it up like a poison inside. How I have missed you the last days and wished you were going to drive up and take me away—for some reason I have thought of one morning (I think it was morning) when you picked me up at Elisabeth's and we wandered round Regent's Park like two people of great leisure, and sat in two deck chairs as if we were going to sit there all afternoon though we only had about ten minutes! You will be glad to hear, by the way, that I have renounced high heels by finally finding some very nice "flats" like men's evening pumps only with a slight heel so I shall never complain about my shoes again in the rain! We can walk comfortably around the world.

Have seen Edith two or three times—something strange has happened to her—all these businesses of recovery are mysterious where nerves are affected—and I have a feeling she is deliberately protecting herself against emotion. So that I have a funny isolated feeling. It is bad business to focus so completely on one human being—I think it is time I read Aldous's new book, don't you? And all these things fit into my depression and make me wonder what to do with my life—when I am not living at an unnaturally taut emotional pitch I produce nothing that's any good, and yet I am sure it is no way to live in the long run.

We had a really lovely Christmas (I'm longing to hear about yours.) Together for the first time in three years for one thing. First I had my stocking in bed with Mummy, an old tradition, then went down and put all the presents round our little tree—then up to Daddy's study to play Christmas carols on the vic.—I am so touched every time I hear them. The words "All is calm. All is bright" brought tears to my eyes and that phrase in one of them "The hopes and fears of all the years"—then down to breakfast with special toasted cinnamon buns—we read aloud a little essay on old streets in Brussels by Jean Dominique and Mummy and Daddy were full of remembrances and funny stories. Then to open all the presents though about this we all feel the same and get rather tired and want to retire with our booty!

I dressed in my Tyrolean dress and we went across the street to the neighbors, I with a wonderful music-box like a hurdy-gurdy over my shoulder that I gave the little boy (the only masculine rival you have!) His name is Binks and when he saw me he said "She has rings on her fingers and bells on her toes" which melted my heart away. There was a tree lit with candles, and eggnog and these two silent ravishing children just standing and staring at their presents not believing. The little girl stood for hours with a toy flute in her hand as if she were in a dream. There we drank eggnog and then came home.

In the evening I put on my pajamas and wandered about feeling like Greta Garbo to say the least—they are really perfect, bless you. And wait till you see me in them—

I'm hoping by the new year to have had an inspiration about a novel—partly about this I was fighting shyness all the time (one does have qualms about using actual people even disguised) and I think I must try to imagine some people about whom I can tell the absolute truth—O la, la. What an absurd life this is.

Love to you, my darling, and so many warm and winged thoughts for this New Year and <u>our</u> part in it.

M—

I see you were in a <u>fog</u> at Xmas—was it exciting? Did you get lost in the Zoo?

---

new novel: In such instances, Sarton used the expressions "throw out" and "tear up" figuratively; *The Waterfall,* referred to here as *A Face In The Mirror,* is extant, though unpublished.

Edith: Edith Forbes Kennedy

Aldous: Aldous Huxley (1894–1963), English novelist and essayist, younger brother of Julian, married to Maria Nys. Had recently published *Eyeless in Gaza* (1936), *An Encyclopedia of Pacifism* (1937), and *Ends and Means* (1937).

Binks: Binks and his sister Sally, children of Anne and Bill Barrett, neighbors at Channing Place.

TO ELIZABETH BOWEN   Jan. 16th, Sun. [1938]
[Channing Place]
Dear Elisabeth,

We have somehow escaped into 1938 which seems little short of miraculous. I don't know why it is that one always feels so sad on birthdays and so certain that a new life is beginning on Jan. 1st. I am always fearfully depressed in December but I expect you are too busy to be even momentarily depressed these days (<u>awful</u> picture!) It seems to me I have been waiting for the novel a fearfully long time—when is it coming out? There will soon be a revolution among your public, and let 'em not eat cake. Will it be soon? Now that I have been given the New Statesman there has not been one article by you and as you haven't time to write I am filled with bitterness.

Today there is one of those flat blue Italian skies incongruous over leafless trees and two feet of snow. It is Sunday. My father keeps looming out of his study next door with the accumulated jokes and facts of the week to tell me—Mummy downstairs is mending my mittens as I am going skiing for two days next week.

I am finding it hard to write this letter in spite of a desire to reach you and say Hello, to come in and find you curled into the corner of the sofa half-smiling like the Primavera—but it is hard to write because except for the interminable inner warmth, the interminable inner story-telling and imaginary woe there are so few events in my life just now. In December I tore up fifty pages of the new novel which I had forced myself to write as discipline while Edith was ill. It was rather a wrench I must confess, but it was inconceivably bad (even I could see). Now I think it is a big step forward as I think it was so bad, so pretty and unimportant because I was writing about real people and a real situation and so kept sliding away from the truth. Now I have started to work with an imaginary situation, imaginary people and perhaps this is a big step forward if I am ever to be a writer. I think you will like it better than the first. God knows, it has got to be better. Much harder work too. I find I have to sit and entrance myself over and over again every morning, catch the imagination and hold it carefully on the wind like a kite, coax and pull it here and there until it suddenly catches the wind and flies. But I adore the characters. The house is one I used to go to on weekends from New York, it was an inn near a waterfall—the waterfall and its sound being part of the theme. It is fatal isn't it to talk about a piece of work? I know it with poems. It gets <u>set</u> too soon if you talk about it. The sap runs out or dries up or something—I talked much too much about the one I tore up. "Silence—silence—like Gogol's Madman." The one thing in the world I would ask for if I could have a wish right this minute would be to see Le Gallienne's production of "Three Sisters." Oh, the scene when her poor husband puts on a false beard and tries to make her laugh in the last act—and the scene where during the fire the youngest sister has hysterics and Masha can't move, just lies on the sofa and can't lift a finger to help her—and the love-scene where the Captain or whatever he is sits in the late afternoon in the dark and says "I love you" and she is sitting on the other side of the room and laughs that queer soft laugh. What a play! Oh Elisabeth, do write a play. When you have finished the novel, please write a play.

Have been reading Angna Enters book "First Person Plural"—I wonder if it's come out in England. It's an extraordinary book because it is five hundred pages entirely about her work—the places, people, painters, music that has been built into it, the reasons and un-reasons the impression and hunches behind each one of her mimes. I sat up half the night reading it. The curious thing being that it is so much more personal than anything she could have said about her self-qua-self apart from her work. Have been re-reading Bovary in a state of acute delight—those wonderful descriptions of her clothes, of the wedding cake with the first layer a Greek temple, the second a romantic garden and so on, the precision of detail in that pure flowing style—the kind of excitement that water creates in a landscape. And who is there to read now? I am fed up with the lack of standards, the sloppiness, the sentimentality and brutality of fiction today—or you get Hemingway whose virtuosity makes you gasp and lack of anything to say leaves you dissatisfied, angry. I do think "Fontamara" and "Bread and Wine" great books, the only new ones I have read that seemed worth the time, and they are not so new.

Have been to some concerts—a Finnish choir singing all songs by modern Finnish composers, wonderful folk-songs and that impact of male voices that always brings tears to my eyes. But music goes right down to the best-defended places in the spirit and I feel vulnerable, not wanting to be touched for awhile. So haven't been spending hours with the victrola (that goes with the months where poetry streams out, where there is some use for emotions).

I am getting awfully sick of personal defeats though I am sure I let myself blindly in for them et c'est ma faute. And now I am in a lonely spot, unpleasant.

But March is coming—I suppose I shall be on English land about April first for two weeks before striking out for Vienna. Do you know at all so soon when you will be in Ireland? I am thinking of sailing back early in August, spending June in London and July in Ireland if you are there, and perhaps even if you are not. It would be too much luck to have you there—and after all there are years and years ahead.

Dear love from
M—

Greetings to Alan—the novel will be out <u>March 10th</u> in England and here. The end is quite childish, but on the whole it is about what one expects of a first novel I think. Perhaps the <u>premonition</u> of a writer.

Elizabeth's novel: The Death of the Heart, 1938.

The new novel: Probably *The Waterfall.*

Angna Enters: (1907–49), painter, dancer, and mime.

"Fontamara" and "Bread and Wine": Both by Ignazio Silone [Secondo Tranquilli] (1900–1978), socialist, anti-fascist activist; wrote these novels while exiled in Switzerland.

Enclosed: "After Silence," see *Inner Landscape.*

c'est ma faute: It's my fault.

TO ELIZABETH BOWEN   March 12th [1938]
[Channing Place]
Oh Elisabeth, my love,

Your letter came at the zero hour of a day of weeping and gnashing of teeth and the sherry-tear made me laugh, thinking if my tears were sherry how drunk I should be! It looks horribly as if I weren't going to be able to come. "The Hound" is simply not being bought at all (I cannot understand this business of a book failing before it has even appeared or being reviewed, but voilà) and so HM [Houghton Mifflin] won't give me an advance which was to pay my passage over, on the new one. They say it is definitely better, but that adolescence is an unsaleable theme (it is not about adolescence but about a family containing two adolescents but they are blind to this) and what with the depression they cannot foster the arts per se. The point of view is understandable but it locks me into prison here. My father just lectures me about my extravagance and says that when he is dead I will obviously starve to death. My darling mother looks worried and harried and that is what I can bear least so that I just want to escape anywhere where I don't have to camouflage my state of mind: There is the mournful picture.

I know I am spoiled and have been too lucky all my life and no doubt this will be the making of me, but O dear, how I want to see you and Kot and Julian and Juliette and Conrad [Aiken]. And then there is this nightmarish sense of insecurity—I have been working hard and probably escaping into work from Edith and a driving sense of loneliness and use-lessness—in a personal way. So it's tough just now suddenly wondering if I shall ever be able to write. And how awful to be one of these earnest de-luded people.

Darling, laugh at me, it is the best thing to do. It is raining today and I am tired, that's all. Meanwhile I am having a very funny time trying to get a part-time teaching-job next year—teaching poetry in a finishing school. I think it will be very good for me to have to formulate things that I guess at now and feel but don't think through. Also I would like to feel that I was doing something besides sit in a room and spread myself over white pieces of paper—poetry is something I have inside that might be transferable. It sounds like the Salvation Army I'm afraid. But apart from the spirit, it would ease up this material question.

There, there's the news. As I am not coming for awhile if at all please write to me. I miss you. And bless you for that note—I didn't dare open it I was so afraid it might not be from you.

Your mouse

Tell me of news—how you are—the book? Whether there are bluebells yet—or crocuses in Regent's Park—

TO VIRGINIA WOOLF   May 16 [1938]
[Vouvray]
Dear Virginia Woolf,

It has rained at last and the roses are lifting their heads which were all nod-ding from so much sun, falling before they opened. This is an enclosed gar-den looking out on vineyards—it is very classic country that makes one think purely. The people live on the earth, work fearfully hard and enjoy it. In cities everyone seems to complain. Here no one complains. When you stop in for a greeting or to admire the lilac bush (there are lots of Persians and great white ones) they laugh a great deal and most always bring out a bottle of wine and tell you that perhaps it will be another 1896 or whatever the fabulous wine year was—the sun is so good for the vines even if it is drying up the garden. And they are full of stories. I never go out without cursing that I am in the middle of a novel and can't stop to write them down. A notebook? Oh God yes, you're right, but when does one have time chiefly? Energy in the evening slides out of me mysteriously.

I have been thinking about Criticism, where one gets it, to whom one apprentices oneself at the beginning. In painting I'm sure painters only go to other painters and to lay-people or professional critics to feel better and to be assured that they have succeeded. In the end the things that have taught me anything have been one or two letters from writers—what the professional critics did was to make me feel that there was a chance if I worked like hell that I might be a writer, nothing more. And then I suppose one learns a great deal from the shame of what one has written a few months afterward. I woke up in a kind of icy sweat one morning seeing my book through your eyes. It is full of so much that is bad and green and artificial—and the character of the boy, mixed up, as you will feel because he is myself in a series of tensions and as a whole character never becomes a man, never in fact becomes a whole character. That is why he is so unattractive and unconvincing. He is always in the process of being and never *is*.

The new one is all imagined people and even if it is worse, I'm sure that's a step ahead.

Well, je tremble. Je vous écrit pour vous dire que je tremble <u>au fond</u>. Ne m'en voulez pas trop d'un mauvais livre. Si vous le détestez entièrement et tout à fait, il me semble que je serai au déséspoir. The suspense is rather terrible.

Yours,
May Sarton

Translation of French: Well, I'm trembling. I'm writing to tell you that I'm trembling in my deepest self. Don't hold against me too much that I have written a bad book. If you hate it entirely and completely it seems to me I will be in despair.

TO ASHLEY-MONTAGU   May 20th, 1938
[Vouvray]
Dear Ashley-Montagu,

I was very touched by your letter which followed me here—the wine country, and I am in the middle of vineyards working hard at a new novel.

I adore Fournier's "Grand Meaulnes" so was very pleased by your comparison.

It is a curious thing what a feeling of peace and confidence it gives to have managed to produce any part of one's inner world and find it has touched other people. For though I hoped it would I had steeled myself to expect mostly slams for so much inward looking amongst the wars! Now I feel it is worth trying still to talk about the heart and the human experiences that go on in any world at any time.

I think probably the new one is worse but a step forward in the end: it is less personal perhaps and I am trying to get away from stream of consciousness and too poetic a style—to be simpler and use a poetic method of approach (that is inevitable) rather than a poetic style.

How are you all? What is your news for next year? Let us meet again. Please give your wife my warm greetings, and thank you again. I suppose letters like yours are the reason for which one writes.

Very sincerely yours,
May Sarton

Ashley Montagu: (1905–), Anglo-American anthropologist, author of books on race, human intelligence, and various subjects concrning man's place in the world. Friend of the Sartons.

"Grand Meaulnes": Henri Fournier (1886–1914), Pen name Alain-Fournier. French novelist killed in the war. *Le Grand Meaulnes,* 1913 a delicate interweaving of fantasy and realism.

TO POLLY THAYER STARR   May 22nd, 1938
[Vouvray]
Darling golden-eyed Poll,

You deserve much better, I don't know where the days go but they vanish, and it is evening before it is morning. I am exhausted with emotion at the moment from drawing a large deer on G's wall—we are painting a "Petit Bois" in her room with birds and flowers and deer looking out like a tapestry and as we are both ignorant and talentless it is a great strain on the mind and soul. You should be here.

I adored your letter and chortled over the dinner-party. Why didn't you say anything about <u>your</u> costume, the one thing I was dying to hear about. I am so anxious to see Cunningham's portrait but please emulate Van Gogh and do one of yourself: this has been my humble re-iterated request for two years—and besides concerns your immortality—<u>please</u> do it. Also am tongue out to hear what you think of pig-like Natalie Hammond. I can't stand the sound of her and quite agree about her work—pretentious and if it is macabre, not macabre because it is herself and inevitable but because she has decided it is effective. I have no faith in her artistic integrity, whatever (but

hardly know her so don't believe me) but tell me what you thought. She is
an out-and-out tuxedo girl too and that goes down even less well with me
than ordinary people—it makes me shiver with horror in fact. Did you go
to Aggie's orchestra party? Is there hence a large picture of you in Life? O
dear, why are you so far away?

Darling, I am so happy and busy and quiet inside it is heaven. And what
happens to the days? In the morning I work, looking out into the garden
now and then to find Jamy (the dog), Grace and Père Bonot in his sabots,
transplanting vegetables, cutting roses, making new steps from the terrace etc.
Then we lunch, then the gate is locked behind Émilienne the maid, and we
read aloud or sleep, then we shine at painting in the afternoon or go for walks
to farms over the vineyards—sit in front of the fire talking with these wonderfully sane people, the peasants, the land-owners, vine-growers, talk of the
state of the vines, of the weather, of God. Yesterday an old woman came to
call and she said, "Mais le bon Dieu se repose en ce moment—faut bien qu'il
se repose comme tout le monde," and she asked me if I believed in immortality. I go everywhere in workmen's honey coloured corduroy trousers with
a big blue belt wrapped around four times, and fame travels fast in small places!
so everyone knows that I write and they are so curious and dear—besides
they all adore G. and one feels as if one were really somebody—then a bottle of wine is brought out, and one's pockets are filled with eggs or a basket
of apples or a bunch of white lilac—and did I tell you? the other day we
went over to "The Belangerie," the farm that belonged to the Chateau of
Moncontour of which the little Baron (a friend of G's) has gone mad so it
is closed. The people on the farm adored him and told her with such pride
that by scraping and going without they had managed to save a hundred
francs to send him! I have seen nothing of the proverbial French tightness—
I think it must be in cities where all people are horrible. These people would
give you their shirt and we spend our time trying to refuse things. That day
we came back after laughing a great deal and drinking a bottle of Vouvray,
with a dear little brown hen in a basket—she lay there without moving and
we have named her Belange. She lays tiny eggs for breakfast. We can't bear
to go out—I am working very hard but have just taken three days off to write
a legend of the country here (a marvelous true story)—Harper's Bazaar has
taken four poems, three sonnets and one I wrote on the boat. And want a
short story so I thought I would strike while the iron is hot. The first part
of the novel is finished and I am longing to get on into happier parts—the
strain of being four unhappy people all at once had begun to tell!

We rarely go out except for errands to Tours once in awhile when there
is nothing left to eat or when my hair looks like a rat's tail. But the other day
we went to lunch at the British Consul's—a moviesque mediaeval chateau,
a vast dining hall, some dreadful Cheyney cousins of G's (she can't abide

them), a darling old Polish countess who lives at Montresor (one of the loveliest small chateaux). We are going there to lunch on Tues. She told me she only had time to read the papers as she had to advise her grandchildren what to do—and is passionately interested in politics.

Reviews pour in from England, some bad, some good—the chief papers have been serious and good and I was amused to have a long very intelligent review in the <u>Sketch</u> of all papers! Also letters from unexpected people, quite a few men to my surprise and delight. I had expected it to be a woman's book.

Is Helen coming over? I sent the book to the Hopkins and have heard from them that they were trying to persuade her. I do hope she does.

Everything in my life at this moment is peaceful and good and I am happier and more certain than I ever imagined I would be. I can't bear the idea of leaving and think I shall come back here after a month in London.

The garden is full of roses but it has been bitterly cold for a week—we have strawberries from the garden and all vegetables.

What else for news? I find that when one is happy one is silent. On ne peut dépeindre le bonheur.

Love from your
[ ]

I'm here till <u>June 10th</u>

G's: Grace Eliot Dudley, grandaughter of Charles William Eliot, president of Harvard University 1869–1909. Sarton had first met her crossing over on the *Normandie,* April 3, 1938 and gone directly to her home in Vouvray for a week. After a week in London for the publication of *The Single Hound,* Sarton returned to Vouvray for five weeks. See "Grace Eliot Dudley: Le Petit Bois" in *A World of Light.*

Natalie Hammond: Wealthy lesbian artist, sister of the founder of Hammond organs.

Aggie: Agnes Yarnall, Philadelphia sculptress whose works include heads of Edna St. Vincent Millay and Gielgud as well as one of Benjamin Franklin which is at the Franklin Institute.

Translation of French: But the good God is resting now; he must rest like everyone else.

the novel: The Waterfall, unpublished.

Reviews: Of The Single Hound.

Helen: Helen Huntington Howe (Mrs. Reginald Allen) (1905–75), monologist who presented her solo performances throughout the U.S. as well as in theatres and supper clubs in New York and London; became a novelist and biographer. Daughter of Mark A. de Wolfe Howe, sister of Quincy and Mark (husband of Moll), all of whom Sarton knew. Howe makes mention of May Sarton in *The Gentle Americans,* her literary and social chronicle of Boston.

the Hopkins: Probably Gerard and Mabel Hopkins who lived in Surrey, England.

Translation of French: One cannot depict happiness.

TO ELIZABETH BOWEN   May 26th, 1938
[Vouvray]
Elisabeth,

I thought of you just before I went to sleep last night with a great longing to jump out of bed and write you a long letter, but must have fallen asleep
between thinking of it and action. Now it is evening, a golden one. The acacia just outside my window in flower looks like a wedding, and the garden
is explosive with roses—strawberries and just beginning peas. I have been
painting a large deer on G's wall, a grandiose and puerile effort after which
I feel as if I had written seven poems. We are making a sort of tapestry on
the wall with a Petit Bois, animals and a little landscape at the back. But the
trouble is there is so much to do the days fly away and it is evening before
it is morning.

I can't remember when I wrote you or what I said and have lost all sense
of time so forgive repetitions. I have only one note at the moment and it is
that I am happy, <u>entirely,</u> in every element of life, and at peace. This seems
little short of miraculous and it makes one silent. I find it difficult even to
write poems about happiness—perhaps it is banal written down. Lived it
seems as rare as a Japanese cock with a tail seven yards long. Je n'en reviens
pas.

Also, my darling, I am 26, an age for embarking on the major course. No
more emotional excursions. Work. Now that I have a little confidence and
think I am not merely charging at a windmill, I see how awfully long it will
take before I can write anything good, rooted, secure and finished, and how
it is like acting in that one writes what one *is,* and under an acquired style
there is the nakedness of oneself. I see so clearly now in the novel its impatient and avid point of view, its superficial pretty sort of wisdom.

Have just finished a short story, a legend, a romantic one of the country
here—it was a great relief to stop digging around for bare essential outlines,
to stop the novel and let myself write something un-profound, unimportant
and charming. The event is that Harper's Bazaar, now run by a nice fairy called
George Davis has just taken <u>four</u> poems and the London Mercury a long
letter to James Stephens—verse—(what a blessing—fifty bucks) and want a
short story. They have gone quite highbrow you know—Virginia had a
queer unsuccessful story in two months ago. She wrote me a most typical
letter in answer to one of mine begging her to hurry up and put me out of
my misery—she seems to be in great agitation about Ottoline, Philip pes-
tering her etc. She says "If you're in London later and still want wild and
random impressions verbally probably we could arrange it. And as for feeling suspense about my judgement—that seems to me absurd in the extreme."
It made me laugh and if I were not twenty six and acquiring a fortress of re-

serve I would write her a tremendous fan letter. But, like Gogol's Madman "Silence, silence."

Damn. I have to dress for dinner. We emerge very rarely from this garden except to walk out into the vineyards after tea but we have to go and dine with a French novelist (passion-flower novels I gather called "Sous le Croix du Sud" and things like that which he writes after spending a week cruising around Constantinople). They are fearfully French and we sit in a tiny stuffy salon full of yellow empire furniture and awful modern oil paintings by some relation. Last week we had a Thckeovian [sic] lunch at the Chateau of "Montresor" a darling chateau (there is no other word) but now lived in by an old Polish countess who has filled it with life-size stuffed wolves shot by her husband, and millions of boars' tusks hanging on the walls on silver chains—ancient retainers in 19th century evening clothes, who pass a little bear holding a lighted cigar in his mouth on a silver tray to light one's cigarettes.

I am coming back about June 10th for a month and then coming back here to work. I really dread cities. I wish I could see you peacefully. Can't Alan and you and I go for a drive as we did once and lie in the grass? I have discovered that Grace is "La poesie." It is very nice to live with one's muse.

There is no other news that I can think of—will you be human when I come back—with the novel almost finished, and full of Ireland, and happy. Shall we sit in front of a little fire and talk? I am bursting with conversation really in spite of my silences (they are further down really)—or shall I only see you through a mirage of voluble Oxford, through a haze of Gladys Calthrop? How is the portrait? I envy that young man. Your young men make me quite wild, just to think of them. I am not entirely reformed, although almost; I am full of jealousy of your young men.

Here is a poem. Here is a pansy. Here am I.

The pansy shrivelled during the night. It was dark red velvet.

Translation of French: I can't get back easily to myself.

Ottoline: Ottoline Violet Anne Morrell, Lady Ottoline, *née* Cavendish-Bentinck, married to Philip Morrell (1873–1938), society hostess, had just died. Philip then began to "court" Virginia Woolf.

Calthrop: Gladys Calthrop, scenic designer whose work included Noel Coward's *The Vortex* and Eva Le Gallienne's production of Ibsen's *The Master Builder.*

Enclosed: "Considerations," unpublished. See Appendix. An entirely different poem, under the same title, appears in *Inner Landscape,* Houghton Mifflin and Cresset, 1939. Also enclosed, "Portrait by Holbein for Elisabeth Bowen," see *Encounter in April.*

July 6th, 1938

[Hampstead]

Dearest Poll,

For a month I have written no letters, a ghastly month of people, very few of them rewarding, of hours wasted in tubes, subways, buses, taxis—I am in revolt <u>utterly</u> against the life of cities and feel like the Mad Hatter, that I have been murdering the Time. This with emotional difficulties, things to settle in a <u>right</u> way once and for all. It is all done but at what expense of spirit! I feel dead like a goldfish panting on a bank—and the day after to-morrow flee to Vouvray for a month—it looks like the Terre Promisé!

It was very startling and shocking to hear of Eliot's death. It makes one feel that there was something fundamentally wrong as he was on the way to personal happiness. That poor girl—I feel so dreadfully sorry for her. How is Mrs. Cabot?

Well, to summarize the month—the one new person I met whom I like was Lord David Cecil (nephew of the Nobel Cecil) who won the Hawthornden prize some years ago with a not very good book on the poet Cowper—but he is flamingly sensitive, charming, the best of the English with a really charming wife—He is about thirty and a real discovery—I only saw them twice but hope it is the beginning and not the end.

Had a good week-end at Basil de Selincourt's—the house full of music as the blind pianist Tom Mitchell was there and played for hours and hours in a Dionysiac way—César Franck, Brahms, Beethoven—he lives in a <u>dark </u>world of sound—by shutting one's eyes one began to imagine what it was like.

Several week-ends with the Huxleys—I have fallen in love with their youngest boy, Francis, 15 with a thatch of hair and a funny sullen face—he has a pet owl and rides their ponies bare-back—he and I spent a day draw-ing animals together (the parents away) and hence have established a firm friendship. Last week-end we went down to see Anthony, the almost too-beautiful blond fragile eldest. Picnicked, had a long lazy afternoon punting down one of those enchanted English rivers full of reeds and flowers with a heron or two flying slowly past. Juliette has been doing a head of me—I sat for ten precious mornings but alas it is not very good.

My business reason for coming was to see about poems. And the deal is on the point of going through with Greenslet buying sheets from Cresset so the new poems will appear both in England and U.S. I haven't heard a word as to sales of the novel from U.S. and haven't had a cent but for once I am not in debt so don't worry much about it.

Mrs. Richard Paine (Grace's sister) is going to be in Vouvray for a few days of which I am glad as I think it will clear up the old misunderstanding of Richard-me! Also the Morrison's (Sam) are coming for a week-end. I met

them at the Huxleys at lunch with H. G. Wells and a wonderful man called
Burnall (the best brain in England, a little man with an enormous head and
a great sense of humour) also Marion Dorn, the designer, a certain type of
beautiful pretentious (intellectually) American, very attractive but how dumb!
I disliked the Morrison's very much except the daughter who is nice. Mr.
was so stiff and New England eating his asparagus with a knife and fork and
looking self-satisfied, so un-cosmopolitan, so very provincial I thought. Mrs.
looked jewish (is she?) and was rather ingratiating but bright. I shall probably change my mind when I see them at Vouvray—this just a lunch-
impression but I'm sure Mr. hated me and I was against him because of what
I had heard of his treatment of his crew on the cruise. What do you think of
them?

I've seen Elisabeth twice for long talks about personal matters—she is a
real friend and I feel funnily that it is not necessary to see her a great deal.
She is there. She is just finishing her book [*Death of the Heart*] which will be
out in the fall, wants me to come to Ireland but I am staying quiet in France.
I want to work. The new novel has got to be re-begun from the beginning
and I want to get very rested and really dynamic about it before I begin again.
It lacks intensity—and I feel every note is just a little off somehow.

Kot is in bed with a poisoned foot but in excellent spirits—it has been
worth coming to see him—he always makes me feel straightened out and
patient about work. I think you will find me changed when I come back—
I feel curiously passive in some ways—you will miss the old panache. But
don't give me up for lost. I see us growing side by side like two trees of which
the branches nod at each other—My darling, how are you? Please write to
me and forgive this silence. This month has been a real nightmare—I am
dreadfully tired.

Very dear love to you as always—

[   ]

Terre Promisé: Promised Land.

Eliot: Theater director and leading man Eliot Cabot (1899–1938) had tried to kill himself a
week earlier and fractured his skull. He left a young wife and child. His mother, Mrs. Cabot,
had met and befriended Eleanor Mabel Sarton as well as May.

Lord [Edward Christian] David [Gascoyne] Cecil: (1902–1986), literary critic and biographer.
His wife was Rachel MacCarthy, daughter of Desmond and Molly.

Basil de Selincourt: (?–1966), literary critic for the *Observer* in London; lived in Kingham, Oxfordshire.

Francis: Francis Huxley (1923–), social anthropologist; author of *Affable Savages,* 1956.

Anthony: Anthony Huxley (1920–1992), author, *Amateur Gardening.*

Mrs. Richard Paine: Ellen Paine.

Richard-me: Richard Paine had been seen taking Sarton to lunch in Cambridge (Mass.); he had also singled her out at a party at his home. Unfounded rumours had spread.

Sam: Samuel Eliot Morison (1887–1976), American historian.

Marion Dorn: Mrs. Ted McKnight Kauffer (1890–1954) American artist and textile designer, became a friend and subject of Sarton's poem "The Clavichord" in *The Lion and the Rose.*

TO ELIZABETH BOWEN   July 13, 1938
[Vouvray]
Dearest E.

Life is always a little more complicated than one expects—I am here— the wheat is all standing up gold in the fields—and the vines just a vast sea— everyone is very busy climbing up tall ladders to pick cherries (there has never been such a year!) Perhaps the peace I have cried out for for the last two years is really here after all. Anyway I am staying as a kind of child in the house, providing tenderness and companionship and that kind of oneness that is possible between two women. Nothing is settled between G. and her husband and I think perhaps never will be but perhaps he will come over sometimes and stay—I see her carefully guarded and built up emotional stability going to pieces and there is nothing to do. Really passion is a frightful thing.

But I am working on arranging the poems—O Elisabeth I think it is really a good book, one I am proud of. A sick heart has its good and bad days but deeper than that I am so glad to be here, to be silent, and in a week or so I may begin furiously at the new novel.

I didn't tell you about Virginia—it was a most painful afternoon—as I realized she really has a phobia about having to say anything about people's work and so we made small talk until almost the end when she suddenly started talking very hard and I had to leave! She evidently hated the "whimsical" old ladies (I know what she means there perfectly and it is true) but liked the second part best (!) Kot says this was a lie and that she just <u>wouldn't</u> say what she thought—but she said I obviously had talent and it would be interesting to see if I really had anything to say. I was terrifically amused afterwards though rather uncomfortable at the time. What a curious woman— I kept wanting to say for God's sake be simple—it was like looking down into one of those spiral shells. She advised me to write essays, and certainly there is the danger of feeling too much and not thinking through and hard enough. In the end I suppose this sort of criticism is interesting from two points of view: the light it gives into the person who is presenting it—I felt I had learned more about her than ever before—and secondly to clarify one's own ideas chiefly through disagreement!

Here are two poems. I think I may write to you often. This is no letter but just to send you a poem I wrote on the frightfully rough crossing and one I wrote earlier which I may not have sent.

I wish you would send me a postcard once in a while—No, I really hear you through your silences perfectly well, so don't bother.

Our three meetings were blessed—

Love

M—

G.: Grace Dudley.

a good book: Inner Landscape.

Enclosed: "Architectural Image" and "The Pride of Trees," both published in *Inner Landscape,* 1939.

TO POLLY THAYER STARR   Sunday, Aug. 17th [1938]
[Rockport]
Dearest Poll,

What a sweet letter and a great blessing. This is an autumn day all the edges so brilliant and the sea very dark blue ruffled by the wind so it looks like feathers. I have just written a long letter to Jean Dominique in French so this will probably be quite wild (I haven't written her for months. We hadn't heard for months and now we have just had an adorable letter, describing the food situation with the single darling phrase "Nous sommes devenues des femmes legères") She will be 68 this year. The school carries on and they had their graduation with crowns of roses (but I fear not medals of choco-lat wrapped in tinfoil as in the old days) They are not touched by the evil of the world.

No, it is nothing except the queerness of life. I feel I am just beginning (rather late!) to find my place in the world which as I see it now is bound to be solitary, for a long time no outward success, financially extremely re-stricted, inwardly I hope rich and growing. I do not belong in your world darling although I love you dearly. I expect it is that. I know Donald thinks of me as a queer bird, not quite comme il faut, and I am perfectly happy and then all sorts of abysses appear from nowhere (in my mind I expect) after-ward. The answer to all this is let's see each other often next winter. I am going to be a hermit but not to you. I am not going out at all for lunch and only Friday, Sat. and Sun. evenings. If one is the kind of creature I am and wants to do the kind of writing I want to do, an undisturbed bourgeois ex-istence with no distractions seems in order. A single meeting outside the fam-ily upsets one's whole inner web, makes one start off on two-days' thinking and weighing, destroys a delicate balance etc. etc. I needn't tell you because you have the same damned problem in your painting and a husband and baby and whole tapestry of rich outer existence as well. I am appalled at how little I have done in ten years (It is ten years since my first poem was published) I now have enough friends to last me a lifetime and that is enough. I am going to close the doors and hibernate at least for a couple of years. I am frightfully depressed about my work. It seems to me perfectly mediocre.

By the way, Moll and I were singing your praises the other day and agreed that you were the most unaffectedly humble person about your work that we know. I wonder if I shall manage to see the New York show? I would like to see many of your paintings all together. Is that the same show that goes to Florida?

Isn't it exciting that Simon and S. have offered Helen a contract for her novel? I have to re-adjust my whole perspective on Helen if she turns into a writer—she would be extremely capable of it. She has the detachment, the powers of observation and the heart. I bet it's a dandy book.

I am just butting along like a "dirty British Coaster" on the book, writing down the whole trip. It is the most boring work you can imagine (because there is nothing to imagine) but it is a good exercise and a necessary discipline. I have no faith in its being published. I wish I had an idea for a novel. I long to get my teeth into something big and real.

I feel much better and calmer now that I have decided to be a worker not a liver.

Do write again—I hope the two weeks is as dazzling as your letter sounds. Dear Poll, you are a marvel to do all you do—

Love from May

Moll seems to me to have grown enormously, to be rich and full of power—I <u>don't</u> like <u>Basil!</u> He is to my mind everything most hateful about England. But there you are! The Torringtons [?] are real—Also B. is such a child, so immature. I can't be bothered. (He hates me too.)

————

Translation of French: We have become thin women.

Helen: Howe.

Basil: Probably Colonel de Basil.

TO MARIE CLOSSET   1 September 1938
[Channing Place]
Dear dear—

I have tiptoed around your letter for days—I've studied the two photographs—I read and reread the line "I have become very old—it is important that you know that, that you see that"—I've gone on feverishly with that end of summer passion, that sense that work is beginning again, that winter is coming—the discipline, the <u>salvation</u> of this precious and terrible work—I've reread all your poems and <u>Une Syllable d'Oiseau,</u> and this wonderful phrase "To stop silence on the lips of love, is better thus" and I have to tell you that as far as I'm concerned you'll never be old—you'll never be <u>mortal,</u> you'll never change either with the years nor with death—because you are the <u>heart</u> of my heart—the bitter sweet seed in the center, Don't you have a picture of yourself at my age—I would love to see it, to keep it near me like an angelic presence that time can never alter.

This summer was strange (I have already moved beyond it and feel autumn in my heart)—I came back here to find everything in *chaos*—the problem of money is once again dire—my hopes for a season in Philadelphia ruined—I've lived through weeks of vast uncertainty in my soul and mind during which one must live from day to day and not think too much about the future. But just now two miracles have happened—at the last minute money arrived (more than I'd ever hoped possible) right after a lecture I'd given which I thought was perhaps the last one and into which I put my whole heart. But there was also a true miracle of the heart—full of pain and grace which left me both dazzled and depressed. Having spent June living out a fierce passion I have finally found the purest most tortuous love for a person I will see only two or three more times, a painter, married, who is trying to build her life on what I can see only as <u>sand</u>—but in the end I was able to help her through a difficult period—she <u>understands</u> everything I am trying to be as no one else (except you) has ever understood. And I have "stopped the silence," because I had to. I feel bathed in light—Dear God! what a <u>treasure</u> this brief life we are given. I believe one must spend it <u>all,</u> keeping only love, which always grows, and is always a little greater then we ourselves are.

I've written a great many poems—I write all the time—it is as if the door which had been closed for so long is wide open—I send you a few—not that they are good but they bring me back happiness, and the joy of <u>celebrating</u> life again.

I am sorry the summer brought you so little silence and peace and your real life. Oh I wish I could take you somewhere for a month, where there would be flowers and sea and hardly any wind—and sun—"dream of peace"—I would come only once or twice a day to tell you my morning thoughts and my evening thoughts, and to fill you with silence—my Gilles.

All my tenderness and anxious love as you return to your work—

M—

---

my Gilles: my sad Pierrot.

TO POLLY THAYER STARR   Nov. 2d [1938]
[Channing Place]
Dearest Poll,

Lovely to get your two letters and hear that you are being cherished as you deserve by Mary Mabon and Aggie—I tottered out on Sat. night and then was violently ill on Sunday again (some sort of intestinal infection that seems very persistent). But this week feel much better, have had all my classes and yesterday got my licence entirely through wearing a hat the officer admired for I did everything possible wrong and was shaking so I could hardly find the gear-shift! But now my car is in Channing Place very shiny and happy and I adore it already and crept over to Edith's in it last night (I literally crawl along, the bane of all other drivers).

This morning <u>at last</u> Ferris [Greenslet] called up to tell me that he would see me tomorrow (in the office, very ominous), that apparently Bob is not enthusiastic about the book and I'm afraid his word goes so I am prepared for the worst—which may turn out for the best if I can persuade myself that it is good enough to take down to New York. I feel quite philosophical about it. Money has always been the pressure that drove me to tears when I saw the only hope of any disappearing—now I am earning and paying off debts things have a better proportion. I can afford to wait and do what is best not only what is expedient. But you're right it is depressing—I just got the final check for Hound $88.00 (immediately sent off for debts) which means that altogether I shall have earned a little over $300 for it in America and about $80 in England. Ah well—

Had a fan-letter from the poet H. D. which was nice. I am depressed in prospect about the poems as it is obvious that nothing will be done. I hope oblivious will be as sweet as the poets say!

About Le Gallienne—your letter pricked a little. The Times review praised her very highly—on thinking it over it seems to me that I have only seen great acting in two people—Nazimova (in Ghosts) and Le Gallienne in Liliom and The Three Sisters, and at the very beginning of Camille when it first opened—<u>because</u> in both cases they illuminated life, opened <u>understanding</u>, and this is the test of an actor for me just as much as for a novelist—I knew more about love and compassion from Le Gallienne's acting in Liliom when she read "Blessed are the pure in heart" than perhaps I shall ever learn again through experience. Perhaps a great actor (one thinks of Fanny Kemble) must hate as well as love the stage—he must pierce through technique and bravura, be more than an actor playing a part—the people like Orson Welles who are all "theatre" and even Cornell <u>never</u> attain that transparency of spirit. It has nothing to do with life—Duse was a dreadful woman, jealous, loving to create emotional situations between members of her company and watch them fight it out, but she had this spiritual quality—she <u>knew</u> even if she could not <u>be</u>—so Baudelaire—so some of the greatest artists, those who must perform because they are <u>less</u> than their vision of what life ought to be, could be.

Forgive this and bless you—When do you come back?

Your devoted

[   ]

Mary Mabon: Friend of the Starrs.

Bob: Robert Linscott (1886–1964), editor who worked for many years at Houghton Mifflin, then at Random House.

H. D.: Penname for Hilda Doolittle (1886–1961), American imagist poet, fell in love with Ezra Pound in 1905; in 1913 she married Richard Aldington; the most enduring of her relationships was with the English historical novelist Winifred Bryher. This letter began her friendship with Sarton.

Fanny [Frances Anne] Kemble: (1809–93), a great beauty, heir to a distinguished acting tradition; retired from the stage at the height of her powers when she was twenty-five.

TO VIRGINIA WOOLF   January 15th, 1939
[Channing Place]
Dear Virginia Woolf,

One begins to imagine the possible renascence of the bulbs which one planted so hopefully and despaired of at every frost—the spring *exists* now in the mind—that is why January is such a hard month—one is already in state of expectation for what can't begin actually for months. We have planted single white tulips—I can't wait for them. Never has there been a year when one needed more to be born again.

But this, I forget, is a business letter. I have been wanting to write to you for a long time but hesitated before the unimportance of what I might have to say, measuring it against the desire to communicate, and finding it outweighed each time. Now there is a reason—a real definite one. It is this: in New York an association for taking care of refugees from Germany has been having auctions of manuscripts. Prince Lowenstein asked me to see if I could persuade Julian, H. G. and you to part with a written fragment of yourself for this purpose. It seems rather horrible, but also necessary as anything that <u>can</u> be done <u>must</u> be done for these people. I rather hate to ask. But I believe that people would almost sell their souls for a single page of yours and if you could send one, the manuscript of a book review or anything small (or big) to the

American Guild for German Cultural Freedom
20 Vesey Street
N.Y. City c/o Prince Lowenstein

it would be a good deed in a naughty world. There are dozens of reasons why you might rather not, and of course don't if one of these seems more persuasive than the need. Woof! I feel now like a man who has had to make a rather painful after-dinner speech. The auction is to be held <u>Feb. 19th</u>. At the last they made $6000 which seems a good augury.

Since I saw you—as I remember it a nightmarish occasion because the end was the beginning, and I had to go at the beginning, with a sharp sense of loss and parting. Since then I have been struggling. It has taken the form of laying aside a new novel, a little better than the first, less facile perhaps, but not good. Of reading Rilke who is like a dense forest into which one disappears, penetrating slowly and often in the dark, but always with a sense of awe and imminent discovery. There are few writers whom one must in some way become before reading. I think he is one and so reading him is more than reading; it can become the most absorbing part of one's life for a time. I am so grateful that he was there this year—just this year and no other where the spirit is towered over by world horror, where it seems like a blade of grass pushing through a pavement (not less miraculous). And then I have been struggling with teaching a class in prose writing and one in poetry. The prose people are six young girls varying from 16 to my age—and it seemed at first as if they would never see, let alone write what they saw. It is appalling the stuffed-ness with things unfelt, unimagined, <u>unlived</u> of people out of schools. I cannot understand why poetry is not taught at schools as a way of seeing, a quick, untiring path to essentials. These girls have a certain amount of knowledge but they do not know anything for themselves. Given a tree, they do not see it for themselves <u>at all.</u> It is not new, not theirs, not given for the first time like a present. It is just a tree that they have read about or passed by in a car—not one would go up and feel the trunk with her hands. So I have tried all sorts of experiments—wondering for instance if they would see better a thing already interpreted by Cézanne or Van Gogh—it <u>did</u> work and I was pleased. Now I am leading them inwards to people and themselves, hoping that by the end of the year they will write a short autobiography.

The poetry class is at present two elderly ladies, a teacher in a progressive school, and a curious aloof creature who once sent you a book about women called "From the Sea." Her name is Mrs. Swift. One is very simple, practical eager and ignorant. The other (Swift) is subtle, learned, out to catch me like a fish in her hands—and it is a game to placate them both. But I am learning a lot even if they aren't. And it is good to feel slightly useful.

Otherwise I am in a flood of poetry—one of the incredible times when I know that I have only to sit down for it to seize me and play a tune. It is so rare when it happens and so unexpected, and usually so intimately bound up with personal emotions. But now it has come out of thinking and not out of myself in the same way—still, the need to <u>solve,</u> to create a balance out of opposing forces inside, to climb to a peak and for an instant rest and look down—but now not the solving of a war in the heart (thank God! at last). For the first time in my life I see that I have grown an inch and I believe that I may in ten years be a poet. It is wonderful.

Dear Virginia Woolf, that is all I have to say. I wish you were near and that I could send you the primroses that I saw in a shop and gave to my mother instead.

Yours to command
May Sarton

Here is a poem or two. They are beginnings and not ends, intimations of perhaps a poem someday that might be written, by someone else or by me.

––––––––––

Never has there been a year: Hitler's annexation of the Sudetenland in September had made Germany the dominant power in Europe; war was imminent.

H. G.: Herbert George Wells (1866–1946), English novelist and journalist, known for his popular fantasies on pseudo-scientific themes, satires on modern life, popular accounts of history and science, and outspoken social and political theories.

teaching a class: At the Stuart School in Boston.

Mrs. Swift: Elizabeth Townsend (Mrs. Rodman) Swift.

The other (Swift): Probably Agnes Swift.

Enclosed: "Progression," published in *American Signature: A Collection of Modern Letters,* ed. by Rae Beamish. Black Fawn Press, Rochester, N.Y. 1941, see Appendix; "Where Warriors Stood" published in the *New York Herald Tribune* November 24, 1948, see *The Land of Silence,* 1953; "Intimation," see *Letters from Maine,* 1984; "Snow and Vivaldi," unpublished, see Appendix.

TO LAWRENCE LEE   Jan. 26th, 1939
[Channing Place]
Dear Lawrence Lee,

Yes, I meant every word of it. Here is what set me off that day—it might be worth quoting somewhere. The death of the Criterion was announced in the Times Lit. on Jan. 7th with the following quotation from Eliot:

"In the present state of public affairs—which has induced in myself a depression of spirits so different from any other experience of fifty years as to be a new emotion—I no longer feel the enthusiasm necessary to make a literary review what it should be. This is not to suggest that I consider literature to be at this time, or at any time, a matter of indifference. On the contrary I feel that it is all the more essential that authors who are concerned with that small part of "literature" which is really creative—and seldom immediately popular—should apply themselves sedulously to their work, without abatement or sacrifice of their artistic standards on any pretext whatsoever."

It is because you stand for that small part of literature that I am all for you! I must confess that when I read of the Criterion's death (though I have never been a subscriber) it gave me a deathly shiver—as much the end of a world— small perhaps but containing an essential grain of human spirit—as, let us say, the fall of Barcelona. At that moment of despair it was moving to be given your Quarterly.

I find my position as a poet today a curious one. I wonder if you do at all? For a long time I have maintained that the poet's affair was the individual human soul, the story of it in one man, in my case the transforming of personal emotions into written events. Now it has become impossible to guard one's soul—death to do it—we are forced to read the papers, and yet I still believe that our job is somehow or other to be above the mêlée, or so deeply *in* it that one comes through to something else, something universal and timeless. This, as I write it, sounds pompous,—what I'm driving at is that although there is a place for Auden and Spender, for Rukeyser and Fearing, there is an even greater need perhaps for Rilke, for Blake. I'm sending you some poems, doubtful if you will want to use them, but just to say the poet's equivalent of "Salud!" and to wish for you all the power of imagination and endurance that you (and all of us) will need! It is splendid what you're doing—

Sincerely yours,
May Sarton

I saw Katharine the other day, looking splendid in a red sweater over bluegreen, so violently alive—she hailed me over to talk about these poems. Scott-James (London Mercury) has the rest of the group. I am sending you too many. Never mind—

Lawrence Lee: Editor of the *Virginia Quarterly.*

Fearing: Kenneth Fearing (1902–1961), American writer, poet.

Katharine: Katharine Sturgis, sculptor and painter; Sarton wrote "Lifting Stone" for her.

TO   POLLY   THAYER   STARR   Thurs. 1:00 A.M. [April 1939 ?]
[New York (HT)]
Dearest Poll,

Your letter and the check filled me with such unashamed shame and blushes and duck-like conscience-less paddling joy—for I went right out in the rain feeling so happy to be cheated out of virtue by friendship—too generous and God knows un-deserved but sweet and world-transforming friendship (Was there ever one before who could bring a family of shells wrapped up in newspaper—like magic—one day, and the very heart's desire for the flesh the next? This is feeding body and soul and this is friendship—I am too tired to write and this must sound quite mad I'm thinking. It has rained all day—I got a darling little black bolero suit with a ruffly blouse and a cherry-coloured bow at the throat and a quite Marlene-Dietrich hat—and for all this bless you my darling. I am reminded of Juliette to whom Julian gave a little ermine cape for Christmas and she wrote that she felt very guilty but would wear her conscience one day and the ermine the next—that is how I feel.

Last night I saw Le Gallienne, a good peaceful talk—I have never been more impressed with her fundamental serenity and <u>purity</u> of purpose—she talked so quietly about failure and success—and had been planting seedlings of petunias in her garden all day—it was <u>good</u> to have faith returned—it happened twice in that evening for I went on to Kappo in some trepidation—but found her looking well and happy (she hasn't had a drink for a year and has worked very hard—she deserved a reward and I have been persuading Hal to take her on and encourage her)—she and Margaret have a little house in the middle of a garden just set down in the middle court of a slum like a Peter Pan house—perfectly <u>darling</u> with crocuses out already and their black cat and black bob-tailed cat sitting at the door when I left. All this makes life worth living again—I mean if the <u>inner</u> person finds a way out for itself, <u>grows</u> (and that is the case with both Kap and Eva) then nothing else matters—

I saw the Dali show—and was conquered I must say—such perfection of madness, such luscious colours and strange <u>clear</u> distances and that horrible but fantastic fecundity of imagination. I hate but admire him.

Ben? In true British style after these quite definitely "Come hither" letters didn't say a personal word—we talked art and literature and left life out! Queer and intriguing I must say. I'll see him in London and sent him an Easter egg to the boat which I hope will not seem too forward! He took me to a new night club called Café Society where I heard hot jazz for the first time and think it is frenzy carried to the pitch where it is perfectly <u>static</u> and so rather boring. He was I think disappointed that I was not a hotter jazz baby but he is *so* tall and held me at finger-tip about two feet away from him so I couldn't dance with him at all (definitely humiliating for both of us)—I think Auden sat beside us and I found it difficult to concentrate being maddened with curiosity.

Then sat for two hours yesterday on Mrs. Colby's immortal bed—with Jack Oakman and Charlie Olsen (who has got a Guggenheim) and poor Bo who gets more ghostly every minute. Mrs. C. spread jam on english muffins and was so charming it melted your heart—the usual men viz. women conversation—but she is wonderful—talking about four-dimensional lovers (the prop of old age apparently) and the fact that the children of drunks were driven by Freud and their father-feeling, always to marry alcoholics and hold-ing her family up as an example of this (!) I suppose she is so much more interesting to her children than any man will ever be that that is the tragedy—so now they all three sit on her bed and talk. What will happen to them when she dies? It is rather frightening to contemplate.

Bob Hale read me a 28-page short story he has just written—really quite good with great charm and rather crazy in a nice way—he sees a lot of Mar-quand and didn't seem to mind the book at all. Rene is going to have <u>twins</u> and goes about enormous swaddled in mink and fox—well, this letter is de-scending to gossip—I'll run out and mail it.

Darling, bless you—I hope the portrait started off well—don't tire your eyes writing but just send me a <u>line</u> about it—My best to Aggie—and to you the warmest and sweetest and lastingest thank you in the shape of love—

[   ]

I go home tomorrow feeling quite renewed—Saw Tallulah tonight—the play is marvelous but so *evil* you can hardly bear it.

––––––––––

Hal: Harrison Smith. Publisher and editor at Harcourt Brace, Cape & Smith, Doubleday & Company, and the *Saturday Review.*

Kappo and Margaret: Kappo Phelan and Margaret English were members of the Apprentice Theatre.

Ben: Benedict Lionel (Ben) Nicolson (1914–78), Art historian. Son of Harold Nicolson and Vita Sackville-West.

Mrs. Colby: Possibly Natalie Sedgwick Colby.

Jack Oakman: Robert Beverly Hale's step-father.

Charles Olson: (1910–1970), poet and critic.

Bo: Sister of Fanny Rogers whose husband, Cameron Rogers, was a poet and author of a life of Audubon and *The Black Winds Blow.*

Bob Hale: Robert Beverly Hale, poet, one of the great teachers of art anatomy. Sarton is re-ferring to John Phillips Marquand's *Wickford Point* (1939) one of his many satirical novels deal-ing with New Englanders struggling to maintain their aristocratic, Puritan standards.

Rene: Renée Orsell, member of the Civic Repertory Theatre; later stage manager of the As-sociated Actors Theatre.

Tallulah: Tallulah Bankhead (1903–1968), played Regina Giddens in *The Little Foxes* that year.

TO JULIAN HUXLEY   May 4th, 1939
[Channing Place]
Dear one,

I have just had your letter from Whipsnade in the middle of that dreary but I hope fruitful treatment—and I wish I were there to be playing bez-ique with you and reading Tom Jones (which I have never read!) I am reading a fascinating fascinating and (repeated ad infinitum) book which you must get at once from the library if you don't know it—but I expect you do— Isak Dinesen's Out of Africa—she is that Danish baroness who suddenly appeared as a full-fledged mysterious writer with seven fantastic tales called Seven Gothic Tales—these she apparently wrote to keep her mind off an awful drought which was ruining her coffee farm in Africa—her descriptions of life in Africa, her relationship with the natives etc. are simply marvelous and she must be an extraordinary person. Do you know anything about her? She had a 6000 acre farm and apparently lived alone there for years.

Since I last wrote I have been a bridesmaid and had a birthday, two events of major importance. Being a bridesmaid is quite solemn and frightening and I had never heard the marriage service entirely—it is so beautiful I was afraid I was going to have to sit down on the floor clutching my flowers and weep. The girl was my best friend at school, a perfect darling of the Barbour type of American, very lively and humourous and when we were at school we had an invented language with some wonderful words like fionsig (funny) and yawflet (awful) in it and even now break into it at once on sight—her husband is a very shy sensitive and brilliant young Scotch engineer (with no amorous experience <u>at all</u> and he is 26 which seems extraordinary.) They are going to live in London and I would love to show them to you and Juliette and vice versa: "Meet my dear friends, the pandas"—except that already there are too many people to be seen (I mean for you) and it is not at all necessary but might be rather sweet as they would be very thrilled.

The birthday took place on a grey cold day yesterday—the spring is a polar nightmare—we drove out to Anne Thorp's beautiful piece of land covered with juniper and cedar trees and tall pines—and rolling pastures divided by stone-walls—the brook full of kingcups, mayflower and bloodroot out—but too cold for a picnic—we were Grace Dudley, Franz, Anne and my family— and it was a very dear birthday (though I kept thinking of Tours and there was a Julian mirage at the back) with a bottle of sparkling Vouvray, ice cream with <u>spun sugar!</u> (Ah!) and I had made little books of my poems for everyone decorated with flowers—Franz's mother brought me from Prague a fabulous leather prince's waistcoat lined with fur and embroidered in blue flowers—too lovely and impossible just like a fairy story—and Grace a book of Lamartine bound by Lavollée—and Anne read Stephen Benét's wonderful story about Daniel Webster's pleading a case against the devil which ends with his chasing him out of New Hampshire for good—"I am not speaking of Vermont or Massachusetts"—a good American story. We sat in front of a huge fire and it was very comforting and nice altogether even though I was mourning my 27th year and its waning, inglorious.

Otherwise I am stupidly tired and just ploughing doggedly on through the spring like a horse in blinders.

In a little over a month I shall be seeing you, my dear one—

Love from your

[   ]

———

Tom Jones: by Henry Fielding (1701–1754). English novelist known for the wit and satire of his picaresque novels.

best friend from school: Barbara Runkle, "Tig," friend from Shady Hill for whom Sarton wrote "A Poem for Women," unpublished; married William Hawthorne, a physicist who was later knighted.

Franz: Possibly Franz Wiener.

Lamartine: Alphonse de Larmartine (1790–1869), French poet and statesman of the Romantic period.

Stephen Benét: Stephen Vincent Benét (1898–1943), American poet, short story writer, and novelist. Particularly known for his narrative Civil War poem "John Brown's Body" which won the Pulitzer Prize in 1929; brother of William Rose Benét. This reference is to *The Devil and Daniel Webster.*

TO POLLY THAYER STARR   [July 1, 1939]
[Whipsnade]
                          [first page missing]
I can now understand why it was that V. talked of Boston as she did. We seemed and were a provincial city built upon character not upon blood and by the very fact that we were originally rebels whatever our blood, standing outside the sacred precincts. But we had a grand talk about poetry and poets and really agree upon most matters—but she is not a first-rate intelligence or character. What she has is the terrific glamour of her past. But compared with V. Woolf's face for instance she is decidedly in the lower order of angels. She has been given a beautiful distinguished and passionate face and she has not done much with it from the inside whereas Virginia's has become a kind of vessel for the mind and spirit. The features are unimportant. She said one interesting thing—that she wished she had never written a novel and would like to destroy them all. In terms of the first-rate of course she is right.

The only new personality that I have fallen for is elephantine Flaherty the movie man who made "Man of Aran" "Nanook" [of the North] "Moana" etc. and is a perfect darling a sort of Santa Claus, with expansive social instincts, always surrounded with people to whom he hands out drinks and American cigarettes, and whom he enjoys and loves like a patriarch—

he took me twice to the Players Theatre—the fashion of the moment— a tiny theatre where at 11:30 actors perform Victorian songs while the audience joins in in the chorus—beer and hot dogs and slot machines lend it a slightly bohemian atmosphere and it is a good mixed audience of everyone from the Duff-Coopers to Bloomsbury. It is very well done and frightfully funny as they never burlesque but do the songs exactly as they would have been done. The only trouble is that it is so late and I am always dead. Gogarty was there one night—rather boring and mercenary I thought—he repeated his stories but Flaherty said he was not in form. He is so anti-Valera that he has left Ireland and is now on the look-out for publishers to give him huge advances on unwritten books of gossip.

Have been having a peaceful time with Julian. All is really well and seems miraculous. I have escaped any personal entanglements and am just feeling happy and busy and at the center of life instead of on the outskirts for a change. Still I think of New England and you with the usual nostalgia and shall be glad to get home.

I go to Belgium Aug. 8th—so write to address above before then—if not it will be forwarded and then to Paris for a week before sailing—had a lovely peaceful week-end at Basil de Selincourts and one at Rye—have been seeing Elisabeth quite a lot (she is bringing Alan down for dinner tomorrow night)—

Very dear love to you, darling—I long for news. Have you seen Moll? How is the family summer working out for Helen? Give them all my love and keep a castleful for yourself—

[   ]

V.: Probably Vita Sackville-West.

the Duff-Coopers: Alfred Duff Cooper (1890–1954), British statesman, conservative, wrote distinguished biographies. His wife Diana, née Manners, was considered one of the most beautiful women of the time.

Bloomsbury: Suggestion that the audience ranges from the swell conservatives to the intellectuals and bohemians.

Gogarty: Oliver St. John Gogarty (1878–1957), Irish physician and writer, said to be Malachi Mulligan in *Ulysses* by his friend James Joyce.

Valera: Eamon De Valera (1882–1975), became prime minister of Ireland in 1938; in 1959 he resigned as prime minister and was elected president.

TO POLLY THAYER STARR   Aug. 6th [1939]
[Le Pignon Rouge]
Darling,

Your letter I expect crossed mine, and I have been the worst correspondent this year. There is never any more than heavenly sense of leisure when one is sitting dreamily in the sun thinking of things one might say in a letter to Polly—and so letter-writing has become a horrible task that accumulates by the dozen and is never finished. Writing this novel is damned hard work—I feel the virtue all gone out of me at the end of the morning and even so it is probably terrible. Anyway it is lovely to be here—in Belgium—with these dear people who knew my father when he was a boy and all my family, and me when I was born—occasionally it is lovely to dip into the past to be somewhere where one has never ceased to be since one was born. My window looks onto a magnificent potager—armies of beans and peas and carrots and beets standing at attention—a lovely little ash just around the corner and a great weeping willow,—all this set against the typical background of a line of poplars. Within the garden live besides myself (the family goes in town every day and I am left alone) a delicious honey-coloured police dog called Flamme who is now asleep on my bed, a wickedly beautiful angora cat, and three goats, one baby who follows one like a dog and can be picked up and held like a little faun. Today there is also a Breughelesque washerwoman who comes up now and then to ask me how I am and to offer to sing. She loves to sing and sings "Pitch a long way to Tipperary" with words of her own invention, very loudly whenever there is an opportunity to do so. She has just sung it to me from the garden for the third time.

Leaving London was like convalescing—I went without a pang but only a sort of relief from pang. I have an idea my London life has come sweetly to an end. I remember now that I didn't tell you about H. D. who turned out to be a huge sculpturesque woman carved out of stone, very kind and neurotic, living in a darkened room, with a high amused voice, whom I got to like better and better as I saw more of her, but not quite sane enough for me, living in too private a world.

Your letter was grand—it made me quite homesick. The news of Helen is marvelous—I guess it means the summer was not the nightmare she foresaw—Moll too sounds happy in her letters and Mark I gather is working all the time as usual.

I sail Aug. 23rd from Havre so ought to be in Rockport by the 28th as I shall go straight there, driving up (how exciting to have a car again.)

The day after tomorrow I see Jean-Do—in Paris, on my way home, Lugné and with all that my heart will be quite full like the camel's hump and ought to last the winter.

About books: read by all means St. Exupéry's "Terre des Hommes" and

David Cecil's "The Young Melbourne" a marvelous brilliant picture of 18th century England—if it isn't published in America he gave me a copy so I'll lend it to you. I hardly saw him because he has just had a baby and he and his wife are staying in the country. But he is so nice—

This will miss the Normandie if I don't send it off—

Love

[ ]

---

potager: Kitchen garden.

"Pitch a long . . . ": "It's a Long Way to Tipperary," a popular song of the World War I era.

H. D.: Hilda Doolittle.

"Terre des Hommes": Translated as *Wind, Sand and Stars* (1939) a series of tales and reflections by Antoine de Saint-Exupéry (1900–1944), French novelist, essayist and aviator known particularly for *The Little Prince;* disappeared while on a reconnaissance flight over occupied France.

TO S. S. KOTELIANSKY   Aug. 31, 1939
[Rockport]
Dearest Kot,

These are the terrible days. The sea beats on and on against the rocks—it is gray—and there is no peace anywhere in the world, and one's nerves stand up like pins in a pin-cushion. O my dear when shall we meet again? When will one be able to live again—the day I sat in the Luxembourg Gardens I knew it would be the last time for that kind of luminous well-being. But there is no point in talking about it—one clings to the small usual things: we have 5 cats (Cloudy has had four kittens—two little black pandas,—they all roll and run about under Daddy's chair so he looks like a gentle mountain)—Mother's garden is a little fête against the rocks—and there are "heavenly blues" a kind of very blue morning-glory that close up every night and then burst open like trumpets in the morning. Mother seems well—though distressed and worn like everyone by this horrible war of nerves—We are all being slowly drained of our virtue I feel, twisted up and hollowed out inside.

Daddy has started driving again—it is a calamity! And I have to take him out every morning for an hour—I will send you my last poems—I am going to work whatever happens—

Whatever happens keep your window open for my thoughts (I feel them flying out into the hurricane so steadfast they will surely reach you)—

Dearest Kot, in the inner world which doesn't change there you are always and it is blessèd to think of—noone will ever be for me what you are—

there are no such fierce and tender lions in these parts—only a few shabby
tame ones—none has such a <u>mane</u> as yours!

Love and love

[   ]

Drawing: This was one of Sarton's familiar hieroglyphs, a homing pigeon carrying a heart in
his beak. Enclosed, "Jardin du Luxembourg," 1939, unpublished. See Appendix.

TO S. S. KOTELIANSKY   Sun. Sept. 10th [1939]
[Rockport]
Dearest Kot—

It is a gray day with a howling wind—the tide has gone down leaving the
pebbly beach looking desolate and the rocks clotted in long black seaweed
skirts—We have had three French guests for the week-end (a nightmare!) I
can't stand my dearest friends for more than three hours at a time but three
<u>days</u>! It reminds me of a story of a very dear Boston lady—Someone asked
why she looked so harassed and she said, "My best friend is coming to
stay"—It is so awful and <u>so</u> true of the really farouche Sarton family! Luckily the kittens were an endless source of conversation, bless them! I managed
to work in the morning—I think this is going to be much better than "The
Waterfall" but it is still not daring enough—and I have a sense of <u>skating</u> along
on this one instead of crashing through (to find the water only a foot deep
after all and solid ground under my feet.)

Am reading T. E. Lawrence's letters—strange, irritating, brilliant little
man—the Saint is there in all these pages—"the holier than thou" which
turned people against him—but the book is like holding a jewel of many
facets in one's hand. There is nothing <u>phoney</u> about it. It is a real diamond
and he cut himself as well as others with the sharp edge. He says some good
things about D. H. L.—but can't stand women-writers—Have you watched
the controversy in the New Statesman? All of it seems to me childish and
besides the point. There is literature and there is not literature. Few men <u>or</u>
women have written <u>literature</u>—they are above controversy and the others
don't matter. But it showed up Naomi to have bothered to answer!

Have you seen Ruth Pitter? Thank God so far they have left London
alone—Has she plans to leave if worst comes to worst? I expect like you she
will stay and see it out. The only comfort is that it <u>had</u> to happen. It is here.
There is the end of Stephen Vincent Bênet's five poems on the Am. Civil
War—

> "Say neither in their way—
> It is a deadly magic and accursed

Nor 'it is blest'—
But only it is here."

That is the great difference between 1914 and now.

I do not listen a great deal to the radio (we would cease to do anything else)—I work as usual. Live as usual, try to abide by the things that may <u>out-last</u>—That is all I can do.

Dear Kot, please write—I think of you so often—Where are the Huxleys? I have sent a letter to Juliette to Whipsnade—Love as always

[   ]

Do not think this letter indifferent—it is a definite effort to keep to what matters between us—in <u>spite</u> of war!

———

farouche: fierce.

better than "The Waterfall": Fire in a Mirror, unpublished.

T. E. Laurence: Thomas Edward Laurence (known as Laurence of Arabia, 1888–1935), English soldier, archaeologist, and author.

D. H. L.: D. H. Lawrence.

Naomi: Lady Naomi Margaret [Haldane] Mitchison, (1897–?), English novelist, poet, classical scholar. Sister of biologist B. S. Haldane.

Ruth Pitter: (1897–1992), English poet with whose work Sarton felt affinities, and whom she saw frequently on her trips to London.

TO S. S. KOTELIANSKY   November 11th, 1939
[Channing Place]
Dearest Kot,

It is Armistice Day, a pale gold and very clear one. Mother is out making holes with a stick to plant the last of the bulbs for next spring—it seems very long since I heard from you—and now there is this darkness of waiting and tension again with our hearts missing a beat for Belgium and Mummy and Daddy remembering the dreadfully tired men that went past our house retreating from Antwerp in 1914. I'll send this air mail but even so perhaps it won't have reached you in time. There is a high wind now that seems full of messages.

I have at least had a letter from Jean-Dominique and she is teaching a great deal and says that her garden is very wild and beautiful—there is something desperately hasty and final about words now but it was a comfort to feel her need for heroism and belief pouring itself out in lessons (Péguy's "Jeanne D'Arc" which she has been reading aloud)—Also had a very dear letter from Ruth Pitter with a very good smiling snapshot of herself that I had asked for. She went for a week-end to Whipsnade and sounds quite cheerful with "business as usual" and long dark starry nights to write poems in. It is a good augury that her new book will be out.

Mine is finished except for one chapter—I took it to Greenslet in a moment of panic least week—no two weeks ago—and he wrote me a good (personal, not official) letter about it in which he said "I liked it very much indeed and am convinced that it is a better book than 'The Single Hound' and a more adult one than "Waterfall"—This was the greatest balm as I had got to a sort of dismal dead state of utter despair but if it is better that is all that matters. Now it is being read by "readers" and they will decide about publishing—G. doesn't think it will sell so I expect the worst but don't much care. I know it is not a really good book, but I think it *is* better and would like to have it published and done with.

This was such a relief but I hardly had time to breathe and to feel human again and alive, when one of my best friends here a boy 22 years old was killed by a hit-and-run driver while bicycling. It seemed so utterly unnecessary and cruel when there are so many necessary deaths that one has to bear. It has made me feel empty and dull. It just shouldn't have happened. It is hard to accept a death like that. And he was one of the few young Americans who made me hope, who was sensible and who had strong convictions and real gaiety as well (That is so rare, one of the few, perhaps the only man among my friends here who didn't depend on me as a sort of mother.) I didn't love him but he was part of my life, a real friend, and now that he isn't there it's as if everything were out of gear, stale and unprofitable. But it will pass. One of the dreadful things is how quickly life takes one on. His mother was in Paris, his father dead, the funeral held impersonally in New York. I believe that a funeral is a necessary thing, a formal farewell—one must be cut off at a definite moment. I would like to have gone but I didn't know his family (distant relations) and didn't dare. Red roses probably shocked them.

It seems that Julian is coming over—though he just wrote very indefinitely "sometime soon" and nothing about where he would go. I'd like to meet the boat.

The light is going—I must go and make tea for my family. Every personal tie seems very strong now doesn't it? One takes refuge in the simple necessary love of every day. I miss your letters awfully and cannot call the postman the "cheri" anymore if he doesn't bring one soon. Have the Nations arrived safely I wonder?

Conrad Aiken and his wife have come back—I am going to see them this afternoon.

Tomorrow night I am giving one of the Sunday evening informal parties

I have begun doing—it is rather a comfort to have the house full of refugees—it is one human thing I can do. We drink beer and talk half the night about the peace and what the solution for Germany is—I'm glad that Julian is working on this. It seems so fearfully important.

I finally read David Jones "In Parenthesis". It is a queer book in that its impact makes itself felt afterwards—now it haunts me and I keep wondering why it is I know so much about the last war—as if I had been there in another life instead of a fat cheerful baby as I was—and then remember that it is this book. But I object to so <u>many</u> quotations that have to be explained for the sense.

I am appalled at the indifference and laziness and general unawareness of my doe-eyed class—roaring at them only makes me feel rather foolish afterward and I'm sure they pity me for a poor misguided lunatic. What is to be done with them? They are not sentimental that is the one good point in their favor—but they do not think and they do not feel except in the vaguest sort of way.

> That is all the news I can think of—
> Dearest Kot, write soon—
> And love from
> [   ]

I think this poem is not good but I wanted to write it for Dick.

––––––––––

Pitter's new book: The Spirit Watches (1940).

a boy 22 years old: Richard Wheeler. The elegy for him is unpublished.

the "cheri": (the dear) Jean Dominique's pet name for the mailman.

"In Parenthesis": David Michael Jones (1895–1974), English painter and poet. *In Parenthesis* is a long poem about the first World War.

the novel: Fire in A Mirror, unpublished.

poem for Dick: Richard Wheeler.

Enclosed "Elegy for R. W.," unpublished. See Appendix.

TO POLLY THAYER STARR   January 2nd [1940[
[St. Petersburg]
Darling,

This is just a little New Year word to hope it will bring you some sweet and unexpected blessing—I am bringing some shells but fear you have them all—Mother and I went quite mad on the long white beaches with waves rolling up the treasure as if they were piles of jewels. But I am still white as a sheet and quite feeble from working till I'm dizzy on the novel and writing over 60 Xmas and New Year letters! The finding of rest is as much an illusion as the Fountain of Youth isn't it? Daddy has been fearfully depressed rather like living with a sick elephant who cannot speak—his little eyes look so sad and weary it breaks my heart. The Carnegie has cut his salary by a third—and the worst is that the new head told Daddy he thought the History of Science "irrelevant," so that he says he feels "hemmed in" for these last two years of the gargantuan struggle to finish his book on the 14th century (12 years work)—Don't mention this please as the whole business is so delicate a word in the wrong place might do a great deal of harm. But it is sad. How little one can do for the people one loves.

I get back Thurs. night late, teach Friday afternoon, go out to Concord Sat. morning to read "Trelawney" to them (That's the play they are doing) and take the midnight to N.Y. to spend the week-end with Julian—It's the last chance of a peaceful time and everything was so sweet and happy and right when he was here I feel I must. Miracles do happen and this friendship that has come out love is one of them in my life. I'll be back Tues. morning and then all hell begins with two plays to direct, the novel to finish etc.—but if you are in Boston we'll surely meet more than once a year! It has been awful seeing so little of you.

Am reading Raushning—which is a must—the most fascinating book I have read in ages. It is just a long analysis of what Hitlerism is after without one horror story or playing on emotion—the most Machiavellian story one can imagine. Please read it even though you don't want to—it's not irrelevant to an understanding of our time.

> Well, love to you, darling, and to Donald
> Your devoted
> [   ]

"Trelawney": On April 16th, 1940 Sarton directed *Trelawney of the Wells* by Sir Arthur Pinero at the Concord Academy.

Raushning: Hermann Rauschning (1887–1982), German political writer, became U.S. citizen in 1947. The book referred to is probably *The Revolution of Nihilism: A Warning to the West,* 1939.

TO ASHLEY MONTAGU   March 30th [1940]
[Channing Place]
Dear Ashley,

Well, we are emerging out of the ice at last though Channing Pl. still looks like the North Pole. Within we have four energetic kittens and lots of flowers, but outside all is dead still. How are you all? It has been an awful winter. Poor mother has been in bed and out and in again with the most fearful acute grippe and an infinite variety of pains from teeth to ears to legs—but today she walked to the Square and it is a great event. It is raining very sweetly just now. I have been utterly submerged in directing two plays (for cash) a thing I'll never do again, so help me. The novel, poetry, life everything buried. I feel dead.

I have not got the Guggenheim and this is what I am writing to ask your august advice about. The plan was to go all over the country troubadour-ing—that is talking about poetry to everyone who will listen, crossing swords with anyone who will fight, getting an idea of Americans and American land-scape—at long last—and I hope writing a sort of "Letters from Iceland" but about America. With the Gugg. I wouldn't have had to worry but I think worry is salutary on the whole. Now I am having to charge twenty five dol-lars (as little as possible for it is not a commercial affair—a "lecture-tour" to drain the cash, and a journey of discovery and exchange of discoveries). I am having folders printed and count on you for some suggestions of where to send them. I have already five bookings ranging from Athens West Va. to Oston-Pray Tennessee, but long for the far west and the Northwest and the Southwest. Have you any ideas? I want to stay two or three days in each place so as to have a chance to talk to small groups and meet people as people.

Have just written to Lawrence Lee and to The Univ. of Kansas.

My novel creeps but I am getting up steam for the final push.

Do tell us your news—we are hungry for it—

Love to all from
May

---

two plays: Trelawney was one. The second play is unidentified.

Athens West Va.: Concord College, Athens, West Virginia.

Oston-Pray Tennessee: Austin Peay State College, Clarksville, Tennessee.

Lawrence Lee: At the University of Virginia.

TO LOUISE BOGAN   April 21st, 1940
[Channing Place]
Dear Louise Bogan,

It has been in my mind to write you for some time, to send a word of thanks for your criticism of poetry which seems to stand almost alone in being based on some absolute poetic value, some standard beyond belief. I have been watching for reviews of Pitter because this seems to me a test-case. When Spender wrote his very mean review a sort of despair came over me: for one had said when the really good, the beyond cavil on "the other side" comes along he and his sort will be anxious to prove their integrity by praising it. When this didn't happen I felt the division to be final and real. One would like to feel a sort of brotherhood in the *craft*—but I guess that is a mediaeval idea these days.

Very sincerely yours
May Sarton

Louise Bogan: (1897–1970), American poet and poetry critic for the *New Yorker.* This is the first letter Sarton ever wrote to her; an important friendship in Sarton's life. See "Louise Bogan" in *A World of Light.*

Pitter: Ruth Pitter's new poems in *Spirit Watches,* 1940, an early copy of which had just arrived, "have been the revelation of the last weeks" for Sarton.

Spender: Stephen [Harold] Spender (1909–1995), English poet.

TO JULIETTE HUXLEY   May 12th [1940]
[Channing Place]
Dearest Juliette,

Your letter was the treasure of the week (like the one they put out at the Victoria and Albert) and I have been carrying it about and reading it over— by the river where now there are hundreds of boys in white shorts with marvelous backs and legs rowing the little "shells" and working in crews, lying half naked on the incredible green grass, studying—running with that wonderful movement as if the chest were leading and it is all like a dream of youth such as the Greeks would have admired—from a distance. Yes, all the leaves have burst out suddenly (how is it that one never <u>sees</u> it happen?) The magnolia trees which have been like presences, striking <u>awe</u> into one's heart are just turning brown and falling—but there are white and pink cherries now and the apples on the way—and our garden a perfect glory of daffodils and violets and bloodroot and scillas and pansies—and cats. Their little faces are always appearing out of a "bosquet" of green and Daddy says "Cloudy is looking for a <u>bower</u>" (such a sweet word somehow). These things are there but there is the possibility that soon one won't be able to look at them or to listen to music or write poetry. We are in hell. But I had said to myself that I wouldn't write about the war because God knows what will have happened when this reaches you and because one simply can't <u>talk</u> about it. And there is no point. One just says the same words over and over and <u>waits</u> for what terror will be loosed next. One has to live the days single like an ill person and <u>hope</u> everlastingly, and <u>believe</u> unshakeably, though the machines know nothing of these (and that is what is terrifying). The hand behind the weapon has so little to do with power. But at least now the thing is <u>locked</u> and there can't be any more compromises. We are in for it. I say <u>we</u> though perhaps it sounds strange as we are so safe and far away. But not really—and very slowly people are waking up from their long drugged dream.

I think often of Dora—and what kind of suspense she must be living in demands of the spirit,

> Essential Oils—are wrung—
> The Attar from the Rose
> Be not expressed by Suns—alone—
> It is the gift of Screws— . . .

And Alan up there. Is he safe? Those are the questions one can't articulate nor stop to imagine the threads of love and anxiety making a web round every man, and so many must be broken. If one could only believe really deeply believe that a new world was being born, that it could be born out of this. One must believe it somehow.

I'm glad there is Kot too. He doesn't write and I know it is difficult. Send him my love. Tell him the novel is finished. That has a virtue even if the book has none—I mean I can go on to something else. I would like to write some poems but one's tongue is thick these days. Nothing easily said is worth saying and the difficult things must have their silence first. In the summer I shall have time to think.

May 19th

I have kept this letter but think I had better send it. One just can't say anything <u>now.</u> There is nothing to say—except love and love and love that somehow or other must set a girdle round the earth in forty minutes, saying we are not divided. Our hearts are all beating together. God bless you and Julian and the boys and Kot and Dora. Your letter is there to remind me of the world there is on the other side of all this if we can come through. It, darling Juliette, petite flamme—and <u>is</u>—the greatest blessing—thank you for it.

Victoria and Albert: A museum in London with a remarkable collection of applied art from all countries and periods.

one never sees it happen: See "Metamorphosis" in *As Does New Hampshire,* written in the 1960s on this theme.

Dora: Dora Clarke.

poem: Part of #675, Emily Dickinson, *Complete Poems of Emily Dickinson.*

Alan: Alan Best.

TO S. S. KOTELIANSKY   Sun. May 19th [1940]
[Channing Place]
Dearest Kot,

   I think and think of you and there you are like a rock in an ocean and
like the little olive leaf that the dove brought back whom Noah had sent
forth. I am too far away and words don't come. I look at the spring fiercely
and the only thing to do is to go out in the fields—just now the apple trees
are out, and the pastures all white with little flowers we call "Quaker
Ladies"—the green is greener than I ever remembered and the spring slower
and more beautiful as if while the man-made world crashed it simply paused
and waited in perfect faith and peace. There is nothing to do but continually re-create and add to the others one's little parcel of courage every morning after that sick moment of waiting for the paper. So you do in Acacia Road
and we do here so far away and so near. Mother takes refuge in the garden
which is just a crowd of blessings, abounding in white violets and great dark
pansies, white tulips, narcissus, a few flame tulips, a great deal of lavender and
white. The cats run up and down the trees. There are no planes. The sky is
perfectly still and blue. Daddy takes refuge in his work (Isis has just been suspended for the second time due to the Germans). I take refuge in things like
cleaning the attic which I have just done. It is good that I finished the novel
before, and so that is done for better or worse. I take refuge in writing dozens
of letters about the tour next year and now I have 15 engagements in remote places like Texas and Tennessee and New Mexico and I shall send James
postcards to remind him of the States. Ralph Hodgson is taking part in the
11th Writers' Congress at the University of Colorado (!)—here is his picture cut out from their bulletin. I do this because it is something to do and
above all one must not fail any part of one's destiny just now through weakness of will. I have heard that the reason Auden has become an American is
for the sake of a boy he met here whom he loves and that has made me mad.
There is this terrible division in him of emotion and mind which colors his
whole work and weakens it. Please send me a postcard. I wish I could send
you the little black kit with a silver lining whom we believe is a negro kitten. He has a very mischievous and sad wise little negro face and a wicked
eye.

   I am reading a good novel, the only good novel HM have published for
ages and which I'm going to review, a first novel by a girl whose name I've
forgotten, called "The Heart is a Lonely Hunter" about a group of people
on the edge of poverty in a Southern Town. The central character is a deaf-
mute to whom they all talk endlessly. It is not a candid-camera novel such
as are the fashion now. She has created an amazing group of living people
and it is the story of their loneliness, an un-affected true talent. I am quite
excited. I had begun to despair of American literature. It has turned into re-

porting of little-known parts of American life. It is useful for the education of a people but it is not an art.

I had such a wonderful letter from Juliette which came like manna at the zero hour.

Now let us hope and believe and love each other forever.

Your

[   ]

James: James Stephens.

Ralph Hodgson: (1871–1962), English poet whose best known poems are passionate protests against cruelty to animals.

Auden: Auden did not meet Chester Kallman until after his arrival in the United States, specifically two days after a lecture which Kallman attended with Harold Norse at the Keynote Club.

"The Heart is a Lonely Hunter": Carson McCullers (1917–1967), American novelist, and short story writer. *The Heart is a Lonely Hunter,* 1940, is a parable on fascism.

TO BRYHER   Sept. 17th, 1940
[Channing Place]
Dear Bryher,

I have to say that because I thought your name was Bryher Macpherson and feel rather confused! I was deeply grateful for the news from Belgium. Very little appears in the papers here—there are so many oppressed peoples now that none receives special attention. They are lumped. We haven't of course had one word from Belgium since. But occasional refugees tell bloody stories—the Belgian army fought for 18 days without sleep, for three without food and finally without ammunition—"c'était les machines contre les poitrines"—Nothing excuses Leopold but this helps to <u>explain.</u> Perhaps we shall never know the whole story.

I haven't heard from H. D. for ages and have been a poor correspondent myself because I am getting ready for an informal troubadouring trip across the country, talking about poetry which is just the only way I know for reaching my contemporaries and imploring them to wake up and realize their inward responsibilities. There is panic and indifference in about equal doses and such selfishness (it is unfashionable to suggest any policy for the sake of an ideal—it is only whether to send destroyers for the better defence of America, not to help England.) Here in America luckily we move fast when we move—already there is a tremendous change toward helping England, and the conscription bill has gone through. But meanwhile one rages because after all there is still hope for life here. We <u>must</u> accept and honor the responsibility and not wait until the guns are at the door before being willing to make personal sacrifices.

It must be very strange to be in that bottled brave little country—one of the few islands of humanity left. But it is an island and you must occasionally get a kind of claustrophobia as well of course as longing to be in England now that war is there.

I wonder if Life and Letters still goes on. The fact that poems and plays and books of all sorts are still being published every day is one of the most thrilling things I think. A book of poems by Dick Eberhart was turned down by the Am. Oxford Press ("No demand for poetry just now") and immediately taken by Chattos ("At a time like this we must have poetry and this is important" wrote one of their editors on his way to join the B.E.F.)—The English are plucking flowers out of the nettles and that is the glory. Also I am glad that it was a defeat (Dunquerque) and not a victory that pulled the whole country together. If only now this state of mind, this unity can be maintained and carried over into peace—if there could be world-pooling of colonies, under an International advisory committee—O well, why talk about it. The work is there to do.

Do write again and tell me your news. I'll see that you get a Nation and New Republic now and then (am sending two off today) and have asked Franz Wiener, 14 Remington St. Cambridge to do it while I'm away. Letters will be forwarded to me from here.

Yours
May Sarton

Bryher: penname of Annie Winifred Ellerman McPherson, English novelist, lifelong friend of Hilda Doolittle from 1918 to her death in 1961; she and Hilda Doolittle are both portrayed as Hilda in Lawrence's *Lady Chatterly's Lover.*

Translation of French: It was arms against the naked breasts of the unarmed.

Leopold: Leopold III (1901–1983), King of Belgium. On May 28, 1940 he surrendered his armies to Germany despite the opposition of his ministers.

Life and Letters: In 1935 Bryher bought the esteemed literary review *Life and Letters* which had been edited by Desmond MacCarthy, changed its name to *Life and Letters Today* and incorporated it with *The London Mercury.* Among the distinguished foreign writers who appeared in it were Gide, Sartre, Valéry, the Sitwells, Marianne Moore, and May Sarton.

Dick Eberhart: Richard Eberhart (1904–) American poet and teacher. Professor of English at Darmouth, 1956–(?) Book in question probably *Song and Idea* published here in 1942.

B. E. F.: British Expeditionary Force.

Dunquerque: Dunkirk, Dunkerque. Fishing port in Northern France, scene of one of the most memorable naval actions in history when some 300,000 Allied troops, cut off by German advance on Channel ports, were evacuated to England. Dunkirk was left in ruins. Germans held out against the Allies until May 1945.

[Black Mountain]
Dearest Poll,

Your letter made me glow all over, I was so happy with all your news—
and your wonderful description of leave-takings (yes, it was a nightmare, a
fearful wrench but now I never want to go back. I see that Cambridge had
become a nightmare. Now I feel useful again and full of life and so excited
all the time I can hardly see)—But what a wonderful year Poll—to have a
little growing girl and an exhibition all at the same time. That was what made
me so happy, that all seemed so very well with you and never has anyone
deserved or earned it more. Isn't it queer how life seems to go in cycles
and there are the long valleys when one thinks one will never see a mountain to climb again—and then suddenly you are high up with all the world
below. When is the exhibition? Do send me a copy of criticisms—I'll send
them back but it's practically impossible to get N.Y. papers here—I am always driving through a town just an hour before they come in, fatally and
always.

I'm sure one must feel absolutely panic-stricken at first and even for quite
awhile—what a responsibility! but also how heavenly to be feeding something out of yourself that grows before your eyes. What is her name? I shall
call her Donald Duck until I hear. What is she like? What color are her eyes?
Who does she look like? I hope a perfect mixture of you two. Donald must
be a darling father though father's don't have so much fun until a little later
I guess when they can proudly make her smile and gurgle.

The trip is all and more than I had dreamed. The country itself more various, more beautiful, grander than I had imagined—there are places where
there is no sense of the past at all and then two hundred miles further on
you suddenly come to a town like Winchester, Va. with red-brick houses and
the light falling through leaves on them, and memories of battles ringing in
the air—(That town changed hands 72 times in the Civil War.) As a northerner in the South, I am filled with shame. If ever anything proved the wrongs
of passion even a passion for justice (so blind as it was!) the war between the
states certainly did. The self-righteousness of us who had never worried about
slaves while we were getting rich in the slave-trade and then when industry
made them unnecessary or at least a different kind of slave, not called by that
name—well, you know it all. We attacked the problem without ever trying
to answer it, destroyed all possibility of its being answered with justice as it
would have been in time. The poverty here is appalling. Country people live
in wooden shacks, one room,—if one sees a prosperous farm it is so extraordinary that you have to stop the car as if it were a monument. But of course
they have lived on their wrongs for too long and there is so little vitality, just

physical vitality even now. There should be a new Lee—after the war you know instead of giving in and retiring to brood he founded a college and devoted his life to the future and to the <u>Nation.</u> I was very thrilled by that. Why are we not taught more about Lee in school?

I am working like a dog—an average day is four or five hours of conferences which means trying to help someone in twenty minutes to learn how to write! An informal lecture or two which is taking over an English class for the day, and then a formal lecture. But it is passionately interesting and I'm learning a lot. There is so much to be done one will never live to do it. Each college wants me to come back for a month and really do some teaching and I think the year after next that I'll choose the five most interesting and do that. This as Meta Glass (Pres. of Sweet Briar) said is administering hypodermics and I'd like to do something more solid. The teachers are saints but haven't a chance—secondary education is so bad, they have to teach them the rudiments of reading and writing. If I were a reformer and not a poet I'd do something about secondary education. I'm glad I'm going to a few teachers colleges. The buildings even in small towns are magnificent but what goes on inside must be pretty poor. They have never been taught to see anything for themselves. They have read nothing. They have no opinions.

As to politics when I come back I'll read your book. I haven't read anything since I left—no time. When I have an hour I write—have done quite a lot toward the book, poetry and prose. I feel myself growing and bursting out of shells. It may be amorphous and may come to nothing but it is alive and I am burning up with things to say. It is a great relief to escape the narrow personal shell which I have so thoroughly explored in the last years. That is finished now. I am out of it.

Julian says that by the end of the war a social revolution will have quietly taken place in England. But there was a moment when every politician and intellectual had a pistol ready to shoot himself and as many Germans as he could first. There was the moment of fearful inner panic in spite of all the courage and outward calm. I was almost glad to hear! it—they had seemed <u>too</u> brave. If I could choose a city to be just now I would choose London. So I suppose you will say there is no hope for me. However whatever you or I hope or believe profound changes are taking place and that is reason for hope in itself. And as at all moments of crisis, inner or outer, it can be the end or the beginning depending on the human mind and on human greatness or weakness. Nobody knows the answer. I am glad to be living at such a time. I consider it an honor.

Well, darling—let us rejoice in our differences—and love each other—I am so happy when I think of you. Write again. I'm here til Nov. 2d and then wandering with no address until

Nov. 13th Austin Peay Normal School, Clarksville Tenn.
Nov. 19th Spring Hill College, Spring Hill, Alabama (Jesuit)
                              Love to all 3, and to the grandmother—
                    [   ]

---

a little growing girl: A daughter, Dinah, had just been born.

the book: Journey Toward America, unpublished as such, although many of the poems in it are in "The American Landscapes" section of *The Lion and the Rose,* 1948.

TO GIORGIO DE SANTILLANA   Nov. 24th, 1940
[New Orleans]
Giorgio,

I was glad to hear from you—and laughed about the boomerang of the shot heard round the world—that is a wonderful image—O yes, one must talk straight from the shoulder, there isn't time to beat about bushes anymore. And as you say a few socks make them sit up! One day in a girls' college, South Ca. I was infuriated by some girls' yawning in the back-row and finally lost my temper and asked them to leave, not for my sake but for the sake of poetry. Afterwards I thought I'd be frowned upon but everyone from students to teachers thanked me with tears in their eyes. None had dared do that. There should be some fierce teaching and some awe of learning. Everything is made so easy and is so second rate. They are so easily satisfied with themselves.

But I am in love with the country—I had no idea how beautiful and various it is from the pink-coloured sedge covered rolling hills backed by blue and purple and crimson (from the oaks) mountains in West Va. to this low tropical land covered with oleanders and myrtles—white egrets darting out from the bushes. I want to live in Charleston—one of the great feminine cities—Venice, Paris. It is so elegant and casual and warm and aristocratic and one could live there so easily! Have you seen it? It is really lovely, full of light, cool sea air, Utrillo streets, secret gardens, high balconies and everywhere the darkies laughing and making a warm current under the life of the city. They have beautiful cries—a flower cry "With a flower's garden on my haid!" New Orleans is a small very crowded claustrophobic "Left Bank" but Charleston is just itself. I am having fun here drinking and having an orgy of conversation. The danger of continual lecturing is that one hears a pontifical note creeping into one's talk! Here I've had some good fights and wonderful meals with Pat O'Donnell ("Green Margins" a good novel about the Delta, the first HM fellowship)—and his gang of WPA organizers, printers, ex-actors etc. He is a very swell guy, son of a locomotive engineer and he knows this country from the ground up literally.

The trip is in other words better than my wildest dreams. I am happy because I am being <u>used</u> and I haven't been <u>used</u> to the top of my bent for years, not since I left the theatre. But it is exhausting. I average about four hours conferences, four hours lecturing, round-table, taking over English classes etc. in each place. Now I would like to go back and stay a month in four or five of the most interesting and really see what can be done with a single project in poetry. The standard is frightfully low.

I think you ought to get a lecture-tour and hammer a little sense into people all over the country, politically—they are all back in post-war days worrying about who makes the money out of war, about British propaganda etc. and just will not look at the <u>facts</u>. Did you see Thompson's riposte to the people who are crowing over the Italians? It was very good and necessary.

I've been writing a lot and enclose a few—the trouble is <u>time</u> and when I put it off I lose the first impression and never get it back.

The best place I've seen is Black Mountain because they are building their new buildings themselves (My typewriter sticks it's so damp) and they are painfully ~~working~~ at least <u>asking</u> the fundamental questions of democracy, not muffling them—It is full of faults but it has <u>some</u> resemblance to life which most colleges ~~don't~~ — I'm sure there is a virtue in building something   with one's hands that has to be put back into education. There's lots of talk about and so much to be done—Well au revoir—God knows we can't help being depressed. Love from

[   ]

~~Do write.~~

––––––––

Giorgio de Santillana: Marquis Giorgio Diaz de Santillana (1902–1974), historian of science, author.

HM fellowship: Houghton Mifflin.

WPA: Work Projects Administration.

Thompson: Probably Dorothy Thompson (1894–1961), American journalist and syndicated columnist.

TO PRESIDENT THURSTON DAVIES   December 4th, 1940
[Channing Place]
Dear President Davies,

This was one of the colleges and parts of the country I was most looking forward to see. I arrived in Colorado Springs with intestinal grippe but so exhilarated by the lean bare magnificent mountains and the air that it didn't seem to matter. But I have been here two days I do feel ill and discouraged and more than that (which is personal) <u>impersonally</u> angry. If this were the 18th century and I were a man I would challenge your English Department to a duel with pistols because I believe poetry has been insulted. When you invite a poet to lecture on a campus and six students come to the lecture that is an insult to poetry. Last night the English Department (who know what I have to say of course) were all present accompanied by six students. I was very touched at the unnecessary presence of the English dept. and charmed that they came. I was hurt and angry to be asked to deliver a formal lecture for six students. As you know I am not in the lecture racket. I am not doing this for money. I am doing it for as little money as I can possibly ask, and still live because I believe in what I am saying and that at this time here in America we have got to set up some spiritual standards or eventually perish as France has done through lack of them. It is embittering to be brought face to face with the fact (and I was warned that this would happen but didn't believe it) that if you <u>give</u> something it is considered of little price. If the college had paid the usual fee for a lecturer coming from so far I suppose some effort would have been made to get him an audience. I realize that there are many activities on the campus and I understand the difficulties of fitting them in. But I think it is a mistake to have a poet at all then. If there is not time for poetry, so be it. But it is then not necessary perhaps to bring poets to a college in order to make them see how little an art for which they live is wanted. It is a rather lonely profession you know. I do not think we are as a whole arrogant. We really are not in need of this kind of lesson. I confess that last night I wept bitterly and it was hard to take.

On the other hand I know how much you are doing for the arts and this is one of the few colleges with as much opportunity for students interested in them. There is then something wrong, an apathy or an irresponsibility at the roots which I find terrifying. I am talking now of the students not the faculty—I must say that I felt very warmly toward the English faculty and admired them and appreciated them very much until the lecture! This morning as I had promised to do so, I addressed a class in writing. I made a plea for greater awareness and more <u>living</u> in the sense of seeing, hearing, *being* etc. as the essential for a writer and the essential for a human being. One boy said that he preferred to be contented and unaware—another that his only object in life was <u>security at fifty</u>. These are the boys who are going out into a tough world at a moment of crisis in civilization. I expect they are the average. If they are there is very little hope for America. If they are allowed to get away with this sort of thing there is no hope for education. They would be better fitted for life if they were sent right off to a military camp where at least they would not be allowed to slouch in their chairs.

When the dancing teacher at the college announced to her class that she was bringing them a group from Denver to dance for them their reply was "Do we <u>have</u> to come?"

I was wrong to be angry with the faculty who are evidently struggling with a mountain of indifference, lack of discipline, arrogance and sloth. Everywhere I go I see more and more that the secondary schools are not doing their job, the families are not doing their job. But on the other hand, the colleges seem to be sitting down under it too. What is the answer? I expect that after this letter you will not want to see me. I would however very much like a chance to talk some of this over sometime. Through the anger, and the hurtness you may be able to discern a hope, an ardent faith, an almost desperate longing that we in America should not fail.

Please believe me

Your obedient servant

May Sarton

President Thurston Davies: This letter was written after having given an evening lecture at Colorado College in Colorado Springs.

TO PARENTS   Christmas Day, 1940
[Santa Fe (AS)]
My darlings,

Here first of all is Ted Weeks' telegram which came yesterday:

"I find little objection and much to applaud in your American journal. It has a good alive run to it and although there are passages you will improve when you have time to catch your breath I can promise unhesitatingly to use some of it in Atlantic. Am at present attracted by Lincoln, Monticello and Charleston Plantations. Send more and tell where long letter can reach you. Merry Christmas.

Edward Weeks."

It was really awfully nice of him to wire and I am so happy that he wants more than one as together they have more meaning. I have sent him the Santos and a few others and a letter. But isn't it a lovely Christmas present?

I am anxious because a telegram from Marie Armengaud (this lovely French woman I met who is in Philly for Christmas) sounded as if something terrible had happened in Europe. There is no paper here today and we missed the radio news. It is such a dreadful Christmas I do so hope for all the world that nothing still more awful has happened. I hope we can get news before the end of the day.

I was so pleased with all the descriptions of the earthquake, Mummy's Daddy's and finally Anne's description of your description! To answer Daddy's letter—I think I can stay here until the middle of February because I have I think got a very nice job at a school here for a month, lecturing on poetry and taking one class a week in writing. It is not quite certain but I am hoping to hear this week. They really seem to want me and it is just the financial question but I gather it is quite a rich school. This would solve my problem of insurance for the car, I owe sixty dollars which is due March 1st. I have been a little worried about it. Also could Daddy send my check to be here by the first as I am short because of Christmas. There will be about $25.00 I think in gas I charged last month. That is the only bill I know of so if you could send a check for $75.00. The gas bill will go directly to Daddy and may not come till next month.

Thank you, my Miutsie for Millay. It is a very fitting book for the times and one I really wanted. I had several little presents to open–the Longs gave me an old silver Indian brooch and I am going there to supper tonight.

Now for the Indian dances—it began to snow about 8:00, fine snow that rested on the trees and made them look quite magical—the lights all went out so we had supper in front of the fire by candlelight and were only sad because we couldn't play any music because the fuse blew that one too. Then we slept for an hour, then went out to some people's for hot buttered rum, then at about 11:00 all piled in with hundreds of blankets, thermoses, sheeplined boots into a big Cadillac with Dorothy Stuart (the nice painter) a silent man called Mr. Wing, the Asplunds (the people here) another girl and I. By then it was a real blizzard and we had forty miles to go—but we all felt gay and sang songs. We helped three or four stuck motorists out of drifts and finally got into the dirt road to San Felipe the village where the dancing was to be.

It was then almost one and mud so deep and thick it was like soup and driving more like swimming. But we finally got there just in time—driving through the dark village to the lighted church from which already could be heard the beat of drums. You have no idea how strange it is to hear their ancient primeval sound coming from a Christian church. It is in the pueblo— a huge barn with a dirt floor, deep in mud too because there were leaks in the roof, rough white-washed walls with colored reproductions of the stations of the cross along the walls, a very primitive wooden pulpit painted in bright colors and stuffed with little Indian boys peeping over the edge when we got there to watch the dancing. At the end the altar on a raised wooden platform with candles and an ordinary plaster virgin—and all along the walls lines and lines of Indians standing in their blankets, squatting on the floor, the men carrying the papooses on their backs. There must have been no more than 15 white people altogether and these dances are done by the Indians for themselves—and they begin when the mood takes them so though it was half-past one they were just beginning. As we got in the drums made a crescendo and started the beat of the dance—the drums are very loud and strong and the earth vibrates with them and your bones vibrate with the rhythm—I felt it in my chest too—Then from the door at the back came two files of Indians, in their soft leather boots, the women's delicate little feet in white the men terracotta with silver buttons—you look at the feet first which carry the rhythm. In their hands they had pine branches or gourd rattles which they shake all the time in rhythm. As they came in the drummers began the song, loud rich men's voices singing a strange penetrating chant that repeats the same thing over and over, swells and dies away, swells and dies away over and beneath the steady beat of the drums that never stop until you can hardly help joining in the dance. The Indians watch with motionless faces and never smile or move their hands or feet while the others are dancing. The costumes are made out of beautiful things mixed with cheap materials they buy—in the first dance the men wore brilliant kilts, white stockings and what looked like long underwear, white too on top, covered with silver jewelry, ribbons round their black heads, feathers—an infinite complication of things, and colors. This first dance was a humourous dance making fun of the Navaho boys who sing very well. The women are fairly static, around them the men move and the women's feet are very delicate and precise in their white boots while the men stamp and sometimes yell, or imitate birds' songs while they dance. The best dance was the last—an animal dance—first came the buffalos, the men's faces painted black and almost covered by a huge buffalo skin with horns. A pine branch in one hand, a gourd in the other. Then the deer with lovely gray masks on their heads, sharp deer-noses, and antlers of course, and tails and covered with branches, so they seemed all green and white and gray. Behind them the antelopes, moving in quick stylized movements, with dear little white tails and in lovely pale beige suits. It gets terrifically exciting as the rhythm penetrates you. At the end of each dance each man or animal goes and kneels a second before the altar. At the end it was strange and rather flat to hear the nasal voice of the priest intoning the mass. One of the priests, Father Chavez is a poet.

Afterwards we had coffee and finally got back here at four so I must go to sleep now again!

Did you get my telegram? I'm hoping there will be one from you soon. If not it doesn't matter, dear love to my dears. Did you have some music? Did you enjoy the funny little packages I sent?

Love and love

[   ]

Ted Weeks: Edward Weeks (1898–?), editor of the *Atlantic Monthly* from 1938–1966.

Marie Armengaud: who had tuberculosis and with whom Sarton fell in love.

earthquake: There was an earthquake in Cambridge on December 21.

a very nice job: A possible job at the Sandia School in Alburqurque fell through.

the Longs: Haniel Long (1888–1956), American poet, novelist, and publisher who settled in

Sante Fe with his wife Alice. He was responsible for Sarton's going there originally. Sarton wrote the preface to a posthumous collection of his poetry, *My Seasons.*

the Asplunds: Beryl and Ted Asplund lived in Agi Sims' house; Beryl did the housekeeping, Ted taught mechanics.

Father Chavez: Fray Angelico Chavez (1910–1996) His first book of poetry was introduced by Witter Bynner and John Gould Fletcher. Author of *My Penitente Land,* reflections on Spanish New Mexico.

TO S. S. KOTELIANSKY   Easter Sunday [April 13, 1941]
[Chicago]
Dearest Kot,

I have been so silent. It is hard to write letters. But all this week I have been thinking of you so dearly and intensely because of the news of Virginia Woolf. O Kot, it is awful. I heard it just before going into lunch at a girl's college, someone ~~just~~ told me quite casually, and I was startled and off guard—~~that~~ I just burst into tears. It matters a great deal that she is dead just now. She was one of the few people delicately and persistently establishing relationships, making a <u>wholeness</u> however much was destroyed. We cannot afford to lose her just now. For three days (off between lectures) I have sat in this hotel room above this ~~very~~ loud ~~and~~ boisterous and cruel city, thinking of her. It is like a hole that nothing will ~~ever~~ fill. And O Kot, I had so hoped I would someday do something she would like—one of the few people who mattered for work's sake, she was. But that is not important except privately. I had the feeling so strongly that in the next years she was stripping down and down and getting closer to her essential truth—this that was so hard for her to do because of her extreme sensitivity and fear of being exposed—and that the best was still to come. One looked forward to a new book of hers with the highest expectation, as to a new marvel to be revealed—and sometimes of course it was not a new marvel at all, but it didn't matter because one knew it was coming. There is I believe noone else of whom this is so exactly true. Of most writers one knows more or less what to expect by the time they are forty. I've been trying to write a poem but cannot do it. I just sit and cry and that is stupid. How I long to be home in my quiet room with the poplar trees outside the window and to be quite silent for a long time. I have been away for seven months and now I feel like a homing-pigeon with his beak outstretched.

My dear, how are you? In his last letter Julian said "You will come back as soon as the war is over" and my heart nearly burst thinking of that—I haven't dared think of it. It has seemed so long. But shall I be walking up Acacia St. to the little green door, and shall we sit and talk again? My <u>dear.</u> I must think of something amusing to tell you, I feel so sad.

O, I saw the Aldous Huxleys in Santa Monica—I liked Aldous extremely, his quiet and simplicity, his interest in what people are doing—it was a very pleasant and easy lunch. Maria looked a little worn, used up (usé is the French word and it is exactly that) but I minded her less than I had expected! They have a small butterfly dog and she was blowing up balloons for him to play with—he looked charming and unreal jumping at them with tiny ferocity. But I don't like miniature dogs on the whole. They both love California. I hate it. Even the grass looks as if it had been unrolled on the ground like a carpet and there are so many flowers that one doesn't care. I would give them all up for one secret violet by a stone. They live in a very queer house, a Victorian idea of Hollywood with lots of Oriental knick-knacks and hideous sofas but big windows opening onto the steep green valleys and a lovely garden. It is on the very crest of a hill. But they are forever and ever wanderers and strangers examining America as if it were an inset, having no part. That is what is awful. Julian is so much a part of everything he does. But they are people (I felt) who look through windows and are never quite in the room. Applied to personal relationships, especially sexual ones, this is quite monstrous.

We had a wonderful vegetarian lunch with mushrooms and all sorts of things made into little cakes, and we talked our heads off.

I have written thirty poems and when I get home must plan the shape of the book. It will be partly prose. There is a great deal to say and not all can be said in the poems. There is so much to be done here, such inertia and lack of zeal among the young, it is quite frightening. They are good stuff but noone gives them anything which is life. By the time they are twenty they are thoroughly in a groove. I get frightfully homesick for Europe and yet I know that this here is my place and my job—and here I am needed. That in itself is a good feeling—except that now at the end I am too tired. But I have done a lot, Kot, and I am happy about it.

There is not much point in sending you individual poems because they belong together. I'll be home May 2nd and just can't believe it.

My dear how are you? Have you enough to eat? Couldn't I send you some tea? It is Easter Day. But what a heavy one in the heart. I think of you tenderly and send you my love. Let us hope.

Your devoted

[   ]

Virginia Woolf: At about 11:30 on the morning of Friday, March 28, 1941, leaving one letter for Leonard Woolf and one for Vanessa Bell, Virginia Woolf, tormented by mental illness, crossed the meadows to the river and with a large stone in the pocket of her coat drowned herself. See "Letter from Chicago" in *The Land of Silence.*

TO FERRIS GREENSLET   April 24th, 1941
[Painesville]
Dear Ferris,

It is the home trail—I'll see the garden and the cat and my darling family and have long hours up in my study to think it all over. The last week has
been terrific, pretty steady going, but no one told me that Southeast Ohio
is one of the most beautiful places in the world—masses of redbud out and
smoky soft green hills and beautiful wide slow rivers, so like England too it
is quite startling. Woods full of dutchman's breaches, adder's tongue, spring
beauty, yellow and white violets, orchards all in-flower, too lovely. The work
less so. I am tired—and a little discouraged. There is almost everywhere a
frightening apathy and inertia and lack of curiosity about intellectual matters. At this rate we are utterly unprepared to take over for a short or long
time the work of keeping civilization going. Well, we must talk.

I am putting a check for half your precious lended lucre in the envelope.
The other half may not be forthcoming until October. I have been paying
bills (including a fat one to HM for given books!) and feel so like the ant
instead of the "cigale" that it is quite remarkable. I hope your backgammon
winnings over Ted Weeks will sustain you until I am earning again in
Oct.?

Long to see you—one aches with the world. and yet in spite of everything

> "Our friends are exultations, agonies,
> And love, and man's unconquerable mind."

I read that poem everywhere I go—

                                                          Yours ever
                                                          M [   ]

_____

"cigale": Cicada.
Poem excerpt: From William Wordsworth's "To Toussaint L'Ouverture."

TO BRYHER   April 28th [1941]
[Detroit]
Dear Bryher,

Please call me May, it feels more comfortable. Your letter dated the 13th
arrived here in record time, especially as it had to be forwarded from Cambridge. It is the first letter from England that mentions Virginia Woolf—how
simply hideous if that damned Times article had anything to do with it. As
it well might. One always felt a terrible fight in her between the communi-
cator and that quivering sense of privacy and a blow could crack her—or

anyone for that matter. The helplessness of writers against critics is always a source of rage to me—when you think what they did to Keats. And one can't even duel with them. There are two people whom I personally will dream of in the grave I'm sure for what they have said—and that in spite of all the hardness and commonsense one tries to knock into oneself—the intrinsic unimportance of critics etc. if the work is good. Still the wound is there.

But the death of Virginia Woolf is a fearful defeat of the spirit. For days it seemed to me just that, the tangible example of what Hitler means. It seemed worse than anything yet but perhaps that is because I have not actually seen London destroyed as you are doing. This is I guess the worst hour since Dunquerque. It has made a flood of reaction in America, caused by fear and a sudden realization of the immensity of the task so many people are saying "Let's not get into it" (as if we weren't in already!) And of course there is the ever-present danger of interpretation of insufficient facts. Everyone knows the defeat but few realize that it has not been at all a proof of english bungling or inferiority as soldiers but on the other hand (like Dunquerque) a magnificent plucking of this flower from this nettle danger. People do not measure the odds but only say "Look, again, why can't they ever win?" etc. etc. There is no point in telling you all this. But it's discouraging. The lack of leadership from our Pres. is discouraging. A few people are working all night on defence but it hasn't yet penetrated the hearts of <u>most</u> people that this is a serious crisis perhaps involving not only the existence of Britain but of us. Until it does nothing much will be done. It is up to the President to get it across and he doesn't seem to be doing it. He pussyfoots about with his hand constantly on the pulse of the public temper, instead of administering the hypodermic and getting on with it. However a society has now been started called "Fight for Freedom" to counteract Lindbergh's "America First Committee." That is a good thing. It must all sound so childish to you over there. My heart aches when I think of it.

The B.B.C. business is bad. What has finally happened I wonder? Julian Huxley wrote me that he had resigned as a result of the censorship.

About the article in the Times. There was an uproar here about 6 months ago when Archibald MacLeish did the same sort of thing accused the intellectuals of a failure in leadership. It was admirably answered by Edmund Wilson in the New Republic. It sounds however as if the Times article were even more unintelligent. There is however this. I realize it after going over the whole country in the last months. There is an almost complete lack of communication between the better poets and anyone but themselves and the critics. It is dangerous it seems to me for a civilization when there is a complete abyss between people in general and the artists. Or is it always so? The poets who are most ardently on the people's side write in such a way that the people cannot see rhyme nor reason to their work.

I realize that one may be sacrificing something in speaking out plain—but I do not think one sacrifices anything <u>essential.</u> But perhaps I am wrong. However even Virginia Woolf finally reached the general public here—it is not technical innovation which shuts the door but I believe a lack of humanity at the root. If that is there—as in Joyce—people will take the technical innovation. But if it is not there they never will. The smug little cliquey critics have become more important to poets than anyone else—and that is grave.

I'll get hold of the Compton Mackenzie when I get home next week.

Thanks for writing—I hope the dried fruit I sent doesn't get sunk. It probably will but I'll try again in a week or so.

Yours as ever

[   ]

Love to Hilda—The best news of all is that I am to have <u>Life and Letters.</u> I'll see that each copy reaches many people and try to persuade some of them to subscribe.

---

poem excerpt: From William Wordsworth's "To Toussaint L'Ouverture."

Edmund Wilson: (1895–1972), eminent American literary and social critic, novelist, short story writer, and poet.

Compton Mackenzie: Sir Compton Mackenzie (1883–1972). Popular English novelist and poet. Prosecuted in 1932 for breach of war secrets in *Greek Memories;* later the ban was withdrawn and the book published as *Aegean Memories* (1940).

TO FRANK DAVISON   May 27th, 1941
[Channing Place]
Dear Frank,

It is because I felt all you say that I went out on a long tour last year. It appears that I am needed. Two nights ago I read my new poems to the Stuart School girls (I am a teacher there) and the reaction was silent and finally perfectly amazing. The school needs me. The colleges which have asked me back need me. You do not need me. You only reiterate that I need you.

Words like total dedication I do not like. One goes where one is needed and does what one can. I'm afraid also that I still believe Gerard Manley Hopkins, Rilke, Marvell, Emily Dickinson to be greater poets than Archibald MacLeish. You referred to the time last year when I was drawn into certain discussion and even wrote for that group "A Declaration of Interdependence." At that moment I suppose you thought I was on the brink of being saved. At that moment I believe I was on the brink of being lost—as an instrument in helping to create a real interdependence.

I believe that for the first time in my life I have discovered the place of maximum usefulness for me and it is in teaching poetry. It is needless to tell you that poetry is first of all a way of life and only secondarily a way of writing. In teaching that, in living it to the best of my ability, I believe that I meet you in your endeavors. Do we not start from the same point and is it a crime that our ways are different? I do not believe it a crime. I believe it the very proof and color of democracy that it should be so. You are fond of quoting Whitman:

"He masters whose spirit masters—he tastes sweetest who results sweetest in the long run;

In the need of poems, philosophy, politics, manners, engineering, an appropriate native grand-opera, shipcraft, any craft, he or she is greatest who contributes the greatest practical example."

It is possible that at the end of our several journeys we shall meet again. Is it not evident to you that we are both doing and believing the same thing? But I cannot now be deterred from a dedication already fully and completely made, any more than you can. Can we not respect and love each other for this?

You will, I know say "No we can't." You will not accept my dedication as valid. For that reason I do not believe that there is anything to be gained for either of us by my coming up.

Very sincerely yours,

<u>May Sarton</u>

Frank Davison: In a letter to Margaret Foote Hawley dated May 21, 1941, Sarton describes Frank Davison: "Last night I was savagely attacked by Jesus Christ in the person of a boy who has founded the William James work camp and believes I am a pharisee because I won't drop everything and lead an expedition to resettle Alaska."

TO ROLLO WALTER BROWN   Aug. 11th, 1941
[Rockport]
Dearest Walter—

Your notes fly in like birds of good omen—Daddy and mother were simply <u>beaming</u> when I got home Thurs. and could tell me they "had heard" the lecture was a great success! You are a <u>dear</u> to have written them as you did—and now your little note this morning.

What I quoted to Arnold "violently" was Agar who said "You have to <u>define</u> peace"—and to define it as "being in the presence of justice"—I then said is Poland peaceful? And told him one story I had on good authority about what is happening in Poland. He said "O that is just a Belgian story." <u>Then</u>

I did blow up! For he is one of the cynical generation who now believe in reverse-gear so to speak that because atrocities were exaggerated at the time, there were actually none at all. He also feels it would not be worse to have a Nazi-dominated world than it would be to fight. But that is because he doesn't know and can't imagine what a concentration camp is like. He said reports from Poland were British propaganda! He and Ciardi are the same sort—it is most sad isn't it? because they are both fine talented people.

It is a terrible thing that has been done to these kids by the "intellectuals," the teachers to turn them into cynics. who to confuse reality with fiction, to be so suspicious that they cannot recognize truth when they see it—and are incapable of faith. That is the worst of course.

The record really does sound quite good—I learned a lot doing it. Any emotion in the voice for instance, sounds melodramatic.

I am longing to hear the story of the children and talk it over but feel I must take this week to get some work done (also we have a sick friend staying with us, Mrs. Bouton, just over a gall bladder operation). Maybe next week?

I hope all is well with you and that the bread upon the water is on its way back a thousand-fold. I'm sure it will be sooner or later.

Lots of love to you and Polly—

it was so good to have you there on Wed!

[   ]

Rollo Walter Brown: (1880–1956), Cambridge friend, author of many books of essays, including *Lonely Americans.* A great supporter of young poets. Sarton, moved by his struggle and financial straits, continually raised monies for him and his wife Polly.

Arnold: Arnold Klebs, historian of medicine, colleague of George Sarton.

Agar: Herbert Sebastian Agar (1897–1980). American author and first president of Freedom House, an organization for the promotion of peace and international cooperation, which he helped found in 1941.

TO WINIFRED BRYHER   Sept. 4th, 1941
[Rockport]
Dear Bryher,

I was simply delighted to find that you like Mallarmé—isn't it strange not to know each other's faces? My whole image of you shifted like a kaleidoscope when you said you liked Mallarmé. Why I should have been astonished I don't know, but I was. It was quite unexpected. Wallace Stevens is certainly a magician, one of the few magicians, pure poets or whatever one wants to call them. Marianne Moore is curious but to me at any rate somehow outside the stream, a bushbaby leaping about in the branches over the stream but never flowing along with it, whereas Stevens is in the stream. Not that it matters. I have lately been enormously irritated by Auden's Popery—The Double Man is such a give-away, such a pastiche, such a grim little patch-work quilt of poorly assimilated, cleverly manipulated other people's ideas and thoughts, gets nowhere that I can see, and O how the notes give him away. But here people mutter that it is a very important poem and a TREND (God forbid!) I am anxious to get back to "imaginary gardens with real toads in them," to the real other world poetry can make, not mental acrobatics within this one. I haven't written for ages (your letter was dated Aug. 6th) because I have been writing away and otherwise lazy. The summer is almost over; our three kittens now seem like an army with banners, invading us constantly and turning our lives upside down. We are now ruled implacably by four cats. When we sleep they wish to bounce up and down on the beds, bite our toes, catch flies off our noses etc. When we are wide-awake and would like to play they cannot be moved, but lie exhausted even forgetting sometimes to put in their tongues. At the end of the week two will be put away and we shall settle down to a free life. I meant "given away" not "put away"—I expect that was the work of the subconscious!

Very interesting what you say about spoken english. I have always thought so except for some actors like Robert Speight who do speak beautifully and without exaggeration. I shall never forget having tea with Fox-Strangways, the music critic, an old friend of the family's and he laughed every time I opened my mouth, literally cackled and grew red with laughter—at my ac-cent as he said. Till I was nearly in tears and it was impossible to converse at all. Which reminds me of a typically American thing that happened the other day. I was having supper with a friend in a restaurant and after awhile the waitress came up and asked us "where we were from" and then congratulated us warmly on "how well you speak"! It was delightful. And could only happen here. I felt I had been decorated by the Lord High something or other. The praise of waitresses is infinitely desirable.

Before I forget, I have received all the L and L's including May with my poem which made me swell with pride, not the poem but to see it there. Have you a victrola? At Harvard they made a record of me saying it with some other poems and it might amuse you to hear it. It is rather tomb-like I think, a voice on a record. Elisabeth's story was a dandy, better than any in her book of short stories, which I found disappointing—the edges never the center of things. And a short story must have a core though all the rest be edges. Of course she is a marvel most of the time.

I have been writing some poems again thank heavens. But feeling sea-dull and cross with myself, here so safe and snug and full of food and without responsibility not to be producing more. But the autumn is coming, the move home next week and then I shall plunge into teaching, lecturing, perhaps a new novel about which I brood fearfully and which is waiting to focus. What I wonder did you think of the last Woolf? I ached with delight during all the first part but cannot understand the Pageant itself taking up so much space—and I keep thinking it must be because I do not get something which is there. Some of it is pure genius. I can't bear to have finished it now—now there will never be another.

We are still sitting placid and smug on the edge of a volcano. Roosevelt has lost a grip on the country—the soldiers do not know why they are there, noone at all will face squarely the fact that we shall someday have to actually fight and send men over to do it. And as long as they don't face that fact everything is half-baked, half-done. We evade the total sacrifice by talking about "Production" and half-believing that that alone will do it. Perhaps we won't have to send an army but until the country is willing to send one, until we declare war in other words, a total effort will not be made. But I am sick of crabbing about it.

The Russians continue to do the impossible. Have you read Edmund Wilson's most lucid book on the writers and actors of modern history from Michelet to Lenin? I thought it a beauty but am too ignorant to judge.

How are you both?

This with my love

M—

Mallarmé: Stéphane Mallarmé (1842–1898), one of the leading French symbolist poets; his *L'Après-midi d'un faune* inspired Debussy to write his well known *Prélude.*

Wallace Stevens: (1879–1955), American poet influenced by the French symbolists; did not receive widespread recognition until 1954. A lawyer by training, was for forty years associated with a Hartford insurance company.

Marianne [Craig] Moore: (1887–1972), American poet, whose work is distinguished by wit, irony, and individual metrical patterns.

Robert Speight: Robert Speaight (1904–1977), actor and author of many books on theatre and theology. Was in the first performance of Eliot's *Murder in the Cathedral.*

L and L's: Life and Letters.

Elisabeth: Elizabeth Bowen.

the last of Woolf: Between the Acts.

Edmund Wilson book: To the Finland Station.

TO KATHARINE CORNELL   Oct. 8th [1941]
[Channing Place]
Dear Kit,

It is very mean to have wrenched such glowing and passionate speech from you by my horrid little skepticisms! But I wouldn't have missed it for any-thing—it was a great hour and thank you for taking the trouble to teach the philistine his lesson. I still don't agree about the play entirely but you justify so completely <u>why</u> you are doing it—you make it into your own life so to speak, how can one mind? One can indeed only be grateful! As I'm sure Mr. Shaw is. Suddenly his desert flowers. And all the time I kept thinking of a poem of Yeats which I adore, because it draws art and life together (as they should be)—there seems to be some connection with what we said but I can't for the life of me put my finger on just <u>what</u>. Here it is anyway—

> We sat together at one summer's end,
> That beautiful, mild woman, your close friend,
> And you, 'A line will take the hours maybe:
> Yet if it does not seem a moment's thought,
> Our stitching and unstitching has been naught.
>   —and thereupon
> That beautiful mild woman for whose sake
> There's many a one shall find out all heartache
> On finding that her voice is sweet and low
> Replied, 'To be born woman is to know—
> Although they do not talk of it at school—
> That we must labour to be beautiful.

For me it was more than enough last night to pass through the theatre look-ing for Gert and suddenly in the silence to hear your voice throb out in the great silence (It was Act I)—Kit, how like a nightingale it is. I mean there is that deep poignance, that heartbreak in it.

And then after that to have the golden chance to hear all your long thoughts and convictions about Jennifer—I went home full of treasures.

I'll come back and say goodbye sometime next week, but don't hesitate to turn me out if you've had too many visitors. I've had more than my share already.

How lovely it was to see Gert so dazzlingly on top of the world.

Love and homage from
May

---

his desert: In 1941 Katharine Cornell played Jennifer Dube in *The Doctor's Dilemma.* "His desert" refers to Sarton's belief that "The trouble is there is never any mystery, any *silence* in Shaw." [to Bill Brown 8 Nov 47] *poem excerpt:* From William Butler Yeats' "Adam's Curse" in *In the Seven Woods,* 1904.

Gert: Gert Macy, Cornell's friend and manager who strongly believed in and supported Sarton during her theatre years.

TO WITTER BYNNER   Jan. 19th, 1942
[Channing Place]
Dear Witter Bynner,

How dear of you to write to me! I had heard that Bob Hunt was gone and felt at once for you and the emptiness of the house and life without him. Perhaps it will drive you from sheer loneliness to write a lot of poetry—in which case it will have to seem a sort of gain as well as a loss! In times like these the temptation seems to be to rush blindly into action and not to realize that those with a talent like yours are keeping alive the very thing others are fighting for. Three people have written me to say that my New Year Poem is escapism! Notes like yours therefore are very precious.

My whole instinct now is to be silent, or rather to speak from silent places and that exhorting-time which seized me on the trip round the country, reaction against the apathy and lack of zest that seemed to possess the young—has gone. There is no need for it now. Other people can do that better.

You are good to say that you liked the review—it was a hard one to write because I really <u>hated</u> Rexroth's book. It seems to me so pretentious not to try to communicate—and then the whole business of criticism seems rotten. But on the other hand I was afterwards (esprit d'escalier!) filled with shame and horror that I had seemed to question your kind of experience or the degree of your struggle at all. I do not really think it is my business to write about my betters—the trouble is that I long for the books, can't buy them, and the only way seems to be to review!

I'm hoping to come back to Santa Fe this summer but at times like this it is such a pure luxury to travel so far that I doubt if I'll ever get there. And I am trying to get some lectures for next year—the colleges of course are scared to death, so I probably won't land a one.

It is splendid of Bob to have volunteered and I think he was right, but that doesn't mean the separation is not cruel, cruel.

The only event here has been Marianne Moore's lecture—which was exhilarating in the extreme. What a queer and lively bird she is! Otherwise I don't like Cambridge much—it is so gossipy and hateful and one is always running into fellow-poets who glare at one as that horror "the female of the species" and at whom one glares for no reason or for any reason! Will noone ever again take up arms against the clever, the pretentious, the slick, the overloaded wordy, self-conscious Freudian batch who rule our roost? Mary

Colum is doing it a bit but unfortunately she has a few bees in her bonnet which get in her way viz. Her antipathy to Louise Bogan—

Ah well, to hell with them, say I! Let us write and rejoice in the Lord.

Yours as ever
May Sarton

Witter Bynner: (1881–1968), poet, critic, playwright, editor, pianist; both American Indian and Chinese poetry greatly influenced his life; was the first American to translate in full a volume of Chinese verse.

Bob Hunt: Bynner's companion signed up for the U.S. Navy; was shortly thereafter released with an honorable medical discharge.

Rexroth's book: Kenneth Rexroth (1905–1982), American poet. Sarton reviewed his *In What Hour,* (1940) together with the lyrics of Wittner Bynner which Bynner appreciated. Of Rexroth she wrote "This is a talented and pretentious book."

esprit d'escalier: To think of a witty retort too late.

struggle: Sarton suggests that in Anglo-Saxon poetry to write great lyrics at fifty involves a struggle with the personality and its relation to the world, a struggle not necessary for the Chinese poets in whom Bynner has steeped himself and with whom he feels affinities.

Mary Colum: Mrs. Mary Gunning (Maguire) Colum (188?–1957), contributed book reviews and critical articles to the *Saturday Review, New Republic,* and others. Her memoirs, *Life and the Dream,* were published in 1947.

TO BRYHER   Feb. 13th, 1942
[Channing Place]
Dear Bryher,

Your letter was like a spell—it rapt me off onto one island after another of Ideas and Emotions—so strange to imagine you and Elisabeth sitting and talking. I am now and then full of the aches and pains of homesickness for her big windows on Regent's Park and the curtains blowing out and in, for the atmosphere of that house with all its undercurrents and tensions (flaring up when the telephone rings) and for Elisabeth moving slightly blindly, with apparent hesitation like a swan, to the very center of things—for she is the very opposite pole from my world with her highly-evolved complicated people-ridden world, her circles within circles, her ability to be an artist and a social being, a wife and a free agent emotionally etc. etc. whereas I feel myself sitting at the bottom of a pool like a frog in the cool and the silence occasionally giving a friendly croak and then going back to sit on the sand. I meant to write to her after V. Woolf died and then didn't. There is no incentive when the answer will be silence.

That was one thing—I had been asleep and your letter fell into my hands as mother came to wake me and the cat (sound asleep in the curve of my arm)—I read it between sleeping and waking, you see how it affected me!

But it is Henri Rousseau, the painter, not Jean Jacques! I really dislike Jean Jacques intensely. But Henri is the pure imagination in a luminous and simple form which is what I like best in art—(I wish I had the painting of the Sleeping Gipsy to send you. Have you never seen it? It is magical—) hence Mozart, Milton's lyric poems, Blake and hence my predilection for 18th century form. I am so glad you came out with it—Hilda hinted that you liked the content of the poem—a graceful way <u>out</u>! But I puzzled a little. A great deal has to do with what the state of poetry is or was at the time of one's emergence into it—you, and earlier, Hilda emerged earlier than I at a time when poetry was form-ridden and inwardly faded. I am already the reactionary against your reaction—can that be it do you think? It is a fact that I love Hilda's poetry passionately but that I think is because the intensity of her language is such that each poem stands physically upright like a piece of marble. I do not find that state of being in any other vers libre. The later Yeats, Edith Sitwell, Valéry, Louise Bogan, Marianne Moore, Ruth Pitter (yes even though you howl with disagreement!) are my modern poets. Each is intensely personal and almost private but each is <u>formal.</u> I believe also that one of the things art does is to translate the chaos for a moment into a form so one can see it, unbewildered, and so at times of terrific outer chaos, there is a tendency toward strict form—whereas in times of apparent prosperity (such as the 1920's) most of the experimentation is done. Sometimes I worry that I am ante-deluvian but one can only write as one feels so there is no point in worrying, is there?

I had to laugh at your ardent paragraph about not getting caught in Volunteer work, for just yesterday after long soul-searching (I have just begun work on a book of modern martyrs as I wrote Hilda—poems) I have accepted to spend hours learning to be an instructor in First Aid. It will mean every evening for awhile and lots of studying. But actually I think it will just cut out all social life and I shall have a radical excuse not to see people! So it may work instead of preventing the book. Anyway I think the longer it brews the better—the longer I can keep it from precipitating so to speak, the longer it hangs about in the air and is felt not seen, the better it will be. I have a passion for getting things down and clear, and it is dangerous for poetry. One is apt to find the idea is there but the poem isn't! I am all with you in your hatred of universities, of what they mean in England anyway. But here you mustn't forget that we are just coming out of savage absorption in materialistic success to the exclusion of all inner life. The colleges have a job to do here in the most general humanistic sense. But perhaps as you say it will make education dearer if it is hard to get instead of given away every day to people who pay no attention!

Politically I am down in my boots. The fact that the Normandie burned as it did proves that Pearl Harbor could happen again—has happened already—right in the middle of New York. Everyone realizes and is dumb before the significance of the Singapore business. If we had had the ships and planes lost at Pearl Harbor we would now be taking the offensive. To put it plainly we are losing the war on every front and it is only a sort of <u>incredulity</u> that holds us up—we cannot believe it <u>possible</u> to lose. But efficiency and organization has got to be added to faith. The Russians seem to have efficiency as well as faith but the rest of us haven't. What is the feel in England? I am angry and terribly anxious to be put to work somehow. That I suppose is why I grabbed at the meagre opportunity offered by First Aid. I wish I could work in a factory.

Sugar is rationed and tires un-obtainable—otherwise life is absurdly normal here. We are putting up black-out curtains. But it is production and not "defence" which is needed. Where are the materials? Where are the men? In 1940 we were told we would be at peak production in 1941, in 1941 it was to be 1942, now it is 1943! Those thousands of planes may turn out to be Snarks. I do not want to be discouraging but things look too damned serious. What do you think? At my garage there are four or five excellent mechanics spending all day fixing up people's private cars—they are married and so not drafted. But they should be drafted for production. To hell with private cars.

I'll seal this up before I explode!

Love from
May

I'll watch out for Mackenzie's Monarch of the Glen. Poor Norman Douglas—still since he is being entertained by you and Elisabeth even in the English winter far from a blue sea, I cannot pity him too much!

––––––––––

Henri [Julien Felix] Rousseau: (a.k.a. Le Douanier) (1844–1910), a customs official until he retired to paint, an entirely self taught "primitive." *Sleeping Gypsy* (1897) is an exotic, metaphorical, surrealistic work. Jean Jacques Rousseau (1712–1778), Swiss-born philosopher, author and political theorist, known for his romanticism and political rebellion.

a book of modern martyrs: Sarton's idea was to do a collection of poems on modern martyrs such as the Italian socialist Giacomo Matteotii, the Roselli brothers, Saint Vincent Ferrer, Jaurez, and Péguy.

Norman Douglas: (1868–1952), British author of many books including *Old Calabria (1915), South Wind (1917),* and *Looking Back* (1933); and scientist known for his rugged sensitivity and diverse interests. For several weeks after the Nazi blitz in 1940 he was reported missing; eventually he made his way from France to Switzerland and with great difficulty to Lisbon and then to London as per this reference.

TO BRYHER   April 12th, 1942
[Channing Place]
Dear Bryher,

Your letter is dated just a month ago. Here we have had an April snow and the crocuses look very lavish and poetic, their rich purples through the snow. The green tulip leaves look violently alive. The garden furniture which we brought out hopefully on the first warm day is extremely reminiscent of that snow-scene in Cocteau's "Sang d'un Poète". I have just been in N.Y. for a week (school vac.) hence am late in answering your letter. Everything piles up when one goes away I can't imagine why. I never realize how many ties there are until I go away and come back and the telephone rings all day, my children have produced an alarming (really wonderful) amount of work on their vac and I had two long papers, seven short stories, ten poems to correct in detail as well as all the mail and to prepare the new term's work. But N.Y. did the trick—I mean at last I am born again. It was really time. I haven't gone so long un-attended by the angels ever and I began to think it was middle age coming on and that I was a bright young thing petering out. Don't bother to scold me about this. I know it was silly. Anyway now I am full of zest, working like a beaver and really seized by my work instead of pushing and pulling it around like a refractory elephant! I shall be thirty early in May. Beginning a new decade is exciting. Anything is possible, even to write a good book! I believe it is. How wonderful and amazing.

In N.Y. I had two good long talks with Marion Dorn and her husband of whom I was very fond in London. They had Janet Flanner over and I was bitterly disappointed. I had met her years ago in Paris and liked her tremendously—a brilliant journalist with a real <u>thrust</u> of intellect. But she has become New Yorkee in a horrible way, was vulgarly cheaply dressed with a large red carnation as big as a human face glaring out from her shoulder and a skirt so short and tight that I watched it fascinated to see if she wouldn't burst out of it like a snake from his skin. All of that wouldn't have mattered if she had made some sense. But she called V. Woolf "Mrs. So and So"—At that I rose up and said very loudly and rudely "<u>Not</u> Mrs. So and So" which I hope rattled her but probably didn't. She then spent five minutes describing the mating of swans. I adore swans but I do not want to hear their mating described by an erotic old woman full of cocktails!

I had a good long talk with Muriel Rukeyser who is just finishing her book of Gibbs, the Physicist. I expect it to be good. She is such a dynamo, such a conflagration of ideas and power. She is rather like Epstein's Adam in the femn.! I saw the Rousseau exhibition and enjoyed watching people's face light up as they entered the room. Best of all I like the small, beautifully composed landscapes, better even than the jungles which do not grow on one. The landscapes do. One sees in the Sleeping Gipsy that the reason the lion's mane is going the wrong way is that there is a slight breeze. I was very excited when I realized that.

I am puzzled about what you say of form. For surely someone like Stravinsky is interesting just because of his pre-occupation with form. There is no such thing as anarchy in art, which frames an experience in color, words, notes, but only of different forms. But as you say it doesn't matter what the form as long as it fits the person who is using it and does what he wants. Do you like Hindemith? I was disappointed in the Shostakovitch 6th Symph. which Kousse conducted here the other day. It seemed clever and skillful mais sans souffle. Marianne Moore is about the most formal writer I can imagine (I for instance do not think English is suited to be counted in syllables and am far more interested in Hopkins' theories of stresses, sprung rhythm)— Horace Gregory is a very intelligent man. I think he writes as good poetry as a very intelligent, sensitive man who knows what poetry is, but is not a poet, can write. (This is all opinion of course, private opinion so don't be cross—you won't I know. It is fun to have someone who makes one define what one does feel instinctively and privately)—Wallace Stevens' great genius seems to me just that he is able to put very complex and dense ideas into comparatively simple classical and lucid form. The ideas are new, the form is old. I do not anyway see any progress in form, only rotating crops— a bit of land is allowed to run to clover for awhile and then someone comes along and re-discovers it because he has exhausted his piece of land by writing too many sonnets or something! It is a pity we can't talk.

I am waiting hopefully about First Aid. I mean I hope they have decided that they have a sufficient supply of young Drs. and Nurses to teach it so that they won't have to use an ignorant enthusiast like myself. I hate to take any time off from work now. It was different when I felt I wasn't doing any good work of my own and so had far better be useful in some other way. Just now I am beginning a campaign to land a full-time teaching or some-sort-of-job for next year. It is quite funny being interviewed and snubbed because I haven't got a college degree! But I'm sure in the end someone will come along with an eye instead of a set of pre-conceived ideas. I am hoping something near N.Y. will turn up so I can escape for week-ends and have some life of my own. I like being on the edge of an entirely new life and not yet knowing what it will be. Someone suggested that I try to get a radio job, but I do not cotton to the idea somehow. Of course one makes a lot of money—

Have just re-read the above—and realize that I haven't said what I meant. Now and then of course someone comes along who adds a new form, who definitely discovers an entirely un-used piece of land like Joyce, and the sum-total of fields to use is thereby increased. But I do not think that only those who expand the form are useful and important—I think Baudelaire is important as well as Rimbaud. I think Wallace Stevens is important as well as Hart Crane.

Well, enough of all this. I am reading Péguy. Some of it is very good. It is for instance: (about Jaurès) "Il savait admirablement expliquer, par des raison discursives, éloquantes, concluantes. Demonstratives. C'est ce qui l'a perdu. Un homme qui est si bien doué pour expliquer tout est mûr pour toutes les capitulations. Une capitulation est essentiellement une opération par laquelle on se met à expliquer, au lieu d'agir."

Well, I must run off to my classes.

Love and write soon, and give Hilda a hug from me—

[ ]

Wish I knew Edith Sitwell—I heard G. Tabouis the other night—liked her better than her book. She gave a good, marvelously organized, passionate speech which ended (so French) with the sentence "Donc nous sommes optimistes non seulement par devoir, mais par Raison!" Only a French woman would end a passionate speech with the word Reason!

"Sang d'un Poète": "Le Sang d'un Poète" ("The Blood of a Poet," 1932) a surrealistic film by Jean Cocteau (1889–1963), French poet, writer, and film director.

(school vac.): Sarton was teaching at the Stuart School in Boston.

Muriel Rukeyser: (1913–80), American poet, biographer, teacher, and fiction writer, became one of Sarton's close friends with whom she later shared an apartment in New York. *Willard Gibbs* published 1942.

Epstein: Sir Jacob Epstein (1880–1959), American born sculptor who became a British citizen, known for his monumental, audacious works.

Mais sans souffle: But without breath.

Hopkins: Gerard Manley Hopkins (1844–1889), brilliant English poet and Jesuit priest, whose intricate rhythm and internal rhymes, what he called "sprung rhythm" and "inscape," provided compound metaphor and musicality and influenced many twentieth-century poets such as Auden and Dylan Thomas.

Horace Gregory: (1898–1982), man of letters, poet, critic, editor, translator. Married poet, Marya (Alexandrovna) Zaturenska (1902–1982), poet, first published in *Poetry* in her teens; won the Pulitzer Prize in 1937, translator of Italian works; collaborated with Horace Gregory on poetry anthologies.

Translation of French: He knew wonderfully how to explain, using discursive reasoning, eloquent, decisive. Impassioned. And this is what ruined him. A man with such a gift for elucidating everything is ripe for compromise. Compromise is essentially when one begins explaining instead of acting.

G. Tabouis: Geneviève Tabouis (1892–?), one of the most brilliant of French journalists; freelance correspondent, especially in international politics. Niece of politician Jules Cambon. Author of *They Called Me Cassandra* (1941).

Translation of French: So we are optimists not only by necessity but because reason tells us to be.

Sunday, May 24th [1942]
[Channing Place]
Dear Bryher,

Your April 30th letter came a week ago which is not bad either! I have
been in bed for two weeks, having finally decided to be ill instead of half-
well (a great relief!) and now tomorrow as two weeks flat hasn't done much
good to my refractory alimentary tract, I am going to hospital to have x-rays
and see if they can find something definite to treat. I hope I swallowed a pin
when I was ten or something definite and extractable like that. I fear they
may come back to the idea that it is colitis which is a bore, as it is a long
weary business to get over. But bed had great compensations. The walls of
my room are dull pale green and all flowers look ravishing against it. Just now
our garden produces a new wonder each day and I have had Siberian iris
one day (it makes all other iris look parvenu) and small white poppies with
their thick yellow crowns of stamens inside, and white violets and lilies of
the valley, and bleeding-heart, and hosts of pansies. It has been a perfect feast.
I have had time to read omnivorously all day the way I used to when I was
about twelve and had to be pushed out of the house because it seemed as if
I would never read all there was to read in time—in time for what I can't
imagine! I have been reading Dickens' Hard Times—I had forgotten what a
breath of passion there was in the man, in spite of the flat cardboard quality
of the characters marked "Good" and "Evil" like the placards announcing
the next act in vaudeville—but back of them there is Dickens' passionate rage
and compassion at conditions in the mills and this comes through like a fire.
It certainly shows up the smug Communists who pretend to have discovered the working-man. It is far better than most propaganda novels written
today. Also a good modern novel, a well-_thought_ novel by Granville Hicks
which I expected to hate and liked immensely: "Only One Storm." It's the
story of a Communist who becomes a small town selectman and a democ-
rat—a very sane, thoughtful, _real_ novel. Worthy is an awful word but that is
what it is. It's like a good salty Maine wind. I think you would like it.

Probably I haven't read enough Gregory—I haven't been tempted to read
more but will get hold of the Collected poems and have another try.

I was very pleased that you liked one or two of the American poems—
they seem very far away now because I wrote them more than a year ago
but when they came they did seem to be broader than anything I had
done—a sort of door flung open from the ivory tower. I am getting slowly
into the martyrs, reading at present a lot about the Risorgimento as background for Rosselli. It is a great question-mark if all this miscellaneous information and emotion will ever fuse, or rather will ever become the _kind_
of experience to me that turns into poetry. But as an experiment it may have
value. One has constantly to branch out and try to conquer a new part of

experience with words,—someday I shall come back to more personal poetry but not yet, not now. And of course every poem is personal if it is any
good, but you know what I am driving at. I get into a sweat whenever I try
to think anything through in my feeble state.

Have you read Miller's <u>Colossus of Maroussi</u>—it is a book for Hilda—I
adored it—it is like listening to a brilliant talker, an improvisation, but it
sweeps and cleans and sets you on bare hills under brilliant skies. I have never
liked Miller at all before and was quite astonished by this—It is published
by Colt in Cal. and costs $3.50 which seems a small fortune to me at the
moment because I'm not earning anymore now school is over. But I must
get it to you somehow. Maybe if I told them it was a book Life and Letters
ought to review, they would send it.

Yours was the first news I got that Julian was all right. I haven't heard how
the battle went from him yet. But I'm glad he fought it out. I loved your
story about the camel-hair and the camel-keeper.

I don't mind the machine-age at all and I don't see where you get that
idea from the poems. I only think ~~as is pretty obvious it seems to me~~ , that
machines can be <u>used</u>—(Boulder Dam is the perfect example)—for <u>life</u> and
not for <u>death.</u> If you have ever travelled for a long time in and out of one
small western town after another, where everything is ugly and cheaply
made by the thousand, and the girls and boys are dissatisfied and empty-
headed because their only vital experience is the movies and they can't have
what they see in the movies, and so have to do with a five-and-ten imita-
tion of it—you would agree. God forbid that I should hate the machine age.
That would be childish. But you must admit that we still have somewhere
to go, for God's sake. (The machine should save labor for <u>life</u>—should be the
great life-<u>freer</u>) We haven't got a <u>perfect</u> country here yet! We have got to
build new traditions for one thing in places where there are none—take a
look at the oil-towns, shot up in six weeks when oil was struck, filled with
people out for money and nothing else, out to capture the earth's riches and
jip anyone they could out of them, out to live in tin-houses and eat out of
cans and never stop to grow a tree or a blade of grass because "next year we'll
get rich and can clear out of this and live in a hotel in Miami all the year
round." Boulder Dam is inspiring because it shows what engineering can be
turned to and points the way to "life, liberty and the pursuit of happiness"
or at least a dignified instead of poverty-stricken harried life for hundreds of
people who have never known it. I loved Boulder Dam passionately because
it was the living proof of the <u>potentialities</u> of the machine age. But to say we
have realized them yet is simply idiotic. I'm sorry if I sound cross but that
sentence seems to me strangely un-understanding as if you hadn't read the
poems. They are certainly not nostaligic for the past! It is not the machine-
age that ruined Kansas, it was the pioneers, who cut down the rich grass-

land and started to grow wheat on it, upsetting the economy of nature so that little by little the land is being blown away and laid waste. That has nothing to do with machines. But it has something to do with thinking in long terms, way ahead, and thinking not for yourself alone, but for the people who will come after you, and thinking not only in terms of yourself but of the land too. That is what Boulder Dam does. That is what central planning and caring about individual lives enough so as to be willing to <u>plan together</u> so people can <u>have</u> individual lives, <u>can do.</u> That is what my book is talking about. Take it or leave it but don't say that I'm a backward-looker or longing for the good old days. The good old days in America were bloody and brutal and I for one am damned glad I didn't have to live them.

Hitler has taken the cruel human element out of education and mechanized it. Mechanize education for what? What are you trying to turn out, human beings or machines? If you want to turn out machines O.K. by me, but I am interested in the other thing. It is much harder to raise up a generation of teachers who are human beings, I agree. And there's lots wrong with education. But people will be in the long run, helped to grow by other people, whoever they are, in or out of school, and no other way. It's what Socrates <u>was</u> not what he <u>said</u> that moves a high-school boy.

Well, I must stop. I might try radio. I still haven't a job. I don't much care. It is one advantage of feeling lousy.

Give my love to Hilda and don't be cross with me for this explosion! Your postscripts are provocative!

Yours with love
May

---

colitis: Sarton had a long history of colitis, the earliest medical record of it in the hand of her Belgian physician, dated November 13, 1914 when she was 18 months old.

Granville Hicks: (1901–82), American critic. Entered theological training before transferring to literary studies. Known for his studies of American literature and works on Christianity.

Risorgimento: In Italian history, the period of national unification (c. 1815–1870).

Colossus of Maroussi: Henry Miller's book about Greece.

the battle: In 1942 after much tension between Julian Huxley and the London Zoo Council, the council took advantage of Huxley's absence abroad to declare the post of secretary merely an honorary one; although he was still nominally secretary, it was evident that the old council would make things increasingly difficult for him, and Huxley had no choice but to resign.

TO GEORGE SARTON   Wed. June 2 [1942]
[Sudbury]
Dearest Daddy,

It was sweet of you to write to me about your similar struggle, though I really believe this is actual mental <u>fatigue</u> rather than the sympton of a struggle. Actually I have given up worrying for the moment. The difficulty in a nutshell is that I know <u>very well</u> what I am and want to do: I am a poet <u>but</u> it is not possible to earn a living by being one. That is a very different matter to desiring riches—You have been angelically behind me, such a solid dear <u>support</u> all these years, but even if it were wise for this to go on forever, it would not be wise for me to live <u>permanently</u> at home. However there is no need for an immediate solution—I am glad to be patient and passive at present and to see what Fate turns up. The <u>inner</u> stream of my work is not touched by all this. But it is a question of making a plan for living <u>and</u> still being able to work. I have to face that I haven't a great deal of resistance.

Thank you for the check! I have cut down 2/3rds of my smoking, you'll be glad to hear. Being at Anne's is purest peace.

Love from your devoted
[　]

TO POLLY THAYER STARR   June 28th [1942]
[Sudbury]
Dearest Poll—

Such a wonderful letter which I re-read and taste sitting out <u>en pleine campagne</u> (in a deck-chair—nothing but cows and trees and lovely luxuriant pasture, full of russet waving grass and black-eyed susans—no sounds but the million country-sounds of crickets, birds, bees and once in awhile the clop, clop of a horse down the road or a distant cock crowing. It is heaven. I am, I see, the most envied person in the world as everyone's <u>secret</u> desire is to be ordered a <u>complete rest.</u> But I am finding out something about living by not living—that it is, in fact, the only way <u>to</u> live. I hope I don't get well too soon is all I can say!

It's not I'm sure <u>what</u> I did which has been abysmally little even for friends, let alone for The Muse! <u>But</u> the <u>way</u> I did <u>everything</u> with this fearful intensity which got <u>me</u> nowhere and accomplished nothing. If I can only somehow keep <u>calm</u> when back in the stream I feel all my problems (except how to earn a living) will be solved. My attitude toward everything was really that of a bull to whom everything from waiting for a train to a love-affair was a red flag to be <u>charged</u> with every atom of the consciousness! No wonder I am flat now! Laugh at me as I am laughing at myself, it is the only thing to do—and yes, envy me! Darling, I am so sorry about the nurse. You have had a Jobish winter altogether and yet have managed to do good work and bring up that ravishing child <u>and</u> be a support to Donald so I can well understand if you are exhausted though, I hope, triumphant.

I don't know why you should value my friendship—I have been such a poor friend for a long time. It was not the <u>will</u> that was lacking but <u>para-</u>

phernalia and I suppose nerves that have made this last winter the lightest grasshopper of an engagement feel like a mountain.

Poor Vicky—is she all right again? I do so hope the perfect nurse you spoke of wistfully didn't escape you when this last one left.

All one's hearts and hopes for <u>justice</u> are with Donald but I fear, as you say, in war-time these decisions are apt to be arbitrary—I shall be so anxious to <u>know.</u>

Am burying myself in novels. Henry James "The Wings of the Dove" which I adore and "The Bostonians" which I'm about to begin—and interspersing them with Jane Austen—

Here is my lunch.

Darling Poll, forgive this feeble answer to your rich and dear letter.

Your devoted

M—

---

en pleine campagne: In the open country.

TO BRYHER   July 31st, 1942

[Sudbury]

Dear Bryher,

It has rained delicious cool rain for three days and now the air is all washed and clear, a very <u>gentle</u> day. The flowers are swarming with bees, simply guzzling honey in the sun, especially the poppies and the bees didn't like it at all when I picked some—I feel much better already, a different person as if a fog had lifted and all the edges were clear again. Solitude is Heaven. I go up and down saying "Glory be to God!" and cannot think delight a sin even in this horrible world. All I can say about Mr. Sachs (whom I met the day Austria fell, he was so dreadfully sad and one felt helpless—I loved him that day)—but to go back all I can say about Sachs is that <u>he</u> is <u>not</u> Solitude and I really don't think analysis is the answer—(However if I am not better later on, I'll certainly go to one. At present I feel I shall be.) I am so awfully unreserved you know it is quite disgusting and I alway spurt out everything that's the matter with me into the awfully patient ears of my friends. When I was worried at one time about the possible ill-effects of bisexuality I did go to an analyst and he said it would be crazy to be analysed that I didn't need it at all. However one never knows—and dear Bryher, thank you for being patient with my cross horrible letters and offering kind suggestions that I take my troubles to a professional ear. I do not deserve such friendship and can only be humbly glad and Praise the Lord! And bless you. What does one mean exactly when one says "Praise the Lord!" I cannot tell you but just the same it comes to my lips and makes me feel warm inside.

Really this place is beautiful—but nothing in America can compare with an english garden—the roses at Edith Sitwell's! and that un-commented sentence 'I have been away for the first time since autumn'—which I shall not comment upon either but I do understand its implications and O, I would send you and Hilda four silver wings to attach to your shoulders, so you could fly merrily down to Cornwall or even over to Bowen's Court when you felt like it—if, if—well, then you would be angels and it might be rather dull. Yes, old-fashioned roses are the best—I have never lived close to a rose garden except in France at Vouvray and now I have forgotten most of their lovely names except "Caroline Testout""Rose d'anjou" and "Rose de France, la plus vieille rose du monde." And once at V. Sackville West's I saw the most extraordinary dark dark red rose wide open called "Night." I wish I could have heard E. S. read—I've only heard the records of Façade and I suspect that the shrill voice she uses there is on purpose for the poems. But I adored "See me dance the Polka said Mr. Wag like a bear." Many of her lines (not *that* one needless to say) are like roses. I cannot imagine a rose without *smell*—is there such a thing? Like the California peaches without taste.

"Été: être pour quelques jours
le contemporain des roses"—

I cannot remember if you like Rilke, probably not. I like best the Sonnets to Orpheus. There is a kind of soft rot in some of the others that is unpleasant—but I can't read him in German so really cannot judge.

Yes, I'm sure you're right about bureaucracy viz. Tories. Names like "Tory" are rather silly now anyway. I have a friend who calls me a Red when I express the simplest belief in democracy or suggest that the negros should have the vote, in practise as well as theory.

About food after the war, I think I must have made myself unclear. Of course Greece, England, Jugoslavia, Spain (if Franco can be done away with in the general holocaust) must be fed first and Poland. I was not thinking of first or lastness but only that the feeding of anyone at all means a great deal of Government planning now—for instance we have a tremendous wheat-crop this year but due to lack of central planning there is nowhere to store it! All building materials have been commandeered for war-purposes as well as labor of course (Carpenters are building Army Camps)—so it presents a real problem. A little planning a year ago or two years ago rather would have solved this but it is against the farmers' individualistic nature to plan in groups and before the war the Gov. Had no power. This is the sort of thing PEP is interested in seeing to. In Brazil they have cast tons of coffee into the sea to keep up prices in times past—some sort of International buying pool could avoid that kind of waste. That's all I meant.

There is much talk here of building hundreds of gigantic flying boats, and flying trailers partly to solve the shipping problem. Last night I heard on the radio figures proving what 300 of these could do (making 24 trips as against 3 of a convoy of ships for instance) and of course such a fleet would be invaluable after the war for carrying food. They are amphibian so don't even need Air Bases. I hope it goes through.

But we are in a mess about steel and copper and a hell of a lot of other things through lack of severe enough central planning. The steel situation is shocking—ships are held up on the ways for lack of raw materials. A contract for 100 ships to be built in New Orleans—has been cancelled for lack of raw materials, throwing hundreds of negros out of work (and they are sure it is racial discrimination)—So it goes.

There is no point in talking about the news. We can only wait and trust to the military to know what they are doing. But one can't help passionately hoping that they will see their way to some offensive action in the west before August is out.

It is quite true that you could go to a restaurant in <u>London</u> with a coloured girl or in Paris for that matter, but could you have in Jamaica or in Singapore? <u>Ten per cent</u> of the population <u>of England</u> is <u>not coloured.</u> That is our problem, and we have handled it with fearful intolerance, prejudice, cruelty and everything else you can say, I know. But that it is a hard problem to solve, there is no doubt whatever in the States where there are 60% coloured people for instance. The first thing to attack seems to be education. At present, given opportunity the negros have been so kept down and badly treated that many would be incapable of using it. But amelioration of education has to go through the States (there is no <u>Federal</u> schooling) and the whites in the South, Talmadge of Georgia for instance would murder, lynch, intimidate in every way to <u>prevent</u> better schools. I have a friend who is organizing cooperatives for the farmers down there and he has had a very hard time keeping his mouth shut. Very very gradually and carefully he is beginning to be an influence to help the negro—he is hated as a "foreigner" by a lot of people down there. But he saved a nearly starving community by starting a coop cannery so his kudos is going up—However the Federal Gov. does help in various ways, by laws against racial discrimination in factories (through the Unions too of course) and the Army is a great democratiser. But O how far there is to go! The sins of the grandfathers who brought the slaves over will go on being visited for a long time—until the great-grandchildren wake up and understand at least, which they are far from doing in the South. I get even angrier with the smug Northerners who have no such problem and over and over again make a mess of things by telling the South off.

How strange to be learning Persian—I mean how small it makes the world that we must know it, and Chinese and God knows what else. Has it iconography as difficult as Arabic? It took my father five years to learn Arabic which he needed for his work on the 13th century—but he had the fun of reading the whole Arabian nights in the original. I shall get hold of Browne as soon as I've finished Taylor's "Mediaeval Mind."

It is such a relief not to have to teach next year! A year of grace—my spirits are soaring. Perhaps I shall be able to do some good work.

Love and a kiss to Hilda—
Your devoted
May

<u>What</u> war work is Elisabeth doing? Can't wait to read B's court. There was a silly review in <u>Time</u> and an <u>awful</u> picture of Elisabeth squinting.

Mr. Sachs: Probably Paul Sachs of the Fogg Museum, who with his wife, Meta, were friends of Eleanor and George Sarton.

Façade: An "Entertainment" by Sir William Walton, being accompanied by small chamber ensemble (six players) to poems by Edith Sitwell declaimed in notated rhythm by a speaker or speakers.

Translation of French: Summer: to be for a few days the roses' contemporary.

PEP: Political and Economic Planning, founded in London in 1931 as a nongovernmental planning organization.

Talmadge: Eugene Talmadge (1884–1946), Governor of Georgia, leader of a "white supremacy" group. Triumphed over the "liberal" group and instituted reactionary, antiintellectual measures.

B's court: Bowen's Court by Elizabeth Bowen (1942). A history of the Bowens in County Cork from the arrival of Cromwell's colonel to the departure of Elizabeth and her mother for England.

TO BRYHER
[Sudbury]
Dear Bryher,

September 7th, 1942
Labor Day

Well you make a great deal of sense and I (I now see) made none about analysis and this is the first thing that has almost convinced the old donkey to move toward the carrot! However I still feel that I can't do it unless I am more desperate than at present as I am at present living <u>on</u> my parents to my growing horror. Well, bless you for being patient with my ignorance.

Your question about my father was dangerous as it is apt to lead to a deluge of information—I don't know why I imagined you knew what his work is—he is writing what he calls "An Introduction to the History of Science and Civilization" which has now reached (published) through the 13th century, three huge tomes and (unpublished) the 14th which he has been working on for ten years and which will be done in two or three. He had to learn Arabic to deal with science in the 13th century. The first volumes are already a classic, not the definitive (because new things are constantly being unearthed about the past) but the nearest thing to a standard work there is. He is a great scholar with a burning faith (the necessity for the humanization of science) and of course this completely international work—that is where it is extraordinary as it deals with science in the world and there has never been anything like it. Previously there have been histories of chemistry or mathematics or astronomy etc.—usually written by amateurs, or rather by scientists who were amateur historians. This ties everything up and he has hence discovered all sorts of amazing parallels as if certain discoveries were bound to be made at a certain time in various places—he also edits Isis, a quarterly devoted to the History of Science in which all new material appears. This he began in 1912 in Belgium and has carried on ever since so there are now thirty volumes which provide a sort of commentary to the books. The publication of Isis has twice been interrupted by a German invasion of Belgium (it used to be printed in Belgium up to 1940). But actually for the work itself it was a great blessing that we were driven out as it brought Daddy to America where he has been supported by the Carnegie Institution and so able to concentrate on research in a way that wouldn't have been possible in Europe. There he would have had to teach to earn a living and as it is he hears Time's wingèd chariot constantly—and works fanatically from nine till midnight every day, Sundays included. After the 14th century he is going to stop in order to be able to write some small books on things he has been brewing all this time. He started out as a young man as a chemist and infuriated his professor, who thought he was mad by dreaming of writing the whole history of science and giving up his career in chemistry to do it. He is an Honorary Prof. at Harvard but only gives a half-course every year on mediaeval science. It has always seemed to me a great stroke of luck that I wasn't born a boy as it would then have seemed necessary that I carry on the work but as it is, I was given up as hopeless!

Of course Arabic as spoken is a different language altogether from Arabic as written, from literary Arabaic—as different as modern and ancient Greek. Is that true of Persian I wonder? Can you read poetry yet? If I were teaching a person a language I would begin immediately with poetry because one can so to speak possess a whole poem even early in studying and it is such a satisfaction!

Was very interested about the new language. Here everyone has gone Jeep-crazy—and it is amusing how in France "Swing" has come to mean deGaullist or at least anti-German! Somewhere I saw an article on Air-Force slang—I wish I had cut it out, but of course it is a different language from yours. I would be extremely grateful for the little book on Political India. Ignorance is the devil here—and there is a growing tendency to simply shut one's ears to facts and either say dogmatically "They must be given their freedom immediately whatever the consequences" to an equally ignorant and dogmatic assertion of the opposite. The Propaganda has not I think been very clever—

a few lists of facts like the number of Mohammedans, the names of the Parties and what they each want (and how they are opposed to each other) and so on. I'll see that the book is lent from hand to hand after I've read it. I myself am bewildered by ignorance and conflicting emotions on the subject. It is of course the sore place in the United Nations, there's no doubt of that. People here simply do not believe in British good-will where India is concerned. This remark I heard the other day is typical "I just don't believe Churchill and the present rulers of England have any intention of giving India up after the war" and The Viceroy's remarks about getting Burma back "for the Empire" have had a bad effect here. For either, people say, it is a war for the people to liberate the people of the world, or it is a war for Empire. They are not of course interested in fighting a war for a return to the Status Quo. They can point with some justification to our dealing with the Filipinos and to the fact that the Filipinos fought like hell on our side unlike the Burmese. I know it is much more complicated than all that but that is the sort of thing one hears.

The whole problem here in a nutshell seems to me that our Home Front is too far from the fighting so there has to be a kind of hysterical and unreal patriotism (much too much mere mud-slinging dirty words applied to Japs and Germans) which as far as I can make out simply didn't happen in England because the civilians were at the front. A strong coarse word is fine if it comes from real anger, from deep fiery indignation but there is very littl of that—people cannot imagine really what is happening. They do not visualize the German horror—they do not identify themselves with the sufferers. There was a moment of hot anger after Pearl Harbor but it has now died down. There is a great deal of empty shouting and "We'll show 'em" business which I find revolting as so far we have done nothing or almost nothing. I don't see what is to be done about this. I suppose you have heard the probably apocryphal but symbolic story of the girl in the bus who said "I don't care if the war goes on forever. I've never made so much money in my life"—and a woman got up and slapped her face and said "That's for my son who died at Pearl Harbor." Another example which my mother actually heard was a woman talking about a friend who had been called up "What's he going to get out of it?" I wish that the factory-workers could be put in uniform and considered soldiers (as they are) wages kept way down just as soldiers are. Instead they are making money hand over fist and especially young boys just out of high school who are earning more than their parents ever have in some cases. It is going to make a bad post-war problem, a poor sense of values and so on. I would guess that the Russians manage this difference between the Front and the Home Front better. In England I gather you have somewhat the same situation as here. Though everyone is working much much harder and the material hardships are so much worse that that evens up the difference. Here the difference between civilian and army life is really shocking.

I loved the description of the rabbit-farm—how strange to comb a rabbit! I am glad the gleaning in Belgium is better—because they are less efficient in harvesting! In one of our last letters from friends they have gleaned basket-fuls of oats and wheat (you <u>buy</u> permission for gleaning from a farmer and they gleaned steadily for a week) If only it will be a <u>mild</u> winter. One cannot bear to think of the agony everywhere—all this is pushing me slowly but surely into some sort of active work. I go out lecturing in November and when I come back hope to find something to do more concerned directly with the war. Lots of love—

May

TO S. S. KOTELIANSKY   Sept. 10th, 1942
[Channing Place]
Dearest Kot,

You will never never guess what I am doing and why I am suddenly impelled to write to you—I am smoking one of your cigarettes! I found it in a box I was clearing out, just one, and the taste instantaneously brought back the smooth wood of your table, the blue ashtray that was K. M.'s, and I am sitting there looking alternately out of the window and at you and we are talking—It is <u>right now.</u> It is not the past at all, that is what is wonderful!

I have heard from Julian about the Zoo—I wonder if it isn't in a way a relief though of course Juliette will now have the horror of moving (Julian said something about a house in the country?) It is bad that they cannot find out more what can help her with her blood trouble.

What do you think of W. R. Rodgers, Kot? I have got to the state where I can hardly read poetry for not writing it! Everything makes me cross—it is all words. But some of his had a freshness, at that. I just do not see that he is <u>the</u> war poet! How can there be one or anyone recognize him until several years later anyway. But over and over again I am struck by the wordiness of modern poetry, as if language had replaced experience and so must be more and more extreme, intricate and in a way divorced from life itself. It seems as if what we all need is a great purification—but how will that come about? As for me I am silent. A great silence has descended on me for the last six months. I am as silent as an Arab in the desert, as dry, thirsty, and full of wonder and rumours which do not materialize into camels or travellers at all, but just vanish into the silent spaces from where they came. I expect this is a good thing though it is extremely irritating—the brink of a voice and never a voice.

The good part is that for the first time in my life I am just living, nothing else. I am a piece of life. It is very curious. Always before I have been holding something back because the next day there would be work and I must have something in reserve for work—I was always hurrying desperately away from life. And life here is of a dreamlike stillness, a river and one is floating down. It is punctuated by tea in the garden when my father comes home from work with a bag full of books for me from the library, and the cat has her saucer of milk in the grass—occasionally too by other people. But mother and I are floating down the river and Daddy comes and goes. That is how it is. It is a pity that you are not here to float down it with us and be fed lots of little red tomatos and jam with your tea, as well as a sugary bun.

Very soon of course, like the Arab, I shall have to fold my tents and go—first to give lectures in the west, in November and then to come back and perhaps (I am thinking about it) then go into a factory to do skilled work. One cannot forever stand apart from the war-effort. It is unhealthy. One must be part of it. If I should find the voice coming back it would be another thing. But I am not worrying at all. It will all be solved in time.

And you, my dear? How are you? How is your hat? The black one? How is your stick? We are not allowed to send tea anymore. It makes me very cross that I didn't send more.

This is really not a letter but to tell you that my smoke is coming your way, and to send you a strangling hug—are you suffocated? You should be.

Love

[   ]

W. R. Rodgers: William Robert Rodgers (1909–1969), Irish poet, script writer for British television. Known particularly for *Awake! and Other Poems.*

TO POLLY THAYER STARR   October 15th, 1942
[Sudbury]
Dearest Poll,

I was relieved to have your letter—and I will try to say something to Moll though I can't imagine how. But I am probably stopping over on my trip—early in November. Until I have to go to Cambridge I can't bring myself to stir from this place because I am working at least and poems come every day—and then in the afternoon I go out on the hill with a pitchfork and dig up masses of horrible stiff red grass that has invaded the place (it used to be all soft blond grass punctuated with cedars and juniper and looked almost like a park)—It is hard work and so far I am exhausted after an hour but am hoping to increase it some every day till I am a Herculean figure and ready to do some sort of manual defence work! This is a good life and I wish it could go on forever, but it's not that kind of <u>world,</u> alas, so it can't. I am very impressed with the letters I get from soldiers, awful fairies who are suddenly pulling themselves together and really becoming men at last with a central <u>core,</u> guts or whatever you want to call it. It is so awful that we succeed in doing this in war-time and fail in peace-time—but there is none of the ballyhoo one gets on the radio from them. They are well enough aware that the big job will be the peace and that they must be thinking and fighting for it <u>now</u>—and there is no hatred. Only a great sadness that it has come to this and a sort of <u>grim</u> laugh that it's up to them. Here in America where I don't suppose the civilians will ever be in the front line in the sense that they are in Poland, Greece or England our greatest problem seems to me how to get <u>across,</u> how to bridge the mock-patriotism of the crooners and bonds-salesmen the civilian end of things, with the growing realisation on the part of the boys "that patriotism is not enough" and that this war is about something else.

As to [Edmund] Wilson—I haven't read the Wound and the Bow, but certainly in <u>Axel's Castle</u> (which came out in the 1920's—the <u>first</u> illuminating analysis of Proust, Joyce, Yeats, Virginia Woolf etc.) he didn't have any marxist axe to grind—and in his book on Marx "To The Finland Station" one is aware that he is far from a party man in any sense of the word. It is acute and fascinating <u>criticism.</u> But what I feel about Brooks is that he has a 19th century point of view, that he has simply revolted <u>before</u> analysing the troubles of the 20th century which cannot be denied by revolting from them—he stubbornly demands sweetness and light in a between-war hell where the greatest artists must be aware that there was very little but suffering around them. He objects to the people who analysed our decadence, as if <u>they</u> were decadent—whereas I believe to show up decadence is a sign of health. In Nazi Germany where they only talk about other people's decadence and their own strength, <u>there</u> is the decadent point. Secondly, at least in The Flowering of New England and its sequel I find his style pedestrian and boring in the extreme—it has a sort of Quincy-Howe-ish vitality which may be all right in a radio commentator but not in a critic. But I haven't read Allston and I must.

I hated Mary McCarthy's book and I'm sure you would. It is petty, sex-ridden and fundamentally boring because somehow <u>flat</u>—I suppose Freud has got her and she can't see except in categories. From a literary point of view it was about on a level with professional cats like Ilka Chase who make their living by wise-cracks. It added <u>nothing</u> to one's experience that couldn't have been got by a pornographic movie.

That is an indignant paragraph and so you will dismiss it. As perhaps you should. But art seems to me to have to do with the triumph of the human spirit (in its power to recognize decadence and expose it as well as in its power to praise and to speak for love)—but when a book debases the human spirit, then I am indignant. And I believe it is a place for indignation. The money-changers you know were chased out of the temple in no uncertain terms and with a certain absence of sweetness and light. Because their act was a profanation of The Light. I suppose Brooks is indignant because he thinks of Eliot and Hemingway as profaners. I would not myself put them in the same category—as Eliot, though mistaken, has made a far sterner and more self-effacing spiritual pilgrimage than Hemingway has. His poetry springs from great discipline (both spiritual and mental) and from great suffering.

The mail-man is coming so I must stop. Did you have fun in N.Y.?

I am still reading William James for whom I have a passion—what a marvelous man he must have been, a pourer out of love and faith and under such nervous and temperamental handicaps all the time.

Here are a poem or two.

Love from
[ ]

How is your work? I take it you have been doing a great deal—

Brooks: Van Wyck Brooks (1886–1963), American critic and biographer. The sequel was *New England: Indian Summer* (1940).

Quincey-Howe-ish vitality: Quincey Howe, son of Mark de Wolf Howe, gave the effect of being highly nervous, talked incessantly, very fast and eloquently, and was always in motion.

Allston: Washington Alston (1779–1843), poet and author of *Lectures on Art* about his theory that lectures should tell a story.

Mary McCarthy: (1912–1989), *The Company She Keeps* (1942).

Ilka Chase: (1905–1978), Actress, author, popular radio and TV personality. Particularly known for her play *The Women*.

William James: (1842–1910), brother of Henry. American philosopher best known for his *The Varieties of Religious Experience*.

TO ELEANOR MABEL SARTON   Nov. 19th Thurs. [1942]
[Granville]
Dearest Miutsie,

It was so good to have your letter this morning—I am distressed at Bridie—she is a brute and needs hitting on the head! Was so glad to know how you are feeling—but you are bound to feel on edge and tired until this horrid business is cleared up.

I was terribly depressed to see that Laval has taken over—and that Pétain did not <u>leave</u> France (there was a rumour that he would.) These are terrible days. But at least one sees the <u>possibility</u> of a swift release—at least by spring though perhaps that is too hopeful. Gerhart is fearfully worried about his parents! They were going to try to escape to Switzerland or Casablanca but he hasn't heard. He did not get the OWI job he had hoped for and now says he is waiting to be inducted into the army. Guenthe has been sent to Carson Camp in Colorado! Fritz is getting married (that is a <u>good</u> thing!)

Do give Anne our love when you see her—I have wanted to write but have been snowed under with letters to answer, very little time off—I am standing it very well which makes me happy: tummy behaving well for a change! I will have given 8 informal lectures (to classes) 3 hours of conferences, 3 hours reading my poems at receptions, etc. as well as lunches in different parts of the campus, every <u>meal</u> in a new place where I am expected to shine! All in three days. It is quite a thing. But the great thing is that I have cracked through and made a <u>dent</u> in the apathy. 8 students came 1/2 hour late to a creative writing class last night (I talked to them for 2 hours) and as much for Miss Shannon's sake as for my own, I gave them Hell. It is <u>too</u> rude. Afterwards they were grateful—they always are. That is the nice thing. The reason most of them were late was some Sorority business. That's what made me mad. The extra-curricular activities have an unholy importance here.

The President's wife has invited me to spend the night over there tonight so I shall escape from the dorm—and I hope have a chance for a talk with the Pres. whom I have hardly seen. Unfortunately his emphasis is on advertising the college, so he speaks of publishing a book of Denison poetry— and I haven't seen <u>one</u> even fairly good poem—yes, just <u>one</u> written of course by one of the girls from the co-op—a swell girl, the thoughtful girls and boys back me up 100% now on all I say to them and I am hoping they will <u>carry through</u> later. And I think I have been a help to Eleanor Shannon who has poured out all her teaching problems on me—and is <u>so</u> grateful and delighted with the little I can do. So it is <u>not</u> in vain—and that is the main thing.

It is raining—the chapel bell is ringing—and I must go.

Love

[   ]

Bridie: The Sarton's maid, suffering from what Eleanor Mabel Sarton calls "convalescent irritability."

Laval: Pierre Laval, Premier of France.

Pétain: Henri Phillipe Pétain, Marshall of France.

Gerhart: Gerhardt Speyer, a German refugee friend.

OWI: Office of War Information.

Guenthe: Guënther Speyer, brother of Gerhardt whose father had been killed in the war; George Sarton became their sponsor.

TO BRYHER   December 12th, 1942
[Channing Place]
Dearest Bryher,

I am filled with the "seraphic shame" of those to whom largesse is given, all un-deserved for I have been the world's worst correspondent for months! But now after six weeks' talking my head off in colleges in Ohio and western Pa. and West Va. I am back in this gray room—and on my desk was Elisabeth's little book, yours on learning German, France Libre, a Life and Letters each a separate blazing coal on my head! What can I do about it except sing hosannahs that there are such people in this year, in this world! I refuse to be motivated by guilt an instant longer—I am not going into a factory until I have to. Six weeks being useful and the month of furious writing poetry before I left have convinced me that I must try to find something more useful first. The need is not great enough <u>yet</u>—of course in another three months we may be all drafted. So that's that. And I refuse to feel guilty about not letter-writing either. There are times when one can, times when one can't. In the times when an enormous amount of living is going on, one can't.

It was great to feel useful again—to feel one had something in one's hand that could satisfy hunger. And God knows fiery and fierce teachers and believers are needed out there. I am going to fight like hell to get a job—you see, they are still isolated in little towns, hardly reading the newspapers. Even Pearl Harbor has only made the war an evil necessity: at heart they haven't changed, have no hope, are not dreaming of building a future, they are pacifists (in a negative sense) at heart. They waste time revolting against war instead of revolting against the inertia which made the war inevitable. Also—and this is even more serious—they are fearfully sentimental. They live in a perpetual BE★KIND★TO★ANIMALS★WEEK. The poems I read were many of them political (though of course I read the great Sitwells and some on a deeper level) and of course the discussions all turned round the world, not poetry—which is all right, for poetry should enter into life, bring life in the moment to a blazing meridian, clarify, deepen, make wholes out of fragments. However when there were questions the question that most concerned them—it came back over and over—was "How shall we prevent too great cruelty to the Germans?" Never never a question about the Greeks, the Poles, the confusion of France. They are mesmerized by Germany. They are mesmerized by a false pity for the to-be-conquered. They have not imagined what the Nazis are. Sentimentality is the greatest danger for America. We are not realists—we are materialists (which is another thing) and sentimentalists, at our worst. At our best we are realists and idealists. All the potentialities are there. But as it is now, we have to wait for a war to make men of the boys—there is no intellectual discipline so the army discipline is better than nothing. I have been amazed and hurt to see how they grow in the army and how we have failed to make them grow outside it. So little is asked of them. Well, you can see that I blazed away and perhaps created a small stir which something else much later will fertilize—or not. It is maddening to stay in a place three days, enter into the life of the place, learn all the needs, and then have to leave just when you are beginning to penetrate and be penetrated. I could only light fires, clear the ground a little, not plant anything. What they need is to learn how to write a sentence, to respect and pay homage to the english language, be <u>seared</u> of their fearful incompetence and laziness.

And then the heroic teachers, here and there, backed up so little, exploited mercilessly by the students (who have no awe) expected to give their <u>blood:</u> "Come on, make it interesting, amuse us"—and then be given a slipshod theme in return. But of this we build the civilization which the politicians like to imagine is the hope of the world. And yet it is not discouraging because the untapped energy and imagination, the power, the will are all there. They are so young, so ready, so un-spoiled and they know what they want in a dim sort of way, only not enough to go out and get it. They come from families where there has never been a book and whose highest ambition is to get their daughter into the right Sorority. Well, I'll stop this spiel.

Things have changed in Cambridge since I got back. It is a great relief to be really cold, as we are here in our house, heated by oil. The oil is going to Africa, glory be to God! We are experimenting with coal in a grate (which covered the walls with soot yesterday) and I sit in a blanket, rejoicing. There is no beef to be bought—no tea for weeks (I managed to get a few quarter-pounds in the west and sent them east—none here)—sugar, butter rationed—<u>at long last.</u>

I spent a wonderful five days in New York, dimmed out and beautifully dark but still horribly the luxury city of the world. But I saw the people I wanted to see—had long talks with Muriel Rukeyser. Her book on Gibbs is <u>the</u> book of the year. A statement of faith. It has majesty. Do you know her? She is the America one believes in, would fight for—huge, magnanimous, as great as her powers, of gigantic appetites—and a sturdy inward <u>line</u> which makes her discipline power that could very easily become chaotic. She tried to get a Guggenheim for this book and was turned down—two weeks ago Moe called her up on the phone and apologized for their fatal mistake! But she is all right now, has a good job on OWI, and a magnificent office on the 25th floor, a cell with a huge window looking down the west-side, seeing the whole span of the river to the tip of Manhattan. She may make lousy posters but she will write good poetry up there—she won't be able to help it.

I am going back to N.Y. after Christmas and stay there somehow until I land a job. It will never happen here. I live so many little lives here—there are so many interruptions and little things to do. It is a sterile place for me now Edith is dead. There is no reason to stay. Long ago I should have cleared out but mother was ill—and what was it? A lack of psychic energy or something. I felt baffled. I keep waiting for something to happen. Now I shan't wait any longer.

In five days in New York I lived more than I have in years, knew more and felt the roots growing—I came back full of powers.

I have sat at this desk for three days clearing it out and getting to the place where I can start writing again. It is awful what six weeks accumulated stuff can take of time. I haven't opened the books you sent because I must finish Gibbs first and because I want to read them well. If I get a job I'll send Gibbs to you on my first check. At present I am saving fiercely to be able to stay in N.Y. a month and don't dare spend a cent for fear I'll get caught and I feel it is now or never.

The Darlan business makes one sad. What a pity that we have had to compromise at the very beginning. The French are confused enough without that! If only it would have been <u>clear</u> where we stood. I do not trust the military mind, at least the American military mind. And I am afraid it has made the English sore which is a pity. I hope they are sore. I hope pressure is brought to bear. O this everlasting <u>politics</u>—what are people saying about it all?

The landscape in West Va. and up the Ohio river was very beautiful— delicate and sober with a <u>fineness,</u> little color but that very fine—sepias and soft beiges and black trees, and the flash of blue on the river. The coal towns are still more terrible than anything I know in America—but the farms are beautiful, the great silos, the white porches, the big red barns.

What are you reading? H. D.'s poem—the shell—was a blessing. I have read it many times. I will write to her but doesn't she owe me a letter? And eventually you will get—very late—a New Year poem I am having cheaply printed. My whole life will be settled—at least for a few years—in the next weeks. Pray for me—or wish—I hope it will conform to what Muriel calls "the wishes of history"—I hope it will.

Love,

Moe: Henry Allen Moe, long-term director of the Guggenheim Foundation.

Edith: Edith Forbes Kennedy died on September 18, 1942. She was Sarton's oldest and dearest friend in Cambridge; the poems in *Inner Landscape* are written for her.

Darlan: French Admiral Jean-François Darlan (1881–1942), important member of the Vichy government whose role as such was ambiguous; assumed position as high commissioner in French North Africa and West Africa with Anglo-American approval, but was assassinated.

TO GEORGE SARTON   Jan. 5th, Monday [1943]
[New York (MHH)]
Dearest Daddy,

It was a great blessing to find your good letter in my box when I got in last night after having dinner with Gerhart—as I knew you would be worried about this year and was relieved to know in more detail—Also I was deeply touched by what you say about my job and I am sure you are right. My plan is to go next week when I come back from Theo's to the teachers' agencies <u>first</u> and then to try to get in touch with people in OWI. There <u>are</u> possibilities I'm sure only one must un-earth them and that means seeing many people before you hit the one person who has a job to offer.

We do not need to decide about the apartment—mother knows more about the cost of living than you—and I am not at all sure that an apartment is the solution. The Browns pay $75.00 for 3 <u>miserable</u> rooms. We would need four at least. We would have to have someone come in to get dinner (that is mother's <u>lowest</u> ebb of the day and I know she couldn't do it). It is <u>very</u> expensive to eat out and mother rarely has the strength to <u>go out</u> and eats periodically nothing at supper time and to get someone to come in to cook one meal would be as expensive as having Bridie stay nearby. I am in favor of looking for a small <u>house</u> in an <u>unfashionable</u> part of Cambridge or part of a house like Agassiz St. off Harvard Sq. for instance, and of having a maid. I do not think mother is strong enough to do the work. <u>Cleaning, beds</u> (heavy work for any one), <u>cooking, washing up</u>—You do not imagine how much work in the house mother does <u>now,</u> even with Bridie—3 or 4 hours of work in the house every day. Of course if I were home I could help—but if I have a job I won't be able to).

I am sure there <u>is</u> a solution and that we can find it—but don't make an <u>arbitrary</u> decision without letting mother go into all possibilities. Perhaps she could do the work for a couple of years but after that I <u>know</u> she couldn't and therefore it is better to find a more permanent solution if possible.

It would be better for mother to <u>earn</u> the extra amount necessary for a maid by giving private lessons in design (which she enjoys) than to do housework which <u>exhausts</u> her without in any way satisfying. Dear Daddy, I know you will do what is best—and this is not meant as criticism but only to beg you to leave some of the responsibility to mother. She will find a way (when she knows exactly what she can have to spend). <u>She always has.</u> I wish you would talk it over together with Anne Thorp who is very sensible—and above all don't worry too much. We have the rest of this year in our dear old house and after that, we will find a way by putting our hearts and heads together.

We are having a sort of blizzard and after doing some errands, I am settling in to write letters for the afternoon. Tonight I am supping with Muriel—tomorrow go out to Theo's—

I won't take a job that means only money, but I am sure that by September I shall have found something. And I hope, <u>long</u> before that.

Meanwhile, all my love, dear Pater Familias—I am so happy that you wrote me as you did—

A hug

[   ]

TO PARENTS   Jan. 6th [1943]
[Poughquag]
Dears,

It is all blue outside with that snow-blue and very cold. I have had such a nice peaceful day—Theo has been working in the barn to make a frame for a Gauguin reproduction she is putting over the mantel—Kate has been resting and feeding the cows, and I have been writing letters and resting and reading. It is marvelous not to have to go out for meals—we have all our meals sitting in front of the fire in the living room. The country is really very beautiful—big windswept bare hills and little farms with red barns sheltered in the valleys—the hills are smooth like sleeping elephants.

I am learning a lot about farming! They weigh the milk each cow gives and then feed her exactly in proportion to the milk—if they are away and the hired man who is lazy doesn't do this, there is an immediate difference in the yield. When it went 25 below in that cold spell one cow's udder <u>froze</u>, poor thing. Noë and Penny, the two dogs patter about the house like two little people and sometime have great boxing matches with the cat who loves them and is always trying to make them play. Then to make up the family there are Flora, a "great person" as Theo says and her husband Simmy, two coloured people—Flora especially is a wonder—laughing all day. She loves the country and hates N.Y. so it is good for her to be here.

Theo and Kate are giving a party on Sunday for all the neighbors.

I was so happy to have mother's letter and all the news it included—darling Miutsie! I hope it is not too cold there. Perhaps by now Anne will be in to see her—I have it in my heart to write to her but I made a list of 30 letters I owed when I arrived here so I am trying to get that off first and then write some of the letters I really want to write.

I have now a long list of people to see about jobs so perhaps something will come of one or other of them. I go back to N.Y. on Sat. and am hoping to see Miss Lockwood of Vassar on that day. There is no immediate prospect but I think it is a good idea to see her anyway.

I had a sweet letter from my friend at Sweet Briar, the girl I helped to get a job there—and she says they are losing teachers thick and fast so the agencies may also turn up with something. Now that I am feeling better I am full of hope. I have stopped taking paregoric and am just taking belladonna which the Dr. said to take for ten days. It is mild and soothing and I have no cramps.

There have been several good letters about the poem, one dear one from Ada Russell—I'll send them along later.

It is too bad about Harper's but I'll try elsewhere.

I am rather tired after writing letters all day—so so long for the present. Give each other a kiss from me—

[   ]

————

Kate: unknown, friend of Theo Pleadwell.

the poem: Christmas broadside, "Celebrations" 1943.

Ada: Ada (Mrs. Harold) Russell, companion and general *factotum* to American poet, Amy Lowell.

TO PARENTS   Jan. 16th, 1943, Sat.
[New York (HA)]
Dear Ones,

It is the warmest spring weather—my cold is a little better but I have an awful cough and feel rather seedy and sleep whenever I get the chance like an old cat!

Today for the first time I see a glimmer of hope at OWI—I had a long good talk with one of the head people in the writing of radio scripts for overseas—Molly Jay Thatcher—a Vassar grad. And she has given me a trial script to write for Tues. on Main St.—the idea of these 15-minutes "platters" (meaning records) is that they are sent over to neutral countries like Sweden and South Africa—countries where there has been considerable Nazi propaganda and are played by small stations. They are not short-waved from here. And their main purpose is to tell the people a little bit about America, what we are like, what we mean and so on. I think it will be quite fun to work on this script—and Gerhardt very kindly went to the Public Library and brought down for me a book called Hometown that he remembered had lots of pictures of small town streets in it. This will be a great help. So there really is hope. The difficulty is that although they need good writers desperately, they are short on funds and this Congress is being very mean. However Miss Thatcher thought there would be a shake-up with some people fired pretty soon and that would be my chance. She was quite encouraging. I don't know what they pay, but I imagine at least $50 a week.

If only I felt well for a change, I would be happy. There was no mail today which is funny, but sometimes it comes late at night.

Gerhardt has been taken back by Bloomingdale's but at a tiny salary—he can't understand why he hasn't been called up. It is out of the question for him to get any interesting job now as he is I-A and I think the waiting around is nerve-wracking.

Did I tell you that I am going out to Van Loon's on Monday for lunch?

Yesterday I had tea with Frances Hawkins who did some publicity for me in the theatre long ago and now works at the Museum of Modern Art—we sat in that lovely big room at the top and had tea and a good talk—before that I spent an hour at the 20th century portraits show—but was a little disappointed. Perhaps it is hard to look at a great many portraits all together— I liked the Vuillards almost the best—there were several hideous portraits by a <u>Balthus</u> (called French)—are there two Balthus's? These were very flat and all in browns. I still haven't seen the big show at the Metropolitan—the fact is, that I just don't feel well. Seeing the people I have to see and writing letters becomes a great task—it is tiresome, but I am cheerful on the whole, and everyone is very kind. Muriel has been angelic and Gert last night was sweet. Her poodle, Porgy, has become absolutely <u>entrancing</u>—I couldn't take my eyes off him!

I'll send this special so you know there is a slight hope about a job. I do not at all count on it, but I shall enjoy having a chance to show what I can do. Of course radio is a very special technique—I hope you have a peaceful Sunday and that it is warm there. Here it is really heavenly and I have great fun riding up and down the buses—

A special Sunday hug to each—

[   ]

1-A: Military draft status indicating extreme eligibility.

Balthus: In 1948 in Belgium, Sarton met an old painter, Georges Baltus who did a drawing of her. His wife was the poet Adreienne Revelard. The Balthus referred to here is Count Balthasar Klossowski de Rola, (1908–), French born of Polish parents, internationally famous for his poignantly erotic work.

TO MARGARET FOOTE HAWLEY   Jan. 21st [1943]
[New York (HA)]
Darling,

A line before I rush out into the snow to have dinner uptown and I am late. Geoffrey is all right, back at work and I had dinner with him very quietly, dearly and soberly on Monday—I felt he was tired—I was tired and something didn't perhaps quite come off. We missed you of course. We drank brandy and he said propaganda was no use which coming as it did on top of my almost landing a job in OWI somewhat dampened my spirits. I expect he is right. Still, the job looks like heaven, a fat salary, writing scripts for radio about America for Turks and Swedes—the mildest form of propaganda in that it is not war-news but a Dept. called Outpost which tries to give some idea of the way Americans live and what we are like. I would like to do a set on different small towns like Amherst, Eureka Springs Arkansas and a small town in Texas. I did them a feeble sample on Main St.—and in about two weeks I'll know the worst. All the people I saw I liked—there are lots of MEN (cheers!) and it really would be a new life opening out. But I don't dare hope too much. Meanwhile I have recklessly turned down two badly paid teaching jobs with a wild sense of relief.

I wish you were here—it was good to know that you are well—I bet the wild life of Fla. must get pretty upsetting at times, but enjoy the sun—and the work. Mrs. H. sounds wonderful but impossible, but maybe it will suddenly come out beautiful. And meanwhile the man sounds good. When do you come back? I'll be here till Feb. 1st anyway—and I hope forever. Love and love

[ ]

I have given a wrong impression of Geoffrey—but I'll explain when we meet. I do <u>love</u> him you know.

———

Margaret Foote Hawley: Portrait painter and miniaturist, sister of Roswell Hawley whom Sarton knew at Gloucester; her works are in the permanent collection of the Metropolitan Museum of Art in New York.

Geoffrey: Geoffrey Parsons (1879–?), American journalist, won the Pulitzer in 1942. He was Margaret Foote Hawley's lover and editor of the editorial page of the *Herald Tribune*.

teaching jobs: One, a school in Vermont, the other in Plainfeld, New Jersey.

Mrs. H.: unidentified.

TO PARENTS   Jan. 21st Thurs. [1943]
[New York (HA)]
Dears,

I had lunch with Louis Untermeyer who is working in Outpost—the dept. I am trying to get into of OWI—he was very kind and hopeful and invited three other men from the dept. for lunch—one was Jerome Weidman who writes for the New Yorker and is leaving tonight for Moscow (we guessed he wasn't allowed to tell.)—I felt they all liked me and I am hoping that they are really considering me there. I haven't heard anything from Thatcher—but Muriel saw Nick Ray the man who introduced me to her and said he was really enthusiastic. Everyone likes him in the office and he is quite a power. The whole trouble is that nothing will be known for at least ten days probably two weeks and I don't dare come home which is what I would like to do as on the other hand, it might be decided quite quickly and if I weren't on the spot someone else would be taken. There is obviously going to be some sort of shake-up very soon.

Then last night I had dinner with Ted Adams who was really dear and very eager to help—he writes the show for "We The People" and thinks that I might get into direct war-propaganda on the commercial radio—there is some Gov. work on that. Not OWI. And he is trying to get hold of one of the top people for me to see. Ted is a wonderful salesman of anyone he believes in and he does believe in me. I found him rather jittery, poor soul—it is a fearful time for a young man, to know what is best to do. He was turned down by the War-Labor board, I mean the draft board, because of his nerves and now he is going to a psychiatrist.

I am feeling fairly sanguine as a matter of fact. It is worth sticking around. The only thing is I would like to get my teeth into <u>something</u> soon—

The Bondis who have a school, in Vermont and whom I saw yesterday at the Teachers' agency are angelic people and they wanted me for the job (called up again today to see if I had changed my mind) but it is a small very family school where there would be no escape, all meals with the children, five hours teaching a day—history and english. History, with no time to prepare at all, frightened me. Salary $800 with board and room which of course is much better than Plainfield. But as time goes on I am more sure that college teaching would be better for me and a writing job better than either. One thing about OWI is that the people in it are swell people, mostly writers and painters and I would be meeting some men for a change! In a school one is pretty isolated. I keep in mind what Daddy said about being very sure it was the right job as whatever I decide now may influence my whole future so profoundly.

Poor Rollo Brown. It is fearful—I wish I could think of something. Has he any lectures?

It is snowing and very cold but I feel fine. I am going up to Gert's for dinner—

Dear dear love

[   ]

Louis Untermeyer: (1885–1977), American poet and anthologist, author of several books of criticism, short stories, a novel, and a collection of compact biographies, *Makers of the Modern World.*

Jerome Weidman: (1913–), American novelist, short story writer, and playwright known for *I Can Get it for You Wholesale.*

Nick Ray: Active in New York theatre groups in the mid-1930s; had a CBS radio program about folk singers; head of the popular and folk music department of the OWI.

TO PARENTS   [January 23, 1943]
[New York (HA)]   Sat. afternoon
Dear ones,

It looks like snow. It is five o'clock and in a few minutes Claude will be here—I am glad as I was a little anxious about him. I have just come back from a good interview with Molly Thatcher who gave me an excellent hour of talk and criticism about my script. Now I am to re-do it and bring it in early in the week and she will then take it to Housman—everything depends on him and, as far as I can make out, what mood he happens to be in so it is quite a peril! She thinks that they might then take me on for a trial week—but she warned me not to hope too much.

I shall rewrite it on Monday and tomorrow have a quiet day with Muriel—we are going to hear Povla Frisjh and I shall go to bed very very early—I did send Giorgio a wire and suggested dinner tomorrow night but in any case I shall firmly go to bed, so as to be fresh in the morning.

Did I tell you that I got an advance copy of Helen's novel? It makes me very sad because I do not think it is very good—somehow it never rises or goes deep enough so that the people do not seem <u>important</u>—but I think the medium, all diaries and letters is most difficult. It is difficult to get any <u>texture</u> or variety. The main thing is that one is not terribly interested in what Helen has to say about <u>life</u> and in the end what one wants from a novelist is, I think, a world within the world, which is that person's <u>creation,</u> an interpretation of life.—but in the end this is an analysis of a second-rate man and she doesn't make one care enough about him one way or another. It is called "The Whole Heart."

This morning I was working here and put on the radio and heard the whole Appassionata Sonata beautifully played by [Rudolf] Serkin. It was lovely!

This is a feeble note but anyway will burst into Sunday—how I wish I was at home just for a few days, but the worst suspense ought to be over by the end of this week and sooner or later I must get back for a few days to get clothes and so on—and <u>bask</u> a little. I wonder how the house near the river was? Are you looking for a house to move into before Sept.? I do not quite understand—

I hope you have a good day and some music—How is the cat? I loved the description of her with the birds—

A kiss to each

[   ]

Claude: Claude Fredericks, a lost young man who attached himself to the Sartons.

Houseman: John Houseman [born Jacques Haussmann] (1902–?) Actor, director, producer. Came to the United States in 1924. Worked in the theatre in the late 1920s and 1930s, particularly with Virgil Thompson and Orson Welles; during the war was head of Overseas Radio Programming for the OWI. Artistic director of the American Shakespeare Festival; head of drama division of Juillard.

Povla Frisjh: Unidentified.

Giorgio: Marquis Giorgio de Santillana, historian of science, author.

Helen: Howe.

house question: The Sartons thought they were going to have to leave Channing Place.

TO HORACE AND MARYA [ZATURENSKA]
GREGORY   August 24th [1943]
[Newcastle]
Dear Horace and Marya—

I have come to ask a boon of your two selves. This is it: Muriel's exhibit "Words at War" made me see how fruitful the connection between writers (critical of the covers of books) and the library might be. For a long time I had also thought of the concerts at the National Gallery in London, open to the public, as a war-gesture and wished the poets here in America could do something of the sort.

After the exhibit Mr. Hopper, director of the library, was anxious to go on from there and I suggested a series of readings, freely offered by the poets and open to the public. The library will get up a show of Mss. and books for each poet.

Would you be willing to make one of these evenings yours? They will be from October 15th–Dec. 1st—You could choose your date I think. I believe it is asking a great deal but on the other hand it seems to me the purest and best gesture a poet can make (better than ostentatious "war-work")—would you? It will be a real blow if you can't. You were the first two poets we thought of—and after you it was even hard to imagine anyone else. The best would be if you would open the whole business.

I am writing to Marianne Moore, Louise Bogan (at the request of the library), Margaret Walker (young coloured poet), Muriel, you two, William Carlos Williams, Auden, Cummings, Langston Hughes and Benét (whom we have to ask as he was chairman of the Words at War thing—I shall suggest that he read some of Stephen and some of his own)—Two poets would read at each evening. If you have any ideas, do let me know. It seemed good to have a rather catholic group to begin with—with as much variety as possible and established enough to command an audience. If it goes well we would do 6 more in he spring and invite some young and less known poets—or old and less known like me!

I'll be here till Aug. 28th—After that 5. East 10th c/o Muriel—
Let us meet soon anyway—

Yours faithfully
May Sarton

Horace and Marya [Zaturenska] Gregory: See footnote to April 12, 1942 letter to Bryher.

Stephen: Stephen Vincent Benét (1898–1943), man of letters, poet, author of *John Brown's Body,* younger brother of William Rose Benét (1886–1950), one of the founders of the *Saturday Review,* writing "The Phoenix Nest" column.

TO HORACE GREGORY   Wed. October 20th, 1943
[22 East 10th Street]
Dear Horace,

The Triumph of Life has travelled out to Ohio and back since I saw you—with Rollo Walter Brown, who was off lecturing, a dear old man. And since then I have had it in my portfolio with stuff for the office, stealing it out during the interminable time-wasting waits and interruptions (a peculiarly hellish five days as a matter of fact) and being nourished. It is a boon and a blessing.

I cannot bear a great many things—to have missed the autumn. There is a small pile of leaves someone sent me to look at but here the trees go dusty. There was just that glimpse of purple asters and goldenrod the day I came out—and this missing of a season seems to me a terrible and wicked thing.

> "I loved my life, I desired joy
> This was a fault, this was a toy"

Of course there are poems everyone who reads at all would choose to put in—an anthology is always a teaser. This seems to me a perfect combination of discoveries and familiar poems. All the modern choices are so good.

Well, I cannot write a letter tonight. But I wanted to remind you that many people are looking forward to next Tues. eve and we shall expect you (and Marya I hope to listen) up in Mr. Hopper's office, second floor on the left as you go up the stairs, at 7:45. Last night was a great success from the point of view of audience—100 people had to be turned away—many stood. Next time there will be a loud-speaker in another room and extra chairs and we hope no one will be turned away. The room only seats a hundred. Also I have a feeling there may be fewer for the second—some will have been driven off by the crowd. Marianne Moore was a delight. Benét was almost unbearable and I felt quite sick at what is spoken in the name of poetry. But you and Williams will be another matter, thank heaven! I sat with my head bent and tried not to look miserable. I will be able to look up and rejoice on Tuesday.

I was hoping Marya would turn up in New York and pay a visit to this gray room which needs house-warming. Perhaps she will come later.

Let's all have a drink on Tuesday after the thing is over.

Yours to command
May

Last night: The first of The Poet Speaks series with Marianne Moore.

TO WINIFRED BRYHER   May 11th, 1944
[Channing Place]
Dear Bryher,

Two letters, from you and Hilda (dated 7th April) arrived yesterday and I answered yours first because I have been wanting to commune with you on paper for months—ever since your Feb. 14th letter! (Shocking!—I mean my silence) The fact is that I have been working like a beaver on the novel and am quite excited about it. It is so wonderful to be using the sap from my roots again, to feel the leaves pushing open. It is about Belgium between wars as I guess I wrote and I am finding it a great boon to have to re-create imaginatively and humanly many of the things I have thought and reasoned so much about. Now there is flesh on the bones, if you know what I mean. (All these images may make for poor style but they only show my fancy-free and liberated condition!) I have just sent 100 pages to the typist and it will go to my agent next week. He will try to get me a contract and a little money to live on while I finish it. It will be a long book as it covers twenty years and all the people have to grow, suffer and change considerably!

I must thank you again and again for the Libre France—every time one comes I catch my breath at the magnificent evocative photographs of France. And then O that heart-breaking magnificence of Sitwell's poem in the March L and L. Let us rejoice that someone other than Eliot now wears the mantle of greatness, the true fire, the wisdom that turns defeat into triumph over and over again. I do admire Eliot very much but I have always missed the "delicate scarlet tree" of blood in him. Which is a quote from Osbert Sitwell's Memoirs which I am reading with the utmost delight. There is a picture of Renishaw at the back of the jacket—do tell me about it, are there any flowers now? Or is still a garden of shade and light and green only?

O dear how I long for a talk. There was a time when I felt I simply couldn't talk in letters any longer and so I was silent. But the spring is here and one must communicate in whatever way there is. When I wonder shall I see you in the flesh and you cease to be a purely metaphysical friend? Perhaps before two more years are out—

The tragic thing about learning from experience is I fear that one can only learn from one's own experience. Other peoples—other nations'—experiences simply do not help. They can be imaginatively learned from. But people do not *act* on other people's experiences.

More and more the war looks to me like a world civil war where over and over again the pattern is repeated—the sell-out to fascism from fear of revolution. The awful thing is that it might still happen here. In England (and you are alone in this) you will as always manage it seems to make the transition quietly and sensibly. With the aristocratic tradition (as opposed to big money interests) a tremendous help. Here there is no aristocracy so the lines will be more hard and fast.

It is interesting that both in China and Jugoslavia national armies are fighting "communist armies" instead of the fascists. Chiang Kai Shek as you know better than I no doubt, keeps his best fighting men on the Chinese Front against the Red Armies—and the Mihailovich armies spend their strength decimating the Partisans. The fear of Russia is beginning to loom large everywhere. O God help us! Let it not all happen <u>again!</u>

I have suddenly become a fierce and passionate gardener after all these years of regarding my mother as a sweet madwoman! I can hardly bear to spend all morning at my desk. And we have finally decided to buy this house where my parents have lived for ten years and where mother has built a garden out of wilderness and Daddy tames a flock of pigeons to nest on his balcony (what a mess they make too but he loves them!) I am greatly relieved that they will be settled here and not have the nightmare of moving ahead. The house was about to be sold and torn down by a speculator who wanted to build three small houses on the land. The neighbors are as relieved as we!

So mother and I have had an orgy of transplanting, sowing a huge seedbed for a picking garden and taking hundreds of tulips out and great masses of phlox and poppies. It has been a job. Mother is planting seeds this minute and calls out what she is putting in like the stations from a train "salpiglossis, zinnias, petunias" etc. etc.

Daddy has at last finished his ten-year work on the 14th century and has already started a book on early science, written book this time (not a giant bibliography) in which he can pour some of his wisdom in his very beautiful and personal style. I think I must get him to send you some reprints from Isis—I would like you to know what he is like.

You are dead right about racial prejudice. Here it is assuming frightening proportions. The Catholic Church may have something to do with it as gangs of Irish boys have been attacking jewish boys right here in Boston. However a citizens' committee is at work now on the problem and people's anger and imagination is at last roused. I cannot see why we do not open our doors to thousand and thousands of jews—there is thousands of miles of arid land that could be reclaimed just as they have reclaimed Palestine. But all we do is agitate about Palestine and blame everything as usual on the British or the Arabs or anyone but ourselves. I get mad as we say in American.

I must go off to the Doctors—trying to get rid of a sinus is like getting rid of a persistent weed in the garden. Why I wonder are weeds so much stronger than anything else?

Have you read Agnes Smedley's wonderful book on China?—If not I'll try to send it over. Be sure to let me know.

Lots of love—

[   ]

I'll write Hilda shortly. Tell her to have nothing to do with Houghton Mifflin. They are making millions on Lloyd Douglas and have hardly published a distinguished work for years. They use up all their paper on best-sellers. They are becoming a sort of Sears Roebuck as far as I can see! Random House is good—I would make a try for Harcourt Brace first. I have a friend at Random House, Robert Linscott if H. D. wanted to write to him. But why doesn't she send the book to an agent? Mine is Diarmuid Russell (A. E.'s son) at 522 5th Ave. Their official name: Russell and Volkening. I hear they are good and care about good writing. So many agents are only interested in the big money—Sat. Eve. Post writers!

———

L and L.: Life and Letters.

Osbert Sitwell's Memoirs: The first of his four-volume autobiography *Left Hand, Right Hand* entitled *The Cruel Month.*

Renishaw: The great Gothic Sitwell estate dating from the fourteenth century.

Agnes Smedley's book on China: Battle Hymn of China, Agnes Smedley (1943).

Lloyd Douglas: Lloyd Cassel Douglas (1877–1942), enormously popular novelist held in ill repute by the critics for his didactic use of the novel form, his emotional effects, and his superficial characterizations. His works included *Magnificent Obsession* and *The Robe.*

Diarmuid Russell: Sarton's literary agent at Russell & Volkening. Son of Irish poet AE (or A.E. or Æ.) pseudonym of George William Russell (1867–1935).

TO MARGARET FOOTE HAWLEY   May 18th [1944]
[Channing Place]
Dearest Margaret,

Heaven knows how long it is since I was so delighted to discover you were reading Flaubert-Sand. Aren't they dear letters? I copied out long passages from them when I read them a couple of summers ago. One forgets what a really grand old bird she was, so full of heart, so warm and wise. And of course

Sarton with her mother, Eleanor Mabel Sarton, Christmas 1914.

Sarton with her father, George Sarton, Ogunquit, Maine, August 1916.

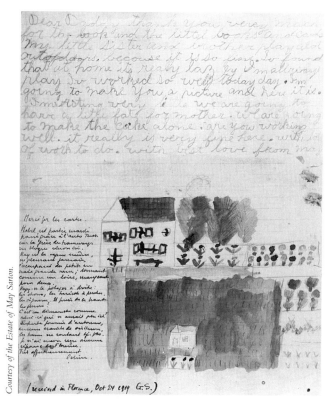

Letter to her father, October 1919.

May Sarton, Christmas 1918.

Program for Nala and Damayanti *performed at the Gloucester School of the Little Theatre in the summer of 1923. Sarton, age 11, was the manager of the play (see footnote page 28).*

NALA AND DAMAYANTI

May Sarton, 1923.

Eleanor Mabel Sarton, June 1915.

Sarton at the Gloucester School of the Little Theatre,
c. 1928.

Anne Longfellow Thorp, c. 1928.

*Marie Gaspar, Blanche Rousseau, and Marie
Closset; the "Peacocks" as Sarton called them,
c. 1931.*

George Sarton, c. 1929.

May Sarton (right) in The Swan, *a play by Ference Molnar performed at the Gloucester School of the Little Theatre, August 8–9, 1930.*

Sarton in an early, unidentified production, c. 1932.

Willem Van Loon, c. 1931.

May Sarton, c. 1932.

Leo Baekeland, March 1919.

Sarton with Theodora Pleadwell,
1934.

Mariea Stiasni and Julian Huxley, Australia, 1937.

Julian Huxley, c. 1937.

Julian Huxley, c. 1937

Polly Thayer Starr, c. 1930.

Edith Forbes Kennedy, c. 1937.

May Sarton with Juliette and Julian Huxley at Savanah Wood, England, June 1937.

May Sarton at work on The Single Hound *in Jean Dominique's studio, Uccle, Brussels, 1937.*

Grace Dudley and "Jammy," c. 1938.

Marie Armengaud, Santa Fe, New Mexico,
c. 1941. Painter unknown.

Lugné-Pöe and Suzanne Duprès,
c. 1939.

Rollo Walter Brown and Polly Brown, c. 1941.

Courtesy of the Estate of May Sarton.

Ruth Pitter, 1962.

Photograph by Tornow of Lausanne.

Hilda Doolittle, 1946.

Courtesy of the Estate of May Sarton.

Judith Matlack and May Sarton, Santa Fe, New Mexico, 1945.

Photograph by Haniel Long. Courtesy of Helen Long.

May Sarton, Santa Fe, New Mexico, May 1, 1945.

Photograph by May Sarton.

Juliette Huxley, c. 1946.

Photograph by Jim Booth.

Bill Brown and May Sarton at Muriel Rukeyser's apartment in New York City, c. 1940.

Photograph by May Sarton.

Celine and Raymond Limbosch, c. 1949.

Photograph by Alice Long. Courtesy of Helen Long.

Haniel Long at Sena Plaza, Santa Fe, New Mexico, 1950.

Courtesy of the Estate of May Sarton.

Marianne Moore, c. 1950.

Eleanor Mabel Sarton, c. 1950.

S. S. Koteliansky and James Stephens, c. 1951.

Peggy Pond Church, c. 1951.

Bill Brown, c. 1957.

Marie Closset (Jean Dominique), 1942.

May Sarton, c. 1930.

I have always had a special feeling for him—the saint of writers because he was so humbly a servant of his art, so truly pure. That is rare. One saw it too in V. Woolf.

What happened to me was that I really fought out those hundred pages of novel (finished early this month) and then of course felt fearfully tired and cross because I couldn't right away plunge into poems! Today I have just corrected the typist's job on the novel and am sending it off to Russell, the agent, to sell. Hold your thumbs for me! I thought as I read it that it was quite good, God forgive me. I was really delighted! I believe it has far more real humanity and appeal to human beings than the Hound. I have grown some since then—and it has some of the magic too that Belgium has always had for me. But it will be a long book—five or six hundred pages I'm afraid so it won't be done for ages. I'll have to write it now even if I can't land a contract on the first hundred.

Meanwhile the great great news is that we are in the act of buying this house so we shan't have to move—the old cellar stairs, the lilacs, even the stains on the ceiling will be ours! The first home we have had of our own since Wondelgem in 1914. It is wonderful for mother. And now we garden with newfound possessive fury! The fever has only just got me this year and I can hardly bear to sit up here and work on a cool day!

It's the end of the morning and I feel wonderfully stupid so forgive this effusion—I felt I must send you a word. As you say, one thinks of people more than one is able to write these strange suspended days. I hope some of the finishings-up, so nerve-wracking are finished up and you perhaps have a spell of peace and quiet or a nice continuity in which to paint someone who isn't always dashing off to war! I expect that won't happen. What of the pianist? Is that done? My mind has left me and I can't remember his name.

O Margaret, if you run into Osbert Sitwell's memoirs at the Club seize it and read it. It is an enchanting book, evoking everyone's childhood though his was such a special grandiose childhood—and what a picture of the english aristocracy, I suppose the most highly cultivated, eccentric and charming aristocracy the world has ever seen. It is rather sad that people will not be able to indulge such cultivated and expensive pleasures anymore! The gardens! The houses! It is all like a grown-up fairy tale. You will love it.

The OWI doesn't seem to need me for awhile as the education picture has been put aside temporarily for more urgent jobs. What are your plans?

Muriel gets back June 15th and I'll probably go off somewhere with her for a month or two. She may get sent overseas eventually as a correspondent. I am at present very happy here at home and would be glad to come back after the summer for several months to finish the book. I am really enjoying the housework, laundry, gardening and so forth. It is awfully <u>healthy</u>—you know?

Dear dear love, my darling—get some rest—when and where shall we meet?

[   ]

The Atlantic has taken a poem—

———

Atlantic poem: "Unlucky Soldier."

T O   B I L L   B R O W N   May 22d, 1944
[Channing Place]
Dear Bill,

It is raining, our first rain in two or three weeks and the garden is soaking it in but it makes such a green gloom everywhere now the leaves are out that the house is quite dark. I have just re-read your poems. The sonnet is almost really distinguished and I liked it better and better. Here and there it limps a little un-necessarily—I would cut "dead" in the 6th line or change haunted. It scans better without dead and both dead and haunted seem suddenly clichés when both used in the same line. The meaning of eight and nine—"the half-formed wish" doesn't seem to me quite as clear as it could be and "vast-complete" sound rather vague and abstract. If you could find a different word for "complete" it would do the trick. Even "concrete future" would give something for the half-formed wish to bounce against, something solid, but that I think is not quite your meaning. The end is beautiful. I like the poem better than any you have sent.

About the other, the last line still isn't quite it, to me. Housman you know used sometimes to wait a year for the line so don't get discouraged. It is too good not to have a perfect last line (and there are lots of rhymes luckily).

Your weary letter after the long march and the "infiltration" morning came just before tea. The heat on top of everything else sounds like sheer hell. At least it won't be as hot as that on the French beaches (at least not actually, I guess it will be figuratively speaking!) I think the crack through in Italy is most encouraging. It shows that long-prepared heavy defences can be cracked once we have sufficient air superiority, artillery and men. I wonder how heavy the losses in men have been. One doesn't hear but it doesn't sound too bad. I'm glad the French and Poles are having their innings!

I have had a too busy week—Ella came for last week-end very weary and bright-eyed and on edge but really so dear and she seemed to bask in the few hours of peace here. She loved the family. I went to a great gathering of poets the other night—the Gregory's, John Holmes, Robert Frost and a lot of aged women who apparently came to sit at Frost's feet. He held forth in a charming way being much the "homely philosopher." But he made me very sore by intimating that the war didn't interest him "now we knew who would win"! As if it were a baseball game and as if there weren't hundreds of men dying every day to see that we do win. The worst of it is that he is listened to as a God. I was the only person who dared talk back at all and I didn't really say what I felt, only suggesting that every day the war was prolonged it meant oceans of human suffering. Then he answered that he didn't need to be told about suffering, that he had lived with death all his life! somewhat off the point and what arrogance anyway. He has not lived in a concentration camp, that is one sure thing. It is a terrible sign of weakness not to be able to face other people's suffering and I fear it is an American weakness. We do not want to believe the worst. I have been writing bitter poems about that very thing—the American letter is turning into a long group of lyrics. I'll copy one out for you. It is very gradually taking shape and today I feel a little better about it. I have been dealing with the negatives and am anxious now to get into the hope and belief, the other side.

Sooner or later most people come to Cambridge if one sits here long enough! This week Freya Stark, that remarkable intrepid Englishwoman, Arabic scholar and lonely traveller all over Arabia and Persia into little explored regions is coming. She writes exquisite serene perceptive books about the near-east. It is curious what great styles Arabian travellers seem to develop: T. E. Lawrence, Doughty and Freya Stark. I think the Huxleys told her to look me up anyway I was immensely flattered to hear that I was one of four people here she had asked to meet and I am going to tea on Saturday. Daddy has dinner with her the night before—I am ashamed to say that I had not read her books which the family have long admired but I am now a convert and wandering the Valley of the Assassins in Persia with delighted eyes.

I'll tell you more about her next week (in our next installment!)

Spring has come and gone and now Cambridge is all leafy and one feels almost shut in by the trees. There are droves of mosquitos to break the peace of sitting in the garden. I suppose you are devoured by them too?

I'll take time to copy the poem—

Much love, dear Bill—O, would that this long horrific business were over and you were in the next part of the experience which may be more dangerous but can't possibly be quite as destructive of the spirit!

A hug

[ ]

Any more rumours about how long you will be there?

Bill Brown: William Theophilus Brown (1919–), artist, amateur musician, and lifelong friend of Sarton's whom she first met by chance in 1939 at Harrison Smith's on the eve of their both sailing on the *Normandie;* they met again on the *Normandie's* last voyage back. "Unlucky Soldier" in *The Lion and the Rose* is written for him.

Ella: Ella Winter, English writer, friend of Muriel Rukeyser's into whose townhouse Sarton moved after the Breevoort, author of *And Not to Yield.* Divorced from Lincoln Steffens, she married Donald Ogden Stewart, one of the "Hollywood Ten." Sarton wrote a poem in 1945, unpublished, for Winter's son Pete Steffens.

Freya Stark: Dame Freya Madeline Stark (1893–?), scholar. In addition to her travel books she also wrote poems and short stories.

Doughty: Charles Montagu Doughty (1843–1926), British explorer and poet, whose principal work is *Travels in Arabia Deserta.*

TO BILL BROWN   November 4th, 1944
[Channing Place]
Dearest Bill,

No word for quite awhile and I suspect you are in the thick of it. I am going to try a straight Air Mail for a change and see if I have better luck than with the three or four V-Mails I have sent until now. I think I'll start numbering my letters so you'll know if you've missed any.

We had our first letter from Belgium from the Limbosh this week via an American soldier! from our dearest friends, the Limbosh—they are all five alive (three daughters, father and mother)—though the middle daughter, Nicole, was in prison with 52 others and only escaped by a miracle. Somehow or other she was tried in Brussels and set free for lack of evidence—the 51 others were shipped to Germany and have not been heard from since! They say this occupation was incredibly much worse than the 1914–18 one—and Aunty Lino the mother devoted herself entirely to trying to help the Jews who were as everywhere abominably persecuted. She is on the village court which tries collaborators. The father has finished a new book of poems! She said that personally the privation of soap, was, next to the lack of liberty, the worst! There is apparently since the liberation no coal, no meat, almost no electricity but nobody complains they are so happy to be free. But one feels the dislocation, the fearful emotions of revenge (on Belgian traitors), the agony of the re-birth all through the letter. The Limbosh themselves are highly civilized and tolerant people with true greatness of soul and suffer from the inevitable injustices in any wide-spread clean-up such as is going on.

Here we are having one soft warm golden day after another and from my window I look out on a pure gold poplar tree against a blue sky—too lovely! I wish I could ship you some of this weather! I fear yours is unspeakable, muddy, cold, wet—how well I remember those grim Belgian winters when it is still dark at 7:30 A.M. and the wet cold eats into one. Do you have a sleeping sack I wonder? Or is that luxury only for officers?

I have been working along steadily at my book, full of doubts and an occasional great lift when I imagine it may be good! I had my first funny experience at the settlement where I had arranged to start a choral speaking group of negro children. Five (out of 17) turned up! They looked about ten years old and several couldn't read at sight. They sat there convulsed with giggles while I read them James Stephens' "Wave" a short poem, depending on sound. When I was through they were laughing so hard I had to ask why. Amid shouts of mirth they managed to say "It's so short!" Their own leader, polka-dotted tie etc. was on a shipyard gang at Pearl Harbor and swore when he came home that he would do something for the kids in Cambridge. I felt at once that he was afraid I would usurp his authority and so it was all rather ticklish. He is very simple minded, good and gentle—but had no idea what poetry or I meant! Well, the next day I called up the Centre and asked to have an older group who can at least read at sight and next week they are going to give me a new lot. I do hope I can do something. It is depressing that the public school education doesn't make it possible for a 14-year-old to read a poem through without a reading mistake, even after four or five times!

The election is getting progressively dirty and I live in terror that Dewey will get elected. They have pulled out the old <u>red</u> rabbit from their hats and are trying to link Roosevelt with the communists. The one thing they haven't had the audacity to say yet is that he is losing the war! They have tried everything else—the '29 depression was brought on by Roosevelt (I can't imagine just how!), he did not prepare for the war etc. etc. It is all rather sad as I think the Rep. under an honest man like Willkie could have made a very good case for themselves. I hope it is true that everytime Dewey speaks he loses votes, but I fear not.

The awful fact is that we are so far away from everything—I feel a terrible lack of generosity toward our Allies. I imagine this is not true among soldiers. It almost never is. But here at home I have recently heard people say such mean-nesses as that the Blitz was "highly over-rated," inferring that the British have been crying over nothing, that they are saving their men and allowing American boys to get killed to save their own, that the French really had a very easy time under the occupation etc. etc. One high Am. officer wrote home to his wife in disgust at the luxury of Paris—and it turned out that he had been living at the Ritz—one of two hotels that have hot water in Paris—and both given over to Allied officers! It makes me boiling mad.

The difficulty is of course to get an over-all picture—every single person in France doesn't bear the outward marks of suffering and so if a soldier sees one fairly prosperous village (and he doesn't see the dead, the sick etc. etc.) he decides that all of France is the same. Everywhere one hears contempt for the Italians because they are dirty and primitive—and I imagine that an army quartered in the deep South and seeing only poor whites and Negros would say the same. How are we ever to understand it all, the whole business and be both just and imaginative? I must say I begin to love the military and hate civilians almost as much as the proverbial soldier does!

Well to go from the sublime to the personal!—I am pleased because two of my poems have appeared in the English Best Poems of the year. I don't know yet which ones but two people have mentioned it in letters.

I sent you a fruit-cake long ago hoping it may get there for Christmas—I expect you'll have a plethora of them! But I didn't know what to send.

I think of you so much and when I get disgusted with people's lack of generosity I think of you dear Bill and your fine delicate sense of justice and your imagination about other people and then I am warmed inside and I think the Americans are about the best there is!

This afternoon I am going down to N.Y. for the week-end to see Muriel and to vote—and I hope, celebrate the election. Shumlin has definitely signed the contract for her play and I think a date of production will be set any day now. It is really marvelous! He liked very much the re-writing she has done. But Shumlin is desperately worried because Lillian Hellman is seven days overdue in Moscow—she was flown from somewhere on the west coast and they fear must have crashed. It would be a great loss. But of course they hope against hope to find them on an ice-floe or somewhere—and perhaps in my next I'll have good news about it.

I've been reading Katharine Anne Porter's book—it is very fine and in the last story about pre-Hitler Berlin, the most terrifying acid portrait of Germans I have ever read. The first stories are beautiful lyrical remembrances of her grandmother and her childhood in Texas. What are they giving you to read in the mud?

Dear dear love—
May

―――――

Dewey: Thomas E. Dewey (1902–1971), governor of New York, Republican candidate for president (1944, 1948). At this time most commentators predicted Dewey's victory; however, Harry S. Truman was reelected over Dewey by 303 electoral votes to 189.

Willkie: Wendell Lewis Willkie (1892–1944), American industrialist and political leader. Led fight (1942–1944) to liberalize Republican party, mainly attacking isolationism.

Shumlin: Herman Shumlin (1898–1979), producer and director of such notable plays as *The Children's Hour, The Little Foxes,* and *Inherit the Wind.*

Lillian Hellman: She was invited to Moscow by the Russians on a cultural mission, perhaps because she had written *North Star,* perhaps because of her Russian sympathies. The war in Europe made it necessary to fly to Fairbanks, Alaska where she was picked up by the Russians for the journey to Moscow. There is some question as to whether or not she visited Dashiell Hammett in the Aleutians. Although her trip had the endorsement of Roosevelt and Hopkins, the F.B.I. dogged her steps. Many stops were made on the flight across Russia merely to keep Hellman warm. Nevertheless she arrived in Moscow with pneumonia.

Katherine Anne Porter's book: The Leaning Tower and Other Stories (1944).

TO BILL BROWN   Dec. 25th, 1944
[Channing Place]
Dearest Bill,

Christmas day—the road is full of foot-prints and cat-prints in the snow and now it is raining and soggy. It is a sad Christmas full of heartache and I miss you and wonder where you are, eating heated up K. Ration and maybe humming carols shyly to yourself. The nicest part of Christmas here was when mother and I went to hear school children sing Bach chorals and carols in the beautiful courtyard of the Fogg Museum. Jaeger, the great German Greek scholar sat in front of us and didn't sing at all—he looked so inexpressibly sad and then when at last we all sang "Silent night all is calm all is bright" (It is the most beautiful of all isn't it?) he did sing and I was so glad—it seemed like a sign that there was a pure Germany to reach toward somehow over the guns and the Hell and all the wrongs done. And then I did enjoy yesterday going from house to house with poems and presents for all the children, seeing the trees set up and the smell of pine cones and snow. I now have on a yellow sweater which I dearly love—and, luxury of luxuries—I have a whole packet of cigarettes to smoke! They are as rare as <u>real</u> camels these days. We have a tiny tree and then we always put up the innumerable <u>Santons</u>, little figures of the crèche, the animals and then fifty or more wondering very <u>French</u> peasants who come to see with presents of a loaf of bread, a branch, a goose etc. They are very primitive little clay figures painted in bright colors but they are full of life and tenderness—and later we will have music in Daddy's study. But it is a lonely day all over the world this year. The Christmas story is really so beautiful and so full of hope and we are still so far from being able to live it in our hearts—

I have had to lay off for a week from the novel because of the old stomach kicking up but tomorrow I shall begin again and hope to carry right through to the end now. It has bogged down in a long conversation from which I couldn't extricate myself so I guess the break was a good idea anyway.

I'll copy a translation of a Rilke for you to find you in the New Year. God bless you dear Bill and keep you safe—

FROM THE LIFE OF A SAINT
And he knew fears, whose entrance closed on one
Sudden and insurmountable as death.
His heart pushed slowly through with labouring breath;
He brought it up just like a son.

Ineffable necessities he knew,
Rayless as lumber-rooms where children cry;
Obediently he gave his soul up too,
When she reached womanhood, that she might lie

Beside her bridegroom and her lord; while he
Remained behind without her, in a place
Where loneliness increased fantastically,
And never spoke and never showed her face.

But in return, after long time, the bands
Were loosed, and he achieved the happiness
Of holding, with a piercing tenderness,
Himself, like the whole creation, in his hands.

With dear love
[   ]

TO BILL BROWN   Jan 14th, 1945
[Channing Place]
Dearest Bill,

I was immensely glad to get your Dec. 29th letter (two days ago) because
I had of course suspected that you were in that Hell. It was reassuring to hear
you sound so cheerful in spite of it—the whole family was regaled by your
description of Dietrich! Poor woman—but you are so right about the New
Eng. faces. I hope I shall have the sense not to wear any make-up as time
goes on. Virginia Woolf for instance was so perfectly transparently beautiful
later on—but that is achieved from within as you say. Something has to go
on in the bean and I fear most of what goes on in Marlene goes on from the
waist down!

I did see the Vercors in Life and thought it very fine, honest and noble. It
did make one understand. I also read The Silence of the Sea—which would
make a wonderful play.

At the moment I am actually smoking a cigarette (great day!) so I can think
of your unsmoked combat ration without too much envy! It is awful that
you can say so very little of what you are doing and running into, but that
will have to wait. Meanwhile it is precious to be in some sort of communication even if the main part of your life is all hidden behind a curtain of snow,
guns and silence.

As for me, I am wildly excited since the novel is done. I have so many
ideas that I can't sleep—it really is a tremendous release of imagination. And
then The Tempest has come to Boston (Shakespeare's not the weather-man's)
Margaret Webster's production with the Negro—Canada Lee as Caliban and
Zorina as the most beautiful Ariel—Le Gallienne is helping out on lighting
and direction (unofficially) and called me up the other night to see it with
her. We had a marvelous talk—she is so fine, Bill, so delicate and deep compared to all other actresses—and so depressed because she needs a play and
there is none. I immediately starting cooking one up about a woman in the

French Resistance. If I could ever do it, it would serve a double purpose, to bring before people's eyes and make them experience something of France—and secondly give Le G. a real part where she can use the qualities she has, which are not sexual but intellectual and spiritual. She really was wrong as Luba in The Cherry Orchard and she talked very well about it—saying it was a tour de force and that she knew she was never really good in it by her own standards. As for my play, I know I must wait until this excitement is past, wait several months and see if it goes on growing and really roots itself in my mind. If it does, I might have a try at it. It would be a serious and grown-up love story as well—in the 3rd act the woman is completely changed, her hair gone white, her body broken by the Gestapo, but France is free and I think the scene when her Underground friend and she meet again could be very moving.

"The Tempest" is simply a miracle—all magic with wonderful strange music written by David Diamond and the set a small revolving island in the middle of the sea which turns before your eyes—the play is the deepest kind of magic. Do you remember "O brave new world, that has such people in it!" and the exquisite love scene with Miranda when she says "Here's my hand with my heart in't." If you can get hold of a copy do read it. It sings on in one's mind and it is really I think about the abuses of power, about freedom, about all the things we think about now.

But yes, how far away and evilly unconscious civilians must seem to all of you out there. We do not live by essentials but on trifles. Our agonies and pleasure are so <u>small.</u> And, worse, perhaps, we do not as a people yet understand The Enemy.

I had a fine letter from Muriel who sounds like herself again with in it this beautiful poem for Bernard (whom we saw for a moment at the Brevoort one night)

THE SURVIVOR
for a friend who went to Greece with the Commandos

Now he has become one who upon that coast
landed by night and found the starving army.
Fed on their cheese and wine. In those ravines
hidden by orphaned furious children lay
while cries and wounds and hour past hour of war
flamed past the broken pillars of that sky.

He saw the enemy. His head is full of faces
of the living, the brave, the pure and blazing alone
      fighting their domination to the end.
And now he sees the terrible rigid friend

whose domination must be fought. And now
he has become one given his life by those
fighting continually under a desperate star
and now he knows how many wars there are.

It occurs to me as I copy this that "Their" in line 3 of the second stanza is curiously weak. Otherwise it seems to me very clear and good and the last line so moving.

What, I wonder does the Stars and Stripes say about Greece?

As long as we do not ourselves take fuller responsibility now before the war is over, politically I mean, I do not think we can blame the British. But it is terribly tragic—there was a moving letter by a British Officer in Greece in the New Statesman, describing all the peasants coming down from the villages to parade in Athens for the EAM—with the priests, old people, children—and he says the Right is an extreme minority.

On Wed. I go to N.Y. to give two lectures at schools, one reading my own poems, and one on "Poets and the War" in which I shall read H.D. and Muriel and Sitwell and Marianne Moore (all the women!) and some soldier poems.

You speak of yours and I realize that I have not written about them yet in detail. I like best "The earth turns." As a whole they do not seem quite real, as if you had not got quite down to the <u>floor</u> of your mind. I wish you could try to get down some of the fighting experience—it would be one way to getting out some of how you feel in letters for one thing! For another, as a purely technical matter, it would force you to use more concrete images. Do have a try!

It is snowing and bleak. I have a wonderful storm coat for Santa Fe.

Darling Bill, all my love and many many thoughts accompanying you—always—

[ ]

Vercors: [Jean Marcel Bruller] (1902–), one of the most lyrical humanitarian writers to come out of the resistance, founder of Éditions de Minuit who published secretly his famous *Le Silence de la Mer.*

Margaret Webster: Anglo-American theatrical director and producer, daughter of Dame May Whitty. She and Eva Le Gallienne formed a professional as well as personal partnership with the American Repertory in 1946; she had her own Shakespeare Company from 1948 to 1951.

Canada Lee: [né Leonard Canegata] (1907–1954), New York-born black actor, first gained recognition in a revival of *Stevedore* at the Civic Repertory Theatre. Best known for his roles in Orson Welles' dramatization of *Native* Son and the film *Cry the Beloved Country,* 1942. He won additional laurels for this performance as Caliban.

Zorina: Vera Zorina (Eva Brigitta Hartwig) born in Berlin of Norwegian parents; became U.S. citizen in 1943. First soloist at the Ballet Russe of Monte Carlo, 1934–1936. Married George Balanchine.

French Resistance play: This was to become *The Underground River,* a play written for Le Gallienne, concerning the French Underground and published in 1947. Not produced at the time, it received its world premiere in October 1995 by the Chamber Players in Thomaston, Maine.

Bernard: Bernard Perlin, the artist. This poem "The Survivor," dedicated to him, was published as "His Head is Full of Faces."

EAM: Greek leftwing party.

Moving letter: See Appendix for "British Officer in Greece," unpublished.

TO BILL BROWN   Feb. 1st, 1945
[Channing Place]

Dearest Bill, I haven't heard from you for some time and wonder what is happening—I expect you are too cold and weary and in the thick of things to be able to write! We have had a small family adventure which has kept me busy—for mother, in trying to rescue our cat (who like Marlene refuses to be her age) from an ardent old Tom got badly bitten by him in her right hand. It swelled up monstrously like a red potato and she had fever and has really been quite miserable. However the Dr. says it is all right now—they feared blood poisoning and she is emerging again! But it meant that I was sole Cook and Housekeeper—it has been great fun and I have become passionately interested in cooking—when you come back I will make you various spécialités de la maison!

We are beginning now to get postcards direct from Belgium and it all adds up to quite a picture—the meekest and dullest of our cousins who was a teller in a bank was tortured by the Gestapo for three months (he is getting well now) for being a spy! One of Jean-Do's pupils hid an American airman (who was shot down and badly wounded for 11 months). Another friend, a dentist, and his son were both in the Underground Army. And then the Limbosh with their activities for the Jews—I have been reading a wonderful book. Did you recommend it to me long ago? Kessel's L'Armée des Ombres about the French Underground. It has some of the human quality of St.-Exupéry but a harder core. And is based on actual stories. Partly as a result of that I have written two poems. Which I'll slip in.

The book is still at Farrar and Rinehart's and I expect to hear the worst any day now. But there are lots of other publishers—this week I have been working on a lecture which I am giving at three schools around here before I go: "The Spirit Watches"—poems that deal with eternal things. It is hard not to go over their heads, but I am using Hopkins and Herbert and Blake of course.

I feel awfully dull today so forgive this wandering letter. It is exhausting trying to choose the right poem from the mass of possibilities—my desk is a forest of open books and papers.

What else for news? Today in a month I'll be on my way to Santa Fe. It seems quite impossible! Quite unreal and I have spasms of wondering whether it is the thing to do. It is if I can really write the poems. But I am stupidly tired, I suppose as a reaction from the long pull on the novel.

Cambridge is in an uproar because the School Committee railroaded through a new Superintendent of Schools who is rotten. It was really a chance, if they had got a good man, to do something about the whole mess here. And I am glad to say that there seems to be a real reaction now and they may be forced to rescind. I am going to a public meeting Monday night. The other home news of the greatest importance is the Wallace fight. I fear he hasn't a chance but we will know tomorrow when the Senate ratifies or does not, his appointment as Sec. of Commerce. The whole idea of full employment after the war which was one of the planks in Dewey's platform is being tested on this appt. If the Republicans kick Wallace out it means they are kicking out his ideas of Gov. help for small businesses and Gov. supervision of the change-over to civilian production. And if they do that and go back to old Laissez-faire it means depression and millions of soldiers without jobs. In that case they are damnably short-sighted as the chances are a Republican will get in and so it will be again a "Republican depression."

The Russians are doing all right and so are you out there. I wish we were doing a little better at home.

I haven't seen much of Ella as she has been dashing back and forth to N.Y. to do broadcasts. Everyone wants to know what the Russian plans for Germany are. By the time you get this, let us hope they will be in Berlin. It is a bitter irony that they are now suffering (in winter too which is worse) exactly what they inflicted on the populations of France and Belgium and Poland—the millions of refugees on the roads, blocking traffic—and so on. It's a grim business and I wish they would give up.

I am also reading a wonderful book on Dickens by G. K. Chesterton. It is a delight and full of good things, "The optimist is a better reformer than the pessimist; and the man who believes life to be excellent is the man who alters it most. It seems a paradox, yet the reason of it is very plain. The pessimist can be enraged at evil. But only the optimist can be surprised at it. From the reformer is required a simplicity of surprise. He must have the faculty of violent and virgin astonishment. It is not enough that he should think injustice distressing; he must think injustice <u>absurd,</u> an anomaly in existence, a matter less for tears than for a shattering laughter."

"We are hard to please and of little faith. We can hardly believe that there is such a thing as a great man. They (in the beginning of the 19th Century, Dickens time) could hardly believe there was such a thing as a small one. But we are always praying that our hearts may behold greatness, instead of praying that our hearts may be filled with it. Thus, for instance, the Liberal party (to which I belong) was, in its period of exile, always saying 'O for a Glad-stone!' and such things. We were always asking that it might be strengthened from above, instead of ourselves strengthening it from below, with our hope and our anger and our youth. Every man was waiting for a leader. Every man ought to be waiting for a chance to lead.—The great man will come when all of us are feeling great, not when all of us are feeling small. He will ride in at some splendid moment when we all feel that we could do without him."

It is really good stuff isn't it?

Darling Bill, write soon—with dear love as always

[   ]

Marlene: Marlene Dietrich whose legendary career as actress and cabaret artist fascinated audiences with her spell-binding beauty and mysterious agelessness.

the book: *The Bridge of Years* was published by Doubleday in 1946.

Wallace: Henry A. Wallace (1888–1965), Served as Secretary of Agricuture (1933–41) and vice-president under FDR. As Secretary of Commerce he was asked to resign in September 1946 following his criticism of the government's policy toward the Soviet Union.

Ella: Ella Winter.

Gladstone: William Ewart Gladstone (1809–1898), British statesman, dominant personality of the Liberal party. Prime Minister four times between 1868 and 1894.

TO BILL BROWN   Sunday, March 11th, 1945
[Santa Fe (ER)]
Dearest Bill,

When I arrived here on Friday I found your Feb. 21st letter forwarded from Cambridge—mails seem to be fast for a change! First, before I forget Jean Dominique's real name is Mlle. Marie Closset, her address 33 Ave. de l'Échevinage, Uccles, Brussels. It takes about ten minutes in a trolley from the Place Louise. O how I hope you get a pass—but I fear you are hurled into the big push now and will be pretty busy for awhile. Claire Limbosh, the daughter of my friends who is a stage designer has an apt. in Brussels—and might be in the telephone book. She could then take you out. She is rather shy and a little cold at first sight, unlike her mother, but underneath is a swell girl. and very talented.

I was interested and have thought about what you said about yourself—I know what you mean. You have antennae out so sensitively toward so many of the arts (Jean Do had a friend whom she called "Tous les Arts" and per-haps that should be your name)—and I suppose that eventually you will have to make up your mind to pour all your concentration for awhile into paint-ing if that is what you want—but I am convinced that all your other loves will enrich the painting. In one letter you said you had been sketching—

have you been able to go on? Have you a decent sketch book you can keep in a pocket? If not, is that something I could supply? There is a superb stationery and art store here which has everything—just send a request! What I deeply feel about you is that when you do suddenly know forever what you want, you will be able to do whatever it is—and I am a believer in people who develop slowly and start late. You have talent and great understanding and now it is isn't it a matter of focus?

I don't know Eliot's essay on Tennyson but will try to get hold of it—I have the whole of "In Memoriam" here in Gregory's anthology but have never somehow got up the courage to read it—it looks so long. Maybe I will now.

O Bill, it is so beautiful here that I want to burst into tears every minute. When the world is in such a state such beauty in its finality and aloofness becomes heart-breaking. Every day since I arrived (on Fri) has been a cristal shining—and the little earth houses lie baking in the sun and far off in the distance there are the mountains so all is brown and red and of earth nearby and all is purple and blue and white and strange and ethereal far off. I have a small white-washed room with three windows through which the sun pours in—and when I lie in bed at night with the window open there is a huge sky of stars right in the room, or so it seems—and in the morning a silvery tree and birds against a solid blue sky. It is not spring yet and I am glad because this is how I remember it. Right past our house is the "mother stream," a small rushing brook which no one would take seriously in N.E. [New England] but here it is life itself. At night when I walk home I find my way back by its sound. After the war this is where you must come and paint, and live for awhile. I am sure it is the place. It is so pure and healing and for people who have work to do it is a blessing. I think it is demoralizing unless one has work.

I am sure now that I was right to come—it is the place where the poems are. I know it now surely. I was rather scared that I had illusions and might be disappointed. It is not the people—though I have good friends and they are awfully welcoming and kind—it is the place itself and my aloneness in it. It is sheer heaven to be alone and to have time. Leaving mother was an awful wrench (you know it is awful for her, I know it is a physical pain) but still it is healthy and right and I had to get away. I feel reborn already.

I'm glad you liked the poem—the snow one—here is another that I wrote in Chicago. I had a wonderful time there—I stayed at Marion Strobel's, now editor of Poetry, a glowing woman with an isolationist Dr. husband and two grown-up daughters. It was suddenly spring the day I came and I thought so much about V. Woolf—you see I heard about her death in Chicago. And then I left Marion's and lived for a day on the 24th floor of the Stevens and wrote the poem. By then, in true Chicago style it was blowing a gale and snowing!

The sun is shining and I must go out—and I must write to Jean Dominique—

Last night having dinner alone in town I was picked up by a Sergeant recuperating here at the Hospital—he talked so well about Belgium and has adopted a family there and I felt again a great surge of love and gratefulness for Americans, especially for this simple tender gentle kind of man—there must be many like him. He used to be a chef in Chicago.

With dear love, Bill—

[   ]

"In Memoriam": Tennyson's "In Memoriam" written after the death of his friend Arthur Hallam.

Chicago poem: Possibly "Letter from Chicago, for Virginia Woolf" see *The Land of Silence.*

Marion [Mrs. James H. Mitchell] Stroebel: Poet, wrote enthusiastically to Ferris Greenslet when *Encounter in April* was published.

TO ELEANOR MABEL SARTON   Monday [March 12, 1945]
[Santa Fe (ER)]
Darling little Miutsie—I am so glad that you felt cheerful about Farrar and R. I did almost myself though it is always a <u>little</u> blow when it comes. I had another note from Diarmiud here enclosing a letter from one of the editors saying "The story is long and its idea does hold the reader's interest, but the characters are not sufficiently sympathetic. We felt that this was particularly true of Melanie who does not come across to the reader as she did to the people in her life." (This I really don't believe is true. It will be interesting to see what others say. Diarmiud has sent it now to Knopf.)

Tues.

This was interrupted by Aggie who came in the station wagon with two dogs and drove me up into the hills where we walked in the sun among the sage with the mountains all around—there is a flat ermine cape of snow on one range otherwise it is all green of pinyons (little low pine trees) and red earth so the hills are mottled like leopard skins.

Then I had tea with Lura with whom I stayed for ten days when I first came here, and a good talk—she made a fire a beautiful one in the oval shaped fireplace that they all have here so the logs are laid pointing upward and the fire is very flaming and pointed. It is good to see all these people again—

The altitude affects me very much—everyone said it would but I didn't believe them—yesterday I walked downtown just a mile downhill all the way and was so shaky at the end that I had to sit down! They say it takes a month to get fully adjusted and meanwhile I go slow and sleep every afternoon. I had fun getting a beautiful book to send to Anne to take to Texas—the book I read in Chicago called Take Three Tenses by Rumer Godden—do get it from the Tory Row lending lib. I know you will love it. I hope it gets to Anne in time. Then I also bought The Way of Life according to Lao Tzu which I am enjoying immensely. He says

> A leader is best
> When people barely know that he exists,
> not so good when people obey and acclaim him,
> Worst when they despise him.
> 'Fail to honor people,
> They fail to honor you:'
> But of a good leader, who talks little,
> When his work is done, his aim fulfilled,
> They will all say, 'We did this ourselves.'

Isn't that fine? Perhaps I will have time to copy out a little of it for Anne for the train.

Then I got some asparagus to have with hard-boiled eggs and spotted tongue and some ephedrine jelly for my cold and a large package of super-sweet peas to send to Ruth Pitter and I came happily back in a taxi.

I have seen Marie Armengaud twice and am greatly relieved to find that everything is really all right and we can now be good friends—she went through some terrible period of rejection of everything and everyone, which was partly fatigue and illness. It was nice to be in her dear little house which is somehow very French in spite of the white-washed walls and Spanish furniture. And we talked of France—she feels that DeGaulle's one great weakness is that he thinks in terms of France and not of Europe—that in that sense he is old-fashioned and I think she is right in that.

I am really terribly happy here and sort of flowing and in my element—and the poems are coming only I am afraid really of doing too much too fast out of sheer excitement and I must try to be quiet—and go slow—I did send you the poem for Woolf didn't I?

The air is full of spring but there are no leaves yet on the trees, no green anywhere—it may be real spring there before it is here. Only the sun is very warm in the middle of the day and I can keep my window wide open without any heat in the room from about 11:00 to 3:00. I have a little gas heater which warms me up whenever I get cold.

Everyone asks after you and Daddy as if they know you very well and O, I hope someday they will.

I am so glad you had a good talk with Miss Campbell—it will have done her good to have someone she could speak to frankly knowing that you love Edith and appreciate her.

I am very anxious to see the Shapley speech—also once in awhile if it is not too much bother I would love to see the Lit. Supplement of the Sunday Times as the papers are terrible here—I get the news on the radio.

I'll put in a little poem—I am still getting started but I want to try using a shorter line and this just came yesterday, a little song.

With dear dear love—

Your mouse

[   ]

Perhaps there will be a letter from Daddy today?

Farrar and R.: Farrar & Rinehart turned down *The Bridge of Years.*

Aggie: Aggie Sims in whose home Sarton was a paying guest.

Lura: Allura (Lura) Conkey, an old lady with whom Sarton stayed when she first arrived in Santa Fe and for whom she wrote "Lura's House," unpublished.

Miss Campbell: Possibly Annie Campbell, friend of the Sartons.

Edith: Edith Campbell Wilder Camp, daughter of Charles MacFie Campbell, friend of the Sartons.

Shapley: Howard Shapley (1885–1972), American astronomer; director of the Harvard Observatory.

TO PARENTS   April 12th [1945]
[Santa Fe (ER)]
Dearest ones,

This is a Red Letter today—first I must say that Daddy's magnificent Easter present arrived—each book is a treasure and I need poems just now as I am so full of them! Bless you, dear Daddy. I am altogether having a delayed Easter—mother's flowers are still beautiful and rich, embaumant ma chambre.

It was a mercy that Marie didn't show up if mother was ill and I shall be anxious to hear how she is—was it migraine or grippe or what? Please let one hear soon.

Now I must tell you about the day—it began with a telegram from Dezke who was delighted with my letter and the poems I sent and said that he was dedicating the performance (secretly I imagine!) of the Shostakovitch symphony on Sat. to me so I shall listen with special attention. Wasn't it sweet of him to say that?

Then I wrote a poem about the little Spanish children who are all in rags and so dirty but always look up at anyone passing and say hello so eagerly. I think the poem needs work and cutting but I'll send it along just so you can see.

Then at 11:00 (I got up at seven to make everyone's breakfast—we take turns) Haniel came and took me out for a drive way out into wild country. I drove the car to save his eyes, which was fun as I haven't driven for so long. He took me to a place where we were high up looking at far off blue peaks of mountains with marvelous clouds making black shadows—and then we went down into an "arroyo" the deep gullies the rain cuts through this soft soil. There we were out of the wind and we looked at everything—the sturdy little pinyons, the dwarf cedars, many covered with blue berries, the fine silvery bushes called "Chamiso," and the old old red stones the broken granite which the frost breaks apart. I had never realized before that even rock disintegrates and is constantly changing. Haniel remembered by heart a beautiful new poem of his and I read him mine and altogether it was a fine morning.

I came back to find the books and a dear letter from Le Gallienne—all about the spring in her garden. She says "I wish you could walk down the lane here with me—daffodils, poeticus and violets all over the place—and at the old house the hillside is covered with masses of naturalized daffodils and the forsythia and bridal wreath are beautiful beyond words. I don't know what I'd do without such things.

I spend my days working in the garden now—and attempting frightful paintings—but at least they soothe me and keep me out of mischief—I am well and peaceful here—

So you see it is quite a day. I shall walk down the Acequia (about a mile) to tea with Haniel and Alice and then come home to supper.

I had a long rather upsetting letter from Brown who I knew would not approve of my writing the play but I'm afraid I have to do what I feel and I have never in my life been so charged with creative power. I feel while it lasts, it is there to be used. And I didn't choose the play, it chose me! I have written far more poems than I planned and once the play is finished shall work them over peacefully. So all is well.

With dear dear love to my family and Cloudy's.

––––––––––

Translation of French: Perfuming my room.

Dezke: Desiré "Deske" Defaux, conductor of the Chicago Symphony for several years. He and his wife Jeanne were old Belgian friends of the Sartons.

poem about little Spanish children: "Always the Children Have Hello to Say," unpublished. See Appendix.

Haniel: Haniel Long.

Brown: Probably Rollo Walter Brown.

Cloudy: The Sartons' cat who had one kitten on April 2 and another on April 4.

TO PARENTS   Sat. April 14th [1945]
[Santa Fe (ER)]
Dearest ones,

I wonder where you were when you heard the news? I was just starting out for tea with Haniel and Alice (they had come for me in the car) and she ran out to tell us. It still seems unbelievable and just now when I was lying down after lunch I thought with a sort of panic "But he won't be at the peace table!" Hardly in the history of the world has a man been so believed in as a man of good will toward <u>all men</u> as he. I wrote this yesterday—it is not as good as I hoped but I sent it off to the local paper and they may put it in today. One of the editors likes it very much but the paper itself is Republican—I like the idea of its coming out here as if I were really part of the community.

This afternoon at two we went to the cathedral where there was no service and so on to the episcopal church (a nice modest little church) just in time for prayers. I felt a great need to be where the people were—and had hoped the cathedral would be full. The stores are all closed here and flags at half-mast.

Dezke had wired that he was playing the Shostakovitch for me so at one we listened and it was very beautiful. But the best of all was the second movement of the "Heroica" which he played magnificently. It is so deeply noble and right, so <u>final</u> and yet full of triumph of the spirit. Of all the music we have heard on the air since the news came over, this has seemed the only really appropriate thing.

I think of all the people in Europe—

I must copy out a part of a letter from Bill that came today (he loved the Window poem which came to him on Easter).

"I talked a few seconds today with a woman who wished to be allowed back in her house to pick up her manuscript book. I asked her (for she spoke English) what it was about—all poetry, she said. She had lived at Muzot where Rilke died—and had apparently written quite a bit about him. She also had written a libretto for Hindemith (I was a bit amazed at this—she said he didn't use it)—but the main thing she said was that they (she and her brother, a surgeon) had helped the Jews, so that her brother is now in a concentration camp—she was keeping up his house for him here, and now of course <u>we</u> have taken it over—"

"These last days have been incredible—seeing the roads filled with Poles, Belgians, Frenchmen <u>walking</u> out of Germany home. I have talked to the

French and Belgians—they are wildly excited of course, after four or five years—also we have liberated some of our own prisoners—They have been living on bread and soup and not much of that."

"We came through Aachen and Düren (did I tell you?) ~~coming on the~~ crossing on the 10th the now famous Ludendorf Bridge—the second day of the bridgehead—It was quite hot for awhile—Some of the towns we have come through are, in their almost completely demolished state, worse than a completely flattened Düren for example—In one building, covered with dust, were 300 civilians that no one had time to bury—a small town near Bonn. And the country is littered with dead horses and cattle; that is really pathetic."

Mother's long letter was a great boon and I meant to answer in detail but it is time for tea. I envy the garden—it is really wintry here with a cold wind blowing and the only thing out in the garden a single dwarf iris. But I expect the spring will come anyday now—

What color are the kits?

Did Anne lend you the book to read? I hope so.

With dear dear love—I have thought of you so much in the last days—

I do think I will stay on, maybe even until the middle or end of July—because it is so good here and I have much still to do. I have written twenty poems and next week start Act III of the play.

Love and love
[   ]

---

the news: Franklin Delano Roosevelt died suddenly of a cerebral hemorrhage at Warm Springs, Georgia on April 12, 1945.

"Heroica": Beethoven's third symphony, the *Eroica.*

Bill: Bill Brown.

Aachen: More than half the city of Aachen was destroyed in World War II.

Ludendorf Bridge: A railroad bridge just above Linz-on-Rhine; the only bridge not bombed by retreating German troops. Bill Brown's company were the first to cross the Rhine, even as the Germans were bombing the bridge. Ten days later, 1,000 Army Corps of Engineers began work to buoy up the collapsing bridge which nevertheless collapsed, killing all the workers.

TO SYLVIA BEACH   April 22d, 1945

[Santa Fe (ER)]

Dear Sylvia Beach,

At last I have heard from Johnny Ames that he was able to see you and now I am sending him a package of coffee, sugar, hot chocolate (instantaneous and already sweetened) and some soap flakes. I hope it will eventually reach you. I feel so badly that I did not hear from him sooner. We have to have a request to send packages to a soldier.

I was enormously touched to hear that you have my books. I have not been able to get anything published for so long (since '38) and it is good to know one is still alive.

Here I am on a miraculous poetry fellowship and writing like mad—as if a lid had popped off.

But what terrible days with the blow of Roosevelt's death with us all, all over the world. There is going to be so much need for men of good will, who have vision and practical sense as well. And he was I think the great mediator in international affairs.

I hear fairly regularly from Bryher and H. D. Isn't it amazing and wonderful that book of H. D.'s? Treasures are coming out of all this. There are the French Resistance writers. There is, it seems to me, much to build on. Much to believe in.

But still it is necessary, supremely necessary that the full horror and the full suffering be understood and realized, first of all in Germany but secondly here in America where I fear our optimism and natural good nature is going to tend to wish to forget and forgive much too soon. We have no right to forgive as we haven't suffered. And we cannot forget what we haven't even realized as yet.

I think of you a great deal. And what you mean and have always meant to those of us who are working for the spirit against such fearful odds. God bless you.

> Yours with homage
> May Sarton

The coffee is a present from my friend Judith Matlack, a Quaker and teacher of English at Simmons College—she sends her greetings—

Sylvia Beach: Owner of the legendary Shakespeare and Company, the first American lending library and bookshop in Paris, meeting place for Joyce, Hemingway, Eliot, Pound and others; publisher of the novel that changed modern fiction, James Joyce's *Ulysses*.

Johnny Ames: John W. Ames, Jr., Boston friend.

poetry fellowship: The Cabot Fund.

H. D.'s book: Tribute to the Angels (1945).

TO BILL BROWN   Aug. 1st, 1945
[Channing Place]
Dearest Bill,

Your letters of July 1st, 2d, 4th, 11th and 18th all arrived simultaneously! Such are the mails. I have sent my typewriter to be cleaned and this is a rented one which scares me because I cannot see what I am doing. I'm afraid I have been bad about letters lately in the general confusion of getting back here—but now I will be better. It is interesting that you have been moved again—does that mean you are more or less permanently with the occupying forces? I really in my heart hope it does. Will you get a 30-day leave eventually? You ask about plans—

FIRST, my dear, when I arrived here I found a letter from Russell to say that Doubleday is taking the novel $1000 advance! Now that this long-awaited recognition has happened I feel completely flat—I can't quite take it in somehow. It is a new climate to which I am not adjusted. I haven't heard directly from Don yet as he is on vacation but I gather he doesn't want radical changes, only "tightening" which means a rather careful revision, nothing more. It really is wonderful. It means too that I won't have to have a job this winter—it is almost unbelievable! As for plans, I am planning two short lecture-trips one in October and Nov. and one in March. The November one is beginning to look quite promising with fairly definite engagements in Wisconsin, Kansas, Mo., Indiana. Between times I shall be in Cambridge. I am moving my stuff out of N.Y. (alas) on Oct. 1st as someone has bought the house and wants to remodel it.

It is possible that I shall move in with Judy Matlack after I come back from the first lecture trip but I haven't broken this to the family and nothing is really definite. In some ways it might be the solution to be living in Cambridge but not at home. It is really a rather un-natural life for me now to live permanently at home I think. I simply never go out. On the other hand mother is not well at all and I see only too clearly what it means to have me here—she relaxes and stays in bed in the morning and so on. I have not really made up my mind about it. It is a very big step.

Meanwhile the play has been turned down by one agent who said they would have been interested four years ago! It has been read by Cornell's first reader who gave it a pro and con review, saying it was better than Maxwell Anderson's "Candle in the Wind" but has too little action, but was full of original, true and deeply moving things. I still have a faint hope that I can find an agent to handle it. It is now at Brandt and Brandt, but I guess the chances of production are slight. Never mind, it is a beginning. Maybe Le Gallienne's play will flop and then she might do it. If you are going to be there for some time I'll send you a copy. Let me know. I long for you to read it.

What a dry letter this is—I am not really out of that floating state of mind between two worlds. Cambridge is like a jungle after the Southwest—so very damp and green. And I miss our dear big puss [Cloudy] who is dead.

I am sure you are right about the Mozart sonnets. But I'm glad I'm glad you liked the two about the dead. I wrote very little at the end—I got rather nervous about the novel and everything and then I hate transitions. I think often of army life which is all transitions and monotony with no roost anywhere—and what it must mean of spiritual strength to stand it and stay mentally as active as you do. It is wonderful. I am so glad you are sketching and singing(!) as well as playing the piano. How perfectly marvelous if you could go to the Sorbonne. How will that be managed? On a leave system or what? When would it be?

Patton's speech is a perfect <u>horror</u>. Thanks for sending it.

I'm glad too that "The Soldier is Very Tired" didn't seem too unreal. I'll try it on the New Yorker, but I fear it is as usual a little late. The Yale Review has taken a lyric called "The Harvest" which I think I sent you.

I talked to Muriel on the phone in Chicago—she was in Iowa City for Hallie Flanagan's try-out of her play. She sounds really awfully happy and wrote me yesterday that she intended to devote the next ten years to having children and will hang them up on the wall like Eskimos while she works in the middle of the room! Her husband is a New Zealander "a British object" as she says.

Isn't it exciting by the way about the British elections. What hope for liberals everywhere, hope for Spain, Greece, India etc. It is really amazing. I didn't expect it all!

I'll see if I can dig up a poem you haven't seen. Could you also if possible mail this letter to a former colleague of my father's? His wife is Norwegian. They were strong anti-Nazis but had to go back as he couldn't get a job over here. I fear they may be dead.

I'll write often now—I do long for your letters too.

Love and love—
[   ]

I'll send poems in my next—

Russell: Diarmuid Russell.

Don: Don Elder, editor at Doubleday.

Patton: George S. Patton (1885–1945). Third Army General in Europe during W. W. II.

Hallie Flanagan: Hallie [née Ferguson] Flanagan (1890–1969), author, teacher of theater, director of experimental theater at Vassar.

British elections: The Labour party's landslide victory.

father's colleague: Probably Robert and Elsa Ulich.

Aug. 23, 1945

[Channing Place]

Dearest Poll,

I was so happy to hear from you and that you liked the poems—that is fine. I'm afraid I rear a little at your emphasis on growth (it would be a pity if one ceased to grow!) but it implies, I think, that my attitude toward the war and the peace has changed. It has not. I have always felt that as long as we were not in the presence of justice, there was war, whatever it might be called. Fascism is one of the great injustices done against the spirit of Christ and the spirit of man: its logical end is Buchenwald or Auschwitz. But I have never hated any country nor any people—and I have always been fearfully anxious to get to the place where we could help Germany and Japan build instead of destroying. We are at that place now. In 1936 I believed that if we had been willing to fight just a little for the thing we believed in (in Spain) we would not have had to watch millions die now. I believed that this war was inevitable but that the <u>sooner</u> it began the less harm would be done. I still believe that.

Now we get letters every day from Belgium, France and from American soldiers in Germany and elsewhere of European background. Gerhardt Speyer's father was shovelled into an oven at Auschwitz. Lt. Einstein (a brilliant young historian of Harvard and student of my father's) has found of his whole family one girl cousin alive. His aunt, uncle, five cousins all murdered in concentration camps. Madame Metzger, one of the great historians of science of France—also shipped off and turned into fertilizer. I could go on and on just with people we know. These were not people at war or in uniform, nor political fighters—these were just ordinary human beings. This was not war: it was fascism. I am not ashamed of having been revolted by it from the beginning nor that I always felt it was a crime against humanity and one which eventually would have to be fought. So do not please imagine that I have changed fundamentally—I think my line has been clear from the beginning and has not wavered. So, I know has yours. Let us respect each other for what we believe. But let us also understand where exactly we do stand.

It seems curious to have to remind you that I was godmother to a German girl (the daughter of Amélie Hanbury-Sparrow all of whose relatives are in Germany) who was later killed by a robot-bomb in England. I consider Amélie one of the great people of this earth. So it is not really I think such a sign of "growth" that I should now be writing poems about Germany that you can like. It is logical.

I was awfully happy to hear about Helen's book and something of Moll—

was she in Hingham this summer? You sound as if you had been close by. I am so sorry you all had grippe. How horrid, to have it in summer—and maidless. My poor lamb! I expect that as far as work goes things will be better soon because you can have more help, thank heavens!

At least I have some good news—the novel has been taken by Doubleday Doran (about Belgium between the two wars) with an advance of $1000, so I am safe from jobs for this winter. I am going west to lecture for a month in the middle of Oct., but otherwise shall be here and around here. Let me know when you are in town—we must meet.

I came back about three weeks ago to find that mother had been quite ill and is still shaky—she had some trouble with the fluid in the ear which gave her violent vertigo, fainting etc. It was for about 24 hours very frightening and exhausting but now Weille is giving her many red pills to eat and she is getting better. I am cook, housekeeper and shopper and these days that is almost a full-time job! We are however going down to the Cape [Wellfleet] for one week after Labor Day. Daddy has not had a vac. in five years so it is quite a celebration.

Then I am getting a book of poems ready to be called The Lion and the Rose—

That is all the news—bless you for writing. I only wrote all the first page so we wouldn't have to talk about it when we meet!

With love as always—I want to see Dinah.

Your
May

Madame Metzger: Mme. Paul Metzger.

Amélie Hanbury-Sparrow: Amélie and Alan Hanbury-Sparrow lost their daughter Gisele. Sarton had been this child's godmother, and became the godmother for the twins they later adopted.

Helen's book: Probably Helen Howe's novel *We Happy Few* (1946).

Weille: Dr. Francis L. Weille, the Sarton family physician.

Dinah: Dinah Starr, Polly's daughter and Sarton's goddaughter.

TO MARIE CLOSSET   30 November 1945
[Oxford Street]
O Jean-Do—
It's snowing; the house is entirely encircled by white veils, the trees are robed in white. When I throw breadcrumbs out the window, they disappear in seconds (the birds come in droves)—<u>and,</u> last night in the storm I went to a concert because one of <u>your</u> poems was being sung in a series organized by

Nadia Boulanger to celebrate Fauré. Oh, you can't imagine! I was in such a state that I could scarcely breathe as the soprano started.

"I must put both hands to my mouth to keep to myself
That which I most want to tell you, beloved one."

Sadly, Olympia di Napoli is a little too much like her name—a young girl (Nadia Boulanger's student), very "bueno", very Italian, with absolutely no soul for these delicate, profound, passionate songs. Nadia Boulanger herself accompanied her and I could not take my eyes from her face—so intense and natural—full of nobility. She is not at all affected—rather she has a sublime simplicity—that greatness which comes from serving one's art rather than imposing oneself on it. That kind of greatness, it seems to me, is becoming rarer and rarer in this age of "personalities". Her hair is almost white now, and her face which used to be rather severe was radiantly tender.

We laughed wildly at your [?]

It's beautiful here but I'm still in a morass of exhaustion—I hope to feel better next week. The house is silent, musing on all the love hiding in every little corner—and I must get to work, but I wanted to tell you that Jean Dominique came to Cambridge.

With all my love, my angel—

[   ]

———

Fauré: On November 29, 1945 at Sanders Theatre Gabriel Fauré's song *Le Don Silencieux* set to a poem of Jean Dominique's (1906) was sung by soprano Olympia di Napoli with Nadia Boulanger at the piano.

TO MR. AND MRS. RAYMOND HOLDEN   Jan. 12th, 1946
[Oxford Street]
Dear Mr. and Mrs. Holden,

I'm sorry to be so late in answering your requests. I was buried under Christmas mail until now. Briefly these are my answers to your questions—the greatest threat to poetry in America is verse and the lack of understanding of the difference between them. A great many poetry groups and societies give prizes and recognition to such inferior stuff that it creates a public who cannot recognize a poem when they see one—and makes them feel smugly superior to what they call "modern" poetry, simply because it requires a certain concentration and effort. I have just been judging Mss. for instance for a literary national sorority. It was all sentimental, trashy, borrowed stuff. The kind of poetry that appears in most newspapers. I think teachers are greatly to blame: they fear to give their classes great poetry or if they do, they make it so damned dull that the students look elsewhere for the rewards poetry might give. In this context Muriel Rukeyser's poem that begins "The fear of poetry is the fear" has much to say (The poem is called "Reading Time: One minute, thirty five seconds"). Our whole American culture fears and resents intensity, clarity of thought, real depth, fears and resents agony, passion, love in the deep sense. What cheap verse does is to give people the illusion that they are feeling without their really having to feel at all. For true feeling is painful, and the true poem would require as Rilke points out in the Sonnet on an Archaic Torso of Apollo: "Here there is nothing that does not see you. You must change your life."

My own talent, such as as it is, has been fostered chiefly by the influence of one or two friends who might be called teachers, and by reading. The thing societies can do is to give recognition, a modicum of which is perhaps essential for one to have the confidence to go on. Poetry is a lonely profession. That is both bad and good—good because it alone of the arts has remained, perforce, pure of commercialism. There are no large rewards so there are fewer temptations. Bad, because in the long run, I believe communication an essential and out of loneliness many poets withdraw from the life of their time.

In my own case my lecture trips have been invaluable in making me feel <u>useful</u> and <u>needed,</u> in giving me a chance to fight for what I believe publicly and to a certain extent, to see the results. I would like to see more colleges bring poets to their campuses for a week or two at a time and then use them to the limit and pay them well.

In the last analysis no one can be taught to be a poet, but I believe everyone can benefit by writing some poetry, and the disciplines and awakenings it involves, and I believe that the teaching of poetry is an essential to the creation of a public for it. At present there is no discriminating public "public" for poetry in America, as there is in England for instance.

Radio would be the channel to create it. I have often wondered why someone doesn't get a five-minute program on the air once a day and read a single poem with a short introduction. One might begin with the Shakespeare sonnets. Radio which has debased everything, has also debased poetry in such inferior programs as Tom somebody or other who croons sentimental lyrics to a musical accompaniment. If people will take Beethoven, they will take Shakespeare!

I do think poets are solitary, but they are also gregarious. What happens now is that the gregarious part of them drives them into cliques, and that is worse than nothing. The solitary part divides them from their fellow human beings, and that has increased the "difficulties" in communication.

Well, I've spilled out a lot. I hope something of it may be useful. Thank you for asking me.

Yours very sincerely,
May Sarton

———

Raymond Holden: Raymond Peckham Holden (1894–1972), American poet, novelist and editor, mystery writer under the pseudonym, Richard Peckham. First wife, Louise Bogan. At the date of this letter, Mrs. Holden is probably Sara Henderson Hay. Mr. Holden's project alluded to in this letter is unidentified.

TO HILDA DOOLITTLE   Jan. 20, 1946
[Oxford Street]
Dearest Hilda,
    Your letter with its wonderful question about the "ration" of poems has been the greatest blessing, for I have been in one of my stupid low spells of fatigue and it was such fun to lie down and consider what poems I would choose—a perfect game! I shall be immensely interested in what others have chosen (of course one is bound to leave out the one poem one really wants!) but here are a few I jotted down on a little pad—

"Fear no more the heat o' the sun—" Shakespeare
Sailing to Byzantium—Yeats
In a Garden—Marvell
"Who would have thought my shrivelled heart would have recovered green-ness" (Herbert)
"The dove descending breaks the air"—Eliot
The Hound of Heaven—Thompson (because I learned it years ago and still love to say it aloud—I don't suppose I would choose it now but it has become part of childhood for me)
Palme—Valéry
Présentation de la Beauce à Notre Dame de Chartres—Péguy
O mon ange gardien—Francis Jammes
"When the present has latched its postern"—Hardy
How Many Heavens—Edith Sitwell
Part I of the Wreck of the Deutschland—Hopkins
The Crystal Cabinet—Blake

I do hope I can get down and see you—or perhaps we could meet in New York—surely the Harvard Poetry people should have you come here—that is what I hope!
    This is no letter—I cannot write letters when I think we shall be meeting and talking—

Love and love—
M

I have been reading parts of 'Tribute to the Angels' in a lecture on poems and the peace—it is <u>so</u> beautiful—Bless you!

H. D.'s "Tribute to the Angels," dedicated to Osbert Sitwell, the second of three book-length poems which came to be known as her war trilogy.

TO BILL BROWN   April 27, 1946
[Oxford Street]
Dearest Bill,

O how lovely that you like the book and all you say is so good, I am beaming all over. I am so <u>happy</u>—the thing is that writing it was such a struggle that I couldn't believe it could come out fresh and healthy—but it seems to have done so, and now I think myself that it has some of the things you say.

I hate it that you have to think of money just now that you are in the full creative flood. Don't for Heavens sake hesitate to beg borrow or steal anything you can lay hands on—one has to make up one's mind I think, if one is a real artist these days that one will be more or less dependent for awhile. Commercial art is such a pitfall and so many drop out of sight in it—I am sure your family would be willing to stake something on a year wouldn't they? Please do tell me just how it is, the whole financial set-up—I want to know.

Yes, why are we so far apart? I too long to see you and hear in person what you think and feel about the book—I can't get used to its being out and I must say it is awfully exciting. I have had one fan letter from an arthritic woman which was quite touching—The squib in the New Yorker was better than I expected from them. I'm glad it didn't fall into [Edmund] Wilson's ghoulish hands! But I have been in a craziness of accumulated people to see and letters and cannot seem to settle down to any work, so I feel rather lost and cross. The trouble is that all winter I kept putting people off and now there is no excuse—and besides I want to see them—but the days seem to vanish with nothing done. I just pray I can get back to poetry in May. Next week I am still going to buzz around and after that try to shut the door and invite the Muse (if that is the expression!)

The Limbosh are really exactly the people in the book except that Paul is a poet and not a philosopher (but a very metaphysical and obscure poet who should have been a philosopher!) The three girls are really portraits too but there was a boy who was tragically killed in a mountaineering accident before the war. I left him out for several reasons—the accident didn't seem to fit into the idea of the book, would have been a digression really. And it would have been too cruel to them to have him go on living in the book. Of course I'm dying to know what they will say—and a little scared too. A lot of the incidents and situations are made up of course—the relation between Paul and Louise, for one—the fight in the forest—the whole character of Jacques and so on. In dedicating a copy for them I said "this mixture of memory and imagination" and that is about it. Much of what I remembered was seen through a child's eyes too—

I'm glad you like Moise—yes, she was real! and that was her name.

Have you seen Muriel? I feel sad about her because I can't really help her—I think I only make her sad for the past and there is no going back—I am reading for the first time Lowe's Road to Xanadu, a most fascinating detective hunt for the sources of the "Ancient Mariner"—it makes me think of Muriel a great deal. He talks about how much Coleridge read of old seatales and how then these facts dropped down into the subconscious and [were] followed by a period of unconscious assimilation and then brought to the surface and consciously fashioned—in other words there are three periods, the first of work, the second unconscious and the third again of work. That is very much the way in which Muriel functions with her accumulations of all sorts of odd lore and then the fusing of it into images for her poems. It is fascinating.

I might stop over on my way to the west in June—or you might come up for a day late in May????

With much much love. Tell me what you are working on now?

[   ]

Shall be anxious to have Amy's reaction to the book.

———

the book: The Bridge of Years.

mountaineering accident: Jacques Limbosch was killed on a mountainside in September 1935.

Lowe: John Livingston Lowes, an English professor at Harvard University; editor of Amy Lowell's Collected Poems; author of The Road to Xanadu.

Amy: Bill Brown's Aunt Amy, Mrs. Evarts Loomis.

TO JULIETTE AND JULIAN HUXLEY   June 13th, 1946
[Carbondale]
Dearest Juliette, dearest Julian, my darling dazzling ones,

What a fearful thing to see you for those snatched minutes and no more—I couldn't sleep for three nights, rocked with memories and images and the frustration of it all! And now, to think you are already back again—are you both back? In all the brouhaha I only gathered that Julian was to be home by today, but did you both fly? Now there is a great emptiness and desolation in the States, a lacklustre, without-Huxley depression, in fact! And did it all go off well? I hope Daddy didn't exhaust Juliette too much with the rhinoceroses and glass flowers???? You seemed indefatigable, fresh as daisies, the delights of the world—but I hope you can flop a little when you get back just the same! I am so sorry that I could match you so little—I felt bewildered, and was somewhat overcome by the blur of that beastly sinus headache, unresponsive as a toad in fact. But perhaps you could glimpse the love shining through?

The minute you had gone out the door Edith Ricketson (our Santa Fe friend, a large rather flat woman) burst into a paean of praise of Juliette so your ears must have practically burst into flame on the way to Channing Place. She said "What a wonderful person Mrs. Huxley is" and went on from there to enumerate your charms, your understanding, your wit, your warmth, your dearness. In fact Mrs. R. was bowled over and for several moments forgot to talk about herself and talked about you. That is a triumph. But I am being mean for she is really an old dear and was most kind to us all last spring—and since then she has made herself a place at the Metropolitan Museum in N.Y. (she is an archeologist by profession) and we are very proud of her, for out in Santa Fe she was going to seed with misery (her husband divorced her suddenly to marry the governess) and we did try to uproot her, so all is well now.

Did you enjoy my parents? Aren't they really darlings? I am spoiled by having such parents.

As for me—it is 90 here all the time and very muggy so I exist from hour to hour gasping like a fish and only getting gleams of joy out of the hours of teaching—that *is* fun—planting the seeds in virgin soil (in this case virgin without quotes, Julian, as the elderly schoolteachers and supremely innocent and foolish young girls who compose it attest!) There is also a Baptist minister and several young men—all virgins is my guess! It is discouraging in one sense that they have read nothing—and here I am trying to get them to read Hopkins, Eliot, Yeats, Rilke and all the time saying "Compare this with Donne's "Ecstasy" or Marvell's "Garden" and then discovering to my horror that they have never heard of either Donne or Marvell! So now I have stopped talking at them and am trying the Socratic method (Boy, is it hard to ask the right questions and keep the form of the discussion going—you both do that so supremely well you cannot imagine how I blunder along like an eager bee!)—But they are waking up and I rage at them and make them listen—you see their idea of poetry is that it is "soothing and relaxing"—I am not going to let them get away with that!

I simply long for a long letter of impressions from Juliette—to comfort myself in the wilderness I am reading Lytton's wonderful essays on Madame Du Deffand and Voltaire and I am also reading Kierkegaard, though I only understand in flashes—"Faith is immediacy after reflection" which I find a good definition of poetry—and I hope, O I hope to have AN IDEA soon and to write a poem or short story—and stop being a fish—

This just to send you all the hugs and kisses and some of the conversation there was no time for. But I count on coming to England next spring and then perhaps having a couple of long quiet evenings with you, each and several—

> With dearest love, your old (gray-haired!)
> May

———

Lytton: Lytton Strachey (1880–1932), English biographer, member of Bloomsbury group. Reference here is to *Biographical Essays.*

TO BILL BROWN   June 25th, Tues. [1946]
[Carbondale]
Dearest Bill,

Letters mean so much here and yours was a dear one to get—Goschman sounds wonderful I must say, if something of a distraction! I'm sorry about Rohr's book which is really awfully good—but I half expected that: they are so stupid! But I hope very much that someone will do it. I'll be eager to hear about Muriel—she never writes (I can understand that too)—she is hurt I think because I didn't stop over on the way, and I cannot explain how wildly tired now it makes me to be taken back into the chaos of her life. You do not feel it I'm sure as a friend, but having lived in the center of it, I cannot help being swung back into the center again and then I get awfully upset. In a year or so when she is settled again, it will be easier for both of us.

I know what you mean about the Rilke—Rodin does seem awfully sentimental and un-sculptural to us now after Brancusi for instance, doesn't he?

June 26th

I was so disgusted by the pomposity of that last statement that I stopped and never did finish—I am a dull fish this afternoon too, but it is nice to sit down and think about you anyway, even if the result is a poor thing indeed—but mine own! I've just had a sweet letter from Ruth Pitter, the poet, saying that my package of food to Dorothy Wellesley (now Duchess of Wellington) got there safely—it gives me a peculiar pleasure to be feeding SPAM to a Duchess! Especially a Duchess-poet—Ruth loves the novel which is encouraging too. But I was very cross [because] in another letter someone said they liked it so much better than the poems—Arriba Aunt Amy, say I to that! She is wiser. The good thing about all this here is that I have come back to poetry and will copy out for you one poem which I think is nearly finished—perhaps not quite. I have ideas for several more but can only get to them at the tail-end of the day when it seems wiser to wait till the end of the month and go at them freshly. The first thing I'm going to do when I get back is make another stab at finding a publisher for the poems—maybe the Harvard Press. The time has come, the walrus said—

Today one of the boys said he was going to drop the course because I was giving him such low marks. I made an impassioned five-minute speech on "standards" and told them I had lowered mine as far as they were going to give anyone in the class an A—and that meant that he was still a C. The class, I'm glad to say, afterwards rallied round and said I was dead right. I gather he is a rather unpopular and arrogant guy without a great deal on the ball but who has somehow ground through very good marks until now. They really have to think for me and that has got him stymied—he can't find the Inf. in a book!

When do you go to Princeton? I leave here Friday the 5th and plan to spend the week-end with Judy in Nyack and then go home on Monday to Channing Pl. I would rather not have Muriel know I'm near N.Y. so don't say anything.

I have a roomette on the train which sounds wonderful—I can go to bed in the middle of the day if I feel like it! Very grand—

I'm deep in Kierkegaard and he is almost making a Christian of me—it is so very deep and honest compared to any other religious writer I have ever come across.

Well, I'll stop this drivel—

Yours with a kiss

[   ]

Goschman: Vladimir Golschmann: (1893–1972), French-born conductor of Russian parents. Founded Golschmann concerts, Paris.

Rohr: Franz Rohr.

Brancusi: Constantin Brancusi (1876–1957) Romanian sculptor, settled in France, known for his radically simplified almost archetypical forms.

Dorothy Wellesley: Dorothy Violet Ashton Wellesley (1891–1956), fourth Duchess of Wellington, poet, lived at Penns-in-the-Rocks, Sussex where Yeats visited her.

Arriba: Hurrah!

the course: Sarton was poet-in-residence at State Teachers College of Southern Illinois in Carbondale during June 1946.

Enclosed: "Before Teaching," see *The Lion and the Rose.*

TO ARTHUR SCHLESINGER   Aug. 14th, 1946
[Channing Place]
Dear Arthur,

I've just finished your book, which I have been slowly imbibing over a period of weeks. Of course I am what my grandfather used to call the Igpub

(Ignorant Public) so I cannot criticize but only admire and I do admire most heartily. It seems to me better than a good book, a really <u>useful</u> book. It has given me, in a time of great depression about this country, a sense of proportion again, a sort of over-all understanding which makes it possible to go on and to continue the fight. My fight of course is very different from yours but they tie in together. I realize more than I ever had what Sherwood Anderson meant by the "selling out of the imaginative lives of the people" when I went out into the Middle West this summer to teach poetry. I realized amongst other things that thin soil intellectually in this age when very few people attain the wisdom of the farmer, say, but everyone gets a veneer of "education," that this thin soil destroys the imagination, and where there is no imagination about poetry or literature there is also no imagination about politics, about government, about the individual's relationship to society. What frightens me about America today is that in the large majority there is no active sense of the value of the individual: few citizens feel that they <u>are</u> the Republic, responsible for what happens. And when the individual in a democracy ceases to feel his importance, <u>then</u> there is grave danger that he will give over his freedom, if not to a Fascist State, then to the advertising men or Publicity Agents or to the newspaper he happens to read.

Your book is fine, wise, deep-going. As a job of synthesis it seems to me masterly.

Please give Marion my best and accept my heartiest congratulations. I hesitated to swell what must be your enormous fan mail and then decided to add my mite! For I really am grateful.

Yours very sincerely,
May

Arthur Schlesinger: Arthur M. Schlesinger (1917–), American historian and biographer who after serving in the Kennedy administration became Schweitzer Professor at the City University of New York. His *The Age of Jackson* was published in 1945; in 1946 Schlesinger wrote a full-length exposure and indictment of the American Communist Party for *Life* magazine.

TO BILL BROWN   Sept. 2d, 1946
[Vineyard Haven]
Dearest Bill,

I was terrifically glad to have your letter about the poems and interested in <u>all</u> your comments—I think you're right about the American Landscapes—they are vintage '40–'41 and I have learned much since then, but they were the very important break-through from personal lyric poems to the world, so to speak—at the time it seemed a great step forward. You are dead right about the last stanza of the Cottonfields and I'm thinking of trying to write a less <u>obvious</u> final stanza. All these were written very much with the idea of being read aloud—I felt deeply the <u>lack</u> of interpretation of so much American countryside in the sense that in Europe every stone is familiar because of the works of art, poems, paintings etc. There is a sort of barrenness here for lack of just that—therefore (too) I think the rather literal painters are a necessary step. Curiously—or perhaps <u>not</u> curiously—the American Landscapes seem to have the most <u>general</u> appeal of anything I've done.

I'm glad you like <u>the Women</u> poems—and more especially glad that you think the Campus ones come off (very wise what you say of the "I" in the second) because they are untested by time and I never quite know. However I believe they enrich the book—It's a different <u>facet</u>—

I'm thinking of taking out "Lincoln Memorial"—I've always liked it but no one else but you does.

I'll think about the "Boy With Waterfall"—this is the kind of criticism that's <u>so</u> helpful, darling Bill, because it makes me look at an old thing <u>freshly</u>—altogether I'm most grateful. I am more and more convinced that the art of criticism consists in <u>loving</u> a work of art sufficiently to take <u>time</u> really to consider it—and that is what you do for my poems.

I have meanwhile had the painting up in my bedroom (at Channing Place) and been considering <u>it</u>. All I say must be prefaced by an admission of really great ignorance of painting—so you can cast it aside at once. These are impressions—questions—

Your sub-conscious is full of memories (which is good in a way) of the paintings you have looked at with most care. For that reason I wonder if it's not dangerous to do still-life <u>removed</u> from the objects themselves. Braque takes a group of objects and interprets them through his own eyes—and isn't there a danger of <u>imitating</u> sub-consciously an interpretation? I always remember a friend telling me, "Don't go to the moderns for your influences—to Elinor Wylie, Millay etc.—go to the sources—<u>they</u> are influenced by Donne, Shakespeare, etc. but if you get the influence <u>at one remove</u>, the result is pale stuff." My instinct would be to tell you to study Italian primitives and Byzantine art and Negro sculpture etc. etc. Then also the invented object is dangerous to me just because it lacks in the painting the <u>tension</u> of a problem.—the solution of a problem—that gives what you do a certain superficiality—a <u>flatness</u> (which may be partly actual lack of technique). I went to the Fogg and saw a small show of French paintings—looked long at an early Cezanne of apples. The painting of [Jim] Booth may be stronger just because it is related to an <u>actual</u> figure, and then the simplification is the simplification of a complex reality and so has the tension. It is so hard to <u>talk</u> about painting isn't it?

It seems to me that you are developing a really original colour sense but that you do not <u>show</u> yet as well as you <u>see</u>. Look at the <u>early</u> Picassos, the

early Van Goghs—(there is a wonderful one of old shoes, for instance—do
you know it?) They did not experiment until they had mastered a certain
technique—that is why I don't think it at all bad that you do an occasional
exercise like the portrait of your father. I feel that you could somehow learn
much more about <u>paint</u> itself, how to get <u>depth</u> (not perspective—depth but
<u>depth</u> in the paint itself)—

I wonder if on the days when you are not working on a painting you
wouldn't do the equivalent of a Czerny on the piano and make experiments
for <u>texture</u> etc. certainly part of which might be just looking at paintings in
the Museum.

My whole feeling is that you must <u>ground</u> your ideas more deeply—but
heaven knows how it is done!

This is a <u>heavenly</u> place and I am really relaxing for the first time in <u>years</u>—
haven't even a typewriter here so I doubt if you can read this—Judy is fine—

Keep the poems as long as you like. I love to think you and Booth are together and you are back in your <u>real</u> life—I'll send this to Princeton—I hope
they forward!

Love and love
M—

"Boy with Waterfall": "Boy By The Waterfall," see *The Land of Silence.*

Czerny: Karl Czerny (1791–1857), Austrian pianist, student of Beethoven, teacher of Liszt,
composer; best known for his one thousand opuses of virtuoso instructive studies.

TO PETER DE VRIES   Oct. 19th, 1946
[Oxford Street]
Dear Peter DeVries,

I'm delighted about the Snail. And here is the clipping from the English
New Statesman and Nation. The clipping in itself is a small masterpiece and
I'm glad it will appear! I want to make one change, if it meets with your approval and will type out the poem marking the change. It is just two words
in one line. If you prefer the old version, stick to it, or if the poem is already
in proof.

I wonder how your double life is going—you manage to be on the two
most interesting mags. in the U.S.A. which is quite amazing! Are you getting any time for your own work? I fear the answer must be No.

The check will be very anxiously watched for. I am broke.

Yours sincerely,
May Sarton

One other thing—
<u>Check</u> the <u>gender</u> of Musik—I have no German dictionary at hand and

hesitated between Eine<u>s</u> Kleine<u>s</u> and Ein<u>e</u> Kleine—It <u>must</u> be right! Someone in the office, if not you, will know for sure—

I've cut one line in the quote to make it shorter.

———————

Peter DeVries: (1910–), American novelist and short story writer; editor of *Poetry* and long associated with the *New Yorker* magazine both as editor and writer. At this time he was editor at the *New Yorker.*

the Snail: "Eine Kleine Snailmusik," later published in *A Grain of Mustard Seed.*

TO BILL BROWN   Jan. 26th, 1947
[Oxford Street]
Dearest Bill,

I am no good at letters—it's time we met in the flesh isn't it? But I loved yours of the 12th and have finally dug down to it through forty other letters I owed—whew! I still haven't heard from Don except that he is back and will get to the book eventually, so I sit in the dark, trying to keep my stomach out of my mouth—

I am so anxious to see your work. I hope the big picture will be done, if I ever do get down (I begin to think I never will!) The quote from André Breton is very fine—it is an almost exact description of Muriel's best poems, it seems to me. Yesterday I felt horribly tired and so took the day off and got at my scrapbook. I had a wonderful time cutting out and pasting in the Moore sculpture and articles about him. The more I see of him, the greater he seems, with a wholly <u>natural</u> greatness, very different from an intellectualization of an attitude.

I'm sure you're right about the subject matter being of little importance, but the quality of vision and emotion being everything. A Still Life to be moving must have been seen and digested so completely—that is, I think why the Cézannes hold up so well—and in another age some of Chardin's Still Lifes. Incidentally re that, here is a little poem by [Walter] de la Mare which I used in a lecture at the Winsor school last week:

> ### STILL LIFE
> Bottle, coarse tumbler, loaf of bread,
> Cheap paper, a lean long kitchen knife:
> No moral, no problem, sermon or text,
> No hint of a Why, Whence, Whither, or If;
> Mere workaday objects put into paint—
> Bottle and tumbler, loaf and knife—
> And engrossed, round-spectacled Chardin's
>   Passion for life.

I was interested to see somewhere that Matisse begins with a literal rendering of an object or person and then gradually reduces it to its essence, drawing by drawing. That is the way I write poems, but many people carry the changes in their heads and many painters I'm sure make the abstraction in their heads too. It is all fascinating.

As to what Hess says—surely if anything literature is dwarfed at present by the immensity of the subject-matter, not the lack of it. We are all stretched out to China, France, England, to absorb politics, art, Freud and Heaven knows what! It is time someone looked quietly at a stone or a bulb growing as far as I am concerned!

My dear, I hope I'll see you soon and will let you know as soon as there is any news. I am embedded in Ernest Simmons's huge Tolstoy, a wonderful book.

With much love

[   ]

Muriel can be reached c/o Marshall, 13 E. 94th St. (at 9-2229) (the last figure is a 9)

Moore: Henry Moore (1898–1986), The most celebrated British sculptor and graphic artist of his time.

Hess: Probably Thomas Baer Hess (1920–), writer, former editor of *Art News*.

Simmons: Ernest Joseph Simmons (1903–1972), American biographer, specialist in Russian literature, professor at Harvard University.

TO GEORGE SARTON   March 18th, 1947
[Oxford Street]
Dearest Daddy,

For some time I have been wanting to have a talk with you about some things that are on my mind. But at Christmas when I thought to do it, you were so worried with the Isis business I did not want to add to your burdens. Now, perhaps,

"The time has come
the walrus said
to talk of many things—"

and before I go, I hope we may have lunch and a good talk. I have gone over your Expenses very carefully—it is really terrific what taxes you have to pay, poor Daddums. And certainly you and mother live as frugally as possible. But it is very hard for mother to explain to you her problems and perhaps that is where I can be of help to you both.

I think mother is very proud—and should be—of having been able to manage <u>all</u> house expenses, clothes, gifts, contributions, replacements (sheets etc.) laundry on her allowance. Living has gone up at least 30% since you decided on the amount and it was as you remember already cut very radically from what she used to have. She has done it and I know it has given her great satisfaction to be able to. I believe also that she gets real satisfaction from proving that she can handle the house and cooking single-handed. At nearly seventy she deserves for this the distinguished service medal, and I know you think so too! It is miraculous that she has recovered as well as she has, though we both know that she gets awfully tired sometimes—and woman's work is never done. She has not only had no vacation, not a single day, but she can never "take a day off" and decide that there will be no supper tonight. The continualness of housework is what is sometimes hard to bear. How can we help her? Well, in the first place I certainly plan to spend at least two weeks this summer at Channing Place taking on all household cares from her back. I had hoped before I left to be able to leave with her a sum of money so that she could afford a few clothes and things she sorely needs—but luck has been against one these months: according to my last year's income I should have earned nearly $1000 in these last three months. Actually I have earned about $300 and had as well to meet a $500 income tax <u>and</u> my passage over. No wonder I am broke at the moment! Judy is helping me to go to Europe. And of course I still hope that I shall have some good news before I leave—

But I feel strongly, dear Daddy, that we must find some way to give mother a little more leeway financially. When she needed a new corset last fall (and this is a matter of health for her as it supports her back) I gave her the fifteen dollars. Fifteen dollars in any month is <u>impossible</u> for her to save. Mother has had no new clothes for almost two years except the things she bought with money Anne gave her and the blouse I gave her for Christmas. She does all her own laundry (which for years she never did) and I feel she deserves as real wages for what she does a little more for her personal expenses. I know that you think she is sometimes extravagant, but if she is extravagant by nature she has certainly learned not to be. Imagine—when she wants to send flowers she goes all that long weary way on the trolley into town to save perhaps <u>a dollar!</u>

I have made inquiries from various friends and all agree that $150 is simply not enough for the expenses it covers. In making your account you must add cigars, Faculty Club, wine, contributions, gifts to friends into your "self" to make it tally with mother's. If you do this you will see that mother spends literally <u>nothing</u> on herself. Now I realize that it is hard to imagine giving her more. But I believe it is quite inconceivable that the house will cost $1500 this year. What I suggest is that you think of raising mother's allowance a little—even twenty five a month would make an <u>enormous</u> difference in her peace of mind. She wears herself out worrying and in the end it simply is not worth it, whatever the cost. Twenty five a month more would mean $300 more a year. Then I wish you could see your way to giving her perhaps an Easter present for some clothes. She will never ask these things for herself as she knows only too well the awful strain you are under and does not want to add one atom to it.

But I see also the strain she is under and perhaps it is part of a daughter's chance to help, to see these things and to let you know of them.

I have not come to these conclusions without much thought. To give you an example: Judy and I live on the whole very frugally. I admit that because of my lectures I have to spend more on clothes than mother does. But I spend $200 a month living and Judy about $160. According to that, mother has about <u>half</u> what we have to spend. I still cannot understand how she has been able to do it. Of these two sums only $22.50 a month goes for rent for each of us.

There is one other way that I think will help mother. That is, she worries because the house really needs some work to be clean and neat. The floors are a continual nightmare and very hard to keep clean. They alone increase her burden immeasureably. Now, if you rent the house next March, please consider setting aside a <u>definite sum</u> out of the rent for repairs such as the floors and paint-washing and having your study painted. Three or four hundred dollars should more than cover it. This would be a great weight off mother's mind in itself.

I hope this letter will not upset you, dear Daddy. I am very anxious for you both when I think of this next year that you still have to work through before you can rest—and I know how sorely you need it. But it is a boon that some of the Isis worries are off your back, at last; and it is also a great boon that mother is so much better. I have no fears that she will not be able to get through if we both help her all ~~you~~ we can. You have been dear too about helping in the house and it has touched her very deeply. Let us have lunch when you come back from Princeton and talk all this over. Meanwhile I shall not tell mother that I have spoken of these things at all. So do not please worry too much. Let us talk it all over.

With dear dear love from your little

[ ]

TO JULIETTE HUXLEY
[Le Pignon Rouge]
My little marvel,

Sunday morning
[June 22, 1947]

Your letter came after all, <u>the</u> letter and with it the gust of tears I have held back so long, and now it is a new beginning. It was at breakfast and when I came down no one said anything, bless them. They are true friends. It is rather terrible that instead of quietly experiencing what happened I have forced you and myself to think ahead to what might happen. But I believe that it will be wise to think that we shall <u>not</u> meet again this time. Heaven knows, your life is complicated enough and then I always am afraid of planning such things. Like the night when we came back from the theatre. It is all flame and air and we cannot hope to hold it. Also I am really afraid of so much emotion. I am no longer capable of much suffering of this kind. Strange—but perhaps that is growing up. When I think how far ahead of me you are in every way, it seems a true miracle that for an instant we were together outside time and you could say, "I am with you." Those words are my great treasure. Never, never shall I come to the end of it or cease to rejoice and praise God.

The little poem is very beautiful. Whose?

If only now I could be alone and work instead of the fearful gaiety, comradeship, physical life ahead in these next six days. But life is always unexpected in its gifts—and I do not know, perhaps a long time on the moving water will be a good limbo.

For you I dread the ten days with your mother, all the business, and the suffering of not loving. That is bad because it can't go out and create but only go in and blacken. The only comfort is, as usual in your extraordinary life, in the certainty that you will give her much. So many children cannot do that for their parents.

As I write all this, it feels like a farewell (beautiful word!). Everything is good, darling, you know that. If it has taken ten years or nearly for this to flower, then ten years from now perhaps there will await us some wonderful strange fruit. More than anything, because I am so frightfully quick, I love and adore slow things. Let us be very slow then, slow and tender and wise. I have so much to learn. Amongst all its other gifts, love humbles. One has to go down so deep, not to die.

I think of you by your lake which I shall see someday and look for your reflection.

It is Julian's birthday. Last night, thinking of you both and our walk on the Ave. Foch that hot night, I wrote a poem. On the reverse you will find it.

If in the end you should come to London before the 25th, it would be of course marvelous. But I have truly renounced all violent hopes. There is only a glimmer which every letter of yours will keep alive. And that is all that matters.

It will be a long time before you get this. Write to here until July 10th. After all Célia [Bertin] is not coming and it will be peaceful here. I leave for

England the 9th or 10th and will send my address. Of course if J. came back later and you said come I would come. But meanwhile, all is <u>well.</u>

With all the silences these words interrupt.

M

these next six days: Sarton was about to leave on a canal trip with Céline Limbosch and her children.

your mother: Juliette often returned to Neuchâtel, Switzerland where she grew up, to visit her mother, Mélanie Antonia (Ortlieb) Baillot.

ten years: In April 1947, Sarton returned to Europe for the first time since the war.

Enclosed: "The Leaves," June 22, 1947. Unpublished. See Appendix.

Celia: Celia Bertin, novelist living in Boston, author of *La Parade des Impiés* and *La Derniére Innocence* published by Bernard Grasset.

TO HILDA DOOLITTLE   June 22d, 1947
[Le Pignon Rouge]
Dearest Hilda,

Your last letter was dated Feb. 14th—I sailed April 21st (I think) for England, then Belgium, then France—it has been two months of anguish, passion, conflict and a sort of burning which has meant many poems and few letters! You must forgive me—I am like an affamée getting back to Europe—just the trees in England made me new. I do miss great trees in America. Paris is an aching glory—the physical presence so utterly beautiful, the soul all gone, dispersed in rags, accusations of everyone but themselves, even the Resistance is now showing up its gangsters—I was so terribly sad. I saw a great deal of the Huxleys there—he is head of UNESCO you know—and had a wonderful afternoon of air, light, space, purity in Brancusi's studio. He is <u>pure.</u> Malraux is pure—I had lunch with him. But in general the moral devastation of the occupation is far worse than I expected. Belgium is another matter—here the recovery is amazing and of course they had no Vichy. Leopold I believe should not come back, but there is the Catholic backing for him and a sort of loyalty to the "anointed king." But I know this will surprise you—the country I respected the most, loved the most was, is England. There is a sort of sober sanity, above all some belief in something outside the individual, England itself perhaps which means that even people who do not believe in this present government will not try to destroy it in every possible way as the communists are doing in Paris to the Resistance Government. Of course there is the fatigue, but I found no rudeness. I had a peculiar weekend at Dorothy Wellesley's—do you know her? That wonderful haunted place of great stones and trees and poor D. so ill, always in pain, and perhaps nearly

always drunk though <u>we</u> (Ruth Pitter and I) were offered nothing but orange pop! I do think here and there she has written perfect lyrics—do you
remember:

> I think myself to be alive,
> Yet died I not that summer night
> When in her arms I lay?
> And knew indeed that joy should kill,
> And stayed so till the day,
> And prayed so till the day.
>
> I think myself to be alive,
> Now in the dying winter light
> When winter time has come,
> Now pain has written heart and limb,
> And the little tits are dumb,
> The little souls are dumb.

I am off now for a week's sail in a tiny boat with the three girls and Melanie
of my book—I'm afraid I am very lazy in my old age. I dread being uncomfortable—above all without mail. But I'll be back here June 30th and
hope for a word from you. Address above will find me till July 10th, then
England until July 25th when I sail: c/o Jane Stockwood, 12 Ormonde Mansions, 106 Southampton Row, W.C.1. If only by some happy chance you were
in England then, what joy!

How are you? I fear the long pull back out of the war years and all the
anguish is hard. It is a very hard time for all souls—I feel the suffering everywhere. I'll copy a couple of poems off of the reverse side of this, sent with
dear love from

May

---

affamée: starved person.

UNESCO: Julian Huxley was first Secretary General of the United Nations Educational Scientific and Cultural Organization.

Malraux: André G. Malraux (1901–1976), French novelist, critic, political activist, and art historian.

Enclosed: "Return to Chartres" and "À Mon Seul Desir" a.k.a. "The Lady and the Unicorn";
see *The Lion and the Rose.*

TO PARENTS   July 4, 1947
[Le Pignon Rouge]
Dearest ones,

What a joy to have mother's two letters and know she is feeling so much better! Yesterday I was able to cash the second cable (O darling Anne!) and took the 5000 francs right to Jean-Do. They were busy in Blanchette's room stringing or rather de-stringing currants. And we had a very merry ten minutes while they spoke of la pluie d'or—I think this and Haniel's fifty dollars have come at just the right time and Jean-Do is afraid of the oculist's bills and also they have less coming in in the summer. It will mean at least one "extravagance Peacockien" as well as a help in the daily problems. The worst problem is that grocers don't deliver and Jean Do and Blanchette have to go out every morning to do the shopping (Bl. can't carry the things alone and Jean-Do has to go slowly, feeling with her cane). I am trying to persuade them to go out every two days and to get stores of canned things so that they could stay home on very hot days. It is a real heat wave here—the grass is brown. The potatoes are dying. The cows have nothing to eat. It is really very serious indeed. It's as if the weather had gone amok this winter and summer and it seems cruel when every scrap is so desperately needed in Europe.

I am sort of flopping today as I feel very tired and have again nervous indigestion, but I know that soon I'll be home in the blessed peace and continuity and so I am not worried. Anyway you know I'll be revived again by tomorrow. Unfortunately I had forgotten that I promised Neufeld I would try to see his mother in Brussels—I only just found the letter—and so I shall have to go in town again on Sunday. I have had to go everyday this week, and it is very tiring waiting so long for trolleys etc. However, all is well really.

Only I have had a shock—dear Kot tried to commit suicide on June 7th. I heard two days ago from Marjorie Wells (H. G.'s daughter in law) who is Kot's faithful friend and neighbor. His wounds are healed (he tried to cut his throat) but he has had to be taken to a sanitorium because his depression is so fearful. They are giving him shock treatment. He is so old and ill and tired I can't <u>bear</u> to think of it. Why couldn't he have died if that was what he wanted? He has no one and is dying (he has thrombosis and some sort of stomach trouble which might be ulcers or cancer?) Marjorie said that my letters have been of comfort and he asked to have them read over to him several times. And I may be allowed to see him in London—

I'm so sorry I had to worry you about the cable. I wrote on Tues. to say that I had finally been able to cash the first so I am all fixed and have my ticket to London. The bank was very inefficient and had simply lost the cable

somehow—the other one got here in two days! Dearest Anne, what a blessing she is!

I am suddenly panting to be <u>home</u> and in the dear garden with you all—
and yes, I dream too of coming with you next spring—

With all my love,
[　]

Blanchette: Blanche Rousseau, one of the Peacocks, Sarton's nickname for Marie Gaspar, Marie
Closset, and Blanche Rousseau who lived together on Avenue de l'Echevinage, Uccle, a sub-
urb of Brussels. They appear as "The Little Owls" in *The Single Hound*. See "A Belgian School"
in *I Knew a Phoenix,* and "Jean Dominique" in *A World of Light.*

Translation of French: The rain of gold.

Neufeld: Gunther Neufeld and his wife Rose were friends who later occasionally housesat in
Nelson.

TO S. S. KOTELIANSKY   July 23rd, 1947
[London (JS)]
Darling Kot,

What happiness to sit in the little house on Acacia Road (where I keep
addressing letters and then having to cross out!) under the photograph of K.
M. and the green painting of you and K. M. and to have a quiet talk with
Marjorie [Wells]. What a blessing. Everything looks so neat and clean and as
if you had just swept the floor and were downstairs making a cup of tea—it
is all waiting for you to rejoice in your homecoming. But I expect you will
have to grow some special patient hairs on your chin like a Chinese philosopher and be frightfully good so that they will see you are getting better. And
perhaps it won't be very quick. A slow rising curve and you yourself perhaps
won't see that it is rising. But it is.

And one has to go so very deep down into such tiredness and weeping
and holy nothingness to be able to come back. It is true of love I think, and
of life, and of everything in fact. People who never go down to the bottom
do not know anything at all.

My sweet Kot, my darling, I shall not see you but I am coming back in
the spring, perhaps when the pear tree is in flower and we will have a great
celebration, silent like fireworks that explode so softly in the sky. We will laugh
a great deal. I think of that and it comforts me for leaving. And it is such a
great comfort to know that Marjorie is there. We met at once. It was very
good. I am so glad she is alive to wreath the days with kindness.

Do you remember in the Bible "Goodness and mercy shall follow me all
the days of my life." I think of your heart so truly good and so truly pure in

this horrible world and I am filled with praise and rejoicing. Dear, get well. Be back in your own life soon. But not too soon, not before you are ready— "Take it easy" as we say in America.

This with my very great love always

[   ]

K.M.: Katherine Mansfield, one of Koteliansky's dear friends, once lived at 5 Acacia Road; her study was on the top floor at the back and looked out on the pear tree celebrated in "Bliss."

your homecoming: Koteliansky was at this time in the Holloway Sanitorium in Surrey.

TO ROMANA JAVITZ   Sept. 6, 1947
[Oxford Street]
Dear Romana,

I carried your wonderful letter around with me all over Europe thinking I would answer it and here I am back again. I wish you were nearer and we could talk—going to Europe clarified many things in my mind as it always does. One realizes there how stifling the American atmosphere is—I succumb to magazines and allow myself to get dulled out of sheer fatigue. In Europe one's soul leaps up close to the skin. I wrote a lot of poems. More about that later—

By now you no doubt know that Muriel is having a baby and it's due around Sept. 20th. She is in San Francisco to have it partly I imagine to be away from her family who do not shine by their power of understanding. She sounds very calm and excited all at once, is hard at work on the Boas and very happy about it and will be east again with the papoose in the spring to work on the Boas in Philly. Of course she hasn't nearly enough money to live on let alone support a child: Doubleday has been very mean in advances in spite of the millions they are making on Costain. It makes me furious. Muriel never mentions the father—he is apparently non-existent and I do not know what name the babe will have. Not that it matters. I wish I could give her a large black friend and Mammie to take care of them both— that is what she needs if she is to do her work and be a mother and in all ways of the heart she will be a marvel, but I must confess to some doubts about the practical end of things!

My poems will be out in February (Rinehart came through, bless 'em!) and you can imagine what a stone it is off my chest to have this work of ten years at last pushed away. It clears the ground for whatever happens next. I think I will now tackle the Santa Fe novel which needs a complete rewriting job, really a new book it will be hard going but fun. Meanwhile I am writing short stories like mad to make some money to live on and going out lecturing in November and again in the spring, three weeks each time. That will be fun too. My only reason for remaining American and not just leaving this country is that I have the right to fight here as I wouldn't there—and things are certainly very dark ahead for all of us.

It is terrible to come back from England and hear the drugstore man say "when will they start to work over there and get back?" Our Gov. is certainly doing the poorest job imaginable about educating America as to its responsibilities and above all the interconnection of everything. We are just noble long-suffering Uncle Sam handing out dough to the poor and needy and despicable (as they seem to most people over here.)

Europe is hog tied between the fear and pressure of communism and the fear and pressure of American capitalism. The only hope I can see is a Federated Union of socialist states, but both Russia and the U.S. will do their darndest to prevent that happening. The Ruhr business is just one example. Russia of course is playing for time with the idea that chaos will set in and all capitalist democracies go under. We are just blundering along, full of good will, ignorance and a profound subconscious refusal to face the facts—it is not a happy picture. On the other hand France is so intellectually alive, it is marvelous—and that in spite of the fearful rackets and difference between rich and poor. Paris has a pre-revolution aspect, big limosines, luxury goods at fearful prices, smart restaurants going full swing, etc. and every honest Frenchman practically starving. But the young people look amazingly healthy, swarm the roads under heavy packs making our kids look "decadent." There is real ferment in the university crowd, violent division of course between Left and Right. But it all feels <u>alive,</u> aware. My feeling about France is that it always suffers the world changes a little ahead of everyone else and is not dead at all, but about to be reborn. England I must say seems like a heavenly human place by comparison, but there is much less <u>inner</u> life. Outward the equality, the sanity are most moving and one feels <u>safe</u> in England. Also one feels acutely the loss which any such levelling down implies and there is no point in denying the loss: it is there in the paper cuts, the very hard time it is for all young intellectuals and the whole middle class etc.

Sunday

I should have talked about people not issues—Malraux (with whom I lunched at UNESCO) saying about France "Il n'y a plus de foi, il n'y a que la colère"—he is a Gaullist and hence many people feel a traitor to France; but he said he was positive DeG. didn't want to be a dictator and it was either DeG. or communism. He was very convincing, that <u>feverish</u> haunted man—he was only saved from the Gestapo at the very end by a miracle (he was high up in the Resistance of course)—Brancusi with whom I spent an afternoon all peace and light—dressed all in white, with Sabots, a long white beard, brilliant black eyes and the most beautiful delight in his work—he kept going around and taking cloths off the shining objects one by one and then smiling with pleasure. And he talked a great deal about being an artist and one felt at peace and pure there—though outside Paris smelled of decadence. Someday if we ever meet, I'll tell you all he said. And in Belgium my dear old friend, Doro of my first novel, who is going blind and with whom I spent twenty or so long afternoons talking about blindness and what one could make of it—she is a marvel of courage. It was I who cried. And my family of The Bridge and in England Elisabeth Bowen and Dorothy Wellesley and Ruth Pitter are so warm and welcoming. It was like a festival of friends. In Paris of course I spent most of my time with the Huxleys.

This is a dull letter but I wanted you to know that I treasure yours—do please write again and tell me what is happening. I am sick of all new books, revolted by the ads, the whole racket—

With much love,
May

Romana Javitz: A librarian at the New York Public Library.

Boas: Franz Boas (1858–1942), German born American anthropologist.

Costain: Thomas Bertram Costain (1885–1965), a popular writer of historical romances; his *The Moneyman* had just been published.

poems: The Lion and the Rose.

The Ruhr business: The Ruhr, the Chief Axis arsenal, was devastated by Allied air raids.

Translation of French: There is no longer any faith; there is only anger.

Sabots: wooden shoes.

TO BILL BROWN   Nov. 20th, 1947
[Oxford Street]
Dearest Bill,

It was simply lovely to go out late yesterday afternoon and find your little letter in the box—I need our correspondence too. After all, it is a rather lonely business, the one we are in! I am very distressed about the cat, perhaps if you show him the enclosed it will inspire him to get well. But it is <u>horribly</u> expensive, even cat Doctors being rather highly paid!

I came back to fabulous news that I had sold a story to Cosmopolitan for $1000 and that the one Today's Woman wanted retouched (for age) also sold for $750. I have put $1000 in the savings bank to go to Europe on and pay my huge income tax (which will take half of it now I have leapt suddenly to a higher bracket!) but I feel very much like Rockefeller and have been having an orgy of packages for Europe. I am off today to get paté de foie gras for Dorothy Wellesley who is in a nursing home run by nuns and so

Pitter says, completely cured, thin and beautiful and sane (so there is some use for nuns after all), and to get bacon for Kot and other things. What fun it is to be rich! It is worth the anxiety of these last months because the contrast is so vivid now.

As a matter of fact Cornell turned out to be marvelous—I had a fine time there and the head of the dept. asked me to come and take his place next year while he is on sabbatical (to teach Milton and Shakespeare). If I weren't going to be away this summer I think I would do it, as I would learn so much beginning from scratch. But I guess I won't, as things are. Only it pleased me with my total lack of degrees that this fine sensitive scholarly man thought I could do it. Also they loved my poems and were so still (about 300 in the chapel—the next day at a required chapel there were 800!) I thought they were bored and stopped after three quarters of an hour. So it was a bang-up finish to the otherwise rather difficult trip. But I learned a lot as I always do, and also it does me good to see the poems get across (Poetry had just sent back a whole batch of the best European ones—did I tell you the "Unicorn" will come out in Atlantic. I had proof on it.)

O yes, how I wish we could see the tapestries. I am very anxious to see what you think of the modern ones (some are hideous, some I liked, though they do not compare with the Unicorns)—I may come to New York to see the Huxleys on their way back and then we might go together just to visit the unicorns—I would love to!

I am deep in Matty's huge volume on the James Family—a rich thing. They are all so sheerly loveable which I hadn't altogether expected. And the father was wonderful. He told Emerson "that he wished sometimes the lightning would strike his wife and children out of existence and he should suffer no more from loving them."

The interruptions are awful—I do not know what the solution is. Yesterday I had a letter from Franz (he is getting married to a girl in Cal. Hurrah!) who wants to come for a week-end—I shiver already at the very idea, but I can't say no. And last night I got absolutely exhausted arguing communism with a lawyer who insists on taking me out to dinner now and then but always exhausts me with these fruitless arguments. I feel quite desperate after seeing him—he reduces everything to economics, says the world is dividing into communism and fascism and one will have to choose (I refuse to choose either one and won't be bullied into communism just because fascism may be worse—and I have my doubts if it is worse.)

I begin with human beings and he begins with theories and never the twain shall meet! What I told the kids on the trip was that democracy predicates rich (in the spiritual sense) individuals and until we grow as individuals we are actually betraying the ideas in which we believe. That is practical and hopeful and you've got to have something you can work on these days.

Well, darling, I must get to work and stop jabbering—I wish you were here. I am writing an odd romantic short story, rather sinister and Jamesian laid in a Charleston Plantation house bought by a Northerner—I invented it on the train. Then I must write the Xmas poem (God knows what it will be!) and then I'll get back to the novel.

With dearest love

[ ]

After reading Sartre's little essay "Existentialism and Humanism" I felt I had come out to some faith. I can't resist copying a few paragraphs from it, I found it a tonic:

"When we say that man chooses his own self, we mean that every one of us does likewise; but we also mean that in making this choice he chooses all men. In fact, in creating the man we want to be, there is not a single one of our acts which does not at the same time create an image of man as we think he ought to be.

The existentialists say at once that man is anguish. What that means is this: the man who involves himself and who realizes that he is not only the person he chooses to be but also a law-maker who is, at the same time, choosing all mankind as well as himself, cannot help escape the feeling of this total and deep responsibility."

This is such a refreshing contrast to Freudianism which excuses everything one may do or be.

Cornell: Cornell College, Mt. Vernon, Iowa.

scholarly man: Probably Clyde Tull.

"Unicorn": "The Lady and the Unicorn, the Cluny Tapestries" see *The Lion and the Rose.*

James Family: F. O. Matthiessen's *The James Family* (1947).

F. O. Matthiessen: (1902–1950), American teacher and critic whose most significant contributions to literary criticism were his efforts at finding a unifying tradition to American literature. He lived in Cambridge and although Sarton did not know him intimately, she was very fond of him. His suicide, his great integrity, and personal agony affected her deeply and were the basis for her novel *Faithful Are the Wounds.*

Franz: Franz Rohr was soon to marry Esther Royce.

a lawyer: Ed Spiegel of the Civil Liberties Union.

TO WILLIAM ROSE BENÉT   Jan. 14th, 1948
[Oxford Street]
Dear William Rose Benét,

Oh bless you for writing! This is the first word I've had from anyone about the book, as it is not out yet and I have been preparing myself inwardly for the <u>blow</u>, expecting the worst from the critics, wondering as one does, if I am quite mad to think I am a poet etc. etc. Your letter is balm. Perhaps you do not remember that many years ago when Encounter in April came out you spoke kindly of a poem in it called "She Shall Be Called Woman." I was particularly happy that you singled out "My Sisters, O My Sisters!" because it is sort of the same theme ten years later! It is hard to be a woman and a poet—in some ways perhaps a contradiction, and yet the challenge and the possibility of doing something new is great. Rinehart made me bury the poem far back in the book—and really wanted me to take it out so I hope you don't mind if I quote you to them!

I waited ten years for this book, trying every year to get it done, weaving and unweaving it as the new poems came along and now I believe it is good that I had to wait so long. I feel myself that it is solid—except when I get into a panic! It is not fashionable stuff either in form or content and I suppose that is what makes me superficially afraid, though inwardly <u>glad.</u>

Your letter was a personal one from one poet to another and not from a critic to a poet—that makes it even more precious. I simply can't tell you what it means. My heart soars.

May I now rudely interrupt and beg that it be reviewed in Sat. Review? They did not review my last novel until almost a year after it came out and after I complained. This was humiliating! I now have a small eager audience in the colleges where I lecture and as they all read Sat. Review they will be watching. Forgive this plea, on top of your generosity—I couldn't help it.

With gratitude, joy, much joy that you are there singing—

May Sarton

TO GEORGE SARTON   February 17th, 1948
[Oxford Street]
Dearest Daddy,

It must seem almost unbelievable that you are at last on the boat, after all the struggle of the last months and weeks to get off. And now I hope you have a little the feeling of adventure, of the wind filling your sail as you smell the sea which you love and settle mother in the cabin and go off to explore. You both did a very splendid job of planning it seems to me, to leave the house and your work and all in such good shape and you should feel very proud of each other.

I wrote a line to the Singers to say you were safely on the way—

Now I have only to hope that you will have halcyon seas and lots of porpoises and that when you are about in mid-Atlantic you feel your European self sigh and wake after all these years and turn your face happily to the green shores. You will find I think that whatever the miseries, still the spirit flour-

ishes there and you will be coming home. Even though you do not think so
while you are still in this half of the Atlantic!

I am so happy to think that European audiences will have a chance to
hear you lecture—you will do them good, dear Daddy!

Now try to get some rest. Do not push yourself to read the proofs till you
can enjoy them and not feel them a nightmare.

With dearest love and all hopes for a fair passage.

[ ]

TO PARENTS   Tuesday, March 2d [1948]
[Fredericksburg]
Dearest ones,

I am longing for your first letter and I wonder when it will arrive! Of
course forwarding takes some time. Last night I read from the book to an
audience of 1200 (!) packed into a huge auditorium with beautiful acoustics
so I really heard the poems ring out. It was very exciting and I got an ova-
tion at the end—the profs. seemed quite astonished! I wove the lecture
round four words from "Before Teaching" Delight, discipline, growth, freedom and ended with "The Tortured" (which is so simple in form it can be
understood at a first hearing) and "To the Living."

There is no spring here yet, alas—and today it is raining hard, and cold.
Luckily I have good rubbers and the wonderful plastic raincoat I bought in
Filene's basement for $.89! Also a new very grand Fall umbrella so I am pre-
pared for the worst. In Boston the storm I left in gave us another 6 inches
of snow, so we have broken all records.

Always in the South I'm terribly aware of the tragedy not so much of the
Civil War as of the bitter and cruel Reconstruction. Virginia, 3 or 4 years
after the war was called simply "Military Zone No. so and so." This is a beautiful old town and this afternoon I am to be taken to see some of the houses.
Mary Washington, Washington's mother lived here. There are no complete
towns in N.E. to compare with these for grace and charm. And the old South
is not dead yet—They send me up my breakfast on a tray with a flower by
my plate and a beautiful linen napkin! The girls are noticeably more polite
than in the North, gentle and kind. I like this college quite a lot. It is not
snobbish, being a State University and the Pres. (whom I haven't met) is relieved of the responsibility of raising funds which is the nightmare of most
small colleges.

Tomorrow I go down to N. Ca. to the Indian College. They are stopping
the train especially for me at Pembroke! Then on Saturday, back to Rich-
mond for the night and on Sunday to Nancy Hale's at Charlottesville for 3
days. I hope the weather will improve.

Sat. night I saw Hedda (a grand performance) and had a talk with Le G.

She is so upset by the savagery of the critics to "Ghosts" and the lack of public support that she says she is <u>through.</u> It was a sad conversation.

> With dear love.
> More soon.
> [   ]

"The Tortured": For "The Tortured" and "To the Living," see *The Lion and the Rose.*

Nancy Hale: (1908–?), Mrs. Fredson Bowers, who was then Professor at the University of Virginia. Boston-born novelist and short story writer; grandaughter of Edward Everett Hale; daughter of Philip L. Hale and Lilian Westcott Hale, both painters.

TO DIANA TRILLING   March 22d, 1948
[Oxford Street]
Dear Diana Trilling,

Just before setting out on a lecture trip three weeks ago I read your illuminating review of Truman Capote and had I had a typewriter with me would have written you to shout a loud hosannah of praise. It was criticism and not reviewing, to the extent that a critic can really help a writer to understand himself and to go forward. This is very rare today, so rare that one is surprised, almost taken aback (having given the critics up long ago). It makes a reversal of judgement necessary and that I think is always a salutary thing to be forced to do.

Now I come back and find your leading article in the Sunday Times on Mrs. Woolf. I am 35 years old. That means that I grew up and began to read when Virginia Woolf was already de rigueur for anyone who wished to understand the literature of this time. Long after I admired and read her and when I myself was beginning as a writer and poet, I had the great pleasure of seeing her now and then in London before this last war. I say this only because it makes it plausible for me to criticize your first premise: the so-often republished photograph which is not one of the best, except that it is one of the best as a starter for an article like yours. When I knew her in 1936, 1937, 1938, 1939 the impression was not at all, I may say, of one who would dress her hair "in defiance of fashion." As Elisabeth Bowen said of her often, "She is such a lady." The impression was always of one completely in command of any situation, and perhaps especially of any social occasion, where her wit overbalanced her sensitivity, her malice shone. You speak of "the higher intellectual circles" but perhaps you are not aware that "The Years" was a best-seller and "Orlando" is now pocket-book! (that does not suggest an ivory tower shut to all breezes from "the common man").

It does seem important always to reevaluate a writer and perhaps the time is now for Virginia Woolf as it surely is for Katherine Mansfield who would have been her contemporary had K. M. lived to be as old as Woolf. What shocked me in your article was that the limitations seemed entirely to over-shadow the achievement. Now this is perhaps valuable in a criticism of a living writer where he is still at war with his limitations. With a writer whose total work we possess, the limitations are only part of the assessment of genius. Proust was a snob possibly, but he managed to write a great novel. V. Woolf was of course, the product of her environment—she was not born a truck-driver's daughter and it seems to me quite pointless to accuse her of being "nurtured among the most civilizing minds of England," as if this were a pity. She wrote as she did because of this fact, with both the limitations and advantages that it implies. My own feeling is that her genius so far outweighed the limitations that they are only relevant in a positive sense. What she did do in her greatest novel, "To The Lighthouse" almost for the first time in English to suggest women's lives are made up of—the daily and [letter damaged] . . . . of a multitude of interruptions the . . . . of strains, stresses, meals to order, lives to appreciate and keep balanced etc. etc. Even in Jane Austen who comes the nearest to it, we do not find just this appreciation of the feminine point of view. Most female writers wish to write as men and succeed more or less in doing so. It is rare to find a woman who will be able to write with such precise understanding about what after all constitutes half the world we live in.

You do not mention Woolf's "feminism" which was certainly at times a limitation as in "Three Guineas." However your main criticism is that she never wrote a complete and final assessment of any writer. Did she mean to? Must one not judge an achievement within the limitations of what the writer set out to do? Did Woolf ever believe or for a moment try to say the final word, say, upon Montaigne? I think she rather enjoyed the very opposite, making some highly pertinent and very personal conversation around a subject. Perhaps it would have been fairer to compare what she said of [D. H.] Lawrence with other critics writing at the same time. Would she have evaluated Lawrence differently twenty years later when she wrote "The Leaning Tower?" The essays that make up the Common Readers were journalism, written from magazines and reviews, just as yours are. What if twenty years from now Truman Capote achieves a certain mastery of material and maturity he now lacks and a critic picks you up on the fact that when his first novel came out you did not entirely foresee the end? It would not mean that your excellent review had no value. It would only mean that about every twenty years there is a shift in the kaleidoscope of values.

But the total impact of the Common Reader is to make us hasten to go back to the sources, to invite us to read and to make our own judgement, to share in the very evident enjoyment V. Woolf experienced for ourselves. This, I think, was their chief and only intention—as bait. She would have been the first person to cry out in alarm if anyone imagined that she had considered any one of them, the last and complete word on any work of art. She was far too circumspect to even attempt such a thing. It was not—as you rightly point out—within her scope. But what was within her scope was a flash of perception so intimate and revealing and (at least for the moment of reading) illuminating that one rushed back to the source. Who today has this power? We have plenty of solid scholarly work, we have hundreds of "definitive" analyses. The Doctors' theses pour out from the colleges. But where is the flash of genius? Where is the original <u>peeled</u> eye V. Woolf had, with all that implies of individuality, limitation, and "specialness."

You say nothing whatever about the <u>style,</u> which is perhaps the essence of the matter—the hesitations, the parentheses, the wonderful evocative images which make a whole period (as in the Chaucer) breathe and live. No—you really cannot do this. Re-evaluate and consider the limitations, yes. Make the limitations take the foreground and obliterate the positive gift, the genius—no. This is not to help understanding but give the new smug generation exactly what it wants—Howard Fast or the really "special" Henry Miller. Was not Virginia Woolf's genius just that being so mad she remained so sane?

Forgive a long letter.

Yours very sincerely

Diana Trilling: Diana Rubin Trilling (1905–1996), cultural and social critic.

de rigeur: required by custom or etiquette; indispensible.

TO WILLIAM ROSE BENÉT   March 23rd, 1948
[Oxford Street]
Dear W. R. B.,

Just back from a lecture trip in darkest Va. and No. Ca. about to secede from the Union for the second time, I discover that Rinehart published your letter to me in the poetry issue of Sat. Review! (as an ad!) I sat alone in the house and blushed to the roots of my hair. I had sent it to them, yes, because I was so happy and grateful and thought they might like a little praise for publishing my book—and I think there was a word in some note from Selby about "using it when the time came." I am so unused to advertising of any kind that I suppose I am innocent be [?] surprised, a little shocked and sad. The beauty of your letter was that it was unofficial and <u>friendly</u>—I did not foresee that it would be turned at once into hard cash, so to speak, and feel rather as if I myself had just auctioned it off for the autograph! Please forgive me and them (they know only too well what they do!) and thank you

again for this new and irrelevant reason. I cannot deny that it is a great boon,
even though I blushed.

May Sarton

[Oxon]
Bill darling,

It is too awful that I haven't written yet, but I was very lazy on the boat
and then had a depression when I arrived, I don't know why—partly I feel
this time more how worn down all my friends are. I feel like a sort of giant
of fatness and health, they look so tired, poor dears. We had a wonderful crossing, very calm, and the woman of the coat turned out to be a darling mother
of a GI Bride on her way home after a visit. She told me long stories of life
on the farm in the most gentle voice alway ending just before we went to
sleep with a sighing "Tis a lovely life." She was hardly ever in the cabin so it
was fine. I plucked up my courage and sent Rebecca West my book with a
note and she came down twice and had a drink with me and seemed quite
thrilled with the poems. She is very warm and eager and simple like all real
people—and I am going down to her country place for lunch on Saturday.
The great thing is that on April 28th I go to Paris for four days to see Juliette alone, on my way to Belgium. I also hear that Julian is to be away again
for a week in late May which sounds almost too good to be true. But the
suspense just now is rather awful as a matter of fact. Auden was in cabin class
but I didn't see him.

Now I am in real country at the de Sélincourts and it is really like a Fra
Angelico Heaven—little pools of blue grape hyacinths under flowering
cherry, a most wonderful magnolia in flower (and full of robins) just outside
my window and then long thick grass dotted with pale daffodils. I am at peace
here for the first time since I arrived and actually wrote five pages of a story
which is a great relief, as I got into a panic last week because I had no ideas
and must get some money in soon. As soon as I've written two or three stories I shall be freer for the summer and think of poems, for which I am already making notes and champing at the bit!

I see Basil going back and forth with a wheel-barrow—they have a very
beautiful cow whom he loves, called Patience—three horses one of which
is about to foal, chickens, a dear little terrier and a huge garden—so there is
a lot of work to do, but he does it at a slow tempo and enjoys it. He has given
up writing altogether and become a farmer.

On the boat I read a very witty book called Prevalence of Witches about
an imaginary country in India perhaps, rather like Waugh but without the
vulgarity and much kinder. I just read Waugh's satire on Hollywood morti-
cians and it is really <u>too</u> horrible, too savage and somehow entirely lacking

in fun. It is just nasty and I hated it. I think he is a little horror anyway.

The most heart-warming thing here is that Kot (who tried to commit suicide last spring and was given shock treatment) is an absolutely changed person, altogether his pre-war self, and so marvelous because he is just himself and I realize how few people are. In himself he is a kind of standard of purity and true values and I'm sure all his friends, like me, feel forced to strip down to essentials in his presence. Also he is rather like a wise old God to whom everyone brings little offerings of Spam and lemons—

I must go out and mail this or it won't go till tomorrow. Write to me in Belgium—c/o Limbosh, 18 Ave Lequime, Rhôdes St. Genèse, Belgium (I'll be there May 3rd)—

and forgive a short letter—I don't feel much like writing letters these days—

Love and love

M—

My flower lasted for days, so lovely! There were 2 horrible GI's at my table who said things like "Why should we respect the British!" and couldn't wait to buy up everything in the Black Market. I argued with them, but to no avail.

---

de Sélincourts: Basil de Sélincourt was a literary critic for the *Observer;* he lived with his wife in Kingham, Oxfordshire and was a great friend and supporter of May's in the 1930s and 1940s.

Fra Angelic: Fra Angelico (Guido di Pietro) (c. 1400–1455), Florentine painter, Dominican friar whose work deeply affected Sarton throughout her life. See "A Little Fra Angelico" p. 205, *Among the Usual Days.*

Prevalence of Witches: Aubrey [Clarence] Menen (1912–), English novelist and essayist of Indian and Irish parentage. His *Prevalence of Witches* (1948) is a satirical novel about the differences between tribal and British civil law.

Waugh's satire: Evelyn Waugh's novel, *The Loved One.*

TO MARGARET FOOTE HAWLEY   May 7th, 1948
[Le Pignon Rouge]
Dearest Margaret,

Here I am in the enchanted garden of The Bridge of Years where your letter of April 20th finally found me—with the lovely news that Geoffrey and Mrs. Ames like the poems (there has been one wonderful review in the Sat. Review of Lit. of April 19th by the way) and your vanishing or metamorphosed subjects—what a damned nuisance. I hope the spring has brought its breath of release even to the pavements of New York, where actually one feels it so intensely in every small visible leaf—here it is all a glory and I am in that state bordering on ecstasy, immense fatigue and everybody so intense and brilliant I can hardly bear it. But all wonderful and the poems shooting out like fireworks as soon as I have an hour to call my soul my own. The chestnuts both here and in Paris where I have just been are simply unbelievable, huge delicate triumphs, towering everywhere—and then from below the intense green light through the ordered fans of leaves—too beautiful! Then there are the beeches, copper ones which are now almost blood-red against the blue sky (I see one from where I sit) and there are still bowers of apple blossom—and everywhere lilac and laburnum (better called in French, pluie d'or) tumbling over the high walls—ah, and my great forest, the Forêt de Soignes like a Bach fugue with its incredible tall straight beeches, making fountains of the freshest green high high up in the air. This I see on my way back from town in the trolley—a green hush which one approaches slowly and which is there half the way home.

I can't believe I have been away just a month (I hardly stopped off in New York, hating to leave Judy until the last possible minute) and sailed April 7th. Rebecca West was on the boat and I saw her several times and went down to her place in Sussex, liked her husband so much too. They are both so <u>human</u>, as real artists always are and who else ever is except some old nurse or peasant? How I wish you were here. One is really born again. I did not think it could happen to me twice and I found Eng. depressing this time because my darling friends look so worn and tired, and one does sense the <u>fearful</u> struggle there. But then the minute I got off at the Gare du Nord and there was Juliette looking like an impressionist painter's dream, and in dove blue and pink and the great shining impossible American car to drive us way up the Seine to where they live now—then I felt everything happen all over again, the wild excitement and everybody too brilliant for words. On the first of May we went to Rambouillet to hunt for lilies of the valley in the forest there, we and all the rest of Paris, on bicycles, in trucks—whole families picnicking under the trees, the toughest looking men and boys with a little bunch of <u>muguets</u> tied to their racing bikes. What a wonderful people, the French! So it is a dream, all this and I shall no doubt wake up to some fearful anguish soon—for instance, Julian who was not there by a miracle but will be there when I go back, at least for some of the time. But everything is all right really in this strangest of worlds. I am appalled at the immensity of the gifts I am receiving from all sides, trees and people, and do not deserve—so I must write some very wonderful poems to justify this purely aesthetic existence!

Darling, how are you now? What are your summer plans?

Before I left I read a wonderful nourishing book called "Cry, the Beloved Country" by Alex [sic] Paton, a South African. Do look for it at the Club, a novel—and now I read poetry and nothing else except St.-Ex's last great work which I am just beginning <u>Le Citadel.</u>

I'll stop now to copy a poem:

Love, darling, and do write! I'll be here till May 24th, from then till June 6th, c.o. Huxley, 38 Quai Louis Blériot, Paris 16e France (Later for a month to Switzerland with the family).

Love to Geoffrey—and to you <u>always.</u>

[   ]

———

West's husband: Henry Andrews.

Le Citadel: The title in English is *The Wisdom of the Sands.*

Enclosed: "The Second Spring" a.k.a. "At the Bottom of the Green Field She Lies"; see *The Land of Silence.*

Geoffrey: Geoffrey Parsons, editor of the editorial page of the New York *Herald Tribune;* Margaret Foote Hawley's companion.

TO BILL BROWN   May 25th, 1948
[Paris (Huxley)]
Bill darling,

I was very happy to find your letter when I got here, rather battered last night—as Julian who was to have been away for a week in N.Y. is ill and can't go—it is, I must say, a rather terrific blow and I am staggering. But I read your letter in bed and thought about you and all the sadness of parting you are in—I have felt that perhaps this was coming for some time. But it is never easy. I do think that living in one room is impossible, however much one loves someone. However I wish you were coming to Europe—the equivalent a piano, solitude and the continent you will be imagining and creating in your work may be even better though. How fine that Mary C. was enthusiastic—one does need now and then the <u>assurance</u> and there are so few people one can trust.

I am learning a lot about myself and life in general. I am more and more convinced, aren't you? that passion is by its very nature tragic and must always end tragically—and the greater it is, the more inevitable the tragic end becomes—(as in the great love stories, Tristan etc.). It is something <u>outside</u> life and that is what makes it so tremendous and so impossible. I am more and more grateful that my relationship with Judy has never been really passionate (I understand better now that it really never was) as that is what will make it last. But how hard it is to learn these things and how much one must suffer to learn them.

It's a great day, rather a blessing, as this apt. is so light when the sun is out that one feels like a skeleton. The Seine is dark green and very still and early this morning the Eiffel tower was shrouded in mist at the top so it looked like Jacob's Ladder. What is rather startling is that on one of the buttresses of the Pont Mirabeau which we see from here stands a small (and I think idiotic) replica of the statue of liberty. Every time I see it I want to laugh.

I wonder what your new apt. is like—do you see the river? Here I watch the barges chug past and wrap myself in Paris. It is so great and calm. I am going off to take cookies and chocolate to the Mayers—

(Dear Bill, I carried this around in my purse for a day—forgive its crumpled state! Everything is pretty Hellish here—I'll write more soon).

Love
[ ]

---

a rather terrific blow: Sarton and Julian Huxley were lovers before the War. Her great and lifelong love, however, was Juliette and when Sarton returned in the years after the war, she longed for quiet time alone with Juliette.

Mary C.: Mary Callery, doyenne of the art world. Well known sculptor; her work is in the garden of the Museum of Modern Art in New York. She had a studio in Paris; took Bill Brown to Picasso's studio for his thirtieth birthday.

Mayers: Friends of the Sartons living in Paris.

TO JULIETTE HUXLEY   Thursday, Aug. 5th, 1948
[Le Pignon Rouge]
My treasure,

What a lovely place—and I think of you sitting in one of the chairs on the terrace, I hope feeling much better. I don't wonder the heat made you ill on top of everything else. We all felt quite queer for a couple of days here, but now it is blessedly cool, autumnal and sombre with rain, dark clouds, nights under blankets (what a relief!). The news of Mother is good—no sign of cancer and the Dr. has decided not even to take out the little lump. So her birthday could be a real celebration. But I had a card from Ellen today to say that Grace has had another rechute, more pleurisy. How bitter the struggle back is and I think often of Brancusi, "Qu'il est doux de mourir," and then the agony of trying to live, of knowing that one must make the effort once more.

I have had two days of exasperating small defeats. In the middle of Mother's opening her presents some devil made us all get into a fearful argument about Germany and German guilt etc. Here they are so anti-communist that they are almost pro-German. I made the long dreary trip to Rhôdes for ration books and found the bon-homme en congé. It takes an hour each way and the heart of the morning is gone and it happens to be an immensely sad village full of idiot children and gross Flemings so going there is a sort of Purgatory to me always. Yesterday spent hours at Cook's to get my ticket for London and when I finally reached the desk was told they were out of Dover to London tickets and I would have to buy it on the train: no pounds. So I went to the bank and was told Americans couldn't buy pounds etc. etc. Lost my gloves. It seemed yesterday as if nothing I could touch would ever go right. But perhaps it was the last bout (for awhile!) with the devils for in the afternoon I felt suddenly all serene and wrote two poems which I enclose. The thing is that I am really rather worried now that nothing whatever sells. I sent off my story air mail and I think it may do, but the winter looms rather huge and hungry and I must really pull something off soon. I suppose it was too good to be true to think I could earn so easily. Perhaps I shall have after all to teach or find some other way. All this makes me wish to get back more than ever. These next weeks seem interminable. Also I heard yesterday that I can't go to my usual haven in London and am rather puzzled what to do. I am really so tired of being a guest that I may try to find a very cheap furnished room for those two weeks. And I can stay at Basil's as long as I like, but must be in London some of the time. The mother of my godchildren (whom I have never seen) is coming from Germany with her older boy. Why do I tell you all this? How dull it is.

I'm glad you liked the strange Blake poems and that they reached you in time, before you left.

How lovely to be in the Vallée of the Lys—such a beautiful book. Really what an astonishing prodigious man Balzac was. On se serait attendu à tout de lui sauf ce livre-là—et il l'a écrit!

For me the recurring image of these days of convalescence has been the great sandy open space in the Tuileries, and our two chairs in the shadow, all that sunlight and that great sky and the little boats and the two men lifting their throats lazily to the sun. I have forgotten everything we said, so strange, but I remember your hands cutting the book, and looking past you at the brilliant green and the incongruous tobacco plants. How cleverly memory sifts what is essential. Nothing we <u>said</u> was essential, but being there together was.

In every letter you ask me to be happy. I do not think it possible quite yet, but there are fine luminous moments as always. Only they have to be created each time. I am very far from peace of mind, but I do not think it just now the most important thing. I am trying to understand in myself the immense weaknesses. Perhaps if I can do that, I may be able to change. But any real change is very slow and one must be patient, not expect too much perhaps, guard what there is carefully and water it every day. Uproot all the weeds of bitterness, even against oneself. Be patient (and you know that is the hardest thing for me to learn to be).

But life is always bringing unexpected gifts. The other day Jean-Do told me a story. It is this. One of her fidèles, the group of women who have been coming to her for 30 years for a weekly lesson and discussion about literature—one of these is a very curious difficult character called Pauline. She looks like a sullen peasant, came of the worst sort of petite bourgeoisie, and made herself, climbing to the top of the teaching profession in the State Lycée, a prof. of literature. At one time when she was very depressed, Jean-Do lifted her out of it little by little, and thus saw a good deal of her for about a year. One day since J.D.'s blindness, Pauline came to her and said, "You used to be fond of me and now I feel you don't care any more." And Jean-Do said, "I am just the same, but I am old now and have much less to give. But now I need you more than I ever did, need all of you fidèles and you have much to give me." Since that day, Pauline is an absolutely changed character. She came to tea once when I was there and having heard how difficult she was, rebutée, silencieuse, I was amazed at how warm and gay she seemed. Hence, the story. Is it perhaps the one necessity of love, that it be needed? And the one great human tragedy that it so rarely is?

Also Jean-Do says that she thinks La Peste is as important to us now as perhaps the great Russian novelists were at their time. We go there today, all three of us, to re-celebrate Mother's birthday—and this time there will be no arguments as we all feel the same about nearly everything! Hurrah!

The morning is ebbing and I must try to do a little work.

Where shall I send this? Perhaps Paris would be safest. After next Thursday write to me c/o Basil de Selincourt, Far End, Kingham, Oxon. and before that to Kot's.

With very dear love

[   ]

Ellen: Ellen Paine, Grace Dudley's sister.

rechute: relapse.

the bon-homme en congé: the kind man on vacation.

Brancusi quote: See third stanza of "A Recognition," in *A Private Mythology,* "How sweet it is to die."

The mother of my godchildren: Amélie Hanbury-Sparrow.

Translation of French: Le Lys Dans la Vallée, one of the books in Balzac's *Scènes de la Vie de Provence.* "We would have expected anything from him *but* this book, and he wrote it!"

Pauline: Pauline Prince, professor at the École Normale in Brussels, one of Jean Dominique's "Fidèles," eleven women, all professors, who came to Jean Dominique's home once a week for help and encouragement.

rebutée, silencieuse: dejected, silent.

La Peste: The Plague by Albert Camus (1937).

Enclosed: #9 of "These Images Remain," see *The Land of Silence;* also enclosed "Sweet Joy," unpublished. See Appendix.

TO JULIETTE HUXLEY   Friday, Aug. 13th [1948]
[Oxon]
Darling,

I agree with you about silence, if we can feel <u>together</u> in it, if it is not a piling up of barriers, all the <u>unsaid,</u> if above all it contains hope. I know that I have a great deal to learn from you now, but at the moment there are very great barriers because perhaps you do not feel with me but only against me and often I do not feel with you but only resent the suffering instead of being able to learn from it and to use it. It has taken all the days since your letter from Bécheron telling me the plans and stating the bare fact that I shall not see you again, to be able to write this letter. I must write it honestly now and really open my heart to you once more, and even if it is to be for the last time, because it seems to me there can be no love otherwise, even the kind that lives in silence and on silence. But that love presupposes real communion and above all the sense of being included and not excluded. Just because our natures and our needs are so very different, we must <u>include</u> each other or everything breaks apart. I know that in order to make this happen I must learn to love you less terribly and more simply and less intensely. But that will take time and with time it is very possible, I think. Only now you mustn't leave me quite outside. If you can make a small act of faith in my direction, then the greatest barrier will fall at once and I believe we can begin to build the foundations of our true relationship as it will grow in the years to come.

However hard these last weeks have been, I have never for one moment doubted in my deepest self that they were necessary and that they would not be wasted. But it has been a matter of remaking that faith every day, of weeding out hatred every day, and then often beginning again half the night. This I think is excessive, in that there must be some rock to which one might hold. I turn to you today and ask your help.

You see, darling, I have come to you so often full of that most vulnerable joy of meeting and love, only to be slapped down and shut out. I know there are valid reasons why it had to be so for you and you couldn't do otherwise, and this is not to blame; and in my letters since I left you, I felt I must go always toward you still and wait and be hopeful and patient, but then every letter held only negatives. You could be tender and anxious about all my small anxieties and never about the big one. And they came <u>after</u> what was a very real torture of the spirit. The fact that it was clear last time that you must be allowed to be extremely cruel but I was not to be allowed to suffer if and when you were. My suffering seemed to become the great sin. To the point that you could write to me over and over "be <u>happy</u>." I wonder if the explanation of this is not that you have so decided that I am "over-intense" and excessive that you confuse this real failing with the reality of my feeling. That even the tears were not <u>real,</u> and therefore the love not <u>real.</u> Oh, I know that another sort of person could do you good where I have done only harm, could have helped not hurt, could have meant peace and comfort. I have hated myself not to be that person, to the point of almost not being able to be the person I may be able to be. It has all become a jungle of negatives, of refusals, of refoulements. The only thing that can make it change, make some peace and clarity is if I can know there is something of me you can still love and believe in. If you can say one positive thing and mean it. It is, I know, a very great deal to ask and I only ask it in humility and because I have come to the end of what I can do alone in this. But if you can't then don't answer this letter. We shall have a real silence and perhaps that would be best.

O my darling, think of me, please try to remember some of the good.

[   ]

The worst thing has been your assumption apparently that everything was happy and peaceful, your saying "do something definite" etc. That is saying to someone with a raging toothache "Why don't you think of something else?" What I don't understand is that now when you know you will not have to see me, perhaps ever again, you cannot be kind and help me through this bad time. It is true that since I left you I have perhaps not done any serious work except a short story and a few poems, but it seems a great deal to expect. There again perhaps we are different. I mean I must live through this out to the other side, and <u>then</u> of course I must get back to work and to life in the U.S. At the moment I parcel out the day into times, into a routine so as not to think too much, but one has to lie down at times. There is no absolute defence against pain, against this frightful loneliness for you. I miss you and miss you and it never stops. How strange it is that to say this to someone one loves risks to seem unforgivable. But I feel now that I must risk it.

———

silence: This was the beginning of a break with Juliette which was not resolved until the 1970s.
Bécheron: The manor house of Jo Davidson in Tours.
refoulements: forcings back into oneself.

TO MARIE CLOSSET   16 August 1948
[Kingham]
Little and big Marie, excellent peacock, and my sweet treasure,

In the peacock's calendar, the 16th of August is encircled with a garland of roses, hawthorne, the song of the magpie, poppies, thyme, sage and lavender—here are a few little samples of the last few. This is a letter which should be inhaled rather than read, you see. A balm to give you at least some idea (even if a poor one) of the balm that flows out from your soul everywhere, whether you realize it or not.

Darling, I am finally emerging from that dark tunnel and I realize now how harmful it really was, I was so far from my deepest and most personal truths, from love and from my self, like an illness from which I have emerged dazzled anew by the beauty of living, of feeling, of growing, of loving, of dying and being reborn. I have read two books which have helped bring me to this point, a very beautiful work by Abbé Brémond on Prayer and Poetry which you doubtless know, and the letters in English of Baron Von Hügle to his niece. I was immediately seized by four words of Von Hügel—"austerity in tenderness, tenderness in austerity." Then there were many passages in Brémond. It's wonderful to hear things we already know but need to hear again, like this, for example, when Brémond quotes Plotin "In order for the soul to achieve the object of its desire it must first go back into itself and through contemplation refind that inner god we each have within us."

These four days of peace in the country have done me enormous good. Something I do every day is to walk among the beds of poppies (a fugue of delicate wings of reds, whites, rose-salmons) to cut their seeds so they won't go by but rather go on blooming all summer long, like poets. Then in the evening before dinner I take a walk in the field with Basil, a great, magnificent field, to feed the hundreds of white chickens and speak a little to the horses and the great lady of a cow, whose name is Patience, and most of all sit with Basil and have a quiet talk. After tea I walk to the end of the garden to see the great golden wheat field, now ready to be cut and hear the wheat tremble in the wind, the most delicate sound, rich and dry like silk to the touch. Now from my window I see Basil in the distance working in the garden—I think he's just your age. And you would love him with his crest of white hair and his great joyous and mischievous laugh. In the evening we listen to the radio, we have the most beautiful concerts every night, yesterday it was Mozart. Basil's wife is in America visiting their children, and his sister is taking care of the house. Unfortunately she's a rather nervous woman who I'm always afraid will take what I say the wrong way. She is thoroughly English, truly believing that God created the English to rule the world, and does not at all understand that the Indians want their freedom from this beneficent power! We had a rather heated discussion in which I dared to say that freedom must be learned little by little, and people have the right to learn it in their way even if it means killing each other (as the English have done for centuries of civil wars) but that to protect them, even if lovingly as dependent children, is not to their advantage. After that I dropped it and we haven't spoken of it again. But I'm afraid she thinks I'm a barbarian! Tomorrow I return to London for the last stage of this journey without end. But now I am at peace.

I kiss you, my dear heart, and send you joyful and tender bravos for being you, particularly today—

Kisses to the peacocks—

———————

the 16th of August: Actually August 16 is Marie Closset's birthday.

Brémond: L'Abbé Henri Bremond (1865–1933), Jesuit historian and critic.

Plotin: Possibly Plotinus (A.D. 203–262), mystic, Neoplatonic philosopher concerned with the highest spiritual mode of life.

Baron von Hügel: Friedrich, Baron von Hügel (1852–1926), Roman Catholic lawyer and theologian.

TO BILL BROWN   Sep. 1st, 1948
[Rathfarnham]
Dearest Bill,

It was wonderful to have your letter as I've heard nothing from Juliette since before then. I should be so happy if you were here with these adorable people (Beatrice—Lady Glenavy is such a wise warm person, old and wise and healing in every way because she knows everything and can look back and laugh and still be wrung, but laugh just the same)—the most heavenly soft green hills, soft changing air, one moment bursts of sunlight, then great clouds heaving up. How I wish you were here—but I hope where you are painting again and glad too to be back in your own life. How thrilling about Picasso! I can imagine what a nightmare your aunt must have seemed after the feasts you had been having but I feel more and more that we must give back in every possible way all that we are given—and so bear with the dull and loving because we can give to them, even when we can't give to the people we love or take from. That is an involved sentence but you will understand. The one loss of this summer for me was not seeing you a little more, but how good that we had that one week-end snatched out of the chaos of feeling. It did me so much good, dear Bill. I feel now a little ashamed of having poured out so much woe upon you—but I know you helped us both. I am so happy that you did see Juliette and Julian and liked him too. He is in his way very fine. I am fonder of him than I have ever been which is strange.

I believe I begin to understand the whole struggle between the other J. and me. She is trying to reason herself out of ever having been passionately in love—that is her way of solving it. But I believe that unless she finally admits her love and lets it in, it will be really destructive. It doesn't have to be passionate (that is incidental and would change in time anyway) but it must be allowed in. She is doing everything in herself now to shut it out and I must just wait and be silent and hope, really for her sake that she will come through in the end. It has taken me a long time and much struggle to come to this point. I am now quite sure that denial never works—one must go on and love more, not less, more purely and deeply but not less. "God indeed is not the cosmos, but far less is he Being <u>minus</u> cosmos. He is not to be found by subtraction and not to be loved by reduction." I was helped by a book by a German philosopher called Buber "Between Man and Man"—it helped me to see that denial and shutting out was not the way and one did not find God by giving up human love but only through it. This Juliette because she has been so hurt cannot admit yet. And someday I shall be able to talk or write to her about it but I know that now I must wait and be patient, stand by, be there, but not insistently there. Darling, enough of all this—you must be tired of hearing about it and all words are beside the point anyway. But I feel deeply that nothing of this summer is lost.

I wonder if you got to the Limboshes? What is 10 East 92nd St? How is Jim? Maybe you can send me a line somewhere. I'll be here till Sept. 8th, then until the 11th c/o E. Bowen, Bowen's Court, Kildorrery, Kirk Co. Cork, Eire sailing Britannic, Sept. 11th, Cabin B45 Tourist Class, Cobh. (How I dread that) I don't plan to stay in N.Y. longer than to get a train and they won't let visitors onto the custom pier (where one waits hours) but I'll try to ring you maybe, or if we got in at some reasonable time you might just be there, but do not make a thing of it if you are working. I have a three-day lecture thing at Briarcliff in October and hope to spend a few days in N.Y. then.

With dearest love—I think of you so much. Isn't it good to be working again?

[   ]

Lady Glenavy: Lady Beatrice Glenavy, married to Lord Glenavy, Governor of the Bank of Ireland. Mother of writers Patrick Campbell and Michael Campbell. Painter, patron of the arts, cultivated close associations with Katherine Mansfield, Middleton Murry, D. H. Lawrence, Koteliansky, Frieda Lawrence, the artist Mark Gertler, Yeats, Chesterton, Shaw and many others.

Buber: Martin Buber (1878–1965), Viennese-born philosopher, theologian, and Zionist, who emphasized the relationships between man and man and man and God, rather than man and state.

TO S. S. KOTELIANSKY   Oct 4th, [1948]
[Oxford Street]
Dear Kot,

Your message to me through Beatrice [Glenavy] arrived this morning with a harrowing description of the dry rot in their house (how awful!), you said that you could not write and to tell me so. I had I think realized that you wouldn't or couldn't. I would not have minded as I think there are long intervals when one cannot write and you have always had them. I cannot really believe that you have, as I hear indirectly, "cast me out." For many years I have thought of you as the unchanging friend to whom one would never change. You were always to be expected and awaited like sunlight and if you didn't write well the sun doesn't always shine either. But one knows it is there behind the clouds and in a plane one could reach it. So there is no reason to despair. But if there were no sun the world would grow cold indeed. We should die of it. And if I thought your estimate of me had been so false that in radically revising it, you had to "cast me out," it would make a terrible cold everywhere I went and inside me. Surely Kot this is not true? I cannot believe it is true. You have not before believed so well of me that you could now believe so ill. You have always been angry with me for some things and I have seen the truth of what you feel. But seeing what is true and being it are years and years apart. One grows so very slowly and is constantly disappointed in oneself and perhaps only goes on because one hopes—often falsely—that one will learn and change. I am terribly dissatisfied with myself.

I do not know how to go on. I have sat here now for half an hour, but there is nothing more to say. I feel so sad.

I will let you know about mother and even if you do not write I'll tell you about mother after the operation. Nothing is very good here, but one goes on. I read the Bible instead of the morning paper now—and only read the evening paper. Otherwise I cannot work at all. Everything is so awful, except to clean the house and work and to think there are friends here and there who do not change.

With my love always,

TO MILDRED BUCHANAN FLAGG   December 5th [1948]
[Oxford Street]
Dear Mrs. Flagg,

I expect you've been getting letters like this ever since last Friday night but I wanted to add my thanks. What a fine evening it was, rich and full of treasures. And what a magnificent job you did of pushing it through (that must have been hellishly difficult!) and getting us all on our feet, and more important, down again. I admired you and felt for you from the bottom of my heart.

Only one thing puzzles me and that is this legend that I am difficult to approach, or anything but humbly grateful to be asked to appear in such company. What did happen was I think that I did not join the Club and for a very simple reason: most of the time I live on such a narrow margin that five dollars is actually a great deal of money to me. These last years sending packages regularly to Europe has diminished that margin so it is nearly invisible. I decided that belonging to the Author's Club was something I could give up for the sake of one more food package. So please forgive me and don't feel that I am high and mighty any more! And ask me again to do anything I can. I would be so happy!

Yours very sincerely,
May Sarton

Those fabulous sums Walter spoke of happen once or twice a year but the rent has to be met every month!

––––––––––

Mildred Buchanan Flagg: President of the Boston Author's Club.
Walter: Rollo Walter Brown.

TO MARIE CLOSSET   5 December 1948
[Oxford Street]
My owl who looks at me with large round eyes—How happy it made me to receive your card except that you are so exhausted after this heart trouble. It always takes longer than one thinks it will to feel better and I know how frustrating it is not to be allowed to do anything but wait and wait to feel better. And all the troubles and sorrows around you, all three of you who are such inexhaustible wellsprings of comfort and understanding. Don't worry about writing to me except now and then. Every word from you gives me a great surge, a breath of love that fills my sails and carries me a little farther along on this long journey through life. I am convinced it was your response to Mother's news in the hospital that encouraged her to write about it. You see how you help us all to survive.

"The Guardian Angel with the car" really got very attached to Mother. And now there is a second angel, a young man who was terribly wounded during the war. He drove her to her radiation treatments while I was away (Anne Thorp arranged for it. He's a student at Harvard and needs the money.) He's grown very fond of Mother and helps her in the garden. Together the other day they planted more than a hundred daffodil bulbs. Mother seems to be blooming like a daffodil herself, but when I called this morning Daddy said she'd had a bad night. I'll see her in an hour when we go there for Sunday dinner.

You say in your card that you had a frost on the 29th. Here we haven't yet had frost or snow. It's wonderfully mild and beautiful, but it won't last! I finally decided to paint each of our bedrooms for Christmas. The ceilings are <u>black</u> and the walls so dirty one can't tell what color they were. So Thursday the painters come and we have to move (and dust) all the books and furniture. We are very excited and can't believe such a cleaning is about to occur. My bedroom will be light gray with the doors and window trim cream-white. Judy's will be a blue gray green, almost turquoise but pale. Her ceilings will be white. We'll be so blinded by those white ceilings that I'm afraid we won't be able to sleep!

I will write to Alice Long for you so you don't have that extra burden. I will tell her everything and that the package has arrived.

Dear soul, I had a terrible blow this week but if I tell you about it I don't expect you to respond or waste your heart or thoughts on it because I've recovered from it already. Poetry saved me, as usual! What happened is that Kot, Juliette and Beatrice Glenavy met in London and talked about certain matters concerning me that were in a way true but which in another way were simply lies, and they all convinced themselves that I am untrustworthy, superficial, dangerous and god knows what. Juliette wrote me a leter telling me that the two others don't want anything to do with me. As far as she is concerned, she'll continue to write to me for the sake of the past, but asked me never to mention the word "love" when referring to her. For the first time in my life I must face the fact that people can deliberately lie (and that is exactly what Beatrice did). When I returned home, a friend of hers told me I must be very careful, and that she is terrible, but it's too late because I completely gave myself to our friendship when I was in Ireland with joy and tenderness. I'm trying to understand, and I think she has been so hurt in life that she has become incapable of understanding others. I am trying to believe that what she did she did not do intentionally to be cruel but really believed she was right, but how dangerous it is to judge others. The worst thing is that I think the only answer to her lies is for me to keep silent. Silence and above all time are on my side because I am very loyal, and in the end it will be known. But dear heart, I've suffered deeply, a suffering without dignity or self respect. But poetry saved me. I took a day off to read poems, old ones like Francis Jammes' which I'm making into a book for Juliette for Christmas. And suddenly I realized deep in my bones that truth lasts and simply nothing else does.

Judy was absolutely furious when she heard and said that these people never really knew me and that they were criminals. (That's not really true, but it made me feel good.) Judy shines through all of this like pure gold, an absolute purity of love.

And I think of you, Edith Kennedy, Lugné, all the true loves which never change and above all always understand. I kiss your dear little hands, and shall try to live better and to learn all there is to learn from this. I believe there is a great deal to learn and that one must grow and become more humble than I yet know how to be, and have the patience which you know I do not have at all.

I've said nothing of this to Mother.

Oh, dear soul, you are so close to me. Thank God that you are.

[   ]

A dear kiss for Blanchette—how is Madame Thuns?

———————

Madame Thuns: Emma Thuns, a poet, one of the Fidèles.

TO BILL BROWN   Dec. 31st, 1948
[Oxford Street]
Dearest Bill,

I wonder if you are back yet—it is so good that you can relax at Moline, play the piano and take comfort in your family—it is so true that one can only do that when one has one's own life apart from them. Then it is all possible and good. I laughed about O'Keefe—I must say, she sounds awful, but I have always felt her painting a bit pretentious, and I expect she is somehow endearing too, as you suggest. We knew a mad Texan girl called Maria Chabot who lives with her and cooks for her in the summer out in the Southwest. If you see her again, ask her what Maria is doing now—she is always trying to make money by taking on vast agricultural projects, with the idea of writing on the proceeds, but of course farming is a full-time job so she never gets to the writing. But she is quite a girl.

We had a really wonderful Christmas, the best I can remember. The family came here to eat curried shrimp on the Eve and then friends came in to sing carols with us and drink mulled wine, and one lonely one spent the night here to have a stocking with us on The Day. Then we separated to our several families and I ended up on the sofa alone (Judy having gone to a party) reading a most adorable life-giving book by a friend of ours in Eng. who does puppets and sets out with his theatre in a barrow and just walks all over, giving a show for nothing when he feels like it and camping out. He writes very well and it all seemed rather like Blake's Songs of Innocence on Christmas Day. A fine day. I knew that the sea of woe I was holding back would have to come to the surface after Christmas and I must confess that I have been feeling rather mad, with awful tensions in my head, not able to sleep and on the brink of tears all the time. But I am going to start my novel in two weeks and that will be absorbing and, I hope, fun as well as the immense effort I dread. I think maybe some of my mad feeling is just the fear of beginning a big job. I have two lectures next week—one on "How to write a poem" for some children at a school. I am basing most of it on three wonderful lines of Edith Sitwell's about a cat:

> "His kind velvet bonnet
> And on it
> My tears run."

I was curiously invited to a small intime tea for the Sitwells the other day, at the Constables (he is curator of paintings at the museum), the only people there except Constables and Sitwells were me, a boy I had brought who used to know Edith, and the Dudley Fitts's (I have never met Fitts who wrote a devastating review of Inner Landscape years ago)—anyway it was great fun, Edith holding forth and then Osbert holding forth and I will tell you more when I see you. I can't imagine why I was invited as I hardly know the Constables—a Cambridge mystery! The only thing I didn't like about the S's was the way they run down the French. It seemed rather provincial. Fitts looks like a butcher and, as far as I am concerned, is one.

Now we must plan when you shall come. I should think maybe the weekend of the 22d Jan. That will give us both time to do some work first—or if that is your busy week-end, then the one after. We are both looking forward immensely to having you here. You will see how fine your collage looks on the gray wall. It is just right. Perhaps we could go to a concert or theatre. There seem to be some things coming.

I saw Paisan, pretty grim I must say, though very good. And tomorrow we go to Symphonie Pastorale. Judy has to work awfully hard this week as she gives a new course next term.

That seems to be all the news. I believe in the bottom of my heart that Juliette loves me and just won't admit it and maybe finally at the end she will have to, though I am now myself so afraid of passion and its disasters that I would rather we never got into that again. I heard from Beatrice who admitted that she lied about the crying and sort of shoved it off as "O well, it all seems to me so silly and unimportant." She is a bastard. But I must say, it made me feel better that she admitted I hadn't cried as I had begun to wonder if I had, and was after all, quite mad. I've written two poems I hope you will like and which I'll put in to weigh this letter down beyond three cents, I fear!

I am glad it is a new year beginning. We must meet in Europe! Maybe this time you could come to Belgium for a few days and see Bruges and Ghent with me—what fun!

I am flat broke again but I think Diarmuid will sell something—he has five good stories now.

With dear dear love from your old

May

I forwarded the card to Muriel—the Chartres is on my desk.—how beautiful!

O'Keefe: Georgia O'Keeffe (1887–1986), American painter, became known for her huge close-up enlargements of flowers, which gradually transmuted into abstract, organic forms.

Constables: W. G. and Olivia Constable.

"Paisan": Roberto Rossellini's landmark film of Italian neo-realism.

Symphonie Pastorale: Beethoven's Sixth Symphony.

TO MARGARET FOOTE HAWLEY   Jan. 12th, 1949
[Oxford Street]
Margaret darling,

Just a word to thank you for the vermilion cigarette case—what a color, the color of elation I think. And with my initials on it too. You are a dear to remember and to always keep me in cases and this is such a beauty. I wonder how things are going with you. It is wretched that we are so far apart and I can't run in and find out now and then and sit down for innumerable cups of tea and talk. I miss you here or wherever I am where you are not. Often I need your wisdom and your saving laughter.

It is good to be through with 1948 I think and the New Year always makes me feel cheerful and full of good resolutions. On Monday I began the novel I've been thinking about off and on for months. Of course I feel and know that I know nothing and am full of fear and trembling but also that wonderful excitement of starting on a big job and knowing that there is a strong underground river of imaginative life beginning; with all it means of continuity. The trouble with short stories is just that one has to make the imaginary effort but then leave the people so fast. Nothing is selling as a matter of fact and last year I made only $2000 and was only saved by the fact that I had sold two in Dec. of the year before. So I get the usual moments of panic but I expect something will happen eventually. I hope to get a contract on 100 pages of the novel and Rinehart seemed amenable to that idea when I talked to them.

Personally I have been going through a hell of a time. A bad shattering experience and the first time in my life when I have been confronted with betrayal. Three people, all very dear to me, and two of them very old friends indeed, got together in London and simply tore me to pieces. Kot my old Russian anarchist friend has decided never to communicate with me again. One was an Irish woman with whom I stayed at the end of last summer when I was in a terrible state of depression and who was very kind at the time but has proved to be either thoroughly neurotic or just plain wicked since. The third was Juliette Huxley whom as you know I have loved very deeply for two years and who did not defend me but believed implicity the outrageous lies the Irish woman told. It all sounds like a nightmare and I still think it can't be true. Why should I have aroused such real meanness in three perfectly good people? I have lain awake at night since Juliette's letter came, severing all connection with me except as a friend, saying "Don't try to defend yourself. It will be worse for you if you do."—lain awake, examining my conscience, trying not to become bitter or full of hate, for that is sheer waste. Of course, Margaret, I know that my great sin is that I become violently attached to people, and I know that this can be destructive though it comes from a real desire to love well and a tremendous susceptibility to share imaginatively in other people's lives. But surely this, though a weakness, has certain values too which are not all bad. And surely it is not the sort of thing to make one cast out as a criminal. I don't know why I am writing all this to you, except that it is a relief to get it out. It has really poisoned me for weeks and I thought I had come out to some peace of mind, i.e. whatever they do they can't destroy my feeling for Juliette and that is pure and deep and fundamentally good. Even if she casts me out, I cannot cast her out.

Then yesterday came a final blast from the Irish which left me in such a sweat of rage I couldn't work yesterday. I'll copy out what she said so you will see:

"We also got your poem The Invisible Bridges and that brings me to the worst crime we attributed to you—worse than any personal temperamental leaning, worse than 'loving' and 'crying' and leaving your room in a mess! I wonder did Juliette tell you? This business of building invisible bridges may be evidence against you, in fact the poem seems full of noble and lovely thoughts if I didn't also have the terrible feeling that it is PROOF that you are a "schemer" for your own ends, building 'invisible bridges'. Anyway, I've said the worst now it is out—the air should be clearer except for one little thing—when your so-called friends attacked you, your terrible humility, your turning the other cheek, your goodness and loving gentleness with only a faint squeak of 'someday you'll know the truth'—was all wrong—it was horrible. You should have said 'get to Hell the whole lot of you and your gossip and attacking. You make me laugh. You make me tired.' The Uriah Heep quality was horrible."

This letter I am simply not going to answer, but I must say it makes me feel like one great bruise inside. I felt all the way through this that I must try to understand and not blame until I thoroughly understood. I never apologized because I did not feel in the wrong so I just don't get "Uriah Heep." Also when you love people really I don't think you stop loving them overnight whatever they do.

O dear, well read all this and throw this letter away. The only comfort is that I have been able to talk about it with my wonderful mother who was terribly angry (a great comfort!) I wish you were here and we could talk. What hurts is that Juliette who did at least once love me, took all this and didn't defend me.

What I think is that these people have all suffered a great deal and that contrary to the pious belief that suffering purifies and makes good, it often on the contrary really blights and distorts people and above all, makes them revengeful against life itself. and against life wherever they meet it. I have been so surrounded by love and trust since infancy that—well—I have just been lucky enough not to get blighted, and so I feel a real responsibility towards people for instance, like Juliette, who was never loved by her mother.

I must get to work—but it is good to know you are there and that however awful I may be, you still manage to love me, dear Margaret, as I love you.

Your old
May

Uriah Heep: Character in Dickens' *Oliver Twist* known for being unctious.

TO PARENTS   May 13th, 1949
[Le Pignon Rouge]
Dearest ones,

Mother's beautiful letter full of spring and the songs of birds arrived this morn, forwarded from London. I am so happy that you too are having this extraordinary spring and that Louise is there to take some of the burden of work so you can concentrate upon the garden, both working in and sitting in it—and I hope mostly sitting! Now I am puzzled as to what happened about the floor as Daddy said mother had done it herself—did Jack never turn up I wonder? I had a sweet letter from Judy yesterday describing Daddy's lecture which she thought excellent—how sad though that Anne couldn't be there. She will have been sad too. And what a splendid group of people for the lunch!

I am happily settled in my nest looking down on the amazing apple trees in flower, woken by the cuckoo every morning! And today at last it is a little warmer and the sun is out. It has been quite bitter cold. Luckily I have an electric heater in my room so that is all right. And I have worked well in these three days—15 pages. Of course I can't tell yet if they are any good, but at least the spell is broken.

The day before yesterday I went to Jean-Do's. It was quite painful—the house feels so still and we sat in Blanchette's dear room talking of her. There is however a real radiance because of all the love, a radiance which transcends death and made it a happy rather than a sad time. They spoke so feelingly of you both and what it had meant to Bl. to have us all three there last year. I remember how we laughed! One of the Giotto's is still pinned up over her bed. There have been many letters from students who remembered her from forty years ago. Just think, Jean-Do and she have known each other for 55 years and lived under the same roof for 25 years. So their roots were really intertwined. I think the mornings are the hardest time—as then Bl. and Jean-

Do always read together and did the errands. Now Jean-Do must spend those long hours alone. Of course there have been a fearful amount of letters to write and people to see. She is trying to get a book of Blanche Rousseau's last works published and all this is a good thing. They had prepared a fete for me—with lilies of the valley and dear little presents and we had a cheerful spoiling tea with delicious cramique [sic] and little extravagant cakes. I shall go every other day—and go both today and tomorrow, then not on Sunday. The only pity is that I can't go in the morning because of working. But I think I must work.

Jean-Do herself looks much better than I expected. Poor Gaspari was chalk-white when I arrived and I was really frightened she looks so ill and worn, but she was rosy again before I left. I think it did them good that we could all talk and remember things together. And I am sure it is good that I shall be here for some time—to help over the transition when the first excitement, that lifted up-ness which even death brings at first, is past. I think Jean-Do has an angelic <u>courage.</u> She says she has become a child again and just does what she knows Blanchette would wish her to do. One of the things I can do—and I hope we shall this afternoon—is to take her for little walks in the park as she can't go alone and Gaspari is too busy. She now does the errands and also teaches still (she has ten pupils). Of course they have been surrounded by the tenderness of many friends—people came from far off for the funeral and to see the two. All this love around them has helped tremendously and also for them to feel how Blanchette was honored and loved and remembered even by people who knew her very slightly. A soft shining radiance goes out from the house and penetrates farther than any of them know. I am sure of that.

Oncle Raymond is very cheerful again. He was in a black mood when I arrived. They have a possible tenant for the apartment which is lovely—but they are quite worried as one tenant has not paid his rent for months and one apt. in town is not rented. This is their only income now so it is quite serious. Aunty Lino seems very well. The Austrian girl is a perfect darling—she looks like a mere child—but the house feels ever so much cleaner and taken care of than when you were here. The kitchen is spotless. The garden is in fine trim—and I was so happy to see the crimson tulips in the grass and especially that the apple tree is still in flower.

Yesterday I had a much needed whole day here to breathe a little in and in the evening walked down to les champs with Sadji and remember so happily when mother and I did the same thing last year. As soon as I know when Bill is coming I shall write Madeleine and plan a day in Ghent. I have written Elsie Masson that Judy and I hope to have a car for a week and drive down to Vouvray and then to see her, stopping there one night or two—and then touring on. What fun it will be.

The last night in London I saw a wonderful new play by James Bridie—
but I think I wrote you that. Now I am going down to have a cup of coffee
and talk to Raymond who is anxious to discuss his new book (shades of Rollo
Brown!)

All is well and happy here.

With dearest love to you both—

[   ]

Louise: The Sarton's maid.

la Gaspari: Marie Gaspar, one of the three "Peacocks".

Sadji: The Limbosch's dog.

Madeleine: Madeleine van Thorenburg, sculptor, Belgian friend of the Sartons.

Elsie Masson: Social worker, friend of Eleanor Mabel Sarton.

James Bridie: Pen name for Dr. Osborne Henry Mavo (1888–1951), prolific Scottish dramatist. Under pen name Mary Henderson wrote *Sunlight Sonata* produced by Tyrone Guthrie.

TO HANIEL LONG   Jan. 19th, 1950
[Oxford Street]
Dearest Haniel,

The book fell into a wonderful day of which it was the most wonderful
gift, consummating three or four others. I have tried to keep from reading
it too fast and while I am pressed, reading proof and getting ready a lecture
on friendship and poetry which I gave today and will give twice more at
three nearby schools. But I did have to read the whole first long chapter at
once, sitting down in a mass of papers and things undone, just <u>rapt,</u> full of
joy and wonder and thanksgiving. It is so deep and true, cutting right down
to the essential matters and to our own essence. It is so filled with your spirit
that I felt as if we had had a sort of talk in Heaven when I put it down.

One of the other gifts was the chance to help the one survivor of Oradour
(which you remember the Germans used as they did Lidice to revenge the
murder of a German officer, burning the women and children alive and
machine-gunning the men and boys)—I was so grateful to be able to do
something, and so put into action and take out of horrible dreams that horror—this I express badly but you will understand. When one can act, one is
saved from the bad dreams. I sent Marie A. a transcript of Madame Rouffanche's story as she told it to my friend Camille Mayran. I trust that she will
let you and Alice see it. I am hoping to raise $200 in small sums to help her
along—she gets a pension but it is tiny and she is ill and old and cold. No,
she is not old, only in her fifties, but old in such grief as we can hardly con-
ceive. Her whole family (husband, three children, one grandchild) gone; her

farm gone, every neighbor and friend gone in a few hours of Hell. She escaped by a miracle, was wounded five times.

On the same day came also a fine letter from Silvia with some excellent criticism of a poem I had sent her. And all this seemed gathered together and given its full deep meaning in your book. I have tried to say it in a poem, too long, but perhaps useful—as a record of that day.

I'll write better soon. I'm out of the worst of my depression, have given up writing short stories (which were the real cause of it) and am just counting on God to feed the sparrow, if I write poems again and do what surely He means me to do.

With dearest love and Oh, untold blessings on this work of your hands and your heart—

Your devoted
May

The book: Haniel Long's *A Letter to St. Francis After Re-reading His Confessions* (1950).

Oradour: The Oradour Massacre, unique in France though not so farther east, occurred on June 10, 1944.

Marie A.: Marie Armengaud.

Camille Mayran: [Mme. Pierre (Marianne) Hepp], French author and novelist, winner of the Prix du Roman de L'Académie Française for her *Histoire de Gotton Cornixloo, Suivie de L'Oubliée,* and the Prix Femina-Vie-Heureuse for her novel *Dame en Noir.* Sarton met her at the Huxleys'. Though they saw each other rarely, they became intimate friends by letter through their respective work. Sarton wrote "Joy in Provence" for her; see *A Private Mythology.*

Silvia: Probably Silvia Saunders, friend from Santa Fe.

Enclosed: "The Empty Day," unpublished. See Appendix.

TO BILL BROWN   March 20th, 1950
[Oxford Street]
Bill darling,

I have been awful about writing, but I just have nothing to say much and so am silent. It doesn't mean that I don't think of you and I did love your letter all about the leopard-epic and the horrors of New York and your starting in again to work. It is damned difficult to get started again I must say—it is just the state I am in myself, but anyway today is a most beautiful blue day and quite warm for a change and E. Bowen is unpacking in the next room and for the moment life looks faintly bearable.

We had our cat [Tom Jones] altered in a burst of decision suddenly one day as he was puking up the house to such an extent and daily came home with fearful wounds and was never here. We now have awful remorse and talk to him as to an invalid as he has become extremely subdued and sad and just sleeps all the time. Last night for the first time he played and we practically fell over ourselves to chase his paper ball and throw it for him! He is very sweet, I must say and a great consolation.

I am busy in a mild kind of way with a few local lectures—one rather good thing, my old school asked me to come and talk to the teachers about "Why Poetry" and try to get them to use more and of course I loved doing this and it was such a success that I am to go back twice more and also talk to the school. Then there is just a possibility that I might get a lecture at a writers' conference in St. Louis in June.

Meanwhile I have also got myself involved in a local fight to try to do something about the police brutality in Boston and here—it is perfectly incredible. A Negro child was picked up by a p. wagon the other day, kept in it two hours and so beaten that she had to go to hospital. A few weeks ago a boy was shot dead on very slight provocation. As this goes on always in slum areas where the people don't dare complain and we others don't know about it—and also it's very hard to prosecute as it is always a bum's word against a cop's, it is a very interesting problem. The meetings are amazing—some violent young kids, black and white who want to take everything by storm, some patient aged Negros and wiser people (like me!) who realize that we must go slow, some Reverends (the way Negros taste the word Reverend is wonderful!) and other odd representatives of various Social Action groups. It takes an hour to decide the simplest piece of business and is altogether a fascinating example of democracy in action. I'm sure it's good for me to get out and do something useful as I am not really working at poems.

I did re-write one of the Santa Fe poems which I think is not too bad and will send (or did I send you "On a Winter Night?") I can't remember. What I have discovered now is that I am learning to use experience which happened a long time ago and that used not to be true. So at least when the poetic burst is on me, I can make notes like mad and know that I can develop and print them later so to speak. Life here is so peaceful and good but what scares me is that I simply do not feel at all in that intense way that makes for poetry and I cannot see what the solution is. Sometimes I feel like a prisoner.

I expect you saw Golshman while he was in N.Y. It sounded like a wonderful concert. Last night I read The Cocktail Party [Eliot] and I must say it haunted my dreams all night. Somehow though it doesn't quite convince me, especially the secret angelic society stuff. This seems an evasion to me so it doesn't seem entirely dramatically satisfying but it certainly is drawing crowds. Have you seen it?

I am eager to talk about Jim's poems with him and hope you really will decide to come up either in mid-April or Mid-May—either of those times would be good for me. I feel that he is needlessly obscure in places but also that he is growing—none of these later poems quite satisfies me somehow. What do you think of them?

Well, I must stop and go and take Elisabeth's dresses to be pressed—

Love and do write soon—

[ ]

---

old school: Shady Hill.

Enclosed: "On A Winter Night," see *The Land of Silence.*

TO POLLY THAYER STARR   June 26th, 1950
[Channing Place]
Dearest Poll,

You are an angel to write such a wonderful letter about the book, but before I answer it I want to set your kind mind at rest about things here. Mother after ten days of really being able to rest, because I am here, is already ever so much better. But not well enough yet to be up and about. However the Dr. was amazed at her progress and it has been wonderful to see her revive like a flower in water, so now she is even feeling well enough to work on an article on English Lowestoft for "Antiques," to write letters and to be plunged into Eleanor of Aquitaine which she says is a masterpiece (the Harvard Press one by an elderly lady who worked on it for twenty years!)

The only Hell is to be divided in conscience and now that I am really here and doing this one thing, I feel so free and happy that I have even been able to write a short story and a little poem. I simply love these days—I think I needed to be active and gardening is a real passion with me—weeding being so much like poetry really. The housework is not hard at all, we live so simply, and having a car makes of course all the difference. I am going off in a little while in it to find some salpiglossis and petunias in boxes to transplant. An adventure. So do not worry—also, I plan to come down sometime next week maybe or if not the following week to see you and have a chance to talk. I'd come for lunch and stay till after tea maybe. I am not being "good" about this, it really is a joy to be here quietly with no arrière-pensée about Judy or the puss at home. And then you know, my parents are such wonderful people. Sometimes mother comes down to lie on a chaise longue in the garden at tea-time, Daddy smokes a little cigar and we watch the birds (whom he feeds immense amounts of grain from a window-box) and the orange cat who loves to roll over on his back and show a wonderful white fuzzy stomach, the picture of voluptuous pleasure.

Now for the book—most discriminating people are not quite convinced by Part III so I gather it does not entirely come off. My intention was simply to show Boston first through Francis' jaundiced eyes (the perhaps usual view!) and then see it again when he comes back wiser and older and able to see more clearly. You are right that mere kindness without explanation seems little, and yet it was exactly my experience when I came back two years ago to be overwhelmed after all the criticisms of Am. civilization, by just this element of New England. I think Francis is not ready himself to probe much deeper, being still absorbed in his own life and world. I do not think it would be reasonable to have him at this stage also become aware of God, at least it seems so to me. Give him another twenty years! The book doesn't set out to do much more than suggest the problem of a person divided between two countries and growing up, in the process of finding out where he really belongs. But there is no doubt that an extra intensity went into the Paris part! I think myself that it would have been more convincing perhaps to leave the marriage in suspense, not tie it up so neatly—but contrary to what some of my friends have felt (that I did it to sell the book) this tieing up was really an inward necessity for me. The book was an act of faith in life and had to end that way for me—but that does not defend it on artistic grounds, only explains <u>why.</u> Anyway, I'm delighted that you did like it at all. You are darling to have given it to people—that is the greatest deed of friendship.

You will be glad to hear that I have found the Letters you sent me, of help, and have been reading them slowly at night. Also to counteract the awful world of Salem in the 17th century which I am having to immerse myself in for Eng A (They are going to give the girls 200 pages of source material on witches to write major themes on)—I must say all this fills me with woe and misery, it is all such a darkness. But also fascinating. And it leads one back into history to try to find out why suddenly the devil became so tangible and why also the fierce persecution of <u>women,</u> and why it was a peculiarly (at least in its most virulent phases) a Protestant disease. At a certain point the dear elves and fairies and all the somewhat charming mythological figures which peopled imaginations became metamorphosed into the single wicked conception of witch and devil. The spirits were all <u>evil,</u> even St. Joan's visions.

The parallel with the present persecutions is also rather interesting, the fact for instance that just as now only the ex-communist is believed (against all honest men) so then the "confessed" witches had power to send many innocent women to the stake. Then of course they had no tradition of justice or of Civil liberty so there was nothing to bank the hysteria. But I suppose communism in the non-communist countries is today the great Heresy, and that also is a point of comparison.

The only ray of light is that in Salem at least it was a fairly short period

of hysteria and the people most involved lived to repent and to make public confessions of guilt. I'm afraid it is too soon for McCarthy to do likewise?

More than anything it seems to prove that the terrible emphasis on
damnation and hell really made neurotics of everyone, especially the "af-
flicted" children who for a time had power of life and death over anyone
and everyone just by pointing a finger at them. It was in a way a revenge of
the children against their elders who had poisoned their souls with fear. And
this is just what the Catholic Church is doing re Communism—Did you
see the report (in Times) of an English Catholic priest and his horror at the
emphasis in the American Catholic Church on hate?

Well, enough of all this—I'll let you know soon when I could come and
look forward—

Bless you for your letter and all your caring—

M—

---

the book: Shadow of a Man.

arrière-pensée: With no qualms or reservations.

TO FRANZ ROHR   July 25th, 1950
[Channing Place]
Dearest Franz,

Your letter made me very happy and you were good to tell me so much
of what you thought—I have myself been dissatisfied with Part III—I think
I should have left the way open for Francis to find Ann, but not tied it up so
neatly, but this tieing up was an inward need in me and I simply had to do
it, even though I had doubts at the time.

I do not think myself that Francis was ready to share Solange's pain—his
state was a selfish state, necessary but selfish, and what Fontanes says to him
in their final talk is I think, true. Only as a friend and not as a lover at this
particular point in their two lives could he have shared the deepest things.
For this was not a happy love affair, or in some ways a "good" one, as I think
I make clear. It was a tragic one which opened the way to Francis to grow
into his true self. I am sure that later Francis and Solange can be friends but
not for about ten years.

Well, enough of this. I am so grateful that you wrote as you did and that
there were things in the book that seemed true to you. It is especially good
for me just now to feel that this work has reality because it is a very dark
time. My mother has been ill for two months—I have been here for the last
six weeks, doing all the housework and gardening and nursing and have been

more and more depressed because she was evidently getting no better. Last week we have finally tracked down the main cause (she also has a very tired heart) and it is that the cancer has spread to one lung. This means that she cannot probably live more than two years. I don't need to say more, you can imagine what strange days these have been. My mother has been my dearest friend and especially after I grew up. I think we have had an extraordinary relationship for a daughter and mother, so free of tensions, so completely understanding. That has made it possible for this too to be faced together. My father is very unable to express himself and so perhaps suffers more. But also I feel isolated from him and do not know if he even quite realizes the truth. Perhaps it's better that he does not.

Mother is in hospital now and feels more comfortable since they have drained the lung and she will be home late next week. Since yesterday we have a maid and already I can feel my spirit breathing a little, for I have hardly had time to think or feel for these last weeks and in consequence felt in a state of chaos. I hope in Aug. to be able to do a little work of my own. Of course I shall stay here and not go to Vermont with Judy as we had planned, but there will be peaceful good days. I think mother will not have much pain and will be able to enjoy coming down to lie in the garden for tea—

I have not said how deeply touched I am by your offer of help. My dear, this is so dear of you, so like you, but since I last wrote the television rights of Shadow sold for $500 and soon my Radcliffe salary begins so I have even been able to begin to pay debts and feel much more self-respecting after a long difficult winter. It is true that I have been depressed and still am, because I sometimes wonder how I shall get time ever to write again. But the whole grave facing of my mother's illness has made such a depression go into the background where it belongs.

Meanwhile it is lovely to know you and Esther are there.

> With much much love and many thoughts—
> May

Franz Rohr: Met Sarton in Grundlsee, and remained a friend throughout Sarton's life.

Esther: Esther Rohr, a sculptor, wife of Franz.

T O   H O W A R D   M O S S   Aug. 19th, 1950
[Channing Place]
Dear Howard Moss,

I'm glad Cornell sent you a copy of the little book of poems, but it was not from me personally. I presume it was meant for review. I have had a good deal more pleasure from it than from any of the books published in N.Y. by a regular publisher just because it was all done for love, or fun. The whole element of sales, money etc just didn't enter into it, and it gave me a chance to put together the poems which for one reason or another have not fitted into larger books. I wish poetry could always be published in small quantities for under a dollar. I believe we would all benefit, but you can't get a publisher to see that.

I meant to say that I thought your poem in a recent issue was a dandy and I'm delighted to see a lot of new names getting a break under your aegis (if that is how you spell that word.) I am not in a stream of poetry at the moment as is evident. My mother is seriously ill and the days get broken up. Also I have to teach at Radcliffe next year. The Atlantic took "Tiger", which made up for my wounds on that score!

Yours sincerely
May Sarton

Howard Moss: Poet, critic, and poetry editor of the New Yorker from 1950 until his death in 1987.

little book of poems: The Leaves of the Tree, Number Twenty Two in the Cornell College Chapbook series, published by The English Club of Cornell College, edited by Clyde Tull.

"Tiger": For "Tiger," see The Land of Silence.

TO MARIANNE MOORE   Aug. 22d, 1950
[Channing Place]
Dear Marianne Moore,

I would have come to the congregation of poets to hear you and Pierre Emmanuel, but my mother is very ill and it seemed at the end of that day as if the better thing were sleep. Also the phoenixes were really a bit too frequent—why so many poets and all to talk about something else than poetry? If a defence of poetry is implied, isn't poetry its own best defence and not poetry and the state of the world, poetry and politics etc.? I was recalcitrant. And yet I had such a pang afterwards to have missed you who sometimes seems the only pureness and humility and greatness left in what has become a deathly scramble for position, prestige, brilliance—everything except a true act of spirit.

I have thought of you very much lately. You have been through the great separation which I must now face. My mother will not live, they think, more than a year, and I feel as if all the flowers were dying. Like you and your mother we have been true friends and surely there is much to be thankful for, but I cannot see beyond each day, nor what life will be like. It all seems like a long journey with no home at the end.

Perhaps luckily I am going to teach at Radcliffe this year and I think it will be good to have to meet classes and be busy, as I feel too agitated beneath the surface to do any real work. The time will come and meanwhile I think of you and others whom I know little but admire much, and of all poetry might be if we were commensurate (not <u>you</u>, but I!)

Yours very sincerely
<u>May Sarton</u>

I hope they didn't <u>kill</u> you—it sounded most exhausting—

Pierre Emmanuel: French poet (1916–), and author of poetic prose.

T O   M A R I A N N E   M O O R E   Sept. 5th, 1950
[Channing Place]
Dear Marianne Moore,

I have read every word of your letter several times. It seems dear that you know all about this time, its pang and how the strength is there because it must be—and because also anyone who has had a mother like ours has been given a store and treasure of wisdom and strength. My mother, as yours, has been my life's lesson and I shall never learn it all. I like the word "reconciled" very much. I am reconciled I think except to mother's suffering. I cannot be reconciled to that. Dying seems a very long difficult business, death an unwinking eye which longs only to close. But there are a few better hours when we gather, my father and I, and have tea at mother's bedside and talk of the garden and plan the spring which perhaps she will not see, but will celebrate her with daffodils and things.

It was good of you to tell me so exactly what Pierre Emmanuel said. Many people had spoken of the thrust and nobility of him but no one had told me <u>what</u> he said. What happened in France during the Resistance and after seems to me such a hopeful thing, a cornerstone for faith, for poetry then did rise so marvelously as it was needed. It did <u>happen</u> in our time. It happened again in your poem about the war. Oh, we have much to be grateful for, even now when it seems sometimes as if earth had become Hell.

I feel it is an intrusion even to answer your letter but felt I could not let it go unanswered, without telling you what an event it was and is, and to bless you for taking time and thought to write it. I am sending you a small book of poems which I like not because of the poems (which are most of them not what I meant—and only the last poem one has written seems any use for a few days) but because of the way it was done, printed by hand by a student in one of the colleges where I have spoken. One would wish poetry not to have to be bought and sold, but always given, so this book made me happy. I feel profoundly dissatisfied with all I have done. It seems to me that I have sacrificed too much to a sort of plainness, so it seems as if there were no overtones. It is all flat and hard. But I shall try again and, I trust, do better, as the years go on.

Meanwhile it is good to know you are there. It is a blessing.

Yours very sincerely
May Sarton

I hope you're still in the North—for the brilliant Sept. light.

TO ASHLEY MONTAGU   Oct. 8th, 1950
[Maynard Place]
Dear Ashley,

Thanks for the good news—I've been meaning to write and tell you a bit how things are going with mother. But it was nice to be told about the poems. I haven't seen the Horney but am hoping they will send me a free copy as I made no charge for the quote (unlike Miss Edna St. Vincent Millay!)

Mother has ups and downs. Last week she suddenly felt much better and we have some golden days. Then it all seemed like a harvest, the slow going out of her tide (forgive the mixed metaphor!) with all her friends able to tell her how much they love her now while she still lives instead of too late. She has been in some ways an exile here—her deep friendships were made before we came over—but I have realized in these last weeks how many people here her imaginative love has touched and helped. She has been lonely, but not for messages and flowers. She does enjoy the flowers and her room is a perpetual fete. Isn't it fine that you did see her last summer? I have such vivid memories of that tea (one of the last) under the arbor and the great wonderful bunch of flowers like a Dutch painting.

Daddy is being quite wonderful and at least is finding in himself the ability to cherish her, instead of its being the other way round, as it always has been. He gets up early in the morning to make her a cup of tea and is angelic in every way. I know too that it means much to him to be able to do more than he thought possible and for that reason it was a good thing that I moved out at the end of the summer. I had got pretty nearly to the end of my tether and knew I could not teach if I was there all the time, but now I run over three or four times a day and it works very well.

The Dr. comes about every three days to drain over a qt. of liquid from the lung—I can't believe therefore that she can live many months, and we just pray that she can slip quietly away before the cancer spreads (and then there might be acute pain). Mother loves this young Dr. who is very grave, cautious and kind and we have perfect faith in him. Then we also have a perfect boon of an Irish maid who seems to be a natural nurse. So things are as good as they can be. We do not think too far ahead but try to live each day. Mother herself is pure and gay as sunlight when she doesn't feel too ill, and always seems herself which is a triumph.

With love from us all
May

---

the Horney: Karen Horney's *Neurosis and Human Growth* which Sarton blurbed.

TO BILL BROWN   Nov. 20th, 1950
[Maynard Place]
Dearest Bill,

Mother died on Sat. very peacefully in her sleep—thank God it is over. The last three weeks were so awful and at the end one felt the slow difficult uprooting, that letting go, so painful and terrible. She just wanted to die and was so frightfully tired and weak. The funeral is tomorrow and I wish you could be there as it will be all Bach on the organ with just that little chapter from Paul on Charity read, and that is all. What is awful is how much there is to do, and all I wish is to sit for a long time silent and alone and just be still and try to be reborn again, for I have been dying with mother for so long.

She was beautiful and herself to the end though literally wasted away, and after it is over I know how I shall feel her radiant presence by my side. Now it is just the emptiness, the telephone calls, the flowers to acknowledge and so many people to tell. I loved your last letter and the doodle—soon I'll come and see you—

Love and blessings
May

TO GEORGE SARTON   Nov. 26th, Sunday [1950]
[Maynard Place]
Daddy dear,

I have been thinking so much about you all morning and wondering how the lecture was going and now thinking with relief that it is over and you can settle in your room and rest and then go out—it has stopped raining here and I hope may clear this afternoon so that perhaps you can go to The Cloisters. This is the first Sunday in a long time when Judy and I have not looked forward to coming to Channing Place and though there is a marmite with a chicken in it cooking on the fire, we miss you, and it feels very lonely without you.

I was upset last night by something Aunt Mary said (not of course meaning to hurt)—perhaps she does not quite understand, but I believe you do, that I do not come now and live at Channing Place. Perhaps she imagines, as some people may, that I could ever be a substitute for mother in your life or that a daughter can in any way replace a wife. What I can be and must be is myself to the fullest limit, your daughter to the fullest limit and mother's, and that means both my life and my work. I think you do understand that Judy and I have now formed a real partnership which will, God willing, last out our lives and though this is not a marriage, it is an abiding relationship with some of the elements of marriage—a real companionship and mutual sharing of joys and sorrows, as well as the material side of living. If we should come and live with you, it would be a different thing—we should be living your life and not our own. I should not have ever spoken of this, trusting to your wise heart to understand without words had not Aunt Mary said this thing last night. I cried all night in a sort of despair at the idea that I might be failing you now, when you need me most. And yet in my deepest self I know this is right. Mother knew it. Anne Thorp knows it.

In the last fearful months I have felt so close to you, dearest Daddy, as I never did before, loving you too in a new way because of your infinite patience and loving kindness with mother and with me. Surely the crown of all those forty years was the last months when I felt you and mother newly wedded through pain.

So now we can go on hand in hand, living our separate lives but truly parallel and sharing so much. I shall never be worthy of my two parents, but at least I do know that and am humble before it.

With all my love, your devoted daughter
May

Everyone is so happy that you have Julia. You must not feel that that is extravagant or out of place. It gives me peace and you peace and time and later we can think of the next step—though I hope there will be no next step for a year or two and that you will stay in the dear house with mother's presence all around and Judy and I dropping in for tea and meals.

———

Julia: Julia Martin, the Sarton's housekeeper.

TO MARK ANTONY DE WOLFE HOWE   Sunday, Dec. 3rd [1950]
[Maynard Place]
Dear darling Mr. Howe,

If love could do anything, you, the most beloved man I have ever known, would be healed at once and have eyes able to see in the dark like an owl! Alas, all we can do is stand by and try to understand and share a little of what it means to be deprived of reading and writing when those two things have been the core of your life. This morning when I woke up I thought of you at once and remembered those beautiful poems which you sent out—was it last Christmas? It may be that you will find lines of poetry running through your head and that you will now become a full-time Bard! I think poems are one of the things one can do without seeing as one can hold a short poem complete and murmur it over. But of course you will first have a long painful time of just getting used to a new kind of life.

I feel I know a little of what it must be because my dear old friend, Jean Dominique (a female poet who uses a pen name) can no longer see more than a dim blur since two years ago. I think of you together, dear valiant spirits, and I send you very much love and hope to see you very soon. As you can imagine my life has been rather full since mother's death because of all the letters there are to write and because I got behind in my Radcliffe work. But I hope to emerge soon.

Yours, with a hug,
May

Mark Antony De Wolfe Howe: (1864–1960), American biographer, editor, and Pulitzer Prize winner. Father-in-law of Sarton's friend Molly (Manning) Howe, and father of Helen (Mrs. Reginald Allen) Howe.

TO S. S. KOTELIANSKY   Jan 7th, 1951
[Maynard Place]
Dear Kot,

I heard only today, indirectly and with no details, that James Stephens has died. I cannot understand that I did not see it in the paper, but I sometimes only read an evening paper, and our best happens to be the Christian Science Monitor which is good in every respect except one i.e. its foolish refusal to mention death; there are no obituaries. So I missed it.

There is no comfort possible for the loss of such a friend. I know that your whole house is mourning too, and I have just been looking at an old snap of you and James under the pear tree in the garden and I think the garden mourns. For those of us who did not know him well, but loved his poems and him for them, it seems as if one of the few pure voices had gone, as if there were never to be again one special bird, like the thrush. How we shall miss him—thank God the poems are there to go back to. We are all now just a little poorer than we were before he left. And I feel all around the terrible poverty of spirit. What does it matter that the atomic bomb destroys our world when the best have gone, and the values they meant are all being destroyed? I think of Virginia Woolf and others here whom you do not know, and of my mother. Of course England is better than this barbarous country. That is something.

And there you are, and I expect the bulbs in your garden are there all right and there will be a spring. Let us believe so.

I send you my love and many thoughts and much gratefulness for the good days when several times I drank tea at your table with James. Do you remember the wonderful drink you made in the square cut glass bottle? How fine it was to be a little drunk on it and poetry, together.

Yours as ever,
May

TO CAMILLE MAYRAN   21 January 1951
[Maynard Place]
Dear Camille Mayran,

Everytime I receive a letter from you I marvel that separated as we are, destiny has brought us together and I am deeply moved. Lucile has already told me that you finally settled with your daughter and that you have refound your real life after so many terrible uprootings. And how happy I am to hear it directly from you. To have a table to write at, shelves for your books, curtains which gently blow in the wind, a quiet place to think, all these things are so very important. And I think now you will be able to get to the difficult book on Oradour, blessed by this new home and the presence of your dear child. I so well understand that she finds teaching miraculous. To make young people grow, or just to help them grow a little, to help them learn real values, to see them start asking themselves deep questions, to help them learn what honesty really is and the joy and surprise of discovering themselves through a work of art and to help them be able to say "yes, I understand" is a miracle, and I don't use that word lightly. On the contrary, I mean it in its deepest sense because in a way, I think, your daughter feels as I do, a profound humility when dealing with the young. One has the feeling sometimes that there is nothing to teach because the sensitive ones will find their own ways, alone, and the others don't seem capable of understanding anything except superficially. Only sometimes, and very rarely God knows, do we feel this moment of illumination when the whole room, filled with entirely separate individuals, becomes a single _whole_ before an idea or a masterpiece, or when, occasionally, we succeed in truly reaching their souls. For me the greatest challenge is to try to make them think and above all to _feel_ honestly. All my students—girls of 18—are filled with the ideas of others. They have felt so little except what has been expected of them at their age. They seem to look at life and art through a window. They write in long, meaningless sentences full of cliché with no style or individuality, without ever having seen anything with what we call in English a "peeled eye."

I have been going back to Mother's long suffering and reliving again and again everything that led up to her death so that I can try to detach myself from it and bring back her essence, her radiant presence. I read very carefully what you were generous enough to share with me about your husband's detachment from his beloved flowers at the very end. It is terrible isn't it, that moment when even love can't help. I hope some day you'll be able to tell me about your husband and what he was like. I'm sure you still feel his presence, as I feel my mother's every minute. I catch myself doing things now which I wouldn't have done before because I know that is what she would have done. How I wish you had known her. Sometimes I feel very bitter that she never found here the kind of true friend who would have understood and appreciated her for the radiant treasure of intelligence and courage that she was, so full of such exquisite sensibilities that few ever understood the noble, difficult, bitter conflicts and suffering hidden beneath her passion for flowers and art and politics. Her real self was all buried as deep as a well. Such lives only God understands and truly loves. My mother was never religious and it was agony for me to feel her absolute loneliness at the end. Oh, if I could only believe that she is loved and truly understood now. I read over and over the end of the letter of St. Paul to the Corinthians: "For now we see in a glass darkly, but then face to face; now I know in part, but then I shall know <u>even as also I am known.</u>" That is the chapter I chose for the service and every word seemed to speak of Mother.

I was glad to hear good news from Mme. Rouffanche. I had written to thank her for the etching she sent me.

I await the book impatiently and with love and send my fervent thoughts toward you and toward it, dear Camille Mayran. Thank God you are in this world that becomes more terrible every day.

Your devoted,
May Sarton

Lucile: Probably Lucille Sumpt, social worker whom Sarton had known in Cambridge as a child and saw several times in Paris after World War II. A friend of George Sarton.

TO J. DONALD ADAMS   Feb. 13th, 1951
[Maynard Place]
Dear Mr. Adams,

I have been meaning for a very long time to write to you, for I feel so greatly indebted. Now on Sunday I was amazed to see another poem from my already old book The Lion and The Rose reprinted in the Times. I had been feeling more than usually isolated, in fact in a sort of despair, and it was like a friendly word of faith and encouragement. At best, poetry is a lonely business. In places of importance, where communications can be made to large numbers of people, I think there is almost no one except you who express the point of view of the common reader (to use V. Woolf's good phrase) about poetry—at least no one whom one can respect, except you.

The other day I woke up early to a moment of revelation, that obvious truth which comes to each of us sometimes as if it were revelation and said to myself, as if it solved a conflict: "But I <u>wish</u> to write for people, rather than for other poets." I do believe that the writing for other poets has deepened and sharpened our technique, that the intra-mural competition has been good up to a point. But it has also set a premium on a certain kind of virtuosity at the expense of what you and I might call "pure poetry." I have been writing professionally for about twenty years, since my first published poems came out just twenty years ago when I was 18, in Poetry magazine. I have never appeared in an anthology. And the anthologies are the one means by which a coming poet becomes known, and by being "known" I mean simply that the people who might like one's work have a chance to find out that one exists. That is why your repeated reprinting of poems of mine in the Times has meant so very much, more than perhaps you can imagine without the above facts.

But I must thank you also for discovering and bringing out in a new light many peoms by other poets whom I did not know. The little column is always a delight and beside it your fine discriminating essays. I was so happy to see Geoffrey Scott's masterpiece "The Portrait of Zélide," referred to again, the other day.

I'm afraid I have complained in this letter. That is not what I meant, for in my heart I believe that good poems exist and will be discovered and I would far rather have my own obscurity than the quick success which can be a real blight. Also I still have a long way to go before I shall even begin to be satisfied with anything—and that is the great challenge.

Very cordially and gratefully yours
<u>May Sarton</u>

J. Donald Adams: James Donald Adams, editor of *The New York Times* "Book Review."

Geoffrey Scott: (1883–1929), English writer who died in New York City shortly after a tragic affair with Vita Sackville-West which she cruelly cut off and which ruined his marriage.

TO JOSEPHINE MILES   March 10th, 1951
[Maynard Place]
Dear Josephine Miles,

I was delighted to hear that you were to be on the jury—I think it's a fearfully hard thing to decide between all the possibilities but after reading the will it does seem clear that it does not have to be someone who published a book this year. I do not know a poet except Wallace Stevens who is

<u>not</u> in need, so I don't think one has to bother about that clause. And I don't see myself from the will why it should have to be a young poet. There are so few recognitions of poetry in this country, I would myself like to see it go to an established but neglected poet—such as Richard Eberhart or John Holmes, whose last book published by Twayne last year seemed to me excellent and way ahead of his previous ones. Mutual respect does not imply mutual agreement and I shake in my shoes to imagine how violently we shall probably disagree; the prospect fills me with woe. However, there <u>is</u> time and maybe one or other of us will hit on a poet so logical and young and poor that it all fits in! I'm seeing Sullivan at the end of the month. He favors Holmes as against Eberhart, but this is only the beginning of a year's discussion.

Sullivan sent me two appalling books of poems of his own—and originally suggested Mary Carolyn Davies and Kenneth Patchen, the latter being my special horror and a wonderful cadger of money from every possible source. There is even a Kenneth Patchen Society or something of the sort to help support him. Well, I am filled with gloom and dismay at this problem.

It would be far better if we could ask an oracle and determine from the intestines of a chicken that the gods had spoken in favor of so and so. No three people could ever agree on anything in poetry, could they?

I wish you and I at least could talk—do unearth a prodigy meanwhile and confound us.

Yours

<u>May Sarton</u>

Josephine [Louise] Miles: (1911–1985), American poet, professor, critic, and literary scholar.

Sullivan: Probably Frank Sullivan, American humorist, author of *A Rock in Every Snowball;* for years composed the annual Christmas poem in the *New Yorker.*

TO MARGARET FOOTE HAWLEY   Sunday April 8 [1951]
[Maynard Place]
Margaret darling,

Just back with the dear little pot of mustard to unpack and show Judy—such a darling thought of yours. Only you and I and Judy appreciate what an important thing mustard can be, intangibly as well as tangibly.

I had a very good though exhausting week. It was so exciting to be alone and I had so much to do, I sat weeping furiously and getting down some of what has been in my heart with no time to get out, since mother died. It is a long poem and I just don't dare even look at it yet. It may be awful but the time and the emptiness was not, was just what I needed. I think I still am a bit grippy though and don't look forward very much to the long haul now teaching. However, I got it all planned and that is half the battle. And by May I shall be teaching Virginia Woolf which will be fun.

Stonington is a most beautiful village by the sea—such dignity and purity and peace, with flashes of blue water behind the white still houses. I went out for a walk at dusk each day, feeling rather like a ghost, a happy ghost, peering into the houses as the lights were lit. Now it is good to be home again. It is high time you came here and early in the fall we must plan it, willy nilly.

It was so good to see Geoffrey, that <u>wise</u> man—and to see you together. I felt afterwards that it was a pity I did not tell him how grateful I am for his frequent reprinting of poems. Please tell him for me how much it means when you see him, will you?

I keep thinking about your show and who might be able to manage it for you. I wish I knew just the right person. Meanwhile I wonder how the Benét portrait goes—it did look fine, that beginning the other day.

Margaret dear, do not give me up for lost because my hair is different—or because I am different. I think it will take me a full year to quite get over this year and I know I am still about half myself, chugging along on two cylinders. But I am here and in time everything will sort itself out.

With dear love
May

---

a long poem: "The Captain's House, In Memoriam E.M.S.," a poem in nine parts written April–1 and 7, 1951 in the Greene's house in Stonington, Connecticut where Sarton went for a week alone.

TO PEGGY POND CHURCH   May 1st, 1951
[Maynard Place]
Dear Peggy,

It is strange that I was talking of you just two days ago with two nurses O'Brian and Sullivan who are studying this year at Simmons College with Judith Matlack with whom I live—we had a wonderful time listening to their tales and sharing our mutual love of the Southwest and it brought it all very near—and you—

Now comes your letter. First, I am honored that you feel the Tilano poem worth including and delighted at the idea, so go ahead by all means. It's so good to know that you are using Edith's [Warner] Christmas letters, those essences.

Of course I have been thinking of her—my mother too died of starvation but it takes longer than one could imagine. The mysterious thread will not break even when the person is at peace with herself and the world and ready to have it break in every way. But finally when my mother did die it happened so peacefully and suddenly and simply—and so it will. But one does pray: soon, soon. It was miraculous that she got home. I do feel that people must have their own deaths and a hospital death is no one's death.

I see I have said "she" rather vaguely. I was thinking of Edith then but it applies to my mother. The only time I felt desperate was when they took her back to the hospital and I was so afraid she would die there, but she got home too. Thank God for that.

The ripples of Edith's life, so still and secret like a source or well, did touch the very rim of the world. Will Tilano go back to the Pueblo then? I think of him too so much. Give him my love when you see him if he remembers me.

Thank you for writing. How I wish I could get out again into the silence and space. I am teaching at Radcliffe this year and find it hard going. I feel about half myself most of the time. All is scattered in little pieces, but I sail for a few weeks in Belgium and shall find my roots again there—sail May 24th.

> Love and blessings
> May

May I have a copy or two of the magazine?

Peggy Pond Church: (1903–1988?), born December 1903 in the Territory of New Mexico, she spent a large portion of her life on the Pajarito Plateau at the base of the Jemez Mountains west of Santa Fe; much of her poetry grew out of her intimate acquaintance with this landscape.

the Tilano poem: See "Letter to an Indian Friend" in *The Land of Silence*. Tilano, an elder of San Ildefonso, worked for Edith Warner who lived for more than twenty years as a neighbor of the Indians of San Ildefonso Pueblo.

TO PEGGY POND CHURCH   May 20th, 1951
[Maynard Place]
Dear Peggy,

I was so grateful for your letter about Edith for the poem which says for us so deeply and simply and well what we feel. The day your letter came I had the most tremendous need to write a poem but instead had to correct papers (or imagined I did!) and so the moment passed and the poem will never be written. I find that after such a thing I get a black feeling of remorse and failure, for surely such moments should be seized and conscience is then a real barrier between goodness in oneself and imagined "duties."

I was interested in the Indians "after four days we do not mourn anymore"—That is health, all right. But my own feeling is that one of the horrors of modern life is that these natural processes are hurried up much too much, that people try so hard "not to give in" "To adjust" (horrid word) that they in a way never live at all. Don't you think that we Americans are very much afraid of grief, of facing death, for instance? But I believe that as Edith did, so we must prepare ourselves for death and then must go through a long seed-time after it, when those close to us die, in which every phase of grief is completely <u>lived.</u> Of course I don't mean a lot of moaning and weeping, though there is a time when that too must be allowed to happen. It all comes down to the fact that you cannot be born again unless you are first willing and ready to die.

I was much moved by what you say about now the time is here that poetry seems an underground river you cannot reach. I think we all go through this—but didn't you always have "dry" periods? I really believe that middle age is a very difficult time, a time of transition in which patience and the power to endure seem the only things to cling to. I have never been as depressed or as empty as I am this year. And when I am not writing, then I really loathe everything I have ever done, so there is no comfort even in looking at the work behind me. But I do believe that the underground river finds its way out again and also that the dry periods are really growing times, though one does not feel it happening and perhaps in the end without them, we would not be poets at all.

I am sailing this Thurs. May 24th so this which wanted to be a long letter is a very short one. I teach up to the 23rd so it is a mad rush—and all this because I have to get back in Aug. to teach at Breadloaf so I wanted to get a good stretch of time to myself. I expect when I'm on the boat it will seem worth the madness of these days. My address till June 20th will be c/o Jane Stockwood, 12 Ormonde Mansions, 106 Southampton Row, London, W.C. 1 after that c/o Limbosch, 18 Ave. Lequime, Rhôdes St. Genèse, Brabant, Belgium. Do write when you feel like it—I so long to hear. One has too few sisters in poetry and I treasure you as one.

Be of good cheer—

With very loving thoughts
May

I was relieved that Edith had been allowed to go—I know all about those last days from my mother.

TO ROSALIND GREENE   Aug. 21st, 1951
[Bread Loaf]
Rosalind darling,

It was a boon to find your letter here—where I am holding forth on the short stay for two weeks at the writer's conference. The Queen E. was stuck in the fog for almost a day so I had just 24 hours to unpack and repack in and am still a bit breathless from the transition from Europe to America, my roots dangling and not quite replanted.

It was the news of you and Harry that I wanted so much to have. I find it very hard to write because words always fail when it comes to the great moments and years in a life, and Harry has sustained this moment of extreme impossible courage into days, weeks, years—you have done it together. Somewhere in your letter you say that it is easier than my brief-by-comparison living out of a death, because you are not divided. But I have an idea that it is very much harder. You have had for a very long time to live at a tempo not your own and wholly another person's life—however deep one's love, that is, I think, a terrific and exhausting feat of the spirit. Darling Rosalind, this love and homage which flows out to you through the rain and across the gentle hills here. It is so beautiful that Harry has been creating the garden in Stonington, building and making life flourish around him even while his own was failing inside him.

For some reason all day—I had had a very sad letter from Jean-Do who nearly died this summer while I was there, and I did for a month become a nurse again, but she is all right now, and she is blind and 78 and very very lonely—well, when the letter came I felt all the tears welling up of these awful separations, and then I remembered a little prayer she sent me last year, just before mother died. Like me, Jean-Do is only a hungry non-believer, but somehow I have been saying this all morning:

> "Ayez pitié de ceux qui s'aiment et qui on été séparés.
> Ayez pitié de la faiblesse de notre foi.
> Ayez pitié des objets de notre tendresse."

The month when Jean-Do hovered between life and death, very gently, not in pain, quite lucid—was for me a sort of balm. I was there and could help and it was almost as if I had mother again, but this time not in agony. I do not know how to explain this but the relief it was to make little meals and that Jean-Do could enjoy them (every meal for months had been an ordeal for mother) it would have been beautiful and right if she could have slipped away while I was there. But one cannot, alas, choose one's death. And now she must try to live and perhaps for some reason we do not yet know.

It was a very marvelous summer and I feel alive again, like Antaeus, the very root which I now see was starving has been nourished. This the faces in Europe do for me, the trees—I don't know what it is. All I know is that I began to feel transparent to life again instead of opaque. The poems come and I have written 70 pages of a short novel, not an important work but it was such fun to be back in the imaginary world again where order and truth do prevail.

I feel the reserve in your letter about the Stonington poem—perhaps someday you can tell me when we meet. What it did of course was to make it possible for me to go forward into my life and I can never never tell you the blessing the house was. I had a wonderful letter from K—about your aunt, about herself, about life and the poem. Here letters are almost impossible as we live shut off together and talk all day and night. I have given two out of three lectures, but still have conferences with nine people to do (that is the hardest work) and to run two long clinics on the short story. It is passionately interesting but I am over-stimulated and at times only long for limbo!

Darling a poor letter, but so much love. I'll be at Maynard Pl. Sept. 1. and shall run to <u>hug</u> you both!

Your devoted
May

Rosalind Greene: Rosalind, her husband Henry (Harry) Copley Greene, and their daughters Katrine, Francesca, Ernesta, and Joy, were friends of the Sarton family. Sarton wrote "For Rosalind"; see *A Grain of Mustard Seed.*

Translation of French poem:

> Have pity on those who love one another and are separated.
> Have pity on the inadequacy of our faith.
> Have pity on the objects of our tenderness.

K: Katrine Greene, Rosalind's daughter.

Henry Copley Greene died on December 29, 1951.

TO MARIE CLOSSET   4 September [1951]
[Maynard Place]
O darling, my heart,

I understand completely the state of despair you are in trying to find the good and wise solution to the empty house, waiting with both anxiety and hope for the changes which are bound to be an upheaval before they are able to feel beneficial and good. I wonder if in the end, Marie Bohez won't actually be happy <u>after</u> that first difficult separation because I often asked myself if the comings and goings, the orders coming from here and there, wouldn't someday force her to rebel. <u>If</u> by some miracle she could become truly friendly with the Curvers, then wouldn't she feel more at ease in a household where the routine was less disrupted? I don't know, but I am thinking out loud that I have a mad desire to take a plane and throw myself into your arms and talk about all this. On the other hand, it seems to me that after you get used to the change, there would be a time of peace for you, too, to resume family life, where there would again be a familiar routine and not this delicious time of "vacation," when friends come and go, taking turns with you, and all this vacation joy. And I say this with the deepest understanding and gratitude for the devotion, imagination, and pure love you give to Mariette, Angele, Rosa and all the "Fidèles." But perhaps now it would be better if they were your celebration, your cake and your champagne instead of your daily bread and wine.

I am so happy when I think that Françoise will be near you when you get this letter, that you have probably seen her already and that you have been able to talk to her about this painful subject. When are the Curvers coming for their trial month? I am in the dark because I don't remember your speaking of them. It all depends on what kind of people they are, and whether they are imaginative, doesn't it? It's not a question of love—I'm sure they love you—but for you to live so intimately with a family requires more than love—it's a question of absolute tact and loving imagination. Will they have all that? I must admit, dear soul, that I'm a little uneasy for you. Fortunately RonRon is there.

I think, too, of those empty rooms that seem to sigh with sadness and will now be filled with life again, but they'll never be filled with the perfect life they contained for so many years. Deep down I know it is true and right that the house goes on living, and never becomes a relic of the past because that is the unique character of the house, and most of all the character of its owner. But I suffer with you, my soul, and more than I can say for the month yet to come, all the upheaval, and as you say "the terrible crime" of moving those silent witnesses of the life in Gaspari's classroom, and of those in yours. It makes me realize more than ever the importance of your dictating passages to Mariette about the school and of all it has come to mean.

After three days of continuous rain, the sun is finally out and Judy and I are straightening the house and picking up a few things—ribbons to hold the curtains in the living room, a lamp—I've just cooked some fish for the cat who is all puffed up now and purring on Judy's bed. This afternoon I will work in Mother's garden.

I had a marvelous letter from Eugénie who really has a genius for understanding everything—she seems to be a saint. I hope that little by little she will be able to talk to you.

We are leaving on Friday for five or six days but will be back on the 12th, so it's better to write here. I'll be waiting for a dictated word when I return—don't use your dear hand too much. I wish I could cover it with kisses. Do you wrap it in gauze at night? Would a hot compress help? Don't stop seeing the doctor until he finds a way to alleviate the pain.

Dear soul, try in the midst of this upheaval to find your real self again, that core which you know is always there when you dictate to Mariette. I beg you with all my heart which is so full of love for you and faith in you for this newly beginning future, this future which the angels perhaps prepared long ago, who knows. How piercingly I can feel at this instant

Blanchette's blue eyes looking at you, loving you and saying that everything you are doing is good. Oh my love,

Your Tobie [   ]

Marie Bohez, the Curvers: The Curvers, it seems, were planning to come to live in Marie Closset's house as paying guests; Marie Bohez was caring for Marie Closset. Sarton wanted Marie Closset to encourage Marie B. to live-in full time rather than commute. It is not absolutely clear.

Mariette, Angele, Rosa: Mariette de la Rivière, Angele Souvein, and Rosa Heughebaert.

Françoise: Françoise Guinotte, friend of Marie Closset who did occasional translations for Sarton.

RonRon: the cat.

empty rooms: The other two Peacocks, Blanche Rousseau and Marie Gaspari, had both died.

Eugénie: Eugénie DuBois.

TO KATHARINE DAVIS   [May 5, 1952]
[Channing Place]   Late Thursday evening
Dear Katharine,

This is just a faint squeak from a mouse wishing you a particular and heartfelt godspeed—I am so happy when I think of you and Helen setting forth on this great adventure in the capacious so steady ship, and I can see you sitting in your deck chairs on the splendid deck (I am glad you are Cabin class for the deck space is ever so much better). I am in this feeble state because I have been cleaning out the attic in a fury for the last three days and I ache in every muscle as well as feeling that life is dust and ashes: "the waste remains, the waste remains and kills" as Empson says in a villanelle. I am sitting in the center of chaos to be exact as I have filled this room, my study right next to the attic, with all the junk which might be sold—eight or nine 17th and 18th century paintings of no great interest in heavy gold frames, masses of old prints and empty frames and old china (odd pieces not from mother's collection of English Lowestoft etc.) and God knows what all. I have been through boxes and boxes of letters and papers and carried down three flights about a ton of stuff to be thrown away. You can imagine and I shall not go into it further, but it's a great relief to have this off my mind as it was a job I was determined to do while I was here.

Thank you for your good advice about the textbook. I don't think I need to do much research as the idea for this book came from Harcourt Brace themselves (and they know what they want). It is to be called Verses and will have good essays pro and con on about ten major issues ranging from women's education (for home or profession) to the neo-malthusian theorists to Civil Liberties to World Government. My job will be to collect material for Benny de Voto to o.k. and then together he and I will think up a list of questions and a brief introduction for each section. The main problem is going to be to find intelligent enough essays on the conservative side of such matters as civil liberties! But anyway I shall not begin to tackle it until I am back again in Sept. The contract expects the book only by mid June of next year. Going back in what people did years ago in freshman english is no help as the world is turned upside down and they are always out (stupidly I think) for a new approach. This I am somewhat equipped to provide because my Harvard plan is a new departure and there is a good deal of interest around it. If the book does what we hope Harvard will take it on at once so I am told. That means 1000 copies right away.

We shall use at least one court case. We have had excellent results with the Majority Opinion and dissenting opinion on The Miracle case now up before the Supreme Court (we used the N.Y. Court of Appeals material)— it is a very good exercise in close and careful reading and analysis. I notice that you wonder whether H-B is new in textbooks—I think, not. Almost all the houses now have a textbook section as it's a great and solid moneymaker these days.

Now that the attic is done I hope to have a little peace and time to pull myself together—I feel more dispersed and empty than at any time I can remember and simply dread my classes, one more drop of blood to wring out! However May 29th is soon coming.

I shall think of you in the green land, the enormous lift it will be and it makes me happy. Give my love to Helen and have a wonderful time!

Love
M-

———

Katharine Davis: Katharine Davis, a retired teacher of English; Helen Chitty was her companion.

Helen: Helen Chitty.

Empson: William Empson (1907–1984), English poet and critic.

Benny de Voto: Bernard A[ugustine] De Voto (1897–1955), Utah-born American historian and critic, taught at Harvard and Northeastern Universities. This idea to collaborate with De Voto on a textbook for freshmen called *Versus* was finally dropped in 1956.

TO MARIE CLOSSET   5 July 1952
[Linkebeek]
My darling owl,

It feels so lonely not to be coming to kiss you today, but I obey you and do nothing but watch the persian kitten purring and now playing with a pink carnation—and stare at the wheat fields outside my window. The muse, seeing I was silent, kindly visited me last night and I even wrote a poem. My old self is gradually returning, and I begin to feel alive again—Monday I will return to you, dear heart, and will have so very much to tell you and will hear you tell of the blue room and of everything, everything. In the meantime feathers balance discreetly on my head and I think I hear the hasty, loving feet of a Marie and her Gilles climbing the stairs and crossing the kitchen to find with me once again love and solitude.

Being deprived of you, and you of me, I send you Eugénie for the entire afternoon, and Monday I will come with wingèd feet, and kiss your little head and put my heart in your hands—

Your Tobie with nothing to do—

Marie and her Gilles: The poet in Marie Closset—Jean Dominique—had chosen the sad white clown, the melancholy "Gilles" of the poetic and grave French painter Jean-Antoine Watteau for her muse. This passage suggests that "Jean-Do," together with her muse, were built into Sarton's own worlds of poetry, love, and solitude.
Marie Closset (Jean Dominique) died July 19, 1952

TO ASHLEY MONTAGU   Sept. 26th, 1952
[Wright Street]
Dear Ashley,

I crave a little boon, as mother used to say. I have been roped in to do a textbook for Harcourt Brace with Benny de Voto as co-editor. The idea is in the title: Versus. It will be essays grouped round specific issues such as civil liberties and the idea is to make the students use their minds. As you know I have been one of the guinea pigs teaching the new writing course called Gen. Education at Harvard, and this book is what we are after.

One of the subjects is <u>race.</u> Naturally we want your best essay-statement exploding the race myth. It will save me some time if you can tell me where in your voluminous works on the subject this is best stated in a <u>single</u> essay. Also—and this is where I cry out for help—we have got to find the most persuasive piece on the idiotic side of the argument possible. The point is to get the most extreme opposites but as far as possible to have both essays by fairly reputable blokes where at least the illusion of impartiality can be maintained. In other words the side we are <u>agin</u> must be given fair play. Have you any suggestions? For instance a chapter from Mein Kampf would not be the best choice possible!

I guess you have in your hands Daddy's wonderful Harvard lectures on ancient science. I must confess that, well as I know him, I have been utterly bowled over by it—the charm and thrust of the writing, and so much learning so beautifully concealed in a simple style. I hope it will get the notice it deserves in the press—as here at last is a book for the layman and which could be reviewed in other than scientific journals. He seems in fine form and I gather the Paris trip was a great success.

Judy and I have bought a small house, address above—it's a wonderful feeling to know we shall not have to move again. Meanwhile I got back ten days ago from Europe and have been moving, starting at Harvard, and making savage brief attempts to clear the jungle of mother's garden. I have a little novel coming out in October, an acorn under Daddy's giant tree. I am hoping to get a year off somehow for poems next year—and am applying for a Guggenheim but with little hope of success I fear.

It would be good to see you again when you are next around—and I shall eagerly await your answer on <u>race.</u> By the way I thought I might use Daddy's defence of science recently out in Sat. Review—would you have any idea about an attack on the scientists which would fit? Have you any other ideas on controversial issues which might fit? I thought of socialized medicine, but have not discussed this with Benny. A good one will be a Supreme Court case with the dissenting views. Another an event in history interpreted by two historians of possibly different nations etc.

Love to all your family and much to your self.

May

TO BILL BROWN   Nov. 23rd [1952]
[Wright Street]
Bill darling,

What a lift your discerning song of praise gave me—and I treasure every word as you have understood as no one else has just what I meant to do, what the difficulties were. I'm especially glad you said what you did about the poetry being organized now (a matter of vision not of language) as that is what I have been working toward. I get terrified when I think of the next book in which all this must help make true and beautiful a big theme instead of a little one—did I tell you that I plan a novel about the effect of Matty's suicide on a group of people? It will be laid in Cambridge and most of the characters will be men which scares me, but a lot of things scare me about it.

I am so glad you are pleased with the paintings. People who produce a lot so often do because they are unable to criticize themselves don't you think? I'm sure it's true in poetry. John Malcolm Brinin said the other day that if he could write five good poems a year he would be more than satisfied.

The Hollywood weekend sounds wonderful fun, I must say! A little dazzle is good for the soul, especially intelligent dazzle—I have been going out more than I like really. I feel it is such a dissipation—so rarely is there an illuminating moment, and one comes home excited and empty. My great joy at the moment is making Christmas presents—I am covering cigar boxes of Daddy's (he has towers of them in the attic, one of his games)—with lovely things like the Tres Riches Heures which Life reproduced so well some years ago. Each box is different and, shellacked, they look quite fine. Anyway for me it is such a rest to be making something. The main trouble with my life is that it is all <u>analytic</u> and so, deadly in the long run. Pasting things on a box is a rather low form of creation, but it <u>is</u> wonderful fun!

Fritz Peters book got a terrific slam in the New Yorker, did you see it? I must confess I was meanly glad as it sounds like a book meant to sell and astound. The review ends "Mr. Peters tries very hard to make this road accident into a moment of blinding revelation for all his characters, but he is not a good writer, and his book is a poor excuse for a novel." (!) It is dedicated to Agi, did you know? She was sure it would be a best-seller when she called up from N.Y. I think the review is a bit strong—he <u>is</u> a writer, of course as the first book proved.

Last night I had dinner at the MacLeishes and Walter Lippman was there, very interesting about Eisenhower and what may be expected. Lippman says the only hope in Korea is a diplomatic peace, founded on recognition of Red China at UN. Pretty hard for a Republican president to manoeuver without loss of face it seems to me. Lippman is quite cynical about Eisenhower, yet he never changed over. He is a queer cautious rather weary man, but I liked him. Well that is all. The puss is wonderful—I'm afraid we have become Cat-worshippers!

Love and love
May

---

a novel: *Faithful Are the Wounds.*

John Malcolm Brinnin: John Malcolm Brinnin (1916–), American poet, director of the Ninety-second Street Poetry Center in New York, known for his works on Dylan Thomas and Gertrude Stein.

Fritz Peters: (1913–), novelist among whose works are *The World Next Door, Finistère,* and *The Descent* to which this letter refers, dedicated to Agnes "Agi" Sims, an artist friend of Sarton's from Sante Fe.

Walter Lippman: Walter Lippmann (1889–1974), American editor, essayist, and one of the most influential and statesmanlike of American journalists.

TO ORVILLE PRESCOTT   Jan. 5th, 1953
[Wright Street]
Dear Orville Prescott,

I have been meaning to write to you ever since your splendid review of Shower of Summer Days, but though I am not under such pressure as a daily review, I have been somewhat buried because of a heavy teaching schedule—and then, Christmas! From the author's point of view your notice was the most discerning of all. It fills me with amazement that you can do this, having both to read and write with extreme rapidity—one can only be grateful and astonished at the same time!

I was so aware of the dangers involved in this little book, so slight a theme, such hair-splitting moods and feelings, that I still cannot believe it is what you and others kindly say it is. I feel rather like a mole who has tunnelled obscurely in the dark for years and suddenly finds himself up in the air, with a host of distinguished animals there to shake his paw and offer congratulations. Now of course I can hardly wait to begin tunnelling again!

Your kind of criticism is the creative kind and that means that it forces one to greater efforts, more joyfully than before.

With very warm thanks
May Sarton

What an unexpected pleasure to meet your wife at the Cosmopolitan Club the other day!

Orville Prescott: (1906–), editor, literary critic, and daily book reviewer for *The New York Times.*

TO LEWIS GANNETT   Jan. 6th, 1953
[Wright Street]
Dear Lewis Gannett,

I have been meaning to write to thank you for the splendid review of my little novel <u>A Shower of Summer Days</u>, but I'm on a rather heavy teaching schedule at Harvard this year and so, almost as pursued by time as someone who writes a daily review! Long long ago when my first novel appeared you gave me that early accolade which means more than any later one ever can, so I have two reasons to thank you.

My fears were so great about this one that I still cannot quite believe that I pulled it off—and now of course I can hardly wait to begin a big novel on a big theme. What your discriminating praise, and that of others, has done is probably to liberate me from having to teach next year. It is such an immense gift that I hope you feel like Charlotte in Charlotte's Web. I certainly do feel like Wilbur the pig, RADIANT.

Yours
May Sarton

Lewis Gannett: (1891–1966), literary critic, known for his daily column, "Books and Things," in the New York *Herald Tribune.*

[Wright Street]
Darling Bill,

I did wonder what had happened but thought you might have gone
home after all—it is much better that you have been painting so well and I
hate being so far away and not able to see anything. What are the subjects?
Is it a series like the football or music stand ones? I wish I could have some
idea—

I am a barbarian about science as I seem to have no curiosity about it at
all, and am just scared to death like an eskimo when I read anything like Limitations of Science though maybe I should look into it for Versus. Versus has
become a kind of albatross of a thing and I wish to God I had never under-
taken it. I am between the devil and the deep blue sea as I get patronizing
letters from the Harcourt editor suggesting books we read long ago or not
liking something we have finally agreed on triumphantly, Benny and I.
Benny is the deep blue sea, an opinionated rather crude man whom I like,
but he hates the whole thing and I have to poke him to get the reading
done—and altogether as you see, it is a Hell of a job. It's much harder than
I supposed it would be to get good pieces on various sides of the subjects.
You find one and then hunt for days for an opposite. And then when and if
we get the material I have to write for permissions and there is endless horrible detail involved. Never again—even if it makes a pile which is the only
incentive, but a somewhat remote one as I shan't get a cent till 1954.

However, everything else is looking up in a wonderful way. I went down
to N.Y. to cadge a poetry prize, $200 for a lyric, offered by that rich mori-
bund institution The Poetry Society of America. I'll enclose the poem, perhaps not one of my best but the 200 bucks was very nice anyway.

In N.Y. I had a talk with Diarmuid and also realized that Harper's and
Harcourt Brace would both like to get me. This means that Diarmuid had
some bargaining power and he has got me a wonderful contract—a book of
poems this year and $1500 advance on the new novel when I need it. If I
get a fellowship (which is dubious) I'll keep that in reserve for the year after
next, but it is very nice to know it is there if I don't get a fellowship, I must
say. But the great thing is the poems and I have been busily typing and arranging. It will be a purely lyrical book, almost no political poems and I want
to call it just New Poems if they will let me. I am rather tired of "poetical"
titles. I don't know yet when they plan to bring it out but I imagine fairly
soon in order to cash in on the interest in Shower. The good thing is that it
clears the decks and I can start in fresh at the end of this year.

I am really very tired of teaching, tired and dried up. I don't see how people do it for long periods of time without withering away. But I guess some

people enjoy being analytic and intellectual whereas I know more and more that I am not an intellectual. The values which interest me passionately have to do with feeling; intellect is only useful for criticizing form in my own work, not for analysing that of other people.

I haven't read Fritz's book either—it sounded rather bad. Agi says he is at work on a new one. She has been painting like mad for a show in Colorado Springs and also to send things to Vivianos. I feel she is about to break through and I hope she will and get away from S. Fe for awhile in the process.

I must say I envy the camellias—here it is dead winter, the iron time. The puss spent three weeks in hospital at Christmas to the sum of $42! He is called The Million-Dollar Cat now, but he is wonderful—

Love and love

M—

(E. Bowen comes for a week day after tomorrow and I am busy fending off the lion-hunters!)

----

poetry prize: Sarton won the Reynolds Award for "Journey Toward Poetry," see Appendix. This poem appears with radical changes under the same title in *The Land of Silence.*

TO BILL BROWN   Feb. 15th, 1953
[Wright Street]
Dearest Bill,

What a wonderful letter—of course I disagree rather violently with the tenets of non-objective painting (which remind me of the discussions of "pure poetry" some time ago)—I would think that non-objective painting was extremely valuable for the painter himself but only as the isolating of one part of a painting for analysis and study—the theory seems to be that "emotion" is something isolated and which has nothing to do with "objects," yet surely this is just nonsense. Isn't it really that a good painting is non-objective in the sense that it could be turned upside down and still hold together as composition, but this is just <u>one</u> element. Subject matter can, of course, get in the <u>way</u> if it is melodramatic as in Delacroix—who seems a great painter in spite of his subject. But does it get in the way in a Chinese painting of a flower or bird? or the Cezanne apples or landscapes? I do not see how one can bring any memories of associations to a completely abstract painting—it pleases as a <u>design</u> and has, to me, all the limitations of the decorative, however subtle and sophisticated. It is just the cutting out of association which seems to short-circuit this connection between the seer's experience and the painter's. One is left outside—and perhaps the proof of this is just the tendency to give complete abstractions fancy poetic titles. Surely the title should be absorbed into the painting and if it has to depend on a title for raising "associations" then it is a failure. However all this does not mean that as a step or discipline needless to say—I do not know what I am talking about! However, I thought the enclosed on Matisse's sculpture might interest you in the context.

I think it is high time the sensuous world came back as it is doing in poetry (Dylan Thomas for instance). Louise Bogan came to Radcliffe to read the other night (more of that later) and read three poems which were a deliberate attempt to use color again in poetry as a necessary element. They are called After the Persian and I found them beautiful. I guess the whole thing as always is a matter of balances—the balance between an emotional and intellectual concept which seems to be the essence of any art and which is well said in the review I enclose; "voluptuous yet austere" would be what I would say I want too in poetry, for instance. It is just this paradox of formal means and anarchic sensibility which is the excitement of art, isn't it?

I got into a fierce rage at the Bogan reading—as about 30 people showed up—most of them my students at that. It was at Radcliffe and apparently they had done nothing to let people know she was coming! I only knew because she said so on a Christmas card and I ferreted out at considerable trouble where the reading was to be held. She herself as Judy said had a kind of "royal simplicity" which carried the whole miserable affair off. Afterwards the Dean had invited of all things, most of the Radcliffe administration to a drink and to meet her, not one student interested in writing was there except a major horror in the shape of a boy called Simon. He is writing his thesis on poems in prose at Harvard and is a teaching fellow. Very handsome with a slight perhaps German accent. He came up to me to say that I might like some news of my friend Claude Fredericks who has been in Rome for some years with James Merrill the young (and very rich) poet. I said I would love some news and Simon proceeded to spill a large garbage can of dirty gossip in my lap—he then took on Bogan and said that the New Yorker had been so stupid as to turn down a poem of his because they (poor fools) had entirely missed the point. "Mrs. White [Katharine] wrote me a four page letter" he sneered. After he had demolished the New Yorker for awhile I rose up and said I thought it was still about the best magazine around, and mentioned Janet Flanner. Then Simon guffawed about "that old rabid Lesbian" (I forgot to say that re Merrill and Fredericks he had said a lot of insane things about homosexuals) well, anyway, so it went on. During the evening he sneered at every one he spoke of—I left at 10:30 so that I would not feel compelled to murder him. What frightens me is to think that he is teaching. Perhaps he is a friend of hers—anyway I did like her and she was very cordial so I shall see her in N.Y. She has, as you know, been rather mean to women poets in general, but I did not feel any of this in talking with her.

I did not see Muriel when I went down as it was just overnight. Apparently there is an essay on her work in the new New Directions—I must get hold of it. I think she is going through a hard time and I am somewhat anxious about her future. I'm afraid she had her heyday in the political period and will not discipline her poetry so it could be all that it should be and all that it is in embryo. Still, she is a giant compared to most of the people who throw mud at her, I must say. One nice thing about E. Bowen is that she is never cruel in comment about other writers, a very warming trait.

I loved your description of Carmel—the actual land and sea is so beautiful and you must go again when the spring comes. I sat in a field there in May and counted about forty wild flowers without moving.

I am definitely taking a year off next year—I thought I had said so—as it's all that keeps me going, to think I'll be a free woman in June. The advance will help if no fellowship comes through but I have some hope that one or the other will. If it does I can save the advance for a later year. I really need two free years—or a dozen!

[Harold] Perry got me wrong about Bowen—it was just that I did not know that The Last September (an early very good novel of hers laid at Bowen's Court) would be reissued this year. But B. seems happy about my book so all is well.

The best poems in the new book are from this summer. I am having quite a time trying to arrange them—at present about 68 but I expect to cut 8 of them. One problem is whether to include a short (5-poem) section of semi-political poems—I think qua poetry they are not my best yet they say some things I can't say any other way. At present, I think I'll shift them into other sections. The best section is pure nature lyric, including "The Swans" from The Leaves of the Tree, "The Second Spring" ditto and some from this summer.

Well, that is all—do write again soon. It is awful that you are so far away—if only you had been there for Bogan!

Love
M—

James Merrill: James Ingram Merrill (1926–1995), novelist and poet, won Pulitzer Prize in 1977 for *Divine Comedies*.

Perry: Harold Perry, unidentified. Possibly a book reviewer.

B: Elizabeth Bowen had just been to visit Sarton in Cambridge and liked *A Shower of Summer Days*, Sarton's 1952 novel set in Dene's Court, modeled on Bowen's Court, Elizabeth's ancestral home in Ireland.

[Wright Street]
Dear Katharine Davis,

It was awfully good to hear from you after all this time, although I am distressed about your eyes. I wish I could have heard you and H. on the Abbey. I expect you listened to the coronation ceremony over the air—I found it extremely moving—this symbol, shorn of its <u>power,</u> which now simply unites many people in love and reverence. I sat with English tears streaming down my face—

I am staying right here this summer. The Bryn Mawr fellowship, by the way, does not involve more than one week's residence at the college at the end of October, but I got it to do a very difficult novel on. And that is what I am plunged in now and shall be for many months, with only two weeks break in August to lecture on the novel at Bread Loaf Writers' Conference. I thought that if by any chance Putney is anywhere near Bread Loaf I might catch a glimpse of you and Helen on your way there or back, but I fear that is a pipe dream. My plan is to push the novel through by February and then to take off for six glorious months abroad—and time for poetry. I have been thinking about this novel for two years now, so I was really ready to begin, but I think it may have been foolish—it was a real compulsion—to start as tired as I was, after the three teaching years. Never mind, I have 140 pages done now and stride along each day. I'm not sure you will approve of this one as it is about the division among liberals, the lack of faith, the giving into false fears which is now making this country contemptible in the eyes of the world. The removal of books from shelves in foreign libraries is just one thing. An atmosphere in which people are held to account and punished for beliefs they held ten years ago (when Russia was our ally for instance) is another thing. It is impossible for any international congress to be held in the U.S. at present, for instance on crystallography which had to go elsewhere. Too many distinguished men would have been kept out by the McCarran act or simply on principle refused to be finger-printed and investigated. What would American tourists think if they were asked the kind of questions we ask and held up for weeks at the borders. I know that you voted for Eisenhower, but I wonder if you are entirely pleased now. At least you did not elect McCarthy as President but major decisions of the greatest importance are made with one eye on his reactions, so he might as well be. My Rep. friends told me not once but many times that the way to get rid of McCarthy was to elect Eisenhower who would fight him and destroy his influence!! I do not think the danger is measureable nor the harm already done. No honest person can stay in the State Dept. If he does he will soon be removed. Our prestige in Europe and India and the near East is at an all-time low. What we have now is power and money but <u>no</u> respect. Imagine sending Cohn and Shine to spend <u>two days</u> in Berlin and then report that Am. Gov. is full of subversives! The irresponsibility and childishness is unforgivable.

Meanwhile the universities (with the exception of Harvard thank God) are allowing first principles to go by the board—we shall soon be teaching "the party line" or be out. Criticism of the U.S. is "subversive." The examination of other economic theories than ours is "subversive." We are simply aping the Russians. Soon it will be un-American to say that an Englishman invented the steam engine. The chauvinism is simply appalling.

Well, forgive me. But the Europeans who came to this country came because it represented certain fundamental intellectual and human values, among them freedom of belief and freedom of speech. It is depressing to see how quickly Americans, under the pressure of hysterical and quite irrational fear, have been willing to give them up. The Germans were much slower about it under Nazi-ism!

One feels quite helpless. However, in my novel I shall try to say some of this as humanly as possible. I come back in my own mind to Camus' statement in The Plague. The way to fight the plague is with "human decency." Public trials with none of the safeguards of the law, such as the investigations have become, is not treating people with <u>human decency</u>. "And what does it profit a man to gain the whole world and lose his <u>soul?</u>" Perhaps we shall get rid of or drive underground the tiny percent of active communists—but at what a price!

It is too hot to continue this—I am enjoying being in Cambridge though in spite of the heat. I need this peaceful time in which I do nothing but work and sleep and go for little walks—cook etc. The puss has taken possession of a window box in which we meant to put flowers, and lies there on his back like a baby in a cradle all day—too sweet! My father takes off for Jerusalem (an international congress of which he is President) next week and will be gone three months. That seems to be all my news.

Don't give me up for lost even if you disagree with the above—

With much love always—
M—

H.: Helen Chitty.

the coronation: George VI of England died on February 6, 1952. His daughter Elizabeth took the oath as queen on February 8, 1952 and was crowned as Elizabeth II on June 2, 1953.

McCarran act: The McCarran-Walter Immigration and Nationality Act permitted naturalization of Asians and established a quota for further admission, but also provided for the exclusion and deportation of aliens and control of citizens abroad.

McCarthy: Senator Joseph McCarthy (1908–1957), whose charges of a large-scale Communist infiltration into the State Department and careless accusations brought great hardships to many people.

Cohn: Roy Marcus Cohn (1927–1986), chief counsel for Senator Joseph McCarthy during U.S. Senate hearings (1953–1954).

Shine: G. David Schine, a private in the Army who was suspected of being a spy for McCarthy and was in fact one of his peripatetic investigators together with Roy Cohn.

Enclosed: Sarton's 1952 Christmas Broadside *Of Friendship at Christmas,* unpublished. See Appendix.

TO JOHN HALL WHEELOCK   Sept. 16th, 1953
[Wright Street]
Dear John Hall Wheelock,

Nat Burt was a fellow at Bread Loaf and so I came to know him and his work. It made me so sad to think that I had not discovered Question on a Kite for myself, sad that such really excellent poetry, such a personal distinguished talent has gone so un-noticed. I do congratulate you on publishing him and wish I could help to make it a more fruitful thing all round. What I would like to do is to send some copies of the book to a few friends such as Archie MacLeish, Rolfe Humphries, Horace Gregory, Conrad Aiken et al with enthusiastic letters. Of course you did this when the book came out, yourself. But I think a totally uncommitted voice some time later might carry some weight. Do you think it would be of any help at all?

The one thorny question is that I cannot afford to buy five copies of the book at the usual rates. Could you give me an author's rate?

I felt appalled, violently moved to some sort of action when I realized that a poet as good as this seemed stifled by almost total non-recognition.

It was a happy thing to meet you in the Ballantine anthology (what a fine job Humphries has done!) <u>Wood-Thrush</u> has seemed to me, among the really memorable pieces in it, bless you.

Tell me what I can do for Nat—

Yours sincerely
May Sarton—

Nat Burt: Nathaniel Burt (1913–), composer, poet. Son of Struthers Burt, novelist and poet, and Katharine Newlin Burt, novelist.

John Hall Wheelock: (1886–1978), American poet and editor at Charles Scribner & Sons.

Rolfe Humphries: (1894–1969), American lyrical poet and translator of Latin, Spanish, and French works.

TO ROLFE HUMPHRIES   Sept. 16th, 1953
[Wright Street]
Dear Rolfe Humphries,

Just before I took off on a two weeks' holiday Sept. 1st, the anthology came, so I had a chance to read it off and on, under pine trees and on beaches, late at night and early in the morning—it is a beautiful job. It seems to me that it has somehow given back poetry to its own country, the country we have all been starving for, call it perhaps lyricism. I have a hunch it will do more to bring the public back to reading poetry and feeling that modern poetry communicates than anything published for a long time. And what variety and richness there is! I was first shaken and taken by Babcock's America (still think it one of the finest single poems in the lot) and so grateful for Louise Bogan's Song for the Last Act where I shall not lose it again. I tore out the New Yorker printing when it came but have lost and found it a hundred times. Now it is permanently <u>found.</u> The Edmund Wilson, too, is such a beauty and I could name many more. I like your finds, all of them, the un-published or little published people.

I wish I could have been at the party, but I have been rather dead tired, in the midst of a big novel and then Bread Loaf like a ton of bricks on my head. It seems to me that the trouble with such conferences is that really only the old profs have the humility and wisdom to learn. I learned an enormous lot, but did the students? That is a moot point! Of course I got a kick out of seeing my name on the cover, such a surprise, I fear undeserved from any point of view, but for that reason all the more received with whoops of il-legitimate pride.

Thanks for all your part in this, a noble selfless work for poetry. I'm afraid your only reward will be a deluge of letters. Do not answer this one. The an-swer is implicit.

Yours sincerely,
<u>May Sarton</u>

P.S. But what a queer world this world of poetry is. At Bread Loaf one of the fellows was Nathaniel Burt. Do you know his work? The second book, Question on a Kite is really a dandy, and yet he said he got three reviews in all and not one letter. I want to send it to you and am writing Wheelock to try to cadge some copies to spread around.

TO CAMILLE MAYRAN   4 October 1953
[Wright Street]
Camille Mayran,

Dear, what joy and tenderness your letter evokes—I'm sorry I left you without news, but here it is: Agnes was unable to come in June and we post-poned her visit here until now. I had an extremely exhausting and full summer with demanding courses to give in a summer school, the new novel which possesses and seizes me like demon, and a sprained ankle that has forced me to become an invalid for six weeks now. It's been only recently that some peace has descended, and I can bury myself in work. I really am extremely agitated and wouldn't dare invite anyone right now, and I don't know when I can go to New York. According to what Vincent has told me, Agnes is like a chrysallis who, inside herself in her silent shell, is creating a new self and the courage that goes with that, and needs to be left alone. I find it terrible for her that she can't find the time for even the small gesture of sending an occasional word to ease her mother's concern. I hope that I can see her before Christmas, but I can't promise. That must sound terribly selfish but right now my first responsibility is to my work. You know the fierce selfishness of a mother protecting her sick child—I feel exactly that way. Try to forgive me. I don't forgive myself, but one can only do what one can. I hope Vincent, whom we love like a little brother, adorable and perfect, will never know what those few days when I had to tear myself away from my real life cost me. I tell you this out of shame. I know too well that art can cost one's life, not only the life of the artist but also the lives of those around him. And there is nothing that can be done about that. The worst part is that this novel might not even be any good! It is extremely difficult. I feel myself totally immersed now in the depths of what I know I must do, in the very human roots of the matter (a suicide that seems political) but actually deals with a man full of love and fervor who could never communicate with others, who could never give himself or forge the true communion that would have saved him and allowed him to create. It took me 200 pages of a false start to discover that. I've just torn up the entire thing.

I'm so happy that you have this wonderful island of time with Vincent. How heartbreaking that he must go so far away to such a dangerous place, and be so isolated over there. I can't wait to hear his impressions. The story of his arrival and incarceration in New York is absolutely incredible! We do live in a crazy world. What frightens me is that the communists (and here the <u>fear</u> of the communists) had succeeded in undermining the basic <u>trust</u> without which men in society simply cannot live. Fear and suspicion become a disease. We are all infected.

It is so beautiful all that you say about the relationship between a mother and son. It touched me the more because my mother lost two little boys—and she would have been such a mother as you are to a son. It is <u>so</u> lovely that Vincent has come into our lives. My father grew so fond of him and both Judy and I almost wept when he left, we had grown so attached. He combines so many beautiful qualities, such sensitivity, intelligence and that delightful shy humour. You must be <u>very</u> proud of him.

Dear one, I hate to send this letter. But you will read between the lines,

I hope—and I trust that before long we shall manage to get Agnes up here (perhaps for Thanksgiving at the end of November)—please forgive me for everything—

Yours devotedly
May

But I did <u>try</u> to get Agnes to come in June.

Vincent: Camille Mayran's son, Vincent Hepp.

Agnes: Probably Agnes Aynard, Mrs. Walter Brennan, a friend who lived in New York and Paris.

TO LOUISE BOGAN   Nov. 4th [1953]
[Wright Street]
Dear Louise,

Not a letter, but just a word to say how beautiful a time it was. I felt like a hunted animal (I always do in New York) who suddenly finds a haven. I walked in and there were the walls that exact green which is my favorite color, and always reminds me of my mother for some reason. And there was the fish, and there were those little framed classical scenes behind me, and there was you. It was just as if some awful constriction and tension eased at once, and I could be myself again. Really a great blessing. And oh, the tea!

On the way back I began Viola Meynell and wanted to go on and on in Howard Johnson's—but now there is the thicket of stuff on my desk to be got through before I can breathe, so it may be awhile.

It is peaceful here (though very shabby)—you must come sometime. The cat is asleep in a tight ball on my bed, one paw over his nose. In a few days I'll have sorted out all that has happened and begin to live again. I feel like an ashcan at the moment.

How very fine and moving that we have finally met.

Yours, with love and homage
May

Realized after I got to Gert's that my face was <u>coal</u> black! I am normally white—strange as it may seem—

---

how beautiful a time it was: Although there had been letters exchanged, and although Sarton had met her briefly at the Radcliffe reading reception in February 1953, this was the first real visit between Sarton and Louise Bogan.

Viola Meynell: Author of novels and short stories. Wrote a *Memoir* of her mother, Alice Meynell (1847–1922), English essayist and poet.

Gert: Possibly Gert Macy, Katherine Cornell's friend and manager, whom Sarton knew well.

TO LOUISE BOGAN   Nov. 13th, 1953
[Wright Street]
Dear Louise,

It was good to hear. I always have a queer sense of suspension, of not hav-ing really landed, when I have been away and seen people until I hear some-thing. I expect you are now beautiful and orderly and wonderfully clean after the upheaval, with books back (I do hope the walls are the same color?) and the fish floating in his place. But it is an earthquake and must at some points have seemed hardly worth it. Anyway, now I think of you at peace—

It was a shock about Dylan Thomas. I shall always remember the flood of relief I felt when I first read October Morning and Fern Hill and "Do not go gentle into that good night," as if a long starvation were at an end. It is cruel that he should go, but it is, I suspect, the Dionysian fate, the exalted feverish climb that cannot make a natural end. How mysterious—these an-gels and self-destroyers who appear now and then. But something has gone out of our world now forever and it does chill one to the bone. Also I get scared because such deaths make one feel responsible, I mean responsible for one's own future—to have more time is such a responsibility. To use it well, to keep on growing, to be implacably self-demanding and self-critical. Given less to begin with, we must become more (but I am talking of myself not of you, of course)—what if Yeats had died at forty? Or Marianne Moore? I like best to think of poetry as a long life with the best at the end.

I finished Viola Meynell's novel and shall send it along after the week-end. A strange, to me, not altogether successful novel—have you read it recently? I got fascinated by Gilda and the subterranean life of her love affair and felt a bit cheated when all that simply dropped out. And I was very much inter-ested in the whole approach to character, entirely (so it seems) by analysis, a very daring thing to bring off so well. Morley is wonderfully real, the girl too. But as a whole it seemed to me almost like an excuse for some won-derfully keen perceptions and almost statements about relationships rather than making them happen for the reader. It has a sheen about it, but to me not a quite real sheen. Probably this is all quite a false view of mine—I read so badly when I am writing. Every book presents a series of private ques-tions, every book one reads I mean. So pay no attention.

                                                            Nov. 14th
I got interrupted. I keep thinking about your book, I mean the prose one you are writing now—I keep thinking of the form of it, not exactly auto-biography you said, but I guess things that do not get said in the same way in poems, which can so rarely suggest the process of growth, one by one. It is very exciting to consider what you may be saying or not saying—when I

saw you I was at the extreme down curve about my novel and now I think I am slowly moving upward, at least I have a little more confidence now. And it begins to come alive. It was for a time, simply hard labor with no joy in it but I do believe it was chiefly that I was dead tired. I cannot bear to waste time being tired, yet it is what I do so much of the time. I have come to believe that one creates time very much as one creates a work of art, and that having no time (which is what makes fatigue) is all in one's own mind. This sounds quite crazy, but I'm sure you know what I mean. The difficulty with being a writer is that one is torn between life and work, all the time having to <u>preserve</u> oneself for work—then seeing that this is all wrong and work is made of life, an endless pendulum swing. The trick must be to learn this way with time which I believe you have—

I felt it very tangibly when I walked into the room and during the hours I was there. Time, which had been boxed, began to flow.

Tell me how you are—Did you see the excerpts from V. Woolf's journal in Harper's Bazaar? So moving and painful—I <u>hate</u> them to be read there— at hairdressers by people who do not care—

Love from
May

Dylan [Marlais] Thomas: (1914–1953), powerful and sensational Welsh prose writer and lyrical poet, died on November 9, 1953. His death at St. Vincent's Hospital in New York City after a night of heavy drinking was regarded as an international event, symbolic of the plight of the artist in modern society.

the prose one: Possibly *Selected Criticism* which was published in 1955; or possibly material that Ruth Limmer later collected in *Journey Around My Room, The Autobiography of Louise Bogan* published in 1980.

TO KATHARINE WHITE   Dec. 18th, 1953
[Wright Street]
Dear Mrs. White,

I am not really as careless of the New Yorker's kindness and belief as I seemed on the phone yesterday, startled as I was out of all politeness even! What I did not explain was that I have been going through a period of what the Dr. calls "nervous exhaustion" and had to keep very still, not even opening mail for a time. This threw off my novel schedule in a bad way and made me put everything else off when I revived. I did mean to write and ask whether I could see one of the contracts which give you exclusive first reading rights. If this could be tried as an experiment on both sides for a year, I think I would like to. I shall certainly be doing some short pieces and especially poems when I am abroad so the chances are that I would this year at any rate, be sending along enough to make it worthwhile from your point of view.

I think my real subconscious fear is the danger of beginning to write <u>for</u> a particular market. But if it works this year, it might be a life saver next when I shall not be on a fellowship—unless by some happy chance I get a Guggenheim (which was put off last year to this because of the Bryn Mawr thing.) I'll write Diarmuid and tell him this today.

Last night I lay awake thinking about another piece—I am dying to get at it, but want some really clear time and this, at the moment (600 poems to get out) is not there. Thank you for calling and for being so patient with my vagaries about a contract.

Yours sincerely
<u>May Sarton</u>

Katharine [Sergeant Angell] White: (1893–1977), writer and editor at the *New Yorker* magazine. Wife of E. B. White.

the Bryn Mawr thing: In 1953 Sarton won Bryn Mawr's Lucy Martin Donnelly Fellowship to work on a novel; *Faithful are the Wounds* was published in 1955.

TO LOUISE BOGAN   Jan. 26th [1954] Tuesday eve
[Wright Street]
Dear Louise,

What a good thing it was to hear your voice say "It's all right" and I am sorry about the man with the check, suspended in the air so to speak. To-morrow I am starting on a stiff work schedule to try to do two more pieces for the New Yorker while I wait for Rinehart to speak about the novel, so after this you will not be quite so inundated with communications, let us hope! But I do have things to say, and want to try to say them.

The first contains all the others really. It is that not since Jean Dominique died two years ago have I been <u>in</u> a place <u>with</u> a person which together meant poetry to me. The first time I came, I felt this so strongly that I almost burst into tears—the green walls, the peace of it, the sense of inward life, the sense that each object has been chosen with love and <u>means</u> something. And of course all I have felt about you and your poetry for many years suddenly <u>there</u>. This was true of Jean-Do's rooms. Here in my own study I feel the same thing, but it is my study and not someone else's <u>ambiance,</u> hence there is no such wild excitement and no possible confusion. To be in your atmosphere with you was like an explosion of poetry, and this after some months of complete being-parted-from-it. The coming back then is always love and always pain. You know this better than I do, I suspect. When I say I love you,

I am saying that I love poetry. And because this is so, to confuse such love with sex is perhaps fatal, at least very disturbing. Yet can I be sorry it happened, for such disturbances also make life seem suddenly overwhelmingly rich and good?—like a huge gift—and perhaps one simply has to accept it all whatever happens, use it, and not ask more of it, above all, than is there. How can I convey the happiness, the richness of that time? Without overweighting them, being completely honest with you which I must be.

I am writing this quite deliberately before I hear from you so that you will know the whole truth and all be clear between us. Oh, I do hope you may come up before I leave March 4th—for N.Y. March 3rd actually. That would be very wonderful. And probably you are saying in your wise self— why is she making so much of this and why go on about what seems rather simple and had no profound meaning beyond what you suggest in "Cup, ignorant and cruel." But it <u>was</u> deeply troubling for me and made me ill and I must try to tell you why. It is not easy. Since last August I have been sort of drowning in a love affair. The details of this don't matter. It's not someone I can see often or ever live with, and my main effort has been to do as little harm as possible (I think that passion if really intense is always destructive if not to the two involved, always to other people) but it is not a small thing, and not something I can cope with simply as my problem because in this case the other person is equally, if not more involved than I. I am extremely unused to being loved (do not laugh). It is a fact. I don't really want to be loved very much—is that the whole truth? Not quite. It is just too devastating, I suppose.

The last thing I foresaw was what it would do to glimpse some immense peace, some coming homeness which I did that night. And it does make me feel rather a criminal type. But I feel better now I have told you. That is all. What I would hope is that somehow some of this aliveness which we have together can go on, somehow. But perhaps I have invented all this! I do know something of the burden that to be loved is and God knows I won't lay that on you, darling. I see some deep and flowing freedom between us. I think of you a great deal. You opened the very deep door that has not been opened for me for a long time and I kiss your hands many times when I think of it. Don't shut me out. And please be happy about yourself, if not about me.

About you apart from anything I feel, there is this anxiety I have because I think you are withdrawing too much and especially that you have not come to terms or something with being grownup. These are your great years—I know for myself that everything will happen to me about work and life in about fifteen or twenty years. This again may make you smile, but it shouldn't and if it does it is you who are wrong this time and not I. One only begins to hold one's life in one's hands if it is a deep life, a life of your kind of genius, at about your age. In your heart of hearts you know this, yet there is something in you which rejects yourself. Please do not imagine that I say this because of anything between us or not between us. It is here real love that speaks, not love for anything I might want, but love for you set apart in your own life. If it is not rejection, it is withdrawal for a bad reason, and you mustn't do it. You simply have no right to, for the sake of poetry which is after all why you are on earth. This is one reason I want so much to see you again, quietly and soberly, before I go, if possible. Because I do love you deeply and I think, perhaps, well.

Isn't life extraordinary? Just after I called you while waiting for someone who was coming to tea, I picked up the December <u>Encounter</u> and opened it to Robert Graves on Juana Ines de la Cruz and this is what I read:

"Every few centuries a woman of poetic genius appears, who may be distinguished by three clear secondary signs: learning, beauty, and loneliness. Though the burden of poetry is difficult enough for a man to bear, he can always humble himself before an incarnate Muse and seek instruction from her.——The case of a woman poet is a thousand times worse: since she is herself the Muse, a Goddess without an external power to guide or comfort her, if she strays even a finger's breadth from the path of divine instinct, she must take violent self-vengeance."

I have ranunculus on my desk and I wish I could put them on yours, really my favorite flower I think—those tightly wadded petals and such colors, one pale pink, one greenish white, one deep red, one a golden yellow, so tightly furled and full of promises.

That is all. I want to send you some of Jean-Do's poems. But that can wait.

Yours with much wonder and gratefulness.

M—

Juana Ines de la Cruz: Sor Juana Inés de la Cruz (1651?–1695), Mexican poet and nun who often attacked the exploitive male attitude toward women.

TO LOUISE BOGAN   March 8th [1954]
[Wright Street]
Dear one,

A good morning's work—five pages; and before I go out for errands into this blue day I have some things to say. It is that you do have some very natural pre-conceptions about women in love and for the sake of understanding, I would like to explain. I do not believe that in such relationships one woman is the man and the other the woman. This is the great fallacy, the dangerous one; it is what makes the masculine woman or the feminine man slightly ludicrous and always pathetic. Such relationships may begin in this way; I suppose the initiative is often taken by one who for the time being is thus the masculine element, one who takes rather than giving. If it is a completed and in the end good relationship this initial balance changes and must change. There is no "aggressor" any longer. It is a kind of reflected double image, hence its difference, its excitement, its limitation. The limitation is that it is not (as in a heterosexual affair) the taking into oneself of something different from oneself, the coming together of two halves which make a whole. It is not an enlargement of the boundaries of the self in that sense. It is not a primal force at work. People who try to make it so are, to my way of thinking, perverting a reality which cannot be questioned.

Perversion is trying to be what one is not and cannot be. A woman is not and cannot be a man. A man is not and cannot be a woman. What then have women to give to each other?

The great difference between men and women is that women cannot separate sex from love and men can. There are no women homosexual prostitutes, but male homosexuality (even in the case of someone as good and sensitive and honest as Auden) tends toward prostitution. The drive is primarily a sex drive. There is nothing wrong for a man in picking up a sailor, but a woman who would do the equivalent would be violating herself (in either a heterosexual or homosexual relationship, bien entendu). The drive which is back of two women who unite in passionate love is therefore, as in any love relationship for a woman, first of all and primarily emotional rather than sexual. Emotion overflows and tries to find a medium of expression. If the medium is physical as it may be, but does not have to be, what the woman discovers is herself in someone else. You break out of yourself through someone else, to find yourself. The excitement—and it is very great in its way—comes from the fact that you give the same pleasure which you receive. This is where it is hard to pin down in words (I am not writing a handbook). It is metaphysical because the caress contains in itself the love and is not a pure drive towards release as it is in a man. In other words, it is exceedingly pure and intense, an exchange of souls. I don't know about homosexual men but my guess is that it's quite a different thing because there the primal drive remains and sex must play a more obsessive part. The chances of a complete and happy mutual response are very much greater with two women and this is why I have always felt it dangerous (and in fact I would not myself do it) to initiate a woman who might be shifted out of her center.

One never reaches the deepest place of feeling part of the almost unconscious universe, of being lost. Instead one reaches a place of extreme consciousness; one is found as an individual. Greater subtlety, less depth, a greater sense of oneself and the other as a person different from others.

The danger—and there is always this danger—is trying to make something more than can be made out of it. Out of this can come violence, exasperation etc. I have never had that experience but I can imagine it. I have never tried or wanted to be a man. I don't know if this makes <u>any</u> sense, without the actual experience from which it has come—But what bothered me was your saying how you should (for some reason) be the aggressive one—this is nonsense—you would simply find yourself being whatever you are meant to be (as <u>you</u>, yourself, unique) in relation to me (myself, unique). You would in fact inevitably make love to me as I would to you—it is <u>inextricable</u> in essence—Needless to say this is an unanswerable letter—let me know about the party—I feel very happy and full of work. Hope you do—

Love,
[ ]

TO ROBERT FROST   March 19, 1954
[Wright Street]
Dear Robert Frost—

I imagined you under the glossy leaves among the oranges—but how fine to get a poem from Ripton. It is <u>such</u> a grand one too—at Christmas when Bill Raney sent me one (but <u>not</u> with your mark in it) I read it and tears rushed to my eyes, those good tears of recognition.

Then—imagine this—I had a letter from Belgium just the other day, telling of just such a visitation, canine, leaving the emptiness of welcome and farewell behind (for I shall send my friends the unsigned copy of the poem as a present)—

I'll see you at least from afar next week at the Celebration—with what deep gratefulness, with what love, dear Robert Frost. I shall lift my glass (champagne, they say!) to you—

Here's a poem. I'm nearly beaten by my new novel, but not <u>quite.</u> It's touch and go—

Love and blessings
May

I don't suppose you can read one word of this. But it's no loss! And <u>do</u> let's meet at last and have a talk later on in Cambridge??

Robert Frost: (1874–1963), eminent American poet.

the Celebration: There was a dinner celebration at Amherst for Frost's eightieth birthday; Sarton was one of only a few women among 100 men.

TO JOHN HOLMES   April 22, 1954
[Wright Street]
Dearest John,

Herewith are three glossies—take your pick and send back the others when convenient. I feel so dreadfully sad when I think of those times which cannot happen again—of Ciardi whom I still love but who has made himself my enemy. However it was good while it lasted and nothing lasts forever: tout casse, tout passe, tout lasse.

I was so happy to see the Easter poem in the Atlantic and now to know that it has had such reverberations. It makes me think of a lot of things—this is a poem for people, John, I mean one that comes from deep feeling and goes right to deep universal feelings in people (as apart from fellow craftsmen and poets, though of course they will <u>see</u> it too). One can almost draw a dividing line right through our contemporaries between those who communicate in this way and those who don't—those who "care" about people as readers, as you would say. I think of William Carlos Williams, who surely does on a grand human scale, of you, of myself, of Ciardi (who does do this I think don't you?), of Frost of course, supremely. I am not trying to make any rules or say this is <u>better</u> than Eberhart and Wilbur, but it is different, and thank God for all the rich differences. I am sure that it is this deeply human quality of yours which Auden is just getting to the point of maturity where he can feel and understand. And that is good news, very. I must confess I felt sore picking up Oscar Williams fat new pocket book of Modern Verse to see that neither you, Ciardi nor I is in it. If one could hurdle the anthologies! But I trust you will be in Auden's Faber book of American poets.

Do let's get together soon—maybe sometime next week? Would Thursday be any good?

I do long to hear more about Mrs. Neal—yes, I may make a book of the New Yorker pieces, but first when I have the novel off, I must be free for a long time for poems. My event of the spring is a new friend, Louise Bogan. Whatever one may say about people it is also very dear to have poets for friends—

> Dear John, bless you and let's <u>talk</u>—
> Love from
> May

John Holmes: (1904–1974), American poet, teacher, and critic was part of the poets' group which met at one another's houses in Cambridge, Lincoln, or Medford, Massachusetts, and in which Sarton participated along with Richard Eberhart [(1904–) poet and teacher]; Richard Wilbur [(1921–), poet, playright and English professor]; and John Ciardi [(1916–1985) poet, teacher and critic] for three winters during the late 1940s.

Translation of French: Everything crumbles, everything passes, everything fades.

Mrs. Neal: Unidentified.

TO MURIEL RUKEYSER   May 4th [1954]
[Wright Street]
Muriel darling,

I did love your wire—the little late object especially (and how lovely to have a present still in the air). I woke as usual in tears because somehow always on this day now woe about my mother rises up—but then, in spite of rain, it turned into a good birthday. Partly the Guggenheims were officially announced (I have one in poetry) and people kept calling up, seeming really happy about it. Partly Daddy had a bottle of champagne and was in wonderful form. He gave me a check inscribed on the envelope "from your Georgian Mama" (the point—so typical of the way his mind works—being that in the Caucasus "mama" means "papa"!). Anne Thorp came with a branch of white dogwood which really seems rather like having an angel captive in the house or a flight of angels.

It is wonderful about the Gugg. I keep praying that I shall at last write some really good poems, invincible ones. It has been sad to have the last book go almost unnoticed, unreviewed. And this is a little balm. Marianne Moore was one of my sponsors and wrote to say "I was urgent—Miss Sarton—urgent."

But the Matty novel is a nightmare. I have finished it now, but it has been ready by one person who advised me to lay it aside for a year and then begin over and now I am waiting for a second reader's view before making up my mind. I am so cross because I want to say what it says, now, but if it is bad of course there is no point.

I do long to see you—maybe I shall be in N.Y. sometime—Daddy is operated again May 17th (to take the gall bladder out) and I shan't get off to Europe till Aug. 1st. I am taking Daddy on a terrifying holiday to the Gaspe when he recovers—will he be bored is the question.

Darling, what a boon and blessing that you remembered my aging self—
                                        Love and love always—
                                        M

---

the last book: The Land of Silence.

TO KATHARINE WHITE   June 9th, 1954
[Wright Street]
Dear Katharine,

What simply wonderful news about A Wild Green Place, I can hardly believe it! In the next week or so I'll put my mind on amplifying as you suggest—actually the strange thing is that mother told me about their taking away her clothes, but did not mention it in the written document (I actually say that in the piece as it now stands.) My guess is that at first even the old woman was wary and not very kind and maybe I can add in a paragraph which would show that their reception of the child was anything but warm. The old lady did get fond of her—but after some time. I am just thinking aloud so pay no attention. I'll send you something definite by the end of next week. At the moment I am just working crazily at the novel and must not stop.

I do understand your reservations about recommending your staff in the case of the Academy Award—there may be others who can be altered such as Rolfe Humphries. I used to be an innocent who believed such awards went to the "best man," but I now have been on some juries and it is certainly true that no harm is done if disinterested people have ideas and say them, that among several equally possible candidates, one has got to be <u>chosen.</u>

Daddy is not very well as yet, so we are now planning to go to Newport for a week and then come home here for a week of small excursions from home base. That means I shan't get a glimpse of you before I fly July 30th. By the way, it would be good if I could go through final proof with someone before I fly. If I get the thing in by the 21st or 22nd of June I take it this would be possible. I could go down to New York overnight and go over it with Maxwell, maybe????

I do hope the house-building is going on apace—

Love from
May

Maxwell: William Maxwell (1908–), American novelist and fiction editor at the *New Yorker.*

TO MADELEINE L'ENGLE   Sunday, July 18th, 1954
[Wright Street]
Dearest Madeleine,

How good to hear! I am too dazed and dead to realize quite how things stand with me but I respond instantly to your problem—and more about that in a minute. I hear two days ago that Rinehart will publish the novel I have been in a death-struggle with all this year—and the relief plus various other things make me feel feeble-minded. I think the book is in some ways a failure and I was very doubtful about their taking it—but it does deal with a major problem of the times and so perhaps something I wanted badly to say will get through, however clumsily. It is called "Faithful are the Wounds" and is about F. O. Matthiessen, the Harvard prof. who committed suicide some years ago. I have revised and redone it so many times (three quite completely) that I am blind and dumb about it. Now it is very wonderful to know that I have a clear year ahead for poems and you are dear to share in this joy so generously, when you yourself are tied hand and foot.

Dear Madeleine, I do understand so well! I got two years ago (at the end of the teaching) so that I couldn't listen to music because it made me cry at once, that door opening into the world where I could not go—my real world.

But remember that a year or two or even five or ten in the total life of a writer is very short; you are digging deep into reality, the reality of being human, being a mother, having to work a bit too hard etc. and all the time you are accumulating or building up the rich human loam from which books will grow in time. I wonder if the path of wisdom might not be to look on this time when the children are small as just that—you are much younger than I and have already accomplished much. There are years and years ahead when there will be time. Sometimes I think (and your crest suggests it) that one of the professional writer's greatest problems is not to write too much, to keep still. Too often we are driven by necessity, financial necessity, or that other necessity which makes us only feel we really exist when we are creating, to write too much. You will be saved from this—and I think it was a danger for you at one time. However, all this is all very well, but I realize too that writing nourishes a part of you that feels starved without it—and how to solve that I do not know. I wish someone would leave you and Hugh some good hard cash so that you could take a year or two off together now and if I had it I'd send it!

Before I forget, you have read the V. Woolf journals I presume? If not, I'll send you my copy before I go so drop me a p.c. if you want it.

I'll be wandering about but this address will always reach me eventually:
c/o Madame Jean Dubois
12 Longue Haie
Linkebeek, Brabant, Belgium.

It has not been all a golden year for me either. My last book of poems The Land of Silence was hardly reviewed at all—five years' work and I'm sure my best work so far. Never noticed in the Sun. Times or Trib. and Louise Bogan who promised a review, finally gave a squib in the New Yorker, one paragraph, of which two-thirds was negative. It began "Miss Sarton begins to show signs of insight" which I felt made me sound like a retarded child who had finally learned to read! I feel bitterly that I cannot reach my readers through this barrier of silence—well, of course the answer is to improve and write better poems. One part of me is dissatisfied with all I have done and I hope I shall write some better poems this year—

Then my father had to have two operations so my trip to Europe on the Donnelly fellowship was put off twice and now has had to be reduced to 4 months—but who am I to complain when others cannot get away at all? And of course the Guggenheim makes up for everything!

Darling, forgive this maundering on, and be of good hope. Try to think in terms of "the long run" and store up your honey like the bees—

With very dear love and faith

from your old
May

Madeleine L'Engle: (1919–), theologian, spiritual counselor, author of novels, poetry, memoirs, books for children; particularly known for her Newbury Award-winning classic *A Wrinkle in Time* and its sequels. She and her then future husband, Hugh Franklin, met Sarton through Eva Le Gallienne and the Civic Repertory Theatre.

Madame Jean (Eugénie) Dubois: (d. 1982), Sarton met her through the Limboschs. A teacher in a school run by her sister, and more sophisticated than Céline Limbosch, she became an intimate friend whom Sarton knew until the end of her life.

TO LOUISE BOGAN   Wed. Aug. 11th, 1954
[Le Pignon Rouge]
Dear heart,

I lay awake a long time in my rather lumpy (but familiar) bed while gales of wind and rain attacked the windows last night and thought about you— the effect, I presume, of having rapidly read over my journal—it is just little notes, nothing really written—because there are some notes for poems I wanted to get at. But it did swing me out on the curve of the last months— since Jan. 21st—and back, the rising and falling curve. Three thousand miles of physical distance only make everything clearer for me, and if that is possible, I seem to love you more than ever before. Or is it just that these turbulent skies and the hosts of trees that I see (a lime, a beech, a plane tree, several oaks, all waving and moving all the time) and, above all, the sense of time opening instead of always closing, release all that is real?

I shall go back to this in a moment—I am longing to know about your birthday party (such a good idea) and feel sad that I did not send a cable, but I had forgotten whether it is the 8th or the 9th and a cable on the wrong day seemed too idiotic, so I didn't. Now you are beginning <u>your</u> new year, and after this year of arrivals, of wisdom, of withholding, of the Collected Poems, I hope you will enter into a foolish, door-opening, troubling journey of a year, in no way an arrival but a departure. I rather hate your having to tackle again the past with the collected prose, yet it <u>is</u> hot, as you say, and the summer is a good time for such jobs—and also, there will, I am sure, come a moment of real fulfillment and satisfaction as if you had tidied all the drawers. And what a gift it will be to all of us who wait for it—I am sure you must be amazed at all you have done, the richness and variety of it and, also, the singleness of its vision. Do you work at this in the morning?

I do not see anything vulgar about a birthday party by the way—but I could <u>hear</u> you saying it and that was nice.

The whole air is purple and dark and ominous and just now four snow-white pigeons flew up, too lovely, and have settled on the red-tiled roof of the house I see through the trees. The weather is Autumnal and has been all through July, nothing but rain and I sit in a heavy sweater, heavy slacks, wrapped in a blanket! Now the clouds have parted and there are glimpses of blue, but this happens all the time, the sun splashes through for a glorious instant and then goes in again. I could watch the sky all day.

Well, what I began to say is that it seems to me you have erected all too successfully barriers against the whole elemental part of your nature and that within this stockade your living self is a prisoner, a prisoner who is beginning to be afraid of ever going out again, who is becoming in fact "adjusted" (God forbid!). Some of your theories are simply justifications and concealed fears, aren't they? It has always been difficult for me for obvious reasons to plead this. I well understand, for instance, your theory that at a certain point of maturity relying on personal emotion, on relationships as motor power would mean going backward rather than forward, or—a better image—not going down one level deeper, which is what you want of course. On the other hand life <u>is</u> relationship and the going deeper, it sometimes occurs to me, may be simply in the wisdom one can bring to them, not on avoiding them, not feeling less, but feeling more and differently. At some moment in these last months, out of some decision—was it a decision about time ("not till next year")? you withdrew and our relationship which—how I saw this in the notes in my journal—had been creative and demanding in a good way, became a kind of gliding along on the surfaces. The effect for me was instantaneous—I could no longer bring to that surface my real deepest self; there were no more poems. I only use the poems here, as an image. It is not important in itself—I mean I could be silent for five years and it might be a very good thing! But it is a sign, that's all and I have been troubled. Darling, this is the last time I shall write one of these letters—and high time I stopped! But I did want to get everything clear, then I'll write you descriptive letters about the places and people and hold my inner peace. It is what you stopped in <u>yourself</u> that is important. You must know by now that I really love you in my own way, and that the very fact that we are in constant communication is an immense joy. For myself I could not ask for more. And the things I say here, have nothing to do with what I want <u>for myself.</u> I should be ungrateful and, worse, stupid, if I did not know that you have already given me far more than I deserve. So please do not imagine that this is a complaint.

You have talked about repeated patterns—as far as we are concerned I cannot see it (maybe for me, yes, but not for you)—but you have perhaps allowed a pattern of resolves to freeze your nature, such as, for instance that enough lies were told for you to refuse ever to use an endearment or express love or affection. But don't you see that if you stop this flow, then you stop all flow? I will go the whole way along with you if you must come to the decision in the end that a passionate relationship is not for you now, or not with me, or not with a woman or whatever. I can meet you on a deeper level than that, but the gift implied is then very great indeed and the intensity just a little greater than it would be were there a simpler release. The idea that everything must be "played out" is dangerous, but the burying of feeling altogether is more dangerous—

I have no illusions as to my importance. This is where all this is new for me—it is more that I look on myself as a sort of pebble in your way or your refusal really to take me in, a refusal of yourself, a pebble in the way of yourself. Coming through this might only be the way to someone else, more suitable—well, I have really said enough. Has it occurred to you that one may be afraid of one's own creativity? Afraid of the troubling of the waters, even by an angel? A psychiatrist in London (not my Chilean wild friend, but a friend of hers) read your poem about the horse and explained the metaphor differently from your own explanation of it: "not the masculine element" she said, "but her own psychic energy." As she knows nothing about you, this amazed me and I pass it along for what it is worth.

By the way, before I forget, Elizabeth remembered your brief meeting very well and said you frightened her just as Virginia Woolf used to—and she read the poems, some in the airport as I was leaving (they have accompanied me on all these flights) and saw them as I do.

The personal part of this letter is now, you may be relieved to hear, at an end.

And perhaps I had better get to work and write another sort of letter in a day or so—Yesterday I rented a little new Volkswagen—Imagine my having a <u>German</u> car, but the alternative was a huge (too expensive) Ford Consul so there was no choice. We are off to see two old friends in the country this afternoon—Darling one, be happy and be yourself—and really, you know, between us all is well, always—

M—

---

collected prose: Selected Criticism: Poetry and Prose.
My Chilean wild friend: Eugenia Huneeus, Jungian analyst.

APPENDIX OF
UNPUBLISHED POEMS

[The text of the following two poems each entitled "Hedda Gabler" appear in the 1928 holograph journal.]

HEDDA GABLER

Her cold careless voice, her pride, her very beauty,
Are all spun out and stretched,
Ready to break
At a touch.
She is fine-cut red wine glass
From Saint Gobin.
She is ice or flame,
A frozen flame,
Burning ice
Terrible and piercing,
Near to heaven
But never Hell.
Always a sort of destiny,
The destiny of boredom, of saturation,
Is fighting in her.
The destiny always wins.
So at the end
When the perfectly chiseled glass
Is shattered into a thousand
Drops of frozen blood
It is destiny you say.
Let it be rather called
A proud will and great beauty
Entering Hell with a sweeping gesture.

[JANUARY 22ND, 1928]

[Beside this poem is Sarton's note: "Influenced by Jean Tatlock. This is not worthy of me."]

HEDDA GABLER (EVA LE GALLIENNE)
I could have run out into the night
And burst into flame, to be blown through eternity.
I could have stayed to be frozen by you, Hedda Gabler.
Into a fixity of ice.
But I did not dare let a burning soul lift me to heaven.
I was afraid lest my heart be frozen forever in your image.
So I am left without anything but words.
There is a great hole smashed in my left temple;
The blood is oozing into my hands.
I am mad with warm blood.
Inebriate of death and sin.
For I have had not enough of Hedda Gabler.
The words are torn into shreds by my fierce mouth.
Hedda Tesman is too smooth; I am prickly with desire,
And Hedda Gabler alone will satisfy my longing—
Hedda—Hedda Gabler.

MAY 22D [1928]

The Tower (J. C.)

Take from me
All hate, all joy, all sorrow,
Above all, all remorse
And I will build you
A tower higher than passion could ever build.
A tower, cruel and clean,
A tower to freeze your heart with beauty
And to gather your pride to its heights.
                    I shall be there,
I, the building,
Waiting with calm eyes for you to come.
Then when we stand there
With only Truth and the tower,
No hate, no joy, no sorrow,
Above all no remorse
For past hurts,
We will face
The mountain at whose foot we stand
Together,
With strength to climb.
When we shall have reached the top,
The tower will fall.

JANUARY 16, 1928

J.C.: Jean Clark, a friend from Shady Hill.

A SENSE OF PROPORTION

It is strange
How little important time is
In life.
For who has not waited months
For the first crows,
And strung life itself
On the decision of a minute?
The difficulty
Is to find a proportion.
He who can do this
Will tread upon the very hem of Truth
And snatch her,
Swift as is her flight,
For his own.

APRIL 14, 1928

A FRIEND (J. C.)

You remember the spicy, special tang of geranium leaves.
You are exact and penetrating in your judgement of people.
But you do not realize, friend,
The strange intoxication
Of forgetting geranium
And breathing it once more
Into a forgetful soul.
You are not possessed
With an extravagant heart—

Friend, forgive me.
Stab me with the quiet passion of understanding.
Explain the lucidity of your eyes
And your austere heart.
For I see I am greatly in need of learning.

DECEMBER 20, 1927

"Despair"

When something beautiful makes a hush
Tears come to my eyes
And I catch my breath.
So it is when a friend is sad.
So it is when I am angry enough
To be insincere.
But I cannot understand
How I can cry at a failure
Which is my own fault;
Why despair has not cast tears into iron
And frozen the heart to a stone figure-head of will.
Now I will beat this clumsy purpose
Into a single keen-edged tool,
And try to keep clear-sighted toward myself.
I will chisel a destiny out of the hardest metal I can find,
And make it proud and cold enough
To have been formed by iron tears—
I swear it here.

MARCH 30TH [1928]

"Flowers After the Ball" (E. Le G)

I am going to lose the key
To the little gilded chest
Where I have kept your words
With perfume and spices,
The tang of exotic adventures.
I am going to forget
Your small white face
And grey eyes
And drift back into still waters
Undisturbed by ~~your~~ swift moods
And your crystalline thought
Like quartz under moving water,
Until there is no ripple of you anymore,
Only my heart beating
And the ~~sound~~ rasp of a cricket
Out of tune.

JUNE 3RD [1928]

St. Joan

I would be a sword in your hands
St. Joan!
I would feel the honest grip
Of a soldier's hand,
Sensitive to the mouths of horses.
I would know
The sternness of France wronged,
And the gentleness, the infinite gentleness
Of a blue fleur-de-Lys.
I would come close to the heart
That turned every doubt to a vision.
Then I could understand
Eyes dreaming with tears
And the Christ, small and silken,
The word "Jésu"
Crooned tenderly
And a sob of love and pain
As the soft, tortured flesh
Melted into fire.
I would be a sword for you,
St Joan.

[AFTER 3 JUNE 28]

L'Âme du Poèt

"L'Âme du Poèt se trouve en son oeuvre seule.
Ne tâchez pas d'ouvrir la porte de sa maison.
Vous ne trouverez, sans doute, qu'un linceul,
Une chambre vide et un mort," me dit-on.

C'est vrai que j'ai aimé d'abord ta poésie,
Aimant tes mots avant de les gôutes,
Aimant ta voix pour ce qu'elle avait dit,
L'aimant déjà sans l'avoir écouté.

Mais un jour vint où j'ai ouvert tremblante
La porte de cette maison—et ton coeur-même,
Et là au lieu d'un mort j'ai vu une petite sanité
Très jeune dont la vie-même est le plus pur poème.

[JUIN 1936]

THE SOUL OF THE POET

Only in the work of the poet will you find his soul.
Don't try to open the door of his house.
Undoubtedly you'll find nothing but a shroud,
An empty room and a corpse, I'm told.

It's true that I loved your poetry at first,
Loving the words before I tasted them,
Loving your voice for what it had said,
Already loving it without having heard it.

But the day came when trembling I opened
The door of the house—and your heart itself,
And there instead of a corpse I saw a little saint,
Very young, whose life itself was pure poetry.

BERCEUSE—POUR LE GILLES

O cette lumière du soir
Qui vous ouvre le coeur,
Qui vous fait ouvrir les yeux tout à coup,
Qui vous donne le petit monde du jour
En vous promettant l'immense monde de la nuit,
Qui vous annonce l'heure des rêves,
L'heure des longs rêves toujours pareils
Dans les petits cimetières verts du coeur,
Qui ne s'alterent jamais.
Vous te reposes entre les fleurs
Autour de ces tombeaux multiples et chere—
Que se repose ici la fièvre de tous les jours,
Que se délie ici le coeur crispé,
Que s'assoupie ici l'âme trop tendere,
Que s'effeuille la sommeil comme une rose sur tes yeux,
Pendant que cette lumière du soir laises tombes
Une pluie diffuse et dorée,
Et s'assombrit en vert
Et se retiré en bleue,
Pour faire entrés enfin l'immensité du noir
Et ses lumières!

LE 13 JUIN, 1936

LULLABY—FOR THE MELANCHOLY CLOWN
O this evening light
That opens your heart.
That makes you suddenly open your eyes,
That gives you the little world of day
While promising you the immense world of night,
That announces to you the world of dreams
The hour of long dreams
always similar
In the little green cemeteries of the heart
That never change.
You rest among the flowers
Around these many cherished and multiple tombs—
May the fever of all the days rest here,
May here the clenched heart relax,
May the too tender soul go to sleep,
May sleep shed its petals like a rose on your eyes
While the evening light lets fall a gilded and diffuse rain
And darkens itself in green
And pulls itself back in blue
To allow at last the immensities of the dark to enter
With its lights.

13 JUNE 1936

PROGRESSION
By an excess of burning
Eyes can reduce the flesh
To skull's immaculate design,
Beyond that early impure yearning
Reach underneath the mortal mesh
Inviolable line.

Vision can burn so fierce
That what was a sweet lust,
Suffering by famished sense alone
Achieves the extra heat to pierce
The soft shell of the skin and rest
On the hard contour of the bone.

Prefers to that love sensitive,
Compart, explosive as a rocket,
Love that was multiple sensation,
An Absolute that will outlive
All sense: the formal empty socket—
For quick lust, steadfast contemplation.

OCT.

SNOW AND VIVALDI
Here in the room
This gaiety so featly
Springs out of time,
Impervious and sprightly.

Outside, snow blown,
Softly and so sweetly
Silence becomes a tune,
Impervious and stately,

And in the mind
Such silence so contrasted
With such sharp sound
So sweeter tasted,

As if all effort wasted
Were sound and healed
And heart, though blasted
Impervious and mailed.

JANUARY 1939

CONSIDERATIONS [APPEARS AS CANTICLE 6 IN
    INNER LANDSCAPE, WITH SOME REVISIONS]
Alone one is never lonely; the spirit
        adventures, waking
In a quiet garden, in a cool house, abiding single there;
The spirit adventures in sleep, the sweet thirst-slaking,
When only the moon's reflection touches the wild hair.
There is no place more intimate than the spirit alone:
It finds a lovely certainty in the evening and the morning.
It is only where two have come together bone against bone
That those alonenesses take place, when without warning
The sky opens over their heads to an infinite hole in space;
It is only turning at night to a lover that one learns
He is set apart like a star forever and that sleeping face
(For whom the heart has cried, for whom the frail hand burns)
Is swung out in the night alone, so luminous and still
The unsleeping spirit attends, the loving spirit gazes
Without communion, without touch, and comes to know at last
That out of silence sometimes, and never when the body blazes
That love is present, that always burns alone, however steadfast.
                                            MAY 13TH [1938]

JARDIN DU LUXEMBOURG, 1939

Someday they will ask, when it is over they will wonder
What you did in that final hour in Paris alone
And why if you knew, if you did foretell the thunder,
You sat quiet in the garden there, half-asleep in the sun.
What will you answer? You who were young who were a poet
And must surely have sealed up in your heart some grain,
Some seed to be re-planted when the time should come for it,
What did you do, they will ask? What was your inner plan?
What will you answer?
The air was very light and clear.
Never in those gardens were the flowers more brilliantly
dreamed,
Formal bouquets of many colors stiff and martial where
Impervious the nurses knitted and the children screamed.
Not a leaf fell. The trees stood there as if transfixed,
Dressed in the extreme luxury of their summer flight.
The fountains alone made panoply of grief and mixed
Their triumph and their tears in the crystalline light.
You stooped there in the path where a feather lay at your feet—
And hid it in your pocket. Just then the clock struck three
Marking the exact hour when happiness should meet
Terror and violence in the mind. But it passed silently.
You cut the pages of a book, You did nothing better than sit
In the sun with poems open and turning the pages found
Each poem dazzling enough without your reading it.
You were dazed. You were half asleep and sun-bound.
This was your action. This your supreme, solitary deed,
This luminous and simple peace. But can you tell then this?
"Remembrance of that garden" say, "This is the precious seed.
This feather in my pocket, this moment without emphasis."

AUG. 22, PARIS [1939]

ELEGY
for R. W.

I would like to give you forever this edelweiss
Because you loved high places and the danger
This cold flower marks out on the cruel ice,
Because your need was mountains, cruel stranger,
I lay this flower forever in your hand,
You the unknown and lost who were my friend.

And you loved speed for that would set you free
(You said) and always then would burst out singing.
Speed was like mountains, a kind of clarity—
O voice in the air, rock-struck and ringing—
I give you forever to keep this edelweiss,
You who are now as strange and clear as ice.

And you escaped since danger was escape, you said,
Climbing and speed and wind like a cutting knife
Burning their wild ways through your childish head:
They were the furies after you to get your life
That was dearer than danger, denser and deeper
Than love of wilderness, O cruel sleeper.

For you were clear enough and dear enough to outlive
Youth: we watched you grow out of the wildness slowly,
Watched you slow down, take pause, take heart, and give—
Since mountains seemed to you always the high and holy—
Thought to the human ways of climbing and to them apply
The canny mountain eye and hand. O did you have to die?

I lay this edelweiss on your heart's love of danger
Let it rest there forever, young and unknown stranger.

I lay Scarlet beside it, this anemone, though you cannot move
Nor take it now, nor know (O dead too young) that it is love.
NOVEMBER 4TH, 1939

———————

R. W.: Richard Wheeler, twenty-two years old, one of Sarton's best friends was killed on his bicycle by a hit and run driver.

SONG—FOR ROSALIND

I saw an old woman with a piercing eye
And this was her wisdom and this was her cry:
"Oh, the world, my child, is crumbling away,
Nothing holds here, nothing that we hold can stay.
So give away your love, my child, be prodigal,
At this end of all and beginning of all.
So give away your love, my passionate child,
For she who goes alone now, goes damned, goes wild,
But she who goes singing in the stern young company
Who have promised their hearts to make the world free
Can lose her heart and find her heart in all humanity."
I saw an old woman with a face like a queen
Stamped on a gold coin, such fire was within,
So proud and so tender the flash of her eye,
And this was her wisdom and this was her cry:
"Give away your heart, child, give away your bone
For the world as we knew it is crumbling and gone,
Be prodigal, my ardent child and never count the cost:
Now is the time for love, my child, or we are lost."

OCTOBER 1942

BRITISH OFFICER IN GREECE

I
(1941)

We had expected the malignant stone,
Dark looks of the betrayed,
For we were leaving Greeks alone
To fight the Terror.
Instead, these, the betrayed, knelt in the streets,
Put flowers in our hats
Our shame consoled with their own perfect honour.
And though we left to fight the war in distant places,
We read its deepest meaning in their faces.

II

(1945)

Now I stand at a window and watch pour
Down those very streets
Old men and children, priests, the very poor,
And women bearing banners,
Flags of all nations, crucifixes
And their own burning memories.
(There is noone left in the villages but the dead)
Almost it is a festival
This coming down of the people to their city
To make known their will.
Many are smiling as they move together
On the strong wave of love.
Once more they kneel—
And now because they know
The war begins here with the people's will
And here must end, though bloodily.
(I bring you not peace but a sword).

Now I stand at a window
Knowing I shall be asked to kill my friends.
O can I do it, England, dear pride, home,
Break heart at your command?
Or—if not—break the patterns of obedience,
Put off false power. Begin the war now. Here.
Divine Justice, help me to do Thy will,
To be not a good soldier, but a man:
Deliver me from fear.

JANUARY 16, 1945

ALL THE CHILDREN HAVE HELLO TO SAY

All the children have hello to say
On the curving road
When you walk to town
They always say "Hello" whoever goes that way.

The little girl in red is always there
Waiting for you to come
And though you have no name
She is waiting for you alone, whoever you are.

And the two dirty cherubs by the gate
Stop playing school
To give you a quick hail
(And maybe you are Love and maybe you are Hate.)

And all the people in the world go walking by
Sooner or later, now or then
The whole world of men
Passes the calling children, passes them by.

The children in the garden smile and stare
When Death himself goes by;
"Hello" to him they cry,
And whoever he may be, he answers "Hello there."

Whoever goes down to town by the mother stream
Thinking the way things are,
Too lonely and poor and hard
All over the world, dreaming a saving dream,

Always whatever he knows, the children are there
Playing the ancient game
For whatever may be his name,
They are wanting Love, they are asking him to care.

They are waiting for an act, for a word, for some
Stranger who will know
The answer to "Hello,"
The stranger who will say, "Your Kingdom come."

[APRIL 1, 1945]

THE LEAVES

We walked under heraldic trees
Under the hot bland street-lamp's flare,
Three shadows in the heavy air
That flowed like water through our knees,
On every side the strong dark breathed,
And overhead the serried leaves,
Leaves stiff as feathers, very black
Shifted like tiny screens,
Mounted the stairs of wind:
Leaves became massive towers,
And all was formal balance, poise,
Arches and domes and bowers
And a little rustling noise.
We smelled night in the green
More potent and more fertile
Than all things heard or seen.
We had to press our hands
On the rough trunks to be sure.
I asked "Where is peace, where?"
"In leaves" was all you said.
From then on it was clear
We would be three, not two,
However separate each shadow:
One grieves, one lives, one gives,
But I do not care or know
Which is he or I or you.

[JUNE 22, 1947]

SWEET JOY

Come in, sweet joy, you who have tarried,
Come in and bless
This love so long to anguish married
And bitterness.

Come in, sweet treasure of this day
When torments cease,
And show my arid heart the way
To pity and to peace.

Possessing nothing, O come in
Fervent and free,
To build your shelter safe within
The bosom of a tree.

Come in and find the secret place
Both cool and deep
Where you will see love's peaceful face
At last asleep.

There in the bower, there in the leaves
Lonely she lies.
Dear joy, will what your heart believes
Open her eyes?

BELGIUM [AUGUST 4, 1948]

[   ]

THE EMPTY DAY

Never had I sat with more empty mind
On a day that was made of solitude and work,
House-cleaning, music-all good things—but I
Empty as a sick man's sigh, wanting to shirk.
But then the mail came and my empty hands
Were filled with presents and with presences
And I was woken alive again in all my senses.

There was a letter from France, from Santa Fe,
And a book on St. Augustine (all this on one day!)
Which was a letter also to a distant friend,
And I knew again for the first time, without end,
How we are moving through each other's minds
At every instant, never alone, but interwoven
Lightly across and through, and always given
And taken, a living complex of human strands.

The first letter spoke of a poem, cast a beam
Of brilliant light on a blundering phrase,
Asking me to mend it. This is the secret dream
Of friendship, that it wake the sleeping days
And set us alive again, hunting the true step
In the poem, in love, in all we mean to keep:
That music which rouses the dull dancer
And by asking the question, becomes the answer.

The second letter was harder to make and keep
For it touched wounds we hide except in sleep,
Told of a woman who lived through Hell alone,
Seeing her husband, her children, her whole town
Burn alive in the church, no hate for Germans here,
But help for the one living soul in lost Oradour.
Oh blessed friend who say you hesitate to bring
Into my life the darkness of such suffering,
You bring the greatest light, the chance to mend
The torn web of our loyalty, to send, Oh to send
Help at last after the long nights when we knew
There was nothing but tears, nothing that we could do.

The third, the book uncracked, shining and new
Brought from deep in the past the always-true
To nourish the long meditations of the heart.
It has come. St. Augustine and you and I never apart.
It speaks of our need for each other, always there,
Of the human loyalty which roots us deep in God,
The search for balance which all humans share,
The search for each other which is our longest journey.
The third letter became the answer and the key,
Took all the threads and wove them into one.
This was not work asked, but deep work done.

And this was the day when I thought myself alone:
Oh friends, I am coming, I am on my way, I run!
                    for Haniel
                                        January 6, 1950

Of Friendship At Christmas
[Published with minor revisions as
"Of Friendship" in The Land of Silence.]
We have boarded ships with our hearts cold,
Aware of the hard geography of distance.
And how little we knew or had been told,
How much might still depend on wind or chance.

We have carried an excess of hopes and fears,
The baggage of anxiety wherever we go,
Yet when the ship unloads its passengers,
We run down the gangplank, and we know.

The handclasp heals. Two continents are meeting.
A gold world merges with a green world here,
And the flat map's a globe again at greeting,
All rounded and resolved, its wholeness clear.

Friendships, the marvelous, nourishing ones,
Bear their cargos of understanding
Or misunderstanding across what oceans,
What wastes of silence to harbor and landing!

Whenever we speak, wherever the silence, spoken, (Letters too
are journeys) and if we dare,
Even the separateness, once it is spoken,
Becomes part of the meeting that we share.

And all the ships, new dear ones and dear old ones,
Burning with brilliant memories and desires,
Float with us like small steadfast constellations
Across the darkness to the unknown shores.

"Tidings of comfort and joy, God rest you merry,"
These messages ring out again tonight,
And like churchgoers who hear the bells and hurry,
We burn our candles now, nor spare the light.

Christmas 1952

"JOURNEY TOWARD POETRY"

After the mad beautiful exploring
Through a multiple legend of landscape,
All the roads opening fast and closing,
And the speed of the car that roars escape
And carries the mind across foreign borders
Into a world of visionary and abrupt disorders,
Where the hills unwind on a running spool
And rivers leap out of their beds and run,
Where the pink geranium against the wall
Stands there a second and then breaks open
To show far off the huge blood-red cathedral
Looming like magic against a bright blue sky,
And marble cemeteries fall into the sea—
After the mad beautiful racing is done,
To be still, to be silent, to stand by a window
Where time not motion changes light to shadow,
Is to be present at the birth of creation
When from the falling chaos of sensation
A single image possesses the whole soul:
So was the fish invented and the beetle, whole.
Here it is this: the curve where two fields meet,
The gold-green, barley, and the blue-green, wheat,
From them the composed imagination reaches
Down and up, up and down to find its own frontier.
All landscapes crystallize in this one signature.

MAY 1953

APPENDIX OF
FRENCH LETTERS

Samedi 15 Aout [1925]
[Lourdes]
Ma Chère Aunty Lino,

   Si tu ne reçois pas des lettres un jour c'est que Daddy à été distrait et a
gardé une lettre dans sa poche jusqua 6 heures du soir! Hier aprésmidi nous
nous sommes reposé jusqua 4 héures et puis maman et moi avons gouté et
puis á 5 heures nous avons rencontré Daddy ici à l'hotel. Il fait si chaud qu'au
milieu de la journée il faut se reposer depuis 11 heures jusqua 5. nous
sommes partis pour un vieux château qui domine Lourdes et qui a était
changé en musée Pyrenéen. C'était très intéressant, montrant les meubles,
les utensils, les costumes et les coûtumes des paysans Pyrenéens d'il y a
quelques années. Dans la chambre d'honneur c'est vraiment l'histoire de la
science. on montre des cahiers des outils et photographies des plus grands
explorateurs des Pyrenées, et il y a une bibliothèque. Quand j'ai dis "explorateurs" je voulais dire non seulement ceux qui ont grimpé ces montagnes
les premiers, mais aussi ceux qui ont fait les premiers cartes, qui ont trouvé
les hauteurs, et qui ont étudié les plantes et les minéraux. C'était vraiment
très intéressant. Nous sommes rentrés alors et nous avons soupé. Puis nous
sommes sortis pour voir la grotte où Bernadette a vu la vierge. Quand j'ai
raconté l'histoire, je ne savais pas qu'elle avait vu la vierge plusieurs fois. La
première fois la vierge n'a rien dit, la deuxieme fois Bernadette à dit "Si vous
êtes de Dieu avancez, si vous êtes du diable partez" et l'aparition en souri-
ant et venue vers elle. La 3me. fois Bernadette a demandé à la Dame ce qu'elle
voulait ~~et elle à re~~ qu'elle l'écrive. La Dame à répondue "ce que j'ai à te dire
n'a pas besoin d'être écrit. Viens içi pour 15 jours et je vous ferai heureux,
mais pas dans ce monde." Après cela elle l'a encore vu plusieurs fois et le Dimanche une grande foule l'accompagnait, la vierge lui a dit, "Prie pour les
malfaiteurs" et le mercredi "Va dire au prêtre qu'une chapelle sera élevé ici

et qu'il y aura des processions ici." Le Vendredi elle lui a dit de boire et se laver dans la fontaine et de manger l'herbe qui était à côté. L'enfant a gratté le sol et un petit ruisseau d'easu est sorti soudainement. C'est l'eau fameuse de Lourdes. Plus tard, elle lui a demandé de dire son nom et l'apparition en mettant ses main dans un attitude d'humilité à repondre "Je suis Immaculée Conception." voilà la vrai histoire. Je trouve extraordinaire qu'un enfant puisse avoir une telle foi et imagination. Il y avait une telle foule qui se préparait pour la procession du soir que nous avons eu de la difficulté à parvenir à la grotte. Il y avait au moin une centaine de personnes à genoux devant. Les murs de gauche sont couverts de becquilles, de plâtres, de fers etc. de personnes guéris là. C'est extraordinaire comme il y en, a mais la procession commencée, c'était comme une rivière d'or. Tous chantent "Ave, ave Maria" et c'était quelque chose de si beau que je ne sais pas te l'expliquer. Ce matin nous avons eté à la cathédrale et à l'eglise du rosaire qui est endessous. ~~Les m~~ Toutes les pierres des murs de la rosaire sont des ex votoret la cathédrale est remplie d'ex votos de toutes espèces. L'architecte de la cathédrale à vraiment du génie je trouve, je t'enverrais une carte postale de la façon dont il la dessiné. J'ai si chaud que maman m'a dit de cesser donc je t'embrasse bien bien fort.

Ta petite fille
May

TO MARIE CLOSSET, MARIE GASPAR, AND
BLANCHE ROUSSEAU   le 26 Août, 1931
[Le Pignon Rouge]
Chères Mademoiselles—

Toutes mes excuses de ne pas vous avoir écrit plus tôt, mais il me semble que j'ai passé un mois entier à dîner (ces interminables dîners!) chez des parents—les chambres étouffantes, entassées de bibelots, où même les fenêtres sont cachées sous dentelle et soie lourde, et d'oú on sort se sentant un peu comme un perroquet en paille! Enfin c'est fini—on a un peu de temps libre pour les amis.

Voici les poèmes—je suis triste qu'ils ne sont pas plus beaux. Justement en les écrivant à la machine j'ai été frappée par la pauvreté de tout ce qu'on fait—de tout ce qu'on peut faire peut-être—en voulant tant faire.

Je reviens et reviens toujours au "Puits d'Azur" et "Une Syllabe d'Oiseau"—c'est un trésor qui ne s'épuise pas mais semble, au contraire, s'enrichir chaque fois que je les relis. Merci de les avoir écrits c'est tout ce qu'on peut dire. Parler du coeur est impossible, au moins écrire un poème, ou envoyer une fleur.

Le petit chat s'est endormi sur mes genoux—son nez enfoncé dans mon bras, avec une oreille alerte et l'autre cachée—je ne peux plus bouger

Je vous envoie un papillon—il entrera
peut-être par la fenêtre legèrement se posera
sur votre tasse de ma part.—

<u>May</u>

T O   M A R I E   C L O S S E T   Vendredi, le 19 février [1932]
[Paris (vanL)]
Cher Jean Dominique—

J'espérais trouver quelque chose un peu comme une fleur à vous envoyer,
mais les mots ne veulent rien de moi ces jours-ci. Peut-être doiton traverser
des déserts d'âme pour gôuter toute la fraîcheur de l'eau à la fin. Mais c'est
vrai que je suis en plein désert pour le moment.

C'est peut-être cela qui m'a fait pleurer en relisant votre lettre. C'est un
tel miracle que vous existiez—que vous êtes-là—que vous m'écriviez et que
je puisse vous répondre—que vous <u>êtes</u> enfin et que je ne vous ai pas imag-
iné—car je pense parfois que j'ai dû vous inventer d'un grand besoin de vous
avoir. Ne vous en allez pas—j'aurai peur de la solitude de mon âme.

Je relis—et ce n'est pas ce que je voulais dire. On voudrait semplement
ouvrir le coeur et on est arrêté, confu, perdu entre les mots et la pensée—
Parce que le coeur est simple mais tout le complique, et c'est difficile de le
montre.

Voilà une anémone—c'est un peu mon coeur—je voudrais vous la donner—

[   ]

J'ai mangé la miette.

T O   M A R I E   C L O S S E T   le 27 décembre—[1932]
[94 Macdougal]   Mardi soir
Cher Jean—

Tu ne peux savoir le délice avec lequel je me place tranquillement pour
t'écrire—"Sable sans fleurs" à mon côté—et le jeune homme Persan lisant
nonchalament sous son arbre en fleurs devant moi—autour de nous le soir—
il pleut. Pour la première fois depuis des semaines j'ai trois heures de grâce.
O Jean, Jean—si tu étais ici (tu aimerais cette chambre—elle est toute petite
mais les murs sont bleus—il y a des livres—et le printemps mélancolique de
Botticelli)—si tu étais là dans la grande chaise, j'éteindrai la lumière: je te
jouerai du Mozart sur le gramophone—je viendrai m'asseoir tout près et il
ne serait pas nécessaire de parler. Il faut m'excuser ce soir s'il m'est difficile
de t'ouvrir mon coeur comme je voudrais—surtout en français mes pensées
<u>guincent</u>—j'ai perdu la faculté de les traduire en mots. (excusez ce griffon-
age)

C'est étrange comme l'atmosphère de ce jeune homme qui lit au printemps ressemble à celle de Proust à la recherche du temps perdu—peut-être la même précision d'images et de détails—par exemple la sensibilité aigue qu'il avait pour les fleurs—fleurs qu'il devait fuir tout en les aimant—il y a peut-être quelquechose de semblable dans l'âme du peintre Persian—j'aime le croire.

Le semaine dernière nous avons eu une neige magnifique—vraiment éblouissante—je suis allée avec une amie à la campagne—là pour la première fois cet hiver j'ai écri quelquechose—ce n'est rien je vois qu'il faudra tout recommencer—aller de nouveau au fond des choses avec une lanterne avant que je ne puisse retrouver le puits. Mais il est là et ne se tarit pas. Et c'est peut-être bon que je vive encore quelque temps aussi fièvreusement—car c'est une fièvre—le théâtre. D'ailleurs tout va merveilleusement bien. Pour la première fois je commence à vivre comme je rêve de vivre en travaillant beaucoup, en aimant beaucoup, mais sans arrêt. Il faut maintenant fabriquer un centre de paix et certitude au milieu du coeur. C'est enivrant—et dangereux aussi, mai je crois que je comprends le danger. C'est difficile de trouver des heures pour être seule—je suis au théâtre de dix heures du matin jusqu'à deux ou trois heures du matin presque sans arrêt sauf deux heures au dîner. Mais alors on est trop fatigué pour créer autre chose qu'une paix intérieure—et même cela est difficile.

Au commencement de 'l'année J'avais espéré faire des études sur la vie des Grecques pour changer completement de nourriture mentale-mais je n'y parviens pas faute de temps? faute d'absorption? Je ne sais pas. En tout cas le travail au théâtre me prend l'âme et le corps pour le moment. J'aime beaucoup les 50 enfants et ils m'aiment et croient en moi étrangement (parce que je ne sais <u>rien</u> en vérité) mais je me sens tout de même fort en sympathie—et donné un pouvoir on ne peut que tirer la force nécessaire. Avec les jeunes j'ai déjà fait trois pièces—"La Mauvaise Conduite" de Variot dont j'ai fait la traduction—"Les Frères Karamazov" et pour Noël un ancien mystère anglais—maintenant j'ai deux projets pour moi-même—comme actrice (j'ai peur de devenir trop critique)—on commence les répétitions de Saint Jeanne de Shaw (je joue Jeanne)—et plus tard "Pelléas et Mélisande" (j'ai toujours voulu jouer Mélisande) tout cela naturellement très simplement comme exercise et sans prétention, joue devant un fond noir sans costumes—on vient de me téléphoner que Miss Le Gallienne est malade et je dois jouer son rôle en "Alice an pays des Merveilles"—la reine blanche—on m'attend pour une répétition—je m'envole!

Oh! Ecris-moi un mot—je t'aime tant—

<u>May</u>

Un baiser à Titi—amitiés chaleureuses à Madame Rousseau—et joyeuse année avec un printemps plein de fleurs à vous trois!

TO MARIE CLOSSET   Vendredi, le 24 Août [1934]
[Rowley]
Cher cher Jean—

Il a plu toute la journée et maintenant il y a une brume blanche et bleue dans le verger, s'étendant comme une longue écharpe jusqu'à la rivière—marée haute. À travers les peupliers une grande lune se lève et semble rose dans le bleuâtre.

En bas les enfants lisent le 4me acte d'une pièce. Il est 8:30. Après le dîner nous avons joué le "Jupiter" de Mozart sur le gramophone en cousant les costumes pour une pièce de Shaw dont nous allons donner quatre représentations ici la semaine prochaine. Dans un coin deux garçons jouent aux échecs. "Noé" le chien est entrain de rotir son petit nez noir au feu. Les deux chats "Bonnet" et "Feathers" jouent sur le sofa—ils sont des chats "manx," c'est à dire sans queue, et ont une allure très spéciale. On les a nommés d'après un poème d'Edith Sitwell.

O si tu pouvais ouvrir la porte du jardin et venir t'asseoir entre nous ce soir—c'est une nuit pleine d'espoir et de tendresse. C'est terrible quelque fois de t'aimer ainsi et de ne <u>jamais</u> pouvoir mettre en réalité cette essence d'amour—te <u>toucher</u>—nos relations sont tout imagination et on a besoin du bon pain et le vin du regard et de la voix. C'est pénible.

samedi, le 15 septembre

Presque un mois c'est passé et je n'ai pu retrouver le moment, le <u>timbre</u> spécial de l'heure où j'ai commencé cette lettre. Maintenant Maman m'écrit qu'elle t'a vu—et mon père aussi—comme je suis heureuse—Mon Dieu quelle joie.

Je n'ai pas tant envie d'écrire longuement les <u>faits</u> des derniers mois—suffit qu'après une crise quand j'ai dû subitement retourner à N.Y.—traverser le continent pour un week-end (j'étais en vacances en Californie)—un moment où j'ai cru que nous ne pouvions continuer, que j'étais une espèce de Quixote d'essayer de créer la loyauté et foi nécéssaire—Deux des meilleurs hommes de la compagne m'ayant écrit qu'ils ne reviendraient pas—après ce coup je suis maintenant arrivée à une idée plus simple et plus claire de la suite des choses à venir—et plus que jamais je <u>crois,</u> j'ai <u>foi</u> en ce que j'essaye de faire. Au lieu d'un groupe <u>rigide,</u> je substitue maintenant <u>groupe fluide</u> un va-et-vient autour de quelques points fixes—moi—même, les deux autres directeurs et deux ou trois des acteurs—cela c'est à dire pendant peut-être quatre ans. Alors nous serons peu à peu <u>arrivés</u> à une compagnie d'une certaine permanence, au lieu de la premièr idée d'un groupe fixe dès maintenant. Cela c'est un changement <u>temporal</u> plutôt qu'<u>essentiel</u>, mais c'est tout de même un changement de point de vue, et qui a pris du temps et de l'énergie à créér.

C'est étrange, tu es peut-être la seule personne au monde à qui je voudrais raconter l'histoire de ma vie dans ses aspects les plus internés. Pour mon age j'ai vécu beaucoup—peut-être trop—vécu dans le sens d'aimer, puisque vivre c'est aimer. Mes poèmes—pauvres comme ils sorts—ne sont que le reflet dans le miroir de la pensée, de choses <u>vécues</u>, <u>senties</u>, <u>souffrantes</u> et je crois que c'est parce que j'ai un peu dédié cette âme-poète à toi que je voudrais que tu le comprennes. Est-ce-que je pourrais un jour te le dire? Je peux l'écrire peu à peu en poèmes, en phrases japonaises, à demi dites. Mais le temps parce la sensation affreuse que nous mourrons peut-être sans nous avoir connus—comme profondément comme l'amour peut connaître—m'effraye. Tu comprends? Je ne me suis pas tromper en croyant, en <u>voulant</u> croire, que tu m'aimes et me comprends mieux que d'autres?—et que cela ne te choque pas d'etre addressé, avec une franchise totale par une petite fille?—seulement la question <u>d'âge</u> n'a pas de place ici. L'âme n'a pas d'âge. Et mon âme n'est pas jeune, ni la tienne vieille—elles sont toutes fraîches et éternelles.

Pendant des mois et des mois je n'ai presque rien écrit—rien d'une grande chose qui passait en moi. Maintenant je voudrais écrire—j'ai <u>besoin</u> d'écrire, et il y a <u>si</u> peu de temps! Voilà quelques poèmes—ils ne sont pas importants. Ils ne disent rien. Tu vois pendant presque deux ans j'ai vécu avec une femme qui ne m'aime plus. Et maintenant je dois écrire cet amour—il n'y a rien d'autre à faire.

Ecris-moi un mot bientôt—je suis un peu effrayée pas cette lettre—je t'aime tant—

May

Cette une petite fleur qui pousse en automne—et qui vient dans tous les pourpres et lavendes. Elle pousse assez haut et est très "hardy" fort—le gêlee ne la touche pas.

[sketch of English asters]

Il y a tout un volume de tes poèmes que je n'ai jamais vu—peut-être deux—et-ce-qu'il n'y a personne qui me les prétera si on ne peut plus les obtenir.

TO MARIE CLOSSET   Juin 28 [1936]
[Le Pignon Rouge]   Mon. afternoon
           la Campagne

Darling Bluebird—

Je suis entrain de boire une bière avant de rentrer—toute la journée a été souriante de cette matinée avec toi et Francis—si bien que la mousse sur ma bière ressemble à une neige miraculeuse, et je suis sans dôute une princesse russe—ou Éve-même (personne n'a reçu de nouvelles de sa mort et on n'en parle pas dans la Bible—alors pourquoi ne serai-je pas Eve?

Je me suis dit que si je t'écrivais maintnant tu l'auras demain matin peut—être—Véra m'a montré la photographie où tu ressemble exactement à Sainte Claire avec un troupeau d'enfants!

J'ai une lettre de mon éléphant. Il écrit "<u>mon cher</u> May." Il est à Avignon, cultivant sa vigne. Il semble heureux et il est <u>sûr</u> que "nous nous rencontrerons et que le temps ne sera point un obstacle—non plus que les distances"—Je suis contente. Je vais lui envoyer tes photos de moi dans le jardin—

Quelquefois je me demande tout à coup <u>pourquoi</u> je suis <u>envahie</u> de joie—et alors je me rappelle que c'est toi-que tu es là comme une petite flamme tout au fond de moi tantôt blanche et tantôt bleue et tantôt rouge mais toujours chaude—et que personne ne peut voir que j'ai le seul trésor du monde—et que je suis illuminée d'amour, que <u>toi</u> tu es l'amour et le miracle. Je n'en reviens pas!

J'ai raté deux trains!

Au revoir, mon oiseau, cher coeur, tu ne peux te reposer vraiment ces jours-ci, mais laisse-moi au moins tenir le <u>poids</u> de ton coeur-je t'aime—et que cet amour t'enveloppe dans le <u>sommeil.</u> [See appendix of poems]

(Elle devait danser!).

TO MARIE CLOSSET   [July 12, 1936]
[Austria]   Dimanche 2 heures
Mon oiseau bleu,

Quelle étrange journée, sans heure—une pluie infinie, longue, comme les pluies de dimanche—sansfin. Et tout à coup en moi des <u>flots</u> de poèmes, qui coulent sans que je puisse les arrêter m'épuissant, mais quelle fatigue adorable!

C'est drôle je crois que je dois mettre une forme humaine dans chaque paysage pour le voir en toute sa grandeur—une petite chose pathétique qui donne l'échelle à un montage. Ici il n'y avait personne pour ainsi illuminer les choses—et maintenant tout à coup <u>Stiasni</u> devient l'image, la statue au fond du jardin lui donnant sa perspective. Ce n'est pas <u>l'amour</u>—c'est une espece de <u>force</u> lumineuse sans quoi je ne vis qu'à moitié—et souvent l'être qui devient soudainement cette force n'est nullement intéressant et ne le sais pas. Marie Stiasni est une femme charmante comme toutes les Viennoises, une étrange figure, yeux très loin l'un de l'autre, une figure irréguliere mais très belle—une grande réserve (le charme est comme un <u>masque</u> dont elle se cache) Je travaille maintenant souvent dans son petit salon ou il fait chaud (ma chambre est froide quand il pleut). Elle travaille tout le temps, reçoit les paysans, parle aux domestiques, nerveuse, se <u>poussant</u> beaucoup trop il me semble. Presque toujours là il y a aussi le Dr. Schwarzwald, mari de la femme qui a fondé <u>Seeblicke</u>. C'est le grand "finance minister" de l'Autriche—un petit juif doux et triste qui boite—il lit dans un coin et moi je travaille sur le sofa avec trois "Scotch" dormant tout autour de moi. C'est bon.

Maintenant il y a une Viennoise qui joue des sonates de Beethoven en bas—comme <u>j'adore</u> un piano lointain à travers une maison—et surtout le dimanche.

Le Czeche est parti ce matin—nous avons diné ensemble à Bad Aussee le soir avant—c'était très gai et très bon—je lui ai parlé franchement le jour avant et la situation qui devenait un peu trop sérieuse et "sentimentale" comme disent les Allemands, s'est éclaircie. Il est très <u>gentil</u> , vraiment. Mais je suis soulagée de son départ.

Je dois changer la robe pour dîner—Bonsoir, ma chérie—je suis heureuse—je t'embrasse—mon coeur <u>vole</u> quand je pense que je te vois dans une semaine.

Lundi matin [July 13, 1936]

Aujourd-hui s'il ne pleut pas nous ferons une excursion à Alt-Ausse—derrière la montagne mais le ciel ne parvient pas encore à se décider—il y a des troupeaux de moutons dans les prairies bleues! Avant de partir je travaillerai sur "Rivalité." J'espére qu'il y aura une lettre de maman me racontant l'histoire de mercredi.

Comment vas-tu? Je crains que cette semaine avec les parents à voir (bêtes fauves) sera pire que celle d'avant—ou au moins tu étais seule avec les élèves. Quand tu dis que tu vas faire des courses, je suis triste de n'être pas là, <u>dans</u> la maison pour faire ces petites choses pour toi. J'irai chercher le courier à Taviton St.—tout les jours—Je ne pars d'ici que lundi matin. Hotel Russell Russell Sq. Londres.

TO MARIE CLOSSET   dimanche
[Austria]   9 heures du soir
                                        July 13, 1936

Bobbie—

demain il y aura peut-être une lettre—ma tête <u>bourdonne</u>—j'ai travaillé toute la journée et rien achevé alors mes pensées continuent à partir comme des flèches et je ne sais pas les faire rentrer dormir! Je suis descendue au village et je suis entrain de boire un café délicieux près du lac—tout le monde rentrant du dimanche me disait "Grüsse Gott"—j'ai passé un jeune homme avec sa main gauchement dans la main de son amie sur un banc—C'était adorable. Je ne peux pas te dire le charme, la bonté des gens ici—ils sont comme tous les gens à qui on pense quand on entend les grands mots simples de la Bible "Aimez-vous les uns les autres" et "Béni sont les humbles."

Ils sont heureux—il me semble que j'ai vu si peu de gens simplement heureux.

Mon histoire est dans une impasse. Je crois que je l'ai trop simplifiée—ce n'est plus une <u>histoire</u>—O, je voudrais tant en ce moment avoir un bien critique sur ces histoires. Il me semble que je suis aveugle—que tout ce que je fais est cru, sans forme, sans exactitude—quelquefois <u>par accident</u> j'aime à faire une phrase qui me semble dire ce que je veut dire, mais si non c'est un aveugle se débattant.

Je pense à un grand poèm—que serait l'histoire de ce voyage—l'histoire intérieure—par une série de rencontres et une espèce de moralité moderne—il contiendrait un ou deux grands chants—par exemple l'experience de Cornwall finissant avec un chant pour les juifs (Singer, l'ami de mon père s'occupe entièrement des juifs). Il y aurait les enfants en Belgique—etc. Seulement il m'est impossible de faire une chose pareille sans être <u>en feu</u>. Je ne sais pas l'écrire froidement et je ne sais pas si ce feu s'allumera ou non. J'aimerai ici dans les montagnes essayer quelque chose de <u>grand.</u> On voudrait mettre un grand cor triste à la bouche et faire un immense cri triste et sauvage et lent. O, je suis allés nager ce matin—l'eau est très claire et très froide—on frissonne délicieusement et puis on se cuit au soleil.

La moitié du temps je m'ennuie et je suis triste mais l'autre moitié j'écris et je suis heureuse!—si seulement tu étais là—O ma chérie, Marie, ma grande soeur, mon âme—Bonsoir—les lettres me semblent si <u>fragiles</u>—Est-ce-qu'elles te parviennent? Cela doît prendre es jours et des jours. Et je ne peux plus envoyer pas avion tout les jours. En tout cas mes pensées mangent tes fraises et tes cerises—vivent dans ton jardin et se cachent dans chaque rose que tu cueilles n'oublie pas de leur dire bonsoir—

Je vais monter me coucher. Je fais une traduction de l'Eventail assez vite et sans trop y penser—puis il faut lentement la corriger—c'est difficile—c'est comme une rose qui tremble quand on y touche—mais cela doit être possible. Je l'adore—et cela me repose et m'enchante d'essayer mais je crains que cela ne sera pas assez bon. On verra.

lundi—

Journée <u>éblouissante</u>—je n'ai rien pu faire ce matin—onéreuse [?] et destraite—finalement j'ai lu "L'Art et la Poésie au Japon" et une grand paix est venu comme un hibou s'asseoir près de moi en me regardant gravement. J'ai écris un poème médiocre. Je t'ai copié quelques petits poèmes japonais—les connais-tu? Je les ai en anglais—la traduction d'une traduction (!) M'enfin il eu restera, pour tes yeux qui peuvent <u>tout</u> imaginer, peut-être quelque chose.

Au déjeuner ton baisser de vendredi, m'est venue—quelle joie! Mais comme tout cela prends <u>longtemps</u>, ma chérie—<u>Que dit Marianne?</u>

Que veut dire "ombelle" et "décharné"? O, n'ai qu'un minuscule diction-
naire avec moi.

Cet aprés-midi je vais en canot avec un jeune homme czeck—il est gen-
til et triste et seul (mais pas <u>très</u> sympathique).

Je t'embrasse—
Une feuille de mon balcon—aucune nouvelle de P__ O, qu'est-ce que "Le
Gaillé" veut dire dans l'éventail. Est-ce-que cela a un sense <u>traduisible?</u>

TO PIERRE DUPRENEUX   le 11 octobre, 1936
[239 East 17th St.]
Cher Monsieur,
    Lugné-Poë m'a dit que celà pourrait vous interresser d'avoir de temps en
temps une lettre de New York pour le Paris-Soir. Je pensai immediatement
à ces articles que Genêt ecrit pour le New Yorker—c'est quelquechose
comme celà il me semble. Naturellement il a enmormement de possibilités—
par example une serie de choses tout à fait americaines: un article sur le "Burlesque," le rite du déshabille qui est aussi frequente par les gens litteraires et
du monde que les Fratellinis. Un article sur "Father Divine" negre qui <u>est</u>
Dieu pour des milliers de negre, qui est enormement riche et a une serie de
"Paradis" au Harlem où vivent ses "Anges" (une historie incroyable!). Un article sur les deux couturieres americaines, Muriel King et Hattie Carnegie,
sur les theâtres des chomeurs et les artistes chomeurs (tout ce plan du gou-
vernement), etc. etc.

    Comme vous voyez mon français balbutie! Mais si je faisais une serie d'ar-
ticles pour vous je ferai re-ecrire chaque fois par quelqu'un ici. Il faut excuser les fautes dans l'article que je vous envoie—je suis en ce moment
terriblement pressé et il me semblait mieux d'attendre un mot de vous avant
de m'y plonger trop profondement!

    J'attendrai un mot de vous avec grand interet.

                            Croyez, cher Monsieur, à mes sentiments
                            distingués—
                            May Sarton

TO MARIE CLOSSET   le 1er septembre 1938
[Channing Place]
Chère chère—
    J'ai marché autour de ta lettre depuis des jours sur la pointe des pieds—
j'ai regardé longuement les deux photographies—j'ai relu cette phrase "Je
suis devenue si vieille—et j'ai besoin que tu le saches, que tu le voies"—j'ai
continué à vivre [?] fièvreusement avec une passion de fruit d'été—le sen-
timent du travail qui recommence, de l'hiver—la discipline, le <u>salut</u> du tra-

vail cher et terrible—j'ai relu touts tes poèmes et le "Syllable d'Oiseau" et "l'Éloge du Poème"—et cette phrase merveilleuse "Arrête le silence sur les lèvres de l'amour. / C'est mieux ainsi"—et il faut que je te dise que pour moi tu ne seras jamais vieille—tu ne seras jamais <u>mortelle</u>, tu ne changeras pas avec les années, ni avec la mort—car il me semble que tu es le <u>coeur</u> de mon coeur—le petit noyau amer et doux tout au centre. N'as-tu pas une photographie de toimême à mon âge—j'aimerais la voir, la garder près de moi comme une presence angélique dont le <u>temps</u> n'a rién a faire.

Cet été fut étrange (déjà j'ai passé à travers et c'est l'automne dans mon coeur)—je suis revenue pour trouver tout ici en *chaos*—la question d'argent de nouveau grave—mes espoirs pour une saison à Philadelphia gâchés—j'ai passé par des semaines arides de suspension complête d'âme et de pensée où il fallait vivre au jour le jour et ne pas regarder trop en avant. Maintenant il y a eu deux miracles—à la dernière minute l'argent est venu—plus que je n'avais espéré <u>possible</u>—après une conférence que j'ai donné—où il me semblant que c'était peut-être la dernière fois que je parlerais et où j'ai mis tout mon coeur. Mais il y a eu aussi un vrai miracle du coeur—une souffrance et une bénédiction dont je reste éblouie et grave. Après avoir passé en juin par la passion féroce je suis arrivée maintenant à l'amour le plus pûr, le plus déchirant pour une personne que je ne verrai que deux ou trois fois de plus, une peintre, mariée, qui essaye de bâtir sa vie sur ce que je ne peux voir que comme du <u>sable</u>—mais enfin que j'ai pu aider un peu à un moment difficile pour elle—et qui <u>comprend</u> tout ce que j'essaye d'être comme personne (sauf toi) ne l'a jamais fait. Et j'ai lu "Arrêter le silence" parce qu'il le fallait. Et j'en suis toute baignée de lumière—mon Dieu, quel <u>trésor</u> cette petite parcelle de vie qu'on nous donne. Et il me semble qu'il faut <u>tout</u> dépenser, qu'il ne faut rien garder sauf l'amour toujours grandissant, toujours un peu plus grand que soi.

J'ai écris beaucoup de poèmes—j'écris tout le temps—c'est comme si la porte qui a été fermée depuis si longtemps—s'est ouverte toute grande—je t'envoie quelque-uns—ce n'est pas qu'ils sont bons mais seulement retrouver le bonheur, la joie de <u>chanter</u> la vie de nouveau!

Je suis triste que ton été a eu si peu de silence, de tranquillité, de vie intérieure—O comme je voudrais t'emporter quelque part pour un mois—où il y aurait des fleurs, et la mer, et presque pas de vent—et un soleil—"Songe à la douceur"—je ne viendrais qu'une ou deux fois par jour te dire les pensées du matin et du soir—et tu te <u>remplirait</u> de silence—mon Gilles—

Toute ma tendresse—tout mon anxieux amour sur ton travail qui recommence—

M—

[   ]

TO MARIE CLOSSET   le 30 november, 1945
[Oxford Street]
O Jean-Do—

Il neige; toute la maison est entourée de voiles blanches, les arbres sont en fêtes; Quand je jette des miettes de pain par la fenêtre en quelques minutes cela disparait (les oiseaux viennent en multitude)—et, hier soir, dans la tempête je suis allée à un concert parce qu'on chantait <u>ton</u> poèms dans une série de concerts que Nadia Boulanger a organizé pour fêter Fauré! Imaginestoi! J'étais dans un tel état que je ne respirais presque plus quand la voix s'est élevée—

> "Je mettrai mes deux mains sur ma bouche, pour taire
> Ce que je voudrais tant vous dire, âme bien chère!"

Malheureusement Olympia di Napoli resemble un peu trop à son nom—jeune fille (élève de N. Boulanger) très brune, très italienne qui n'a absolument pas l'âme pour ces chansons—si délicates, profondes et passionnées.

Nadia B. elle-même l'accompagnait et je ne pouvais retirer mes yeux de sa figure intense, simple—le grandeur y habite. Elle n'a aucune "manière" de concert—mais une divine simplicité—et la grandeur de ceux qui <u>servent</u> un art sans s'exploiter eux-mêmes par le moyen d'un art. Cette grandeur-là devient de plus en plus rare il me semble, dans un temps de "personnalités." Ses cheveux sont presque blancs maintenant et sa figure autre-fois assez sévère, était illuminée de tendresse—

Nous avons ri follement de ta carte du <u>poivre</u>!

Il fait bon ici mais je suis encore dans une mare de fatigue dont j'en sortirais j' espère, la semaine prochaine. La maison est silencieuse, couvant les tendresses qui se cachent dans tous les coins—et je dois travailler, mais je voulais te dire comme Jean Dominique est venu à Cambridge!

Avec tout mon amour, mon ange

                                                          [   ]

TO MARIE CLOSSET   le 16 aout, 1948
[Oxon]
Petite et grande Marie, peacock en excellence, et mon doux trésor,

Dans le calendrier des peacocks le 16 aout est tout entouré d'une garlande de roses, d'aubépines, de chants de merle, de coquelicots, de thym, de sauge, de lavande dont voici quelques échantillons au moins des derniers. C'est une lettre qu'il faut sentir plutôt que lire, tu vois. Un bâume pour te donner une idée (bien pauvre) du bâume que ton âme répand un peu partout, le sachant et ne le sachant pas—

Ma chérie, je suis sortie enfin du trou et je vois maintenant comme il était néfaste et surtout loin de la vérité intime et profonde et de mon amour et de moi-même, comme une maladie dont je sort toute éblouie de la beauté de vivre, sentir, croître, aimer, mourir et re-naître. J'ai lu deux livres qui m'ont aidé à cela, un très beau livre de l'Abbé Bremond sur La Prière et la Poésie qui tu connais sans doute, et les lettres en anglais du Baron Von Hügel à sa niece. La chose qui m'a saisit d'abord c'était quatre mots de Von Hügel "L'austérité dans la tendresse, la tendresse dans l'austérité"; puis en Brémond plusieurs paragraphes. C'est très bon d'entendre dire les choses qu'on sait mais qu'on avait besoin de retrouver comme par exemple ceci: il cite ici Plotin "Le moyen pour l'âme d'atteindre l'object même de son désir sera de rentrer en elle-même et de retrouver par le recueillement le dieu intérieur dont elle porte la trace."

Ces quatre jours tranquilles de campagne m'ont fait un bien énorme. Une chose que je fais chaque jour c'est d'aller dans le parterre de coquelicots (une mereille d'ailes légères, rouges, blanches, roses-saumon) pour couper les graines, ainsi ne pouvant pas faire leur fruit elles continuent de fleurir pendant tout l'été, comme les poètes. Puis les soirs avant le souper je vais avec Basil au champ, un grand champ magnifique, pour donner à boire et à manger à des centaines de poulets tous blancs, et parler un peu avec les chevaux et la grande dame, la vache qui s'appelle Patience, et surtout pour nous asseoir après et parler tranquillement. Après le gôuter je fais une petite excursion au fond du jardin pour voir un grand champ de blé, bronze, qu'il est grand temps qu'on coupe. J'y vais pour écouter le blé, qui frémit dans le vent avec un petit bruit délicieux, riche et sec, comme de la soie qu'on touche. Maintenant de ma fenêtre je vois Basil au loin qui travaille au jardin— je crois qu'il a juste ton age. Et tu l'aimerai avec sa crête de cheveux blancs et son grand rire malicieux et joyeux. Les soirs nous écoutons la TSF et avons eu chaque soir des concerts ravissants, hier du Mozart. Sa femme est en Amerique pour voir ses enfants, et la soeur de B. entretien la maison, malheureusement une femme assez nerveuse à qui j'ai toujours peur de dire une chose de travers, où qu'elle prendrait de travers plutôt. Foncièrement anglaise, croyant que les Anglais ont été crées par Dieu pour diriger le monde, elle ne comprend pas du tout que les Indes ont voulu leur liberté de cette présence bienfaisante! Nous avons eu une discussion un peu acerbe où j'ai tâché de dire que la liberté doit être appris petit à petit et les peuples ont le droit de l'apprendre à leur facon, et même en se tuant (comme les anglais on fait pendant des siècles de guerres civiles), mais que de les garder même avec amour dans l'état de l'enfance dépendante n'est pas leur vrai bien. Après cela je me suis tue et nous n'en-parlons plus. Mais je suis considérée je crain comme une barbare!

Demain je rentre à Londres pour l'avant dernière étape de ce voyage qui ne finit pas. Mais maintenant je suis en paix.

Je t'embrasse ma toute-chérie et je te félicite avec joie et tendresse d'être
<u>toi-même</u> et surtout aujourd'hui—

Baisers aux peacocks—
[ ]

TO MARIE CLOSSET   le 5 december 1948
[Oxford Street]

Mon hibou aux grands yeux ronds qui me regardent—comme j'étais contente d'avoir ta petite carte, sauf que je sens comme tu as été épuisée par cette
maladie du coeur—c'est toujours plus long qu'on ne croit et si embêtant, je
le sais, de ne devoir rien faire que d'attendre et attendre de se sentir mieux.
Et puis, les troubles et chagrins autour de vous, qui sont toutes les trois des
puits inépuisables de consolation et de compréhension—il ne faut pas tâcher
de m'écrire sauf de temps en temps. Chaque mot de toi me donne une longue
haleine, un long souffle d'amour qui me gonfle les voiles et me pousse un
peu plus loin dans le long voyage de la vie—

Je crois que c'est le fait de ton appréciation de sa petite nouvelle de
l'hôpital qui a poussé maman à vraiment l'écrire—tu vois, comme tu nous
fais tous vivre.

"L'ange tutélaire à auto" s'est attaché à maman véritablement. et il y a un
second ange, garçon terriblement blessé pendant la guerre, qui est venu pour
la conduire aux rayons pendant que j'étais partie (Anne Thorp a arrangé cela,
c'est un étudiant à Harvard qui a besoin de gagner de quoi vivre). Il s'est attaché à maman et vient l'aider au jardin. Il parait que l'autre jour elle et lui
ont travaillé et mis en terre des centaines de narcisses pour le printemps!
Maman surgit comme une narcisse elle-même, mais quand j'ai téléphoné ce
matin Daddy a dit qu'elle avait eu une mauvaise nuit. Je la verrai dans une
heure quand nous y allons pour le déjeuner du dimanche.

Je vois que tu dis qu'il gelait le 29 de ta carte—ici nous n'avons pas encore eu un vrai gêle, ni de la neige. Il fait merveilleusement doux et beau—
mais cela ne va pas durer! Je me suis enfin décidé à faire peindre pour Noel
les deux chambres de Judy et moi—les plafonds sont <u>noirs</u> et les murs tellement sales qu'on ne sait plus quelle couleur ils étaient. Alors jeudi les pein-
tres viendront et il faudra enlever (et épousseter) tous les livres et les meubles
et nous sommes très excitées et ne pouvons croire à cette proprete si proche!
Ma chambre sera gris pâle avec les bois des fenêtres et porte blanc-crême, et
celle de Judy un gris-bleu-vert presque turquoise, mais pale. Et les plafonds
seront blancs enfin—nous serons tellement éblouies par les plafonds je crains
que nous ne pourrons dormir!

J'écrirai à Alice Long pour toi, alors n'ais pas cela comme petit fardeau
en plus—je lui dirai tout et que le paquet est arrivé.

Mon âme, j'ai eu un sale coup cette semaine, mais si je te raconte cela ce n'est pas pour que tu y répondes ni épuises un grain de ton âme a même y penser, car j'en surgis déja. La poèsie m'a sauvé comme toujours. Le fait est que Kot et Beatrice Glenavy et Juliette se sont recontrés à Londres et ont échangé au sujet de moi des propos qui <u>touchent</u> à la vérité d'un côté, mais de l'autre sont de vrais mensonges—et se sont convaincus les uns les autres qu'je suis un personnage auquel on ne peut se fier, superficiel, dangeureux, mauvais, je ne sais quoi. Juliette m'a ecrit une lettre où elle a dit que les autres ne voulaient plus jamais me voir, mais elle, par égard au passé continuerait à m'écrire, mais que le mot "amour" ne passe jamais mes levres à son sujet. C'est la première fois de ma vie que je dois regarder en face le fait qu'on peut délibérement mentir (c'est ce que Beatrice a fait. Quand je suis rentrée ici une amie d'elle m'a dit qu'elle etait terrible et qu'il fallait prendre garde, mais alors c'était trop tard, car je m'étais plongée avec tendresse et joie dans son amitié quand j'étais en Irelande) Je tâche de comprendre—et je crois qu'elle a été tellement meurtrie par la vie qu'elle est devenue incapable de vrai compréhension pour les autres. Je tâche de croire qu'elle n'a pas fait exprès ce qu'elle a fait, mais qu'elle croyait vraiment servir la vérité. Mais comme c'est dangeureux de <u>juger</u> les autres! La chose la plus terrible c'est que je sens que le silence est le seul moyen de répondre à ces mensonges, le silence et surtout le temps qui era de mon côté. Car je suis loyale et à la fin on le verra. Mais, mon âme, j'ai beaucoup souffert d'une souffrance dépourvu de la dignité et du respect de soi-même. Mais la poésie m'a sauvé. J'ai pris un jour pour lire des poemes, de vieux poemes comme celui de Francis Jammes et dont je fais un petit livre pour Noel pour Juliette. Et tout à coup j'ai senti dans la moelle de mes os que la vérité <u>dure</u> et que rien d'autre ne peut durer.

Judy a été absolument furieuse en disant que ces gens ne m'avait jamais compris et était des criminels (cela n'est pas vrai mais cela ma fait du bien!) Judy rayonne dans tout cela comme de l'or pur, d'une pureté, d'un amour absolu—Et je pense à toi, à Edith Kennedy, à Lugné, aux vrais amours qui ne changent pas et surtout qui comprennent. Je baise tes chères petites mains, et je tâche de vivre mieux, et d'apprendre ce qu'il y a à apprendre dans tout ceci. Je crois qu'il y a beaucoup—et qu'il faut grandir, et qu'il faut être plus humble que je ne sais être encore, et surtout d'avoir une patience que tu sais que je n'ai pas du tout.

Je n'ai rien dit de tout ceci à maman.

O mon âme, tu es près de moi. Tu es là. Dieu soit béni!

[   ]

Un doux baiser à Blanchette—Comment va Madame Thüns?

TO CAMILLE MAYRAN   le 21 janvier, 1951
[Maynard Place]
Chère Camille Mayran,

Chaque fois que je recois une lettre de vous je suis émerveillée d'une destinée qui, de si loin, nous a rapproché l'une de l'autre et je suis touchée à fond. Lucile m'avait déja raconté que vous êtes en fin installée avec votre fille, que votre vie quotidienne reprend des racines après tant de terribles déracinements. Comme je suis heureuse de le savoir aussi par votre main. Avoir une table pour écrire, des rayons de livres, des rideaux qui s'enflent doucement dans le vent, un nid pour la pensée, comme c'est nécessaire. Et je pense que maintenant le livre si difficile à dire sur Oradour pourra s'accomplir, béni par le foyer et la présence de votre chère enfant. Je comprends très bien qu'elle trouve l'enseignement une vie presque miraculeuse—de faire croître des êtres humains, ou de les aider même un peu à croître, d'apprendre de vraies valeurs, de commencer à s'interroger sur les profondes questions, d'apprendre ce que c'est que l'honnêteté, et la surprise et la joie de se retrouver dans une oeuvre d'art, de se dire "Oh oui, c'est ainsi—je le sais"—Tout cela tient du miracle. Et je dis ce mot sans légèreté, mais en pesant sur son sens profond. Car, d'un côté, je suis sûre, que votre fille sent comme moi une humilité profonde d'enseigner car les êtres sensibles trouveront leur chemin, seuls, et les autres ne semblent pas capables de comprendre sauf la surface. Seulement, quelques fois, bien rares d'ailleurs, il y a ce moment d'illumination quand la salle d'individus différents et disparats devient une communauté devant une idée ou une oeuvre, ou quand, par hasard, on arrive à toucher la moelle de leurs êtres. Pour moi, le plus grand problème c'est de tâcher de leur faire penser et surtout peut-être sentir honnêtement. Elles sont (car toutes mes élèves sont des filles de 18 ans) tellement, garnies d'idées empruntées; elles ont si peu senti sauf ce qu'il est convenable de sentir, ce qu'elles attendent d'elles-même, qu'elles semblent voir la vie et l'art à travers une vitres. Elles écrivent en employant des lieux communs, de grandes phrases vagues, san style, sans individualité, sans avoir v u une chose avec un oeuil pelé (on dit a "peeled eye" en anglais)—

Je reviens assez lentement de la longue agonie de maman. J'ai du refaire et refaire en moi le chemin qu'elle a fait pour enfin, il y a quelques jours, pouvoir m'en détacher et revenir à l'essence de sa personne et de sa vie; toute lumineuse. J'ai lu avec une attention d'âme complète ce que vous avez la tendresse de me dire de ce détachement des fleurs de votre mari à la fin. Ce qui est terrible n'est-ce pas, c'est ce moment où même l'amour ne peut plus rien. Un jour j'espère que vous me parlerez de votre mari, comme il était. Je suis sûre que vous sentez comme moi, cette présence à chaque instant. Je me vois faire des choses que je n'aurai pas fait avant, en me disant "C'est cela que maman aurait fait." Comme j'aurai voulu que vous la connaissiez même, je me révolte parfois qu'elle n'a pas pu trouver ici les vraies amies qui l'auraient appréciée et comprise pour le trésor de flamme, d'intelligence et de courage qu'elle était—toute fleurie aussi de sensibilité exquise, au point que beaucoup de personnes n'ont jamais compris ce qu'il y avait de grand et de noble et de difficile, que de conflits amers et de souffrance cet air délicieux de jeune fille émerveillée et passionnée de fleurs et d'art et de politique—cachait. C'était une vie toute en profondeur comme un puits. Ces vies-là Dieu seul les voit et les aime assez. Ma mère n'était pas croyante, et c'était aussi une angoisse pour moi de sentir sa solitude totale à la fin. Oh, si je pouvais croire qu'elle est maintenant aimé, connue à fond—J'ai lu et relu la fin du lettre aux Corinthiens de St. Paul; "For now we see in a glass darkly; but then face to face: now I know in part; But then I shall know even as also I am known." Pour le service c'est ce chapitre—là que j'ai choisi—et chaque mot semblait parler de ma mère.

J'étais très contente d'avoir les bonnes nouvelles de Madame Rouffanche—et je lui ai écrit dernièrement pour la remercier pour la gravure qui est bien arrivée.

Comme j'attends avec impatience et amour, le livre et comme j'envoies mes pensées les plus ardentes envers lui et envers vous, chère Camille Mayran! Dieu soit béni que vous êtes là dans ce monde qui devient plus horrible chaque jour.

Votre dévoúee
May Sarton

TO MARIE CLOSSET   le 4 septembre [1951]
[Maynard Place]
O darling, mon coeur,

Je sens tout à fait l'état de désarroi où tu es, tachant de trouver la bonne et la sage solution à la maison vide, attendant avec angoisse et espoir les changements qui seront bouleversants avant qu'ils ne puissent devenir bienfaisants et doux, peut-être. Je ne sais pas si à la fin Marie Bohez ne sera pas plutôt contente, après la première et dure, abdication, car je me suis souvent demandee si le va et vient, les ordres venant d'ici et là, ne la jetteraient pas un jour dans une révolte. Si—par un miracle des anges—elle pourrait se trouver en véritable sympathie avec les Curvers, alors ne serait-elle pas finalement plus à l'aise dans une maison où le rhythme serait moins souvent brisé? Je ne sais pas—mais je pense à haute voix et j'ai une envie folle de prendre un avion et de me jeter dans tes bras et puis de parler de tout cela. Comme je suis loin, mon hibou adorable!

D'autre part il me semble que pour toi aussi il y aurait après une periode d'apistement de la paix à reprendre une vie de famille, où il y aurait la routine d'une vie familiale et non pas cet état délicieux de vacances où les amis

vont et viennent, se remplaçant auprèsde toi avectout la joie des vacances—
mais pour la vie quotidienne autre chose serait peut-être une libération pour
toi—et je dis cela avec la plus profonde compréhension et reconnaissance
pour le dévouement, l'imagination, l'amour pur qui te sert et te chérit en
Mariette, Angèle, Rosa et toutes celles qui sont les petites soeurs de L'Échevinage. Mais peut-être serait-il mieux qu'elles soient ta fête, ton gâteau, ton
champagne et non pas le pain et le vin quotidien?

Je suis tellement heureuse en pensant que Françoise [Miomandre] sera près
de toi quand tu recois cette lettre, que tu l'as deja vu sans doute et que tu
auras pu lui parler de toute cette question douloureuse et passionnante.
Quand et-ce que les Curvers vont venir pour le mois d'essai? Je suis dans le
noir car je ne me souviens pas de t'avoir entendu parler d'eux—et tout
dépend, n'est-ce pas, de la qualité de leur âme, et leur capacité d'imagination. Ce n'est pas une question d'amour—je suie sûr qu'ils t'aiment—mais
vivre si près d'une famille cela depend pour ton bien-être d'autre chose que
l'amour—du tact complet, et de l'imagination du coeur. L'auront-ils? Je dois
avouer, mon âme, que je tremble un peu. Heureusement que Ron Ron est
là!

Je pense aussi à ces chambres vides qui semblent pousser des soupirs de
tristesse, et qui seraient de nouveau remplies de vie—mais jamais la vie par-
faite qu'elles ont contenu depuis tant d'annees. Au fond de moi-même je
sens qu'il est vrai et juste que la maison continue à vivre et ne devient pas
le reposoir du passé, que c'est cela qui est dans la nature de cette maison et
surtout dans la nature de sa propriétaire! Mais je souffre avec toi, mon âme,
et plus que ne puis dire du mois à venir, de tous les remuements, et comme
tu dis "le crime sauvage" de déplacer les temoins silencieux de la vie de Gaspari dans sa classe et la tienne dans ta classe. Cela me fait songer plus que jamais à la necessité que tu dictes à Mariette des pages sur l'école et sa
signification—

Après trois jours de pluies continuelles, voilà le soleil et Judy et moi
arrangeons la maison, faisons des achats—des rubans pour tenir les rideaux
dans le salon, une lampe—je viens de cuire du poisson pour le chat qui dest
gonflé maintenant et ronronne sur le lit de Judy. Cet après-midi je vais me
mettre au travail dans le jardin de Maman—

J'ai eu une lettre éblouissante de Eugénie qui vraiment comprend tout
avec une imagination de génie, et peut-être aussi de sainte. J'espère qu'elle
pourra te parler—petit à petit.

Nous partons vendredi pour cinq ou six jours mais serons de retour le 12
alors il vaut mieux écrire ici. J'attendrai un mot dicté au retour, mon âme—
ne tâches pas de fatiguer ta pauvre main. Oh, que je voudrais la couvrir de
baisers.

Est-ce-qu'on l'enveloppe d'oûate la nuit? Est-ce-que des pansements à l'eau chaude ne feraient pas de bien? Ne lâches pas le médicin avant qu'il ne trouve un moyen d'àlléger un peu cette peine.

Mon âme, tâches pendant cette période de dé sarroi de te retrouver et de retrouver le centre qui ne s'ebranle pas ne dictant à Mariette—je t'enprie de tout mon coeur qui t'inonde d'amour et de foi dans ce futur qui se prépare, et qu'ont peut-être prépare depuis longtemps les anges—qui sait? Comme je sens profondément en cet instant les yeux bleus de Blanchette qui te re-gardent et t'aiment et disent que tout ce que tu fais est bien—oh mon amour—

Ton Tobie [   ]

TO MARIE CLOSSET   samedi 5 juillet [1952]
[Linkebeek]
Mon hibou cheri,

Il me semble bien étrange ce ne pas venir t'embrasser moi-même au-jourd'hui mais je t'obéi et ne fais rien sauf regarder-jouer le petit chat per-san qui ronronne et joue en ce moment avec un oeillet rose—et regarder le champ de blé devant la fenêtre. Mon âme, qui voyait qu'<u>enfin</u> je me taisais, a bien voulu me rejoindre et hier soir j'ai même écrit un premier poème. La vieille seve monte doucement—oh, que je me sens revivre, et lundi je te retrouverai, cher amour et te dirai tant et tant de choses, et t'écouterai par ma voix raconter la chambre bleue et tout et tout. Entre temps les plumeaux balancent discrétement sur ma tête et je crois entendre les petits pas hâtés et amoureux d'une Marie et d'un Gille Blanc monter les escaliers et traverser la cuisine pour retrouver avec moi la solitude et l'amour.

En me privant de toi, en te privant de moi, je te donne Eugénie pour toute l'après-midi et lundi je viendrai les ailes sur les pieds embrasser ta petite tête et metter mon coeur en tes mains—

TO CAMILLE MAYRAN   le 4 octobre, 1953
[Wright Street]
Camille Mayran,

Chère, quelle joie profonde, quelle tendresse votre lettre évoque—je suis triste que je vous ai laissé sans nouvelles, mais voilà: Agnes ne pouvait venir en juin et nous avons remis son séjour ici jusqu'á maintenant. J'ai eu un été extrèmement fatigant et plein—avec de grandes conférences à donner à une école d'été, le nouveau roman qui me possède et me secoue comme un démon, et en plus une cheville (sprained ankle) qui m'a forcé à ralentir tout comme une infirme depuis six semainess. Ce n'est que depuis quelques jours qu'un peu de paix commence à descendre et je m'enfonce dans le tra-vail. Je suis vraiment à bout de nerfs et de tout pour le moment et n'ose pas invitér quelqu'un, et je ne sais pas quand j'irai à New York. Mon impression d'après ce que Vincent m'a dit c'est qu'Agnès est comme une chrysalide qui tout au fond d'elle-même et de cette carapace de silence—se crée une nouvelle personne, le courage de cette nouvelle vie- et qu'elle a besoin qu'on la laisse tranquille. Je trouve affreux <u>pour elle</u> qu'elle n'arrive pas à faire le petit geste d'écrire souvent qui juste mettrait un peu de baume, sur l'anxieté constante de sa mère. J'espère vraiment la voir avant Noël, mais je ne puis rien promettre—cela doit vous sempler terriblement égoiste. Mais ma première responsabilité en ce moment est mon travail. Vous savez cette égoisme féroce de la mère qui protège un petit malade. Je suis dans cet état exactement. Il faut tâcher de me pardonner. Je ne me pardonne pas d'ailleurs, mais on fait ce qu'on peut. On ne peut faire ce qu'on ne peut faire. Vincent— que nous aimons comme un petit frère adorable et parfait—même n'aura jamais, j'espère, aucune idée ce que ces quelques jours où il fallait que je <u>sorte</u> complètement de ma vie intèrieure m'ont couté. Je vous dit ceci par honte. Je sais très bien que l'oeuvre d'art <u>coûte</u> la vie, et hélas, non seulement la vie de l'artiste, aussi la vie des autres qui le touche. Il n'y a rien à faire à cela.

Le plus terrible c'est que ce roman sera sans doute mauvais, extrèmement difficile—je me sens plonger maintenant tout à fait en dessous de ce que je croyais faire, jusqu-aux racines humaines de la chose (un qui semble politique) et vraiment il s'agit maintenant de la vie d'un homme plein d'amour et de ferveur, qui ne <u>pouvait pas</u> communiquer avec les autres, qui n'arrivait jamais à se donner, ni à créer la communion vraie-qui l'aurait sauvé, et qui lui aurait permis d'agir en créateur. Cela m'a pris une fausse, piste de 200 pages pour arriver là. Et je viens de tout déchirer.

Comme je suis heureuse que vous avez eu cette isle merveilleuse, le temps avec Vincent. Quel déchirement qu'il doit partir si loin dans une atmosphère dangereuse et qu'il sera si isolé la-bas. Je serai passionnément curieuse d'entendre ses impressions. L'histoire de son arrivée et incarceration à New York est tout à fait fantasque. Nous vivons d'ailleurs dans un monde de plus en plus fou.

ACKNOWLEDGMENTS

I am, and for all of my life will be, illimitably grateful to May Sarton for her legacy to me of unconditional love, and the richness of her companionship, support, and trust; during the past ten years of my work she shared unstintingly of her personal archives, her confidence and belief, and even as she lay dying, gave her blessing and certitude that I would complete the editing of her letters as she had intended—the final stage of what she called our *ineffable rencontre.*

The following have aided my work in varied and incalculable ways; I hereby acknowledge their contributions with ardent gratitude: Mary Shelley Carroll for her enthusiasm and loyalty; Marianne David for her hard work and alacrity; Philip Lyman for unearthing essential books at essential moments and extending imaginative help beyond the bourne of duty; Liam O'Hagan for providing order and lyricism; Fred Streitfeld, *in memoriam,* for being the anchor and ballast.

Special thanks to Shelley Armitage, Mr. and Mrs. Robert Barber, Lenora P. Blouin, Bill Brown, Christopher deVinck, Margaret English, Edythe Haddaway, Beverly Hallam, Helen Long, Tom McKitterick, Lewis Pyenson, Liz Rosenberg, Helen Sheehy, and Mary-Leigh Smart.

Very special thanks to Polly Thayer Starr for her grace of heart and grace of mind, and unwavering friendship.

My thanks to John Gulla and Roger Bookcock of the Riverdale Country School for granting me a one-year leave following May's death.

Great thanks to Shoji Masuzawa who over the past ten years at both godly and ungodly hours made available his steadfast and patient support and expertise.

I am particularly grateful to Joyce Mannis, *deux ex machina,* for her uncommon, imaginative and boundless friendship.

Loving thanks to Karen and Will Balliett for their friendship, support, and superb editing advice.

Once again my gratitude to Nancy Jahn Hartley far exceeds the limitations of this acknowledgement; her work as May Sarton's secretary and archivist for twelve and a half years has provided the bedrock for my own and all future Sarton scholarship; the help and professional guidance she has extended to me and to this ongoing project have been the *sine qua non* of its fruition. Her expertise, humor, and steadfast friendship during the past ten years of my work and throughout the dark year following May's death, are imperceptibly woven into every page of these volumes.

I have benefitted from the assistance and kindness of librarians and curators across the country and wish to thank in particular Amy Hague of the Sophia Smith Collection at Smith College; Carol Knauss of Breadloaf; Lori Misura at Beinecke; Francis O. Mattson, Lisa Browar, and Phillip Milito at the Berg Collection; James H. Hutson and Alice Birney at the Library of Congress; Helga Borck of the New York Public Library Access Services; Margaret Sherry of Princeton; Wendy Thomas at the Schlesinger Library at Radcliffe.

To various special collections for permission to use Sarton's unpublished letters, grateful acknowledgement is hereby made: to Amherst College Special Collections for letters to Louise Bogan and Rolf Humphries; to the Beinecke Rare Book and Manuscript Library at Yale University for letters to William Rose Benét, Winifred Bryher, and Hilda Doolittle; to the Henry W. and Albert A. Berg Collection of English and American Literature for letters to Elizabeth Bowen, Rollo Walter Brown, William Theophilus Brown, Marie Closset, Katherine Davis, Julian Huxley, Mary Garden, Margaret Foote Hawley, John Holmes, Romana Javitz, S. S. Koteliansky, Eva Le Gallienne, Muriel Rukeyser, Giorgio de Santillana, Eleanor Mabel Sarton, George Sarton, Anne Thorp, Katherine Warren, and Virginia Woolf; to Boston University, Mugar Memorial Library, for letters to Mildred Buchanan Flagg; to Bryn Mawr College, Miriam Coffin Canaday Library, for letters to Katharine S. White; to Columbia University, Butler Library, for letters to Orville Prescott; to Dartmouth College, Baker Memorial Library, for letters to Robert Frost; to Harvard University, Houghton Library, for letters to Witter Bynner, Lewis Gannett, Ferris Greenslet, Mark Antony de Wolfe Howe, and George Sarton; to Indiana University, Lilly Library, for letters to Katrine Greene; to the John Fitzgerald Kennedy Library for the letter to Arthur Schlesinger; to the New York Public Library for the Performing Arts, the Billy Rose Theatre Collection, for the letter to Katharine Cornell; to the New York Public Library Rare Book Collection for letters to Peter de Vries, Howard Moss, and Katharine S. White; to Princeton University for letters to Raymond Holden and Sylvia Beach; to Radcliffe College, The Arthur and Elizabeth Schlesinger Library on the History of Women in America, for letters to Mildred Flagg Buchanan, Rosalind Greene, and Katherine Taylor; to the Rosenbach Museum and Library for letters to Marianne Moore; to Syracuse University Library for letters to Horace Gregory; to Tufts University for letters to John

Holmes; to the University of California at Berkeley for letters to Josephine Miles; to the University of California at Los Angeles for letters to Haniel Long; to the University of Chicago Library for letters to Harriet Monroe (*Poetry* Magazine Papers); to the University of Texas at Austin, Harry Ransom Humanities Center, for letters to J. Donald Adams, Elizabeth Bowen, and the *Saturday Review of Literature;* to the University of Virginia, Alderman Library, for letters to Lawrence Lee; and to the Vassar College Library for letters to Hallie Flanagan.

To those individuals willing to share their Sarton letters for this volume, my inordinate thanks: Vincent Hepp for letters to his mother, Camille Mayran, Madeleine L'Engle, Ashley Montagu, Mary Dewing Morain for letters to herself and her sister Abby, and Franz Rohr.

Letters to all correspondents not listed above came from Sarton's personal archives in York, Maine all of which have now been transferred to the Henry W. and Albert A. Berg Collection of English and American Literature at the New York Public Library.

CREDITS

Library Acknowledgments

Henry W. & Albert A. Berg Collection, The New York Public Library, Astor, Lenox and Tilden Foundations, various letters.

The New York Records, Rare Books and Manuscripts Division, The New York Public Library, Astor, Lenox and Tilden Foundations, various letters.

Department of Special Collections, The University of Chicago Library, *Poetry* magazine Papers, 1912–1936, Box 21, Folder 20, six letters to Harriet Monroe.

The Hallie Flanagan Davis Papers, Special Collections, Vassar College Libraries, letter to Hallie Flanagan.

The Beinecke Rare Book and Manuscript Library, Yale Collection of American Literature, various letters.

The Burndy Library, Dibner Institute for the History of Science & Technology, letter to Ashley Montague.

Amherst College Library, Louise Bogan Papers, Box 3, Folder 9, and Rolfe Humphries Papers, Box 14, Folder 18.

Houghton Library, Harvard University, letters to Ferris Greenslet, Witter Bynner, Mark de Wolfe Howe, and Lewis Stiles Gannett.

Billy Rose Theatre Collection, The New York Public Library for the Performing Arts, Astor, Lenox and Tilden Foundations, letter to Katherine Cornell.

The Horace Gregory Papers, Syracuse University Library, Department of Special Collections, letters to Horace and Marya Gregory, and to Horace Gregory.

Manuscripts Division, Department of Rare Books and Special Collections, Princeton University Libraries, letters to Sylvia Beach, Mr. & Mrs. Raymond Holden, and John Hall Wheelock.

Harry Ransom Humanities Research Center, The University of Texas at Austin, letters to Elizabeth Bown and J. Donald Adams.

Virginia Quarterly Review Archives (#29-A), Special Collections Department, University of Virginia Library, letter to Lawrence Lee.

Text Permissions

INDEX

Page numbers in *italics* refer to recipients of Sarton's letters. Page numbers beginning with 375 refer to letters in French.